OFF THE RECORD
Political Interviews, 1933–1943

ALSO EDITED BY A. J. P. TAYLOR

FROM THE BEAVERBROOK LIBRARY ARCHIVES

Lloyd George: A Diary by Frances Stevenson

W. *illiam* *P.* *Crozier*

OFF THE RECORD

POLITICAL INTERVIEWS 1933–1943

Edited
with an introduction by
A. J. P. TAYLOR

HUTCHINSON OF LONDON

HUTCHINSON & CO *(Publishers)* LTD
3 Fitzroy Square, London W1

London Melbourne Sydney Auckland
Wellington Johannesburg Cape Town
and agencies throughout the world

First published 1973

*This book has been set in Baskerville type, printed in Great Britain
on antique wove paper by Anchor Press, and
bound by Wm. Brendon, both of Tiptree, Essex*

ISBN 0 09 116250 5

Contents

2. Before the War, 1936–39

Biographical Index

(The information about ministerial and other offices is usually given only for the period covered by the interviews. During this period there were so-called National governments under Ramsay MacDonald, 1931–35, Stanley Baldwin, 1935–37, and Neville Chamberlain, 1937–40, and a genuine National government under Winston Churchill, 1940–45.)

A V Alexander, MP (Labour), first lord of the admiralty, 1940–45

26	7	40
20	3	41
18	7	41
3	10	41
19	3	42
29	5	42
23	10	43

L S Amery, MP (Conservative), secretary of state for India, 1940–45

6	8	40

Don Pablo de Azcárate y Flórez, Spanish ambassador in London, representing the Republican government, 1936–39.

22	4	38
11	7	38
8	12	38

Stanley Baldwin, MP (Conservative), leader of the Conservative party, 1923–37, lord president of the council, 1931–35.

12	6	34

Lord Beaverbrook, minister of aircraft production, 13 May 1940–1 May 1941; minister of state, 1 May–29 June 1941; minister of supply, 29 June 1941–4 February 1941; minister of war production, 4 February–19 February 1942; member of the war cabinet, 2 August 1940–19 February 1942.

24	8	40
21	5	41
18	7	41
25	10	41
21	11	41
19	2	42
16	3	42

Eduard Beneš, president of Czechoslovakia, 1940–48

3	10	41
21	11	41
16	1	42
28	5	42
2	7	43

Brendan Bracken, MP (Conservative), parliamentary private secretary to Churchill, 1940–41; minister of information, 1941–45

18	1	40
29	3	40
26	7	40
20	11	41
19	3	42
26	3	43
1	7	43

Viscount Cecil, president of the League of Nations Union

5	5	34
2	10	41

Neville Chamberlain, MP (Conservative), leader of the Conservative party and prime minister, 1937–40; member of the war cabinet, 1939–40

17	12	37

Winston Churchill, MP (Conservative), first lord of the admiralty, 1939–40; prime minister and minister of defence, 1940–45; leader of the Conservative party, 1940–55; member of the war cabinet, 1939–45.

13	10	39
18	1	40
29	3	40
1	5	40
26	7	40

David Lloyd George, MP (Liberal), former prime minister

10	5	34
10	1	35
12	6	35

Viscount Halifax, foreign secretary, 1938–40

| 12 | 7 | 38 |

Arthur Henderson, MP (Labour), president of the disarmament conference, 1932–34

15	9	33
9	12	33
5	5	34

Sir Samuel Hoare, MP (Conservative), secretary of state for India, 1931–35; foreign secretary, 1935; first lord of the admiralty, 1936–37; home secretary, 1937–39; lord privy seal, 1939–40; secretary of state for air, 1940; member of the war cabinet, 1939–40; British ambassador to Spain, 1940–44

12	6	34
14	2	35
21	11	35
8	12	38
10	11	39
15	2	40
28	3	40
3	4	40
24	10	41

Leslie Hore-Belisha, MP (Liberal National), minister of transport, 1934–37; secretary of state for war, 1937–40; member of the war cabinet, 1939–40

12	6	35
19	7	35
15	7	36
16	12	37
11	3	38
26	5	38
15	12	39
20	1	40
16	2	40
29	3	40
23	8	40
18	7	41
21	11	41

Introduction

W P Crozier became editor of The Manchester Guardian on 6 May 1932. He had not expected this elevation. The Manchester Guardian had always been a dynastic property. For its first half-century it was directed by its founder, John Edward Taylor, and by his son of the same name. In 1872 the younger Taylor appointed as editor his cousin C P Scott, who became also the proprietor of the paper in 1906. When C P Scott retired in 1929, he was succeeded by his son Ted, a man of Crozier's own age. Crozier assumed that the editor's chair was filled for his lifetime. On 22 April 1932 Ted Scott was drowned in Lake Windemere. No member of the family was available to take his place. John Scott, the manager and now sole proprietor, turned to Crozier, who had been on the paper since 1904.

Crozier, son of a Methodist minister, and a classical scholar at Manchester Grammar School and Trinity College Oxford, was an accomplished journalist of great experience. He had been news editor since 1912, had directed the foreign news service since its establishment, and was for a time also the military correspondent. During C P Scott's prolonged absences in London and elsewhere, Crozier kept the paper running in Manchester. He did more. Scott, as the chief sub-editor once complained, 'never cared a bit about news in his paper'. Crozier cared a great deal. Thanks to him, The Manchester Guardian was transformed from a provincial organ of opinion into a national newspaper pre-eminent also for its news. Crozier was not only a news man. He was a first-rate writer of leaders, carefully argued in a style of classical simplicity. Crozier was fortunate in the moment of his appointment. In home affairs he was by no means radical. During the financial crisis in 1931 he had supported the National government until rescued from this error by Ted Scott. In foreign affairs it was the other way round. The Scotts, father and son, tended to be soft on

Germany. Crozier took a harder line, and no English editor stood up to the impact of Hitler more firmly than he did.

C P Scott spent much of his time in London talking to leading politicians and especially to Liberal cabinet ministers.[1] Crozier, too, began to go up to London soon after he became editor, and he too talked to leading politicians. His talks were of a different character from Scott's. Scott was an important political figure in his own right. He had been a Liberal member of parliament from 1895 to 1905, when he and Lloyd George established bonds of mutual esteem as pro-Boers. Scott was also a leader of Lancashire Liberalism. When Liberal ministers came to Manchester, Scott often took the chair at their meetings, and they sometimes spent the night at his house. When he went to London he was as much concerned to press his own views and those of Manchester Liberals on ministers as to find out what ministers were doing.

Crozier was a stranger to London and its political world. He took no part even in Manchester politics except to be a member of the local Liberal party. Among the many prominent figures whom he interviewed between 1933 and 1943, Amery was apparently the only one he had met previously—an odd exception.[2] This detachment had its advantages. Crozier saw those whom he met with a fresh eye. He noted the personal characteristics of, say, Baldwin, Lloyd George, and Sir John Simon with a penetration that he would not have shown if he had been used to them. On the other hand, the interviews were rather official, mostly formal meetings in the minister's room. Only Churchill and Beaverbrook regularly invited Crozier to lunch. Maybe Hore-Belisha, no doubt emulating Lloyd George during the first world war, sometimes gave him breakfast, or perhaps Crozier watched while Hore-Belisha ate. Amery once gave him a cup of tea from a silver tea pot. None of the others seem to have offered even that.

Crozier listened, asked questions and departed. Occasionally, during the war, he hazarded a suggestion about strategy. For most of the time he was there to be informed, not to push ideas of his own. The interviews were not for use in the paper. They provided background for Crozier himself. Later, I suspect, he began to think that they might make material for a book. The interviews reflected Crozier's own interests. He was not much concerned with politics in the routine sense, though, being a good journalist,

---

1. Trevor Wilson has published a selection from these talks, entitled The Political Diaries of C P Scott, 1911–1928 (1970).
2. Perhaps they had met when Amery was on The Times (1899–1909).

he livened up when changes of office were actually being aired. Otherwise foreign affairs were what mattered to him. They were what he himself wrote about in the paper, and its treatment of foreign affairs was what distinguished The Manchester Guardian during the nineteen-thirties.

Crozier's choice of subjects largely determined his choice of the men he talked to. He wanted to know the state of the armed forces. Hence he endured the defence ministers, even though most of them were dull fellows. There was one omission during the war. Crozier appreciated that, after Eden left the war office, Churchill could tell him all he needed to know about the army and he did not bother to meet later secretaries of state for war.

With foreign affairs he did not confine himself to cabinet ministers. Vansittart was the only Englishman not a minister whom he saw regularly. But he widened his range by including the spokesmen of foreign countries. Some of these—Masaryk before the war, President Beneš during it, perhaps Maisky—may have suggested themselves. Others were Crozier's own idea. His choice was curious and significant. He did not trouble himself with the ambassadors of the great powers, never talked to the French or Italian ambassadors and rarely to the American. He preferred the representatives of the smaller powers, such as Denmark and Sweden, men who were on the fringe of diplomacy as Crozier was himself and as, one might say, Manchester was in relation to London.

This concentration on ministers and diplomats gave a somewhat one-sided picture. Crozier carried his Liberalism just far enough to have occasional talks with Sir Archibald Sinclair, the leader of the Liberal party. He was not in touch at all with Labour opinion. Before the war he talked to Arthur Henderson, but as president of the disarmament conference, not as a Labour spokesman. Even during the war, when Labour was in the government, Herbert Morrison was the only Labour minister with whom Crozier talked at length.[1] He met Bevin once and Citrine once when lunching with Beaverbrook and met Cripps once when lunching with Churchill. He made no comment about any of them and did not record their opinions. He never met Attlee or Greenwood or Dalton. Maybe he thought that Labour was the affair of A P Wadsworth, his colleague and successor.

There was another factor that influenced the choice. Like Mr

---

1. A V Alexander, first lord of the admiralty, though also a Labour man, stuck almost exclusively to naval affairs.

Guttmann in The Maltese Falcon Crozier was a man who liked talking to a man who liked to talk. He went back to the men who welcomed him and let themselves go. He struck others off his list. Reading, for instance, the account of Crozier's one meeting with Neville Chamberlain, it is easy to foresee that it will not be repeated. The men who talked well sometimes got more than their due share of attention. Vansittart was a captivating talker, as anyone who knew him can testify, but his opinions on foreign affairs became increasingly wild. Hore-Belisha is an even more remarkable case. He was the only minister whom Crozier continued to see after he had left office. Did Crozier really think that Hore-Belisha was an important political figure, perhaps even a rival to Churchill as Lloyd George suggested? Or was it just the fascination of a ready talker who had got his affairs into confusion? The later interviews with Hore-Belisha are, I think, exercises in self-indulgence, touches of comedy to relieve the seriousness of war.

Most of the long interviews are fully justified. Churchill plays every role from grave to gay—growling at his critics, laboriously explaining that he does not interfere with the chiefs of staff, offering whisky which Crozier refuses. Beaverbrook is also at the top of his form,[1] showing off as the tornado of aircraft production, provoking an unprintable epithet from Citrine by slipping out of the room, commenting mischievously on his colleagues. Even the drab figures have their redeeming moments. A V Alexander shows a paper he had written during the hunting of the Bismarck and is innocently pleased that the first sea lord had commended it. Sir Samuel Hoare reveals a sincerity that makes Crozier, and John Scott too, favour him as the next prime minister.

Sometimes Crozier arrived in London at a moment of crisis. This is true about the preliminaries to the Czech crisis in the summer of 1938 and even more so about the interminable discussions over sending an expeditionary force to Finland in the winter of 1939–40. Crozier was in London at the height of the battle of Britain. Politically the most interesting episode is in February 1942 when Churchill was reshaping his government. The speculations in 1943 over a postwar coalition are also revealing. Most of the interviews are what Crozier intended them to be: background that conveys how events seemed at the time.

Crozier went to London about once a month, though with long

---

1. The interviews with Beaverbrook reached me later than the rest, too late for me to use them in my life of him.

and often regrettable gaps. He spent two or three nights at the Cumberland Hotel and managed to see half a dozen or more men during each visit. He noted down the heads of each conversation as he went by taxi or tube to the next one. Then at night in the hotel or travelling back to Manchester by train he wrote out in longhand verbatim accounts of his interviews, with occasional cross-references from one to another. Next day at the office his secretary typed out the manuscripts. Though there is only one comment on the interviews,[1] there are indications that Crozier sent them round the office—to John Scott, Gordon Phillips, A P Wadsworth, and J L Hammond.

On the approach of war Crozier resorted to a primitive form of security. He recorded those he interviewed by arbitrary initials, A, B, C, etc. Later he sent round the names in a separate envelope. During the war itself he sometimes learnt secrets that it would be dangerous to disclose. These records were copied out by his wife, often in the small hours. The most secret Crozier kept only in his own hand. They are not difficult to decipher despite the abbreviations usual with journalists.

Crozier died on 16 April 1944. John Scott and A P Wadsworth, his successor as editor, regarded the interviews as Crozier's private papers and handed them to his widow. Some years later his son Stephen began to prepare the papers for publication but died before he could proceed far. Stephen Crozier did not use the schedules of engagements that Crozier kept and so got some of the ascriptions wrong. These schedules have enabled me to get them all right. The schedules also indicate that some of the accounts have been lost or perhaps that the interviews were not held. After Stephen Crozier's death, the records passed to W P Crozier's younger daughter Mary (Mrs McManus), an old friend of mine, who at my suggestion deposited them in the Beaverbrook Library. Researchers have found them of considerable interest. Seeking employment after concluding my life of Beaverbrook I have prepared this selection for publication.

What is printed here represents about a half of the whole series. I have cut many passages where the man talking is merely repeating what was in fact general knowledge. On the same grounds I have often omitted entire interviews. Where I have done this, I have kept the heading of the interview, so that the reader has a full record of those whom Crozier saw. I have not interefered with the long interviews in Crozier's own hand. After all he was a great

---

1. By John Scott on the interview with Sir Samuel Hoare, 21 November 1935.

editor, and his judgement of what should be recorded is likely to be right. To add a personal note, Crozier was the first editor for whom I wrote, and I welcome this opportunity to pay tribute to him.

Beaverbrook Library A J P TAYLOR

I

From the Disarmament Conference to the Hoare-Laval Plan, 1933–35

When the year 1933 opened, the international order created by the Paris peace conference of 1919 was still intact. Germany was still disarmed and still ostensibly a democratic republic; the Rhineland was still a demilitarised zone; and a disarmament conference at Geneva, presided over by Arthur Henderson, was seeking to promote an agreement on general disarmament. The League of Nations was wrestling, not altogether unsuccessfully, with the Manchurian crisis—at any rate, the immediate conflict ended with a truce in May 1933.

Three years later, all was changed. Hitler had become ruler of Germany and had established a Nazi dictatorship. German troops had reoccupied the Rhineland. The disarmament conference had failed. Germany was preparing to become a formidable military power. The League of Nations had attempted to end the war between Italy and Abyssinia by imposing sanctions. That ingenious device, the Hoare-Laval plan, instead of ending the war, plunged the League into irremediable discredit. 'Versailles', to use the popular parlance, was dead.

Crozier's early interviews cover this period with accidental precision. The first with Arthur Henderson was held exactly one month before the decisive meeting of 15 October 1933, when the Germans withdrew from the disarmament conference and so, for all practical purposes, killed it. The last with Sir Samuel Hoare was held a fortnight before the meeting in Paris that produced the Hoare-Laval plan. In the years between, Crozier charted the changes of opinion from the time when Hitler was regarded as sincere, pacific and well-meaning, to the realisation that there was nothing to be done with him, though there was still bewilderment as to what should be done against him. Crozier had his own views even if he did not obtrude them. The Manchester Guardian, under his editorship, was the most firmly and effectively anti-Nazi of British newspapers. On the other hand, Crozier, unlike some of his staff, doubted the value of sanctions against Italy and favoured conciliation as the policy of the League of Nations. In fact, as his comments show, he stood close to the attitude of Sir Samuel Hoare.

There are subsidiary themes. As editor of a newspaper serving a region which was still deeply involved with the cotton trade, Crozier was naturally concerned with the attempts to pacify India and with the Government of India bill. He was a member, though not a very active one, of the Liberal party and followed its fortunes with some interest. He was interested in personalities as any good journalist must be. But the essential theme is the collapse of the international order.

15 September 1933

10.15 A.M. ARTHUR HENDERSON AT TRANSPORT HOUSE

Arthur Henderson was a leading figure in the Labour party from its beginning. He had been a member of Lloyd George's war cabinet, home secretary in the first Labour government, and foreign secretary in the second. When Ramsay MacDonald set up the National government, Henderson became leader of the Labour party. He lost his seat at the subsequent general election and, though later returned to parliament, devoted himself thereafter to his work as president of the disarmament conference. At the time of this interview the conference was approaching a crisis from which it never recovered.

Henderson said that the situation was critical—very critical indeed and he was not confident now that he would be able to obtain a Convention. If no Convention, the political position (France and Germany, etc.) would be extremely grave. They would have to settle it before Christmas or the end of the year; he could see no reason in going on and on after the coming months.

The French were now extremely difficult. He had found Paul-Boncour[1] difficult enough when he saw him in Paris in June and tried to find out from him what the French wanted or would consent to. But he found him much worse lately when he saw him after his (Henderson's) tour of the European statesmen—'I could do nothing with him'. He would have to find out from the French next week what they would agree to—that must be discovered, for everything depended on it. The British (Captain Eden,[2] going to Paris next Monday) were also going to insist on finding out; they were not going to give the French just what they wanted without raising and settling the question of what the French would concede.

The French wanted a preliminary period of supervision for (they said) four years. It was called a 'trial period'. He did not like this term because it sounded like a trial of Germany. He preferred 'period of transition'. This period of supervision or contrôle could be coupled with the change from the Reichswehr system to the short term service system, etc., which would take some years.

---

1. French foreign minister and leader of the French delegation at the disarmament conference.

2. Anthony Eden, parliamentary under-secretary for foreign affairs.

Then came the question of the second period. In this there ought to be, year by year, reduction of the aggressive weapons, until at the finish of the second four-year period (or three years followed by five) there was something like equality with Germany. The French would not say whether they would accept any reduction in this second period, let alone what reductions. If they would not budge, then Germany would get nothing and would rearm— rearm openly, he thought, and if there was a war he thought that France would get no sympathy from this country. (The arms 'reduced' would be handed to the League, to be kept or scrapped at its discretion.)

.   .   .   .   .

He urged the importance of having a system of international inspection set up and functioning for the first time in history. Also, the immense importance of getting Germany to enter freely (for the first time) into an armaments treaty.

He had seen Hitler and believed him to be sincerely pacific— Hitler had talked about the powerlessness of Germany, etc. Henderson believes that Germany would certainly accept the scheme which he had outlined.

.   .   .   .   .

He talked of MacDonald, who, he said, would support a good disarmament plan because he was bound to get the 'equality' formula honoured. In general, he said, the trouble with Mac-Donald was that both in respect of the League and of disarmament you never knew where you had him—he blew hot and cold.

He then went on to give some experiences of MacDonald.

(1) In 1924 he had insisted that Henderson should stop at Geneva to put the Protocol into an 'instrument'. Henderson stopped six or seven weeks. At the end he read suggestions in the press that there was going to be a dissolution. On getting back to London, much disturbed he rang up Mac-Donald at Chequers and asked what the rumours meant. MacDonald told him to ask Thomas, who 'knows all about it'. Clynes, that same night, knew nothing. Next morning he and Clynes rang up Thomas, who said briskly that he and MacDonald had decided a week before to go to the

country. He, Henderson, Secretary of the Labour Party, had not been consulted or even told.[1]

(2) In 1931 MacDonald, in going to Buckingham Palace to see the King about a Coalition, had assured him (Henderson) that it would be a Coalition for a short time only—six or eight weeks—; then they would return to ordinary Party conditions, and also there would be no election.[2]

2.30 P.M. NORMAN DAVIS AT THE HYDE PARK HOTEL

Norman Davis was chief USA delegate to the disarmament conference. This interview, like its predecessor, provides evidence of the favourable views taken about Hitler during his early days in power.

His view was that Hitler was sincerely pacific. He had talked to Hitler and had said to him, 'What do you want—rearmament or disarmament, peace or war?' Hitler had replied that they wanted disarmament and peace. But they were helpless, etc.; he talked about all the armed nations round Germany and said they must have equality. However, Hitler added, no doubt the armed nations would come down a lot and Germany would go up a little—she would thus have a few of the prohibited weapons— until they met ['meet on the staircase' formula]. Davis said, 'I said no, that would not do at all—disarmament but no rearming was what we must have'.

'I think', said Davis, 'that Hitler is a *good* man—stupid and uneducated but still a good man.' When I said that for a good man Hitler had done and said some pretty bad things, he qualified and said that at any rate Hitler 'had good in him'. (He used this phrase also of Goering, whom he had not met.) He said that the American correspondents in Berlin, who were keen and experienced men, disagreed with him about Hitler and thought that he meant war in his own time. (In general he, Davis, took the line that we must get the best out of Hitler.) He also cited a friend who has said how fortunate it was that the Germans were always politically the most stupid of peoples. Otherwise they would dominate Europe.

He was against any 'Sanctions' if Germany or anyone else broke

---

1. The Labour cabinet decided to ask for a dissolution on 7 October, the day before the debate on the Campbell case. It seems unlikely that neither Henderson nor Clynes knew of this.

2. MacDonald in fact set up a National government and remained prime minister of it until June 1935.

the Convention. He thought that only some countries would be inspected. He thought it ridiculous that England should be inspected. France would want Germany to be inspected and Germany France. The USA would want inspection in Japan, and Japan in the USA. (This amused him.) He was against rigidity, definitions, etc., and said that they defeated their own ends; someone would always find a way of getting round them.

. . . . .

He was most insistent on the US and England working together in general. Said everything in the future depended on it. US and England could do almost anything. Roosevelt had impressed on him that they must work for this—just before he came away this last time. In this respect the Russo-Japanese business had been badly managed. England had not supported the US well over that business. Nowadays Eden was good and had all the Tories behind him (Eden must have told him this—he had just seen him). I mentioned Baldwin. He said he believed that Baldwin could not forget that the US Senate had repudiated Wilson and therefore he could not trust anything they said nowadays. I said that we all felt that when the President or Secretary of State said something we did not know whether it would be carried out in practice because of the Senate. I instanced the statements of Stimson and himself about the US and the Kellogg Pact. He said those statements were dependable because it was a matter for the President and not for the Senate; it was executive action. They would see to that by putting it into a protocol attached to the Disarmament Convention and the Senate would be unable to get at it except by throwing out the whole Treaty, which it dare not do even if it wanted to. Further, no President had ever yet gone back on an undertaking by a predecessor. He was much concerned about this point; obviously they do not like our scepticism about their undertakings.

4 November 1933

REX LEEPER AT THE FOREIGN OFFICE

Rex Leeper was head of the foreign office news department and a strong anti-German.

Leeper began first to talk about Germany. He said that there were two views held in the Foreign Office. One, that the Nazi system would eventually result in a quite new sort of Germany which would have abolished a lot of the old distinctions and which would be genuinely pacific; the other, which most people held, and which it appeared that he shared, that the Nazis were a dangerous and threatening force in Europe.

He indicated that the British idea was to improve, if possible, on the present disarmament proposals. I said that what troubled me was not the making a beginning of disarmament but the question of what we were to do with Germany if she were found undoubtedly to be rearming. He said it would be very difficult for the British Government to commit itself to anything at all because 'the country' would not like it. I was surprised to find how often in the conversation he suggested that the Foreign Office were afraid of 'the country', meaning sometimes the Daily Express and sometimes questions in the House of Commons, and sometimes a by-election.

He was, however, not so much interested in Germany as in Japan. He said that when they got through the German trouble there was the much worse business of Japan in the background. If they did not get an agreement with Japan in the present negotiations, and he was not hopeful of an agreement, the outlook would be extremely gloomy. They might then be driven to shut Japan out of certain markets, whereupon immediately Japan would become politically hostile in a very active manner and would also make intensified commercial war on us wherever she could. He said plainly we were very weak in the Far East—'How could we protect Hongkong if we were called upon to do it?'

I suggested that British policy in the Far East had been a complete failure since we denounced the Japanese Alliance. Having denounced it, we put nothing at all in its place and had no means of restraining the Japanese or of protecting ourselves. He said that we had relied upon Japan continuing to have a civilian and pacific Government and had not reckoned on these present people getting control of her. I suggested, in reply to that, that the character of Japanese policy should have been made clear to us by the fact that when her own allies were in distress in 1915 she seized the moment to force the '21 demands' on China. He then said that the situation was extremely serious in general because we ourselves were weak, we had no force in those regions, nobody could rely on the United States, and China was now definitely at the mercy of Japan. Moreover, he said the fact was that, although the United States had been more unfriendly than we towards Japan over the Manchuria business, we were getting far more of the odium than they. Some diplomatist who had recently come back from Tokyo had stated that we were literally hated by the Japanese and were blamed for the whole trouble.

SIR HERBERT SAMUEL

Sir Herbert Samuel was leader of the Liberal party from 1931 to 1935. He was home secretary in the National government from 1931 to 1932 and resigned in protest against the Ottawa agreements. He and his followers gave general support to the National government except over tariffs until November 1933.

He spoke first of his recent visit to Canada. He said there was complete confidence there, that Bennett would be swept away at the next election, and that the Liberals would come in.[1]

He then referred to domestic politics. He insisted that with regard to the position of the Liberal Party in the House he had all along realised fully the disadvantages of remaining on the Government side. It was, however, essential that when he moved he should take with him the great bulk of the Party. If he had gone over when the Liberal Ministers resigned on Ottawa the group would have been seriously split and all the enemies of the Liberal Party would have declared that he was leading it to final destruction. Now he could hope to take over the whole, or almost the whole, of his followers—he hoped the whole lot.

. . . . .

He then said that what he had most against the Government was their mishandling of the World Economic Conference. There was no reason why they should not put forward a policy with regard to tariffs even after the currency breakdown.[2] A lot of States were positively waiting for a lead on our part, but they got none. Neville Chamberlain, he thought, had not been averse from a low tariff plan, but having got his protection and imperial preference had lost initiative. Runciman did not greatly care and

---

1. This proved correct. R B Bennett, who had been Conservative prime minister of Canada since 1929, was defeated at the general election of 14 October 1935. This returned 169 Liberals, 41 Conservatives and 35 others.

2. The world economic conference, which met in London on 12 June 1933, broke down when President Roosevelt refused to stabilise the dollar.

simply stuck at his bi-lateral negotiations, while MacDonald had lost grip of everything.[1]

I then mentioned Simon. He said Simon was a complete misfit in the Foreign Office. When the Government was formed Simon had to be rewarded with something big and, on the other hand, there was no strong claimant to the Foreign Office so they gave it him. He was always the lawyer, and a lawyer ought never to be Foreign Secretary.[2]

.   .   .   .   .

He indicated, but did not want it said, that the Parliamentary Party would decide in the interval before the new session to cross the floor and would appear in a new position in the debate on the Address. I gathered they would vote against the Government for the first time in an amendment to the Address, which would be equivalent to a vote of censure.[3]

9 December 1933

IVAN MAISKY AT HARINGTON HOUSE

Maisky was Soviet ambassador in London from 1932 to 1943. His range of political contacts was much wider than was usual with ambassadors, especially Soviet ambassadors, as is shown in Ivan Maisky and parliamentary anti-appeasement, 1938–39, by Sidney Aster in Lloyd George: Twelve Essays (1971).

The early part of this interview describes the negotiations for a new Anglo-Soviet trade agreement. It was signed on 21 February 1934.

He seemed to be rather amused about the subject of disarmament. He said, 'I can tell you one thing. I have been in Moscow, and I have been in Berlin, and there is not the slightest doubt that Germany is re-arming.' He said that she had given orders to four factories for military aeroplanes, and would shortly be producing three hundred a month, and that she had begun on both guns and tanks. Then he said, 'Nothing at all can stop Germany re-arming.' He suggested, however, and this seems to be an idea which is

---

1. Neville Chamberlain was chancellor of the exchequer, and Runciman president of the board of trade.

2. Sir John Simon was foreign secretary and leader of the Liberal Nationals, i.e. those Liberals who supported the National government without reserve.

3. On 27 November the Liberals moved an amendment to the address. Unlike the Labour party, they did not vote against the address itself.

floating about everywhere, that France might 'legalise' whatever illegal arms Germany at present has got, and make a start from that. He then said, without any prompting of mine, that the all-important thing was control, and he seemed to think that it would be a tolerable situation, though not too hopeful, if Germany were allowed what she has got and a sound international control were instituted. I asked him about penalties for infractions of an agreement and whether Russia would join in, and he said that he thought she certainly would (this, of course, apart from any re-actions of the Japanese situation). He did not really, however, seem to expect that there would be any sort of eventual agreement at Geneva. Litvinoff,[1] he said, was right in calling the Disarmament Conference a 'corpse'. Germany would re-arm, he said, and nothing would prevent her. Then he shrugged his shoulders and said 'except, of course, preventive war', conveying that he did not think, or at any rate did not know, whether that was likely to come about or not.

When I asked him about Japan he became extremely serious, and he said that he recommended us as a paper to give a great deal of attention to events in Japan and Manchuria during the next few months. He had found in Moscow the greatest uneasiness about the way in which events in Japan itself were now going. Not only the civilians, but the more moderate military people were being steadily pushed into the background, and it seemed extremely likely that by the Spring Araki[2] would be in complete control—'and Araki means war'. Even if it were not Araki, there were still more extreme men behind him. He told me a long story to the effect that in September, 1931, it was not the Japanese Commander in Chief in Manchuria who ordered the army to march, but subordinate officers who had received their instructions direct from the General Staff in Tokyo. He said that once the military were in complete control in Japan there was no security at all that some one, it might be Araki, it might be some of the other military men, would not give an instruction for an advance into Russian territory, and the mischief would be done. 'So', he said, 'we are making all our preparations for it.' And he suggested again that we should get as much information as possible from Japan. His tone was quite different about the seriousness of the situation from what it was when I saw him in the early summer.[3]

---

1. Soviet commission for foreign affairs.
2. Japanese war minister.
3. No record of this interview has survived. Probably the idea of making these records had not occurred to Crozier at that time.

Then he said that Russia was prepared, but he did not think there would be a conflict. Now he clearly thought that the odds were on a breach.

ARTHUR HENDERSON AT TRANSPORT HOUSE

Henderson showed some resentment at the attempts which had been made to make him responsible for any severe expressions directed against Germany's action in leaving the Conference. He said that various attempts had been made at Geneva to saddle him with the responsibility for such expressions and that he had had to resist them firmly. He also said that when in the House of Commons Simon had been referring to the matter he took care to say the President said this and the President said the other, although the reponsibility was as much his own, or more his own, than anybody else's.

.   .   .   .   .

With regard to the disarmament position he had now little hope. He thought that a possible way out might be for the French to accept German rearmament, whatever it amounted to at the moment of the Convention, and to make a fresh start at that point, asking no questions about anything that they had already got. He did not like the idea of any sort of German rearmament that really mattered. If they got it he could not see how the Conference could conclude in anything that could be called 'disarmament', and he did not see how he could very well, as President of the Conference, accept a result which was not disarmament at all.

With regard to any sort of sanctions I inquired whether it was proposed that all these countries should sign an agreement of this sort and that no penalties should be provided for infractions of it. He said that penalties were essential, and he had said so at the FO. He spoke strongly of the vacillations and changes in British policy, implied that MacDonald had overridden the Foreign Secretary, and said that in his day at the FO he would not have put up with such a thing; in those days the Secretary was the Secretary and that was the end of it.

He repeated what he had said last time, that Hitler had twice assured him personally that all that Germany wanted was disarmament and not rearmament. Finally he said that his information was that supposing the rest of the scheme was satisfactory

Germany was prepared to accept both automatic control and penalties for breaches of the agreement.

29 January 1934

LORD MARLEY

Lord Marley, formerly Dudley Leigh Aman, served in the navy and the artillery during the first world war. He was an unsuccessful Labour candidate on a number of occasions, was made a peer during the second Labour government, and was under-secretary for war from 1930 to 1931. He was now Opposition chief whip in the house of lords. He became a prominent anti-Fascist and acted as the innocent cover for many Communist-inspired movements, such as the Reichstag fire counter-trial. Later he was active on behalf of the Spanish government during the civil war.

The British Union of Fascists had been founded by Sir Oswald Mosley in somewhat belated imitation of Mussolini. It never had a serious impact, and the agitation against it probably provoked more trouble than the Union did itself. However, with Hitler triumphant in Germany, it caused some alarm as Marley's remarks show.

Lord Marley began by saying how grateful he was for the assistance rendered by the paper with regard to Fascism, both abroad and at home.

He said he and his friends were much exercised about the progress of Mosley and the Fascists in this country, and he gave the customary figures of their supposed strength, the character of their headquarters in London, etc. He went on to say that he and one or two other people—Ellen Wilkinson among them—were about to found an anti-Fascist society. It would be a national society and non-party in character. They hoped to get hold of important people belonging to all parties and none. He instanced a bishop or two and said he had hopes of Austen Chamberlain. He had been promised already substantial sums and had very little doubt they would obtain more as soon as their intentions were known. Their immediate object was to keep track of Mosley-ite activities, and wherever Mosley had a big meeting—like those recently at Oxford and Birmingham—they would organise a really big meeting also. He said he thought there was danger of Mosley-ism growing owing to the indifference of its opponents, and it would be the object of his society to induce public attention and discussion and to expose the Fascists.

I pointed out to him that up to a certain point it was advisable not to advertise Mosley and his people and that the inevitable result of having a big national anti-Mosley society would be to give Mosley an importance, which he would welcome, before perhaps he actually deserved it. Marley said they fully realised this and one of the things which they had still to make up their minds about was when actually to take the field. But he repeated that he took a serious view of Mosleyism, and especially of Mosley. He thought he was a dangerous and a cruel man. He believed that Mosley really had plans for carrying out a 'march on London', and he referred to reports that Mosley had actually organised a private aeroplane squadron; and he said that he thought Mosley was so violent and hot-headed that he was capable, if his march on London were interfered with, of ordering the squadron to drop bombs on the city. He thought also that a certain section of the public was sheeplike enough to put up with this sort of thing, and that conditions were conceivable under which certain Tory politicians and Generals would connive at Mosley's coup and abstain from putting it down. He mentioned as persons whom he regarded as 'dangerous' Trenchard of whom he seemed to have a thoroughly bad opinion, and Maurice Hankey.[1]

When I was disposed to be sceptical about such developments, he said they might seem incredible in the Manchester region—and this he attributed largely to the long educational influence of the MG!—but he said things in the South of England were quite different. He thought a time might arise when Mosley would suffer some rebuff and that he might then lose his head completely and order his various sections to take any violent measures that were within his power.

·   ·   ·   ·   ·

5 May 1934

10.00 A.M. ARTHUR HENDERSON AT TRANSPORT HOUSE

The early part of the interview discusses ways in which the disarmament conference might be brought back to life. None of them proved effective.

·   ·   ·   ·   ·

He criticised MacDonald severely on the ground that although he was the first British delegate to the Conference he did no steady

---

1. Lord Trenchard, known as 'Boom', was a former chief of the air staff. Sir Maurice Hankey was secretary to the cabinet. Though both men had highly conservative principles, neither had any dealings with Mosley.

work. He put in an appearance on rare occasions and then did nothing more for many months. Thus, in December 1932 he had helped to bring about the famous declaration of equality within a régime of security and then had done nothing to fill in these phrases although it was absolutely essential that they should be filled in quickly. After the formula had been accepted he (Henderson) had pointed out to Davis that they should get to work at once and try and fill it out. They had gone together to MacDonald who said he would not have time to go abroad again to take on the task. Davis suggested that they should meet in London in a few weeks, but MacDonald saw difficulties in finding the necessary time. That was how opportunities were wasted. Similarly, MacDonald turned up in March 1933 to introduce the British Plan and then vanished again for many months. As for Simon, he was always running away back to England to attend a Cabinet meeting, leaving sometimes unimportant people to take his place.

At the finish I asked him about the question of co-operation between Liberals and Labour. He said that twenty years ago the same question had been asked him in the Cross Street office by C P S[cott] and he had made the same answer as he would make to me, only it was still truer now than it was then. It was that if the Labour Party made any attempt at accommodation with the Liberals it would be split into fragments and would play fatally into the hands of the ILP and the Communists. Besides, he did not believe in accommodation; he was a sincere Socialist though Socialism would have to come gradually, and actually there were plenty of Liberals who were prepared to go a long way in the direction of nationalisation. He could produce a report signed by C F G Masterman and other leading Liberals in favour of nationalisation, and he told very graphically of how Lloyd George in December 1916 had spoken of nationalising industries.

'I was sent for to No 10 Downing Street', he said, 'and there I found Asquith surrounded by his Liberal Ministers. "Mr Henderson", said Asquith'—Henderson delivered this in a deep sonorous voice—' "my Liberal colleagues assure me that Mr Lloyd George will be unable to form a Ministry. They will not serve under him and I am informed that none of the Unionist Ministers will serve under him. Further, that Labour is unlikely to enter his Ministry." "Mr Asquith", I replied, "I disagree with your Liberal colleagues entirely. The Unionist Ministers will join Mr Lloyd George as soon as ever he offers them posts in his Ministry and I can assure you that he will make such a statement of policy to Labour that Labour will join him too".' A little later, said

Henderson, a Labour deputation went to see Lloyd George at his request. It included MacDonald, Snowden and Henderson. 'It is no longer a question of controlling industries', said Lloyd George with great energy (here Henderson threw his arm out with an ample gesture), 'it is now a question of nationalising—and I am going to nationalise.' So Labour went into his Ministry.[1]

I suggested to Henderson that if Labour would make no accommodation the Tories would be prolonged in power. He replied he would sooner see a reactionary Government in Office for ten years and more than make any sort of an arrangement with Liberals. His proposal simply was that Liberals should vote Labour if they agreed with Labour sufficiently, and otherwise had better vote Conservative. I said that what he was proposing was merely a return to the two Party system and the voluntary extinction of all Liberals, and from this he did not dissent.

11.30 A.M. LORD CECIL AT 16 SOUTH EATON PLACE

Viscount, formerly Lord Robert, Cecil had been a Conservative and now devoted himself to disarmament and the League of Nations. Most of the interview, like the preceding one, discusses how the disarmament conference might be saved.

Cecil talked stretched out in a low arm-chair, with his legs extending most of the way across the room. He was constantly slipping down a little further in his chair, and his coat became pushed up more and more at the back of his neck, so that he looked more storkish than ever. When he had slidden completely down he would give a prodigious wriggle and hoist himself upwards, after which the downward process began immediately. At intervals in his argument he turns on one the most benevolent and inviting smile.

.   .   .   .   .

It was the fact that a large part of the rest of the world was simply thirsting to have Great Britain give a decided lead. Unfortunately, nothing was to be expected from the three men who

---

1. Henderson's reply to Asquith is confirmed by contemporary accounts. Lloyd George's remarks however, according to the verbatim report preserved in the Beaverbrook Papers, were less positive than Henderson makes out. Lloyd George said only: 'The control of the mines should be nationalised as far as possible' and 'Personally I am strongly in favour of the same line being taken with shipping.' But apparently this only meant 'a man to control Shipping and Shipbuilding'.

directed policy:[1] MacDonald used to be strongly in favour of the League, pooled security and all that sort of thing, but nowadays he had no ideas or drive left in him: Baldwin often had the right ideas, but unfortunately it never occurred to him that ideas ought to be followed by certain steps A.B.C., etc. in the way of action or else they would not come to anything: Simon suffered from a 'repulsion from any sort of action'; he was concerned solely with the presentment of a case. The famous speech at Geneva on behalf of Japan was mentioned here.

Germany, Cecil said, had a strong moral claim to the beginnings of practical equality, and he thought that Neurath strongly desired a settlement (on the other hand he thought that Barthou was a bad man and that Herriot was also dangerous.)[2] Both Germany and France at the present moment were extremely nervous. Germany was the more nervous of the two. He thought that at the present time she was seriously frightened of the danger of a preventive war. The French were shortsighted in trusting to their power alone. It was conceivable that some of the French were thinking about a preventive war, but if they were he doubted whether the French people would 'march'.

Cecil agreed that the Services were very powerful and that the three Service Ministers were no more than their mouthpiece. But he said also (what I had heard from other quarters) that Sir Maurice Hankey, the Secretary to the Cabinet, was a most dangerous man. 'He believes in war, you see,' said Cecil, 'and not in disarmament. He thinks war is the right and proper process by which things move in this world.'

·   ·   ·   ·   ·

10 May 1934

DAVID LLOYD GEORGE AT CHURT

Ll G greeted me with great energy and liveliness. 'Well', he said

---

1. Ramsay MacDonald was prime minister and in failing health, Baldwin lord president of the council and the real centre of government. Sir John Simon was foreign secretary. He was much c...ised in League of Nations circles for his legalistic line during the Manchurian affa'~

2. Neurath was German foreign minister and supposedly more moderate than Hitler. Barthou was French foreign minister. Strongly anti-German, he promoted close relations with Soviet Russia and the idea of an Eastern Locarno. At a later date, when the 'peace' men became anti-German also, Barthou became their hero, particularly after his assassination at Marseilles in November 1934. Herriot was a leader of the French Radical Socialist party. His heart was stronger than his head.

bustling into the room and beginning to speak almost before he was in the door, 'I have been a long time in getting to know you. I kept in touch, and very glad I am that I did, with C P[1] right up to the end. He did not always approve of what I was doing or saying, but he used to come to see me all the same, and he used to sit down and tell me what I was doing wrong and what I ought to do. He was a bit of a prophet.' I interpolated that C P always reminded me more of the Hebrew prophet than anything else, and he agreed energetically. 'He was tremendously right in his convictions', he said. 'He used to look at a thing and then put his finger on the course that he thought should be followed, and after that he would not budge. I kept in touch with Ted[2] too', he added, 'and liked him very much. His death was a great misfortune.' Then he went on 'There are not many newspaper Editors that count. Rothermere, well'—he made rapid motions to and fro with his hands—'you never know where you have him. First he is here and then he is there. Beaverbrook—well he is a puckish creature, and Geoffrey Robinson (he meant Dawson)[3] does not really count for a great deal.'

I started by asking him about disarmament. Did he think there was any hope? 'No', he said, he did not think there was any hope at all, and he straightaway proceeded to make the point in any case Japan's attitude was making any substantial agreement impossible. He enlarged on the friction between Japan and Russia, not that he was expecting immediate trouble, but that the Russians maintained, and were compelled to maintain, among other things a big air force in the Siberian region with which to tackle Japan if necessary. His information (which from things he let fall later I think was from Maisky, the Russian Ambassador) was that the Russian air force is highly efficient and formidable. He thought it was capable of devastating the coastal ports of Japan, whereas Japan could do Russia little harm; but Russia, however reasonable she was now, could not reduce her air force unless she got compensating reductions of various kinds from Japan, and if she could not reduce her air force the result would be felt right across Europe from East to West.

However, not only had he no hopes of the Conference but he would like to see it exploded and come to nothing. He thought that collapse would make people realise the situation for the first

---

1. C P Scott, editor of The Manchester Guardian from 1872 to 1929.
2. E T Scott, editor of the MG, 1929–32. Drowned in Lake Windermere.
3. Geoffrey Dawson, editor of The Times. He had changed his name from Robinson in 1917.

time and pave the way to a more sincere attitude later. His view was that as it was neither making or going to make progress, and as everything eventually was bound to come to grief on the Japanese obstacle, the sooner we had an end to the Conference the better.

I inquired what in his opinion had been misdone or left undone most conspicuously to make the Conference fail. He said that the capital mistake was that the British Government did not at the start of the Conference bring forward a clear-cut plan giving the beginning of practical equality to Germany. He said a great deal with much energy about the Conference of party leaders in England in the summer of 1931, which unanimously agreed that the English policy to be pursued at the Disarmament Conference should be the grant of practical equality to Germany. All evils, he thought, sprang from the action of the British Government in shelving this resolution. The Conference had been presided over by Ramsay MacDonald and each party had its representatives. Baldwin was not there, but no doubt the Tories present had referred to him throughout. They had been able to obtain from the Services whatever documents and particulars they wanted, and the Services had been very helpful. He indicated that the Service documents showed that the French armaments were really much greater than anyone would expect. The recommendation of the Committee in favour of equality for Germany had been unanimous. Nevertheless, so far as he could understand, the Government (then, of course, a Labour Government) had turned it down. When I asked why, he said he did not know, but he thought that Ramsay had reported adversely on it to the Cabinet. Anyhow the British representatives at the Disarmament Conference did not, as they ought to have done, immediately bring forward and push that policy on our behalf. He said he understood that Ramsay had now gone round about and had become rather anti-German, while Simon had become anti-French. He seemed, however, to have the idea that the Conference had actually begun in the autumn of 1931 and that the Labour Government was responsible for dropping the equality policy; he was at first reluctant to accept my assurance that the Conference never started until February, 1932. He was insistent that if during the early months of the Conference the equality policy had been pushed it would have saved the Liberal régime in Germany and there would have been no Hitler Government at all.

If the Conference failed there was no reason to be apprehensive. There would be no war. Germany had seen enough of war and would avoid one in future; besides she did not want war. He paid a tribute to the 'sagacity' of Hitler. 'No German Government,' he said, 'would ever in future be so foolish as to take away Alsace Lorraine from France.' There was only the Saar question between the two countries and that would soon be settled.[1] There was, of course, a standing difficulty with Poland, but recent events showed that Germany had for the time being settled that amicably and he did not anticipate any danger. In any case there was no serious question about the Corridor being restored to Germany; he rather indicated that the Germans had no serious ambitions in that direction and that something might be amicably arranged in the shape of a Corridor to East Prussia across the Polish Corridor.

He was not hopeful of the French attitude at the present time. It had to be remembered that although the Radicals, etc. of France appeared to be more conciliatory you always eventually came up against a hard core in French politics which was fiercely national and would not give way. You had to fight against it all the time when you were in conference with them; no one knew it better than he. Briand had tried to do something in the international spirit, but Barthou had supplanted him, and he told the story of how Briand at the moment of his betrayal had asked Barthou how much thirty pieces of silver were worth 'at the current rate of exchange'. Poincaré was the man who represented the hard core of French policy, and now it was represented by Tardieu, Barthou and, he thought the most typical of all, 'Pertinax' who writes in the Echo de Paris. However, what could France do? People talked of the possibility of a preventive war. Well, if the French tried any such plan the Germans would resist them. He doubted, though he was not sure, whether even at the present time the French would not encounter a successful resistance. He said that when the Germans were engaged in their great retreat in Sept.–Oct. 1918 they held up the allied armies most disagreeably, and the weapon with which they held them up was machine guns. They would have lots of machine guns now if the French ventured in.

His view, however, was that when the Conference came to an end it would be best to let disarmament alone for the time being and approach the problem from an entirely different angle. The important thing was to get people actually co-operating together on a specific piece of work. Once they had actually worked to-

---

1. The Saar was returned to Germany in 1935 after a plebiscite.

gether you were much more likely to be able to persuade them to come to agreements and make concessions to each other. Very well, then the European countries should come together on a policy of co-operation on behalf of China against Japan. Everybody should come in on this, including not only the United States but Germany who had no axe of her own to grind in China. He said we had always been lamentably weak in our attitude towards Japan. He would not have put up with it when Japan invaded Shanghai in 1932. He would have made definite proposals to the United States for co-operation. He would have said to her 'Your fleet is at present in the Atlantic. Well, bring it into the Pacific as a guarantee that you mean business and then we will see what we can do.' And having decided on our methods we would have said to Japan 'Out you go!'—and at this he threw out his arm with a gesture of great energy. At the present time Russia would join in any such co-operative scheme as he suggested and so he was sure would Roosevelt. He would get them together and then he would say 'Out you go!' to the Japanese and prevent their establishing any sort of protectorate in Northern China. I inquired whether he meant out of Manchuria also, and he thought a second and said 'Yes, I do.' He was sure that the Japanese would go. He thought they were prepared to 'expand' to any extent so long as the rest of the world gave way to them and were divided. But he was convinced that as soon as they recognised they were going to be tackled decisively they would yield.

The united effort made in settling with Japan would create a basis of goodwill on which it should be possible to grapple with our troubles in Europe. He did not believe that Germany intended trouble, but he thought that something would have to be done to make her contented. He would be in favour of Britain making a great gesture of generosity and proposing that Tanganyika and the Cameroons should be restored to Germany as mandated territories. He would, however, only do this as part of a big scheme of settlement which would make Germany a contented member of the family of nations. He said that Germany would not bother about S W Africa and Samoa, but Tanganyika would mean a great deal to her. She needed its products and, moreover, she was a really good colonial administrator—better in some ways, he said, than we were. He repeated that there was no danger on the Polish frontier thanks to the recent agreement and he did not appear to attach much importance to the idea that the German Government had ambitions which could only be satisfied at the expense of Russia, though he admitted that that remained a doubtful point. He mentioned parenthetically that if we were willing to restore Tanganyika there would be trouble with the Belgians. At the Peace Conference, he said, for some entirely mysterious reason Milner had consented to let Belgium have the best aad richest part of Tanganyika, leaving to Britain the poorer sections. He had never been able to understand why on earth Milner should have done this, but he thought the fact was that in 1918 Milner had had a collapse which had deprived him of all grip on affairs—a sort of stroke which, though not physical, had made him a different man.

However, he had no thought that the present lot of Ministers would ever have any clear and far-reaching plans about getting things right in Europe. Baldwin had a good idea now and then, but that was all and it never came to much. Simon was incapable apparently of coming to a decision. It was not true that Simon could not take action: his trouble was to come to a decision that could lead up to action. What he liked was that someone else should present him with a decision and then he could put up the case for it in the most brilliant manner possible. He (Ll G) had been told that Simon was just the same in legal consultations: he would not come down with a clear definite view. He liked the people at a conference to take the view for him and then he made a very good show in court. As for MacDonald, Ll G said not only had he lost vigour and clarity of mind, but people in the House seemed to be no longer interested in what he had to say. You could see them hunch up mournfully when Ramsay spoke, leaning their heads on their hands; and he went through a little pantomime in his big chair to show what it looked like.

Some further points he made were these:

(1) That Irwin (now Lord Halifax) was the principal inspirer of Dawson of the Times.

(2) When I mentioned that the French suspected that the Locarno Treaty, because of our whittling it down in speeches, was dead, he said 'So it is. There is no doubt about that.'

(3) He expressed great interest in what was going on in the United States, and said that neither could he himself make out exactly what the 'new deal' amounts to, nor had he found anyone—American or other—who could tell him. He inquired whether we had had anything on the subject recently, and expressed great interest when I told him Bliven was now engaged on a series of articles for this purpose.

(4) Apropos of Japan, he said that the British Government was extremely timid and nervous. He had seen J H Thomas not so long ago, who had spread out his hands and said 'But what can we do? We have not got a Fleet, at any rate out there.'

(5) In talking about the present Foreign Secretary, he considered the question of who might succeed him, and he mentioned, as Cecil had done, Sir Samuel Hoare. I said I had heard Irwin mentioned. 'Well, but you know,' he said, 'he is very pious—and I do not know that I like the idea of having such a very pious man for Foreign Secretary', and then suddenly his eyebrows went up and the corners of his mouth went down, and he gave a most diabolical grin. In talking about Eden, he said he did not think that he was frightfully good. After there had been such a lot of talk about Eden's achievements at Geneva he had gone specially to the House to hear him and, of course, he was a very agreeable fellow and speaker, but he could not see in him any great signs of strong character or mental force.

SIR ROBERT VANSITTART AT THE FOREIGN OFFICE

Sir Robert Vansittart was permanent under-secretary for foreign affairs from 1930 to 1938, when he was elevated to the empty dignity of chief diplomatic adviser. He was a strong advocate of 'hitting Germany on the head'.

Most of the interview, which is very long (nearly 3,000 words), again goes over the barren ground of the disarmament conference.

Sir Robert Vansittart said he would see me at 4.30, and I told him that if he could spare so much time I would like to stop till 5.15, when I should have to leave for the train. He continued talking, however, after we had got up, and at the door, along the corridor and in the waiting-room, so that I could only get away at 5.30 and almost missed the train. He talked with great rapidity all the time and answered almost every question apparently with great frankness and freedom.

.   .   .   .   .

I suggested that, on the argument so far, we were in for an extremely uneasy and dangerous period of politics, and I asked him what sort of policy he himself had in mind to deal with it. He

said that the danger would be greatly minimised if it were made
perfectly clear that the democracies of Europe were going to stand
together. German arms were not a menace at the present time,
but what was a menace, and a serious one, was the militarisation
of the mind of the whole German people from childhood onwards.
The German Government was working to construct a nation with
one mentality, and that a warlike one. He thought the only thing
to do was for the democracies to make clear that if and when
trouble arose from this mentality they were going to stand together solidly against it. I asked him how this solidarity was going
to be demonstrated, as by his own admission there were to be no
alliances or exclusive understandings. I inquired whether it was
not desirable that our own Government, if the Disarmament
Conference collapsed, should say something formal and explicit
of the kind which he indicated, or were we just to go drifting along
without any evidence that in fact we intended solidarity of that
kind? He waved his hands and said he was a civil servant, but
personally he thought it highly desirable that the Government,
having secured the co-operation of the Opposition leaders, should
make a formal declaration of that kind.

I pointed out that there were not many democracies left to act
together, and asked whether it was not desirable to bring in
Russia into a future working policy. He said, By all means; Russia
had shown increasing signs lately of being willing to act with the
rest of us, and although he did not think that she desired at present
to come into the League he would be quite willing to have her in
if she would.[1] Russia, he said, had her own troubles to think about;
Japan on the East and Germany on the West, she was naturally
concerned to preserve peace in Europe if she could. It was true
Poland was there as a sort of buffer between her and Germany,
but then, as for the Poles—he shrugged his shoulders—'Well, you
know.'

.   .   .   .   .

Finally I raised the question of co-operation with the United
States and inquired whether it was not essential, especially in
dealing with the Japanese question, to work as closely as possible
with the United States. He showed no great enthusiasm for the
idea and remarked that in actual practice the United States were

---

1. Soviet Russia joined the League later in 1934.

somewhat difficult people to work with. He thought that before
we could get very far the United States would have to come to
realise that 'The world is one.' He had been discussing this matter
a few days before with an important American, and I gathered
that his point had been that if America would lend more assistance
in settling the troubles of Europe the prospect of dealing successfully with the Japanese problem would be much better. We had
in the first place to keep Europe peaceful, and that would help
matters greatly in the Far East.[1]

.   .   .   .   .

12 June 1934

3.15 P.M. SIR SAMUEL HOARE AT THE INDIA OFFICE

Sir Samuel Hoare was at this time secretary of state for India and as such in
charge of the proposals for constitutional reform which ultimately became the
Government of India Act, 1935. The proposals had been embodied in a White
Paper which was accepted by the house of commons in March 1933. The White
Paper was referred to a joint select committee which sat from April 1933 to
November 1934. In the course of its deliberations Churchill, a fierce opponent
of the proposals, alleged that Hoare and Lord Derby had committed a breach
of privilege by inducing the Manchester chamber of commerce to change the
evidence that it proposed to give to the joint select committee. The charge was
referred to the committee of privileges which decided that there was nothing
in it. The chamber of commerce had consulted Hoare and Derby while preparing its evidence and had changed the draft after hearing them—and for
other reasons. The house of commons gave a crushing dismissal to Churchill's
charges on 13 June 1934.

The omitted passages cover general topics in regard to the White Paper
proposals.

He was very business-like but also extremely earnest and, it seemed
to me, anxious both in his looks and in his tone. He seemed to me
'fine-drawn', as though he were a nervous man suffering under a
heavy burden of anxiety. He began at once by saying 'What would
you like to talk about first? The Privilege report or the White
Paper policy?' I said the Privilege report. He thereupon remarked
that it was 'a very nice one' and he thought also interesting in its
arguments. I asked him whether Churchill was going to raise a
lively debate, and he said he thought there was no doubt that

---

1. Vansittart did not believe that any effective action could be expected from the
United States in the Far East. He therefore tended to favour some sort of agreement
or compromise with Japan.

Churchill was going to go 'all out' and make a very bitter speech attacking him (Hoare) violently. He thought that if Churchill had chosen to accept the report and say that he would not press the matter further the House would have been pleased.

.   .   .   .   .

He complained strongly of the methods which Churchill had adopted towards him personally in dealing with this question. Churchill had sat at the same table with him at a luncheon on the Friday before the bomb was exploded (that was a Monday) and had spoken to him throughout as though they were good friends sitting together in the same Cabinet. It was not until late on Sunday night, a few hours before the attack on Monday, that Churchill had given him warning. He added incidentally that Lord Lloyd had had the same documents in his possession and had been intending to use them by bringing them out in public meetings in his (Hoare's) constituency. Churchill had just anticipated Lloyd and had then, by making it a question of privilege, shut Lloyd's mouth, and in consequence Lloyd was at present much annoyed with Churchill.

.   .   .   .   .

4.40 P.M. STANLEY BALDWIN AT THE HOUSE OF COMMONS

Baldwin was in his private room. It communicated with Palace Yard by a narrow little back staircase and a side door, so that it is rather like something out of Dumas. Baldwin's face, seen close to, was most interesting. I had never seen him before, and in his photographs his face had always seemed to be chiefly amiable and a little whimsical, just as his speeches sound simple, honest and ingenuous. Actually he is not like that at all. His face is rugged and nobbly; his right eye is either going wrong or has some sort of a cast in it and was mostly half-shut. But the characteristic of his face is its determination and shrewdness—or rather, because it is much more than shrewdness, a sort of deep rustic craftiness. More than any other politician he reminded me of Lloyd George in this, but while L G is gleefully and maliciously cunning, Baldwin seemed to me to look shrewd and crafty in a rather grim and hard way. I got quite a new idea of him and for the first time understood how he had come to be leader of the Tory party and

Prime Minister. The good-natured mellow look of the photographs was only there when he greeted me and when he said good-bye, saying that I was to come again whenever I would like a talk. During most of the conversation he tried vainly to light his pipe.

.   .   .   .   .

We discussed the Privilege Report. He said it was a great pity Churchill had not decided simply to accept it. He would have got a cheer from all sides of the House and the matter would have been finished. But, said Baldwin with much energy, Churchill was going to do nothing of the kind. He laughed and said it was reported that Churchill had sometime ago prepared two speeches —one in case the report went in his favour and the other in case it went against him, and that the latter was much the more bitter of the two.

.   .   .   .   .

He could tell me something about Churchill. In 1929, after the Conservative defeat, the Tory leaders had been in the habit of meeting in committee to frame a policy with a view to the next election. They decided that they would advocate duties on meat —or it might have been wheat, he was not sure which—Churchill had refused to agree to this and had walked out from among them. That was all right, but what he actually did was to go to Rother-mere and Beaverbrook and see what support he could get for his position. Of course on such a point he could not get support from them. He could not very well go back to the Liberals and he did not want to join Labour, so after a week he came back to the Tories in a chastened mood. When, however, the India business came up he thought he saw a great chance and leaped at it, and on this he had at any rate got the support of Rothermere. Incidentally Rothermere had provided large sums for Churchill's anti-Government campaign on India.[1]

---

1. Baldwin's account of Churchill's behaviour in 1929 is by no means accurate. A proposal to advocate food taxes was made at the Conservative shadow cabinet in July 1929. Churchill opposed the proposal and it does not seem to have been adopted. Beaverbrook, erratically supported by Rothermere, launched the Empire Crusade, of which food taxes were an essential part, in January 1930. Churchill was never associated with it. In January 1931 Churchill left the shadow cabinet over the India proposals. He was now running an India Defence League which was mainly financed by the Indian princes.

Baldwin added that Churchill's judgment was always wrong. He said that when Churchill was in the Cabinet with one this was not so disastrous if there was a week or so in which it was possible to delay action and persuade him to change his mind, but if it was a case where action had to be taken at once, then 'eight times out of ten' Churchill's judgment as to what ought to be done was a bad one. Of course it was the fact that the White Paper policy aroused some deep-seated opposition in the Tory mind. I suggested that it was the same as had been the case with Ireland: he replied that he could not admit any analogy with Ireland. He then proceeded to summarise the history of the Irish question; declared that it had been a great misfortune that it had become a purely party question so that each side was absolutely rigid and the result in Ireland ultimately was revolt and civil war. He had all that in mind with regard to India and it had been his object throughout to put the Indian question on a non-party national plane. It had been a disappointment to him that Labour split over the National Government so that now he had on the side of the National Government 'only about half a dozen of these fellows'. I suggested to him that anyway Labour supported and would support the White Paper policy, and he said yes, of course, only it did not go far enough for them. Nevertheless he would like to have had Labour co-operating in the whole thing.

. . . . .

In this connection I asked him where Lloyd George stood, and he said he did not exactly know: 'He keeps a free hand. He is very busy with his books, getting up early and working hard at them. He has made a lot of money out of them. They are well-written too, the last two not quite as well as the first two [a curious slip, as L G has only published two altogether]. Of course he makes out that no one thought of anything or did anything right except himself. I like the little man, but I cannot work with him. I got Hankey,[1] by the way, to "vet" those two volumes to see what Cabinet memoranda L G had used, but it was pretty well all right. About India L G is on the wrong track. He says that we ought to deal with Gandhi because it is no use dealing with anyone who cannot deliver the goods. He says this because he thinks that with regard to Ireland he himself dealt with the people—Michael Collins,

---

1. Sir Maurice Hankey was secretary to the cabinet from 1916 to 1938.

etc.—who could deliver the goods. There are two objections to this policy in India. First of all that Gandhi is an impossible person to deal with and, secondly, that he cannot deliver the goods anyway. There are three people, you know, who are impossible to deal with—De Valera, Gandhi and Beaverbrook.' (To these he afterwards added Poincaré.)[1] Baldwin added also with regard to L G 'He does not, of course, count for much in this present House of Commons.'[2]

.   .   .   .   .

Finally I asked him about foreign politics and air armaments.

.   .   .   .   .

He said the upshot was that we could simply not avoid increasing our own air force. It ought to be realised that the whole situation had been altered for the worse by the rise of the new Germany. 'No one,' he said and repeated more than once, 'knows what the new Germany means—whether she means peace or war.' He said that he himself was no alarmist. He did not believe in war in the near future and he did not think about it, though he was bound to say that most of the people who talked to him on this subject took a gloomy view about Germany's ultimate intentions. At all events he held that the Government could not take risks. It was the trustee for the people of the country and it had got to have adequate means of defence so far as those could be provided.

10 January 1935

DAVID LLOYD GEORGE AT THAMES HOUSE

Lloyd George started by offering me a cigar, and when I declined

---

1. Baldwin had had rough dealings with all four men. De Valera was locked in conflict with the National government over the land annuities and other aspects of the Irish treaty. Gandhi was demanding Indian independence and was, as Lloyd George said, the only Indian worth dealing with. Beaverbrook had almost unhorsed Baldwin during the Empire Crusade. Poincaré had been in dispute with Baldwin at the time of the French occupation of the Ruhr.

2. Despite this remark Baldwin sought Lloyd George's support for the National government later in 1934. A cabinet committee examined his proposals for a New Deal, and he was led to believe that he would be offered a high place in the cabinet. Neville Chamberlain kept him out.

he took one himself, and said 'Well, I am not a heavy smoker; I only smoke four or five cigars a day. But I like smoking, and if ever the doctor tells me that I have only a short time to live if I go on smoking, I shall ask him how long, and consider the matter carefully.'

With regard to the Independent Liberals, he hoped that they would not attempt to crab his programme.[1] I said that I thought there was little in it that could offend them. He replied that there was nothing at all. I pointed out that the official Liberals in their expositions of policy were much more cautious than he was in this programme; that they were rather timid people. Not timid, he said, but cowardly. 'It will be much better', he said, 'if they will let me go into the jungle for them.' (He *does* sense the battle afar off.)

Although the young Tories would support him, it was impossible to expect that anything would be done by this present Parliament in carrying out his programme. To get anything done it was necessary first to 'destroy this Parliament'. It was possible that in the next Parliament there might be a Government with so narrow a majority that a group of even twenty Liberals devoted to this new programme would be able to exert a decisive influence. Of course it was possible that the Government might do worse than he now thought. In his opinion things were going badly for it. Two things would possibly bring disaster on it. The first was unemployment, and the second was the dissension in its own ranks over India, to which he had already referred. On the other hand, the country was no longer afraid of Labour policy. He did not believe there was, or would be, any panic now about Labour. It was quite true that the personnel of Labour was poor; there were only a handful of really capable men—he mentioned Morrison, Addison, Tom Johnston, and Greenwood (subject to the condition of his health).

He had something to say about himself and Labour. He said that sometime back he had been very strongly urged to join the Labour party, but he could not do it, and he had no intention of doing it. He had been a Liberal all his life and he would die one. It was no use; he had got Liberalism in his bones and he could not now join another party. Liberalism, he said, was much more a living thing in North Wales than it was in England; it still meant a great deal to them there, whereas in England it was more or less dead. And he thought that in Wales it meant more than anything else a belief in, and sprang from the sense of, Liberty. 'We have the

---

1. Lloyd George was now preaching a New Deal.

mountains, you know,' he said. I mentioned the famous sonnet
'Two Voices are there, one is of the Sea, One of the Mountains;
each a mighty Voice'. And he said 'Yes, and in North Wales we
have got them both—both the mountains and the sea. Who wrote
those lines?' I said Wordsworth, and he said Wordsworth was a
poet that he had never taken to very much. He went on to say that
he had told his children that if they felt like it they should join the
Labour party without worrying about him or what he did, but
they had said that they could not do it either, and it was not only
because he himself proposed to remain a Liberal.

·   ·   ·   ·   ·

4.15 P.M. SIR ROBERT VANSITTART AT THE FOREIGN OFFICE

I asked him first to tell me something about the new Franco-
Italian accord and its possible effects on the German question:
to put it crudely, would this agreement be likely to improve the
prospects of a disarmament convention?[1]

He replied that he very much hoped that it would, and he said
that most certainly they were going to take up and press this point
with Laval and Flandin when they paid their visit to London
shortly. He had been working steadily at the idea of an understanding between France and Italy for the last five years. It had
always been desirable, but now, of course, it was enormously
important because of the German situation.

With regard to Germany, he said he was afraid it was a case of
the Sibylline Books; we should have to pay more in the future
because of the our failures in the past. The Germans were undoubtedly rearming, especially in the air, and it was, indeed, this
and nothing else which had put the fat in the fire.

·   ·   ·   ·   ·

He spoke of the Reichswehr and the SS and said that in his
opinion it was probably true that the Reichswehr were gaining
more and more power over German policy,[2] that they did not

---

1. The Franco-Italian agreement claimed to remove all disagreements between the
two countries and thus to secure a united front of resistance against German aggression. Laval was French foreign minister, and Flandin French premier.

2. The belief that the Reichswehr was increasing its political power in Germany
was a common delusion of these years,

want a war, and therefore would go cautiously, but that they did mean to have armaments, and that in point of fact they were probably not in the least desirous of having disarmament or limitation at all; they would prefer, if they had the choice, to go on steadily manufacturing arms and increasing their forces until from the military point of view they were roughly as strong as they wanted to be. It followed, therefore, that if we were going to get a convention at all we had better be quick about it. He said that in his opinion 'The sands were running out fast' and 'if we do not get a convention within the next six months I doubt whether we shall get one at all.' He was not in the least alarmist about the dangers of war, but merely insistent that Germany was going on steadily in re-arming, would probably put her demands up, might put them up so much that the French would not look at them, and in a short time would not be interested in the idea of a convention.

I asked him about the Eastern Pact and whether there was any change in the attitude towards it by either Germany or Poland.[1] He said no there was not, and I gathered that he was of the opinion that their refusal, including that of Poland, was probably final. I inquired whether in that event Russia would not be much more sticky on disarmament or limitation because of her fears of Germany's ambitions, and he said that was so. 'On the other hand,' he said, smiling, 'you have to remember that Germany and Poland may feel some uncertitude about Russia; they may have their doubts about her.' (I was not able to ask questions about this, as I ought to have done, because I could not make out why at the present time Germany should have any fears of Russia, which is obviously in a disagreeable position between her eastern and her western neighbours.)

.   .   .   .   .

As I was going out he referred to Lloyd George. He said that he had only read the first volume of Ll G's Memoirs, but he did not at all like the references to Grey. Ll G, he said, represented that he did not know of the diplomatic events leading up to the war, and this was certainly untrue because of the invariable custom of circulating all the most important documents to

1. Louis Barthou, the French foreign minister, assassinated at Marseilles in November 1934, had proposed an 'Eastern Locarno', which both Germany and Poland refused to join.

Ministers.[1] He also spoke of the publication of memoirs, and attributed it principally to the necessity that public men were under, or thought that they were under, of making money.

11 January 1935

IVAN MAISKY AT THE RUSSIAN EMBASSY

The principal topics were Japan and Germany. Nothing of importance was said on either topic.

14 February 1935

3.00 P.M. SIR SAMUEL HOARE AT THE INDIA OFFICE

I asked Sir Samuel Hoare how he felt after the recent field days in the House of Commons on the second reading of the India Bill. He said that he felt not much like tackling the forty days that were to come. He had been over the ground so often during the last four years, had sat on so many committees and heard so much evidence that he felt now that there was nothing new that he could say, and nothing new that he was likely to listen to. He was extremely glad that the Government had been able to come to an arrangement with the Churchill people about a reasonable time-table; if he had had to face the prospect of insistent obstruction, closure, and all the rest of it, he could not have borne the prospect, and he thought the willingness of the Churchill people to come to this arrangement was promising. It showed at any rate that they were not disposed or prepared to take extreme measures and that they recognised that the Bill would go through.[2]

. . . . .

I asked him whether he thought the strength of the die-hard movement was growing within the party, and whether the extension of the field of attack by Churchill at Wavertree from India to the general field of politics was likely to threaten the Govern-

---

1. Lloyd George was certainly kept fully informed between 1911 and 1914. Perhaps he did not read the papers he received.
2. The Government of India Act reached the statute book on 24 July 1935.

ment.[1] He said he did not think so. He thought it possible that Churchill was taking the view that apart from India he had better go rather cautiously at present. 'It is to be remembered,' he said, 'that although there is great discontent in our party about the India policy there is scarcely a single Tory who would be willing to accept Churchill as the leader of the party or Prime Minister.' (Contrast this with what Sir Joseph Nall said to me later the same day.) He admitted that the Government stock and the MacDonald stock were both low.

.   .   .   .   .

I then asked him about the recent reports of the reconstruction of the Ministry. He said the situation was undoubtedly 'very fluid', but that he did not believe that there would be any major reconstruction during the next few months. Even if there were a reconstruction that brought into office a new Conservative Prime Minister, it would make no difference to the India Bill. No Conservative Prime Minister was conceivable who would not put the India Bill through. They were all of them, including the real Tories like Hailsham, on his side. He added parenthetically that if an election came earlier than was expected and the Labour Government were returned—which he did not anticipate—it would, in his belief, have to introduce an India Bill which would contain most of the things like the safeguards that the Labour people now criticised. I asked him about the Lloyd George reports,[2] and he said that he never believed that Ll G could come into the Ministry at present. The whole idea, he said, was too sudden, too abrupt. A change of that kind could only be brought about by the pressure of actual events so that it forced itself on the situation, and so far there were neither the events nor the pressure; there was not any sufficient reason behind the idea of Ll G coming into the Ministry to secure its adoption.

.   .   .   .   .

---

1. In January 1935 Randolph Churchill presented himself at Wavertree as an Independent Conservative candidate, championing the cause of the Indian princes. The seat was lost to Labour. Winston Churchill had no prior knowledge of his son's escapade but gave it his blessing.

2. The government's consideration of Lloyd George's proposals and the hints that he would be invited to join the government dragged on until the beginning of July 1935. Perhaps there was no serious intention behind all this. Or perhaps Baldwin dropped Lloyd George when he found an easier winning ticket for the general election in foreign affairs. If so, it was Hoare who saved the government from Lloyd George, though not with much ultimate profit to himself.

4.00 P.M. SIR JOHN SIMON AT THE HOUSE OF COMMONS

Sir John Simon was foreign secretary from November 1931 to June 1935. As a Liberal National, he was of course the wrong sort of Liberal for Crozier. All the same, it indicates Crozier's remoteness from the great world of politics that he had never met Simon in earlier days, particularly as Simon sat for a north of England constituency.

The interview was mainly devoted to a proposed Air Pact which came to nothing.

Simon received me in his private room, which he said used to be the drawing-room of Lady Ilbert, wife of Courtenay Ilbert, for many years Clerk of the House of Commons. It was in that room, Simon said, that when he first entered the House he had been introduced to John Morley and the old Liberal veterans. I mentioned that I had frequently heard about Ilbert from C P S, who had been his contemporary at Oxford, and Simon said that Ilbert was a man who had had an extremely brilliant academic career but had somehow failed to achieve the eminence which had been expected of him. Simon said that Ilbert had been at the Bar in the Chancery Court and that he thought he lacked one or two of the essential qualities. A barrister, said Simon, needed sometimes to have the courage and determination to tell a client that he was entirely in the wrong, and that something which he wanted simply could not be done.

Simon went on to say that in 1900 C P S[cott] had asked him whether he would attach himself to him as a sort of lieutenant during the election at Leigh. At the same time he had been invited to stand himself as candidate and had taken the advice of Ilbert and others who had recommended him not to. This, said Simon, had proved to be extremely good advice, because he would probably have got in and have had little time for the Bar; it was during the two or three years following 1900 that he really founded his fortunes at the Bar.

Simon said he would give me the choice of two chairs—one which involved a draught from the window and one which involved my sitting in the light. I chose the light, but discovered that Simon's face was completely in the shade, so I changed over to the draught. He then said that he could not allow this and insisted in my sitting in his chair at his desk while he himself sat in the light. This was very useful, as it gave me an extremely clear view of his face and expression. He has a much less pleasant face than I had supposed, but it is not unpleasant in the way represented by Low: that is to say, smug and sly. It is distinctly a determined, hard, and sometimes sneering and bullying face. There is nothing anywhere soft or gentle about it, as there is, for instance, in the face of Baldwin, who also can look hard and determined. Much the most striking thing about Simon's face seemed to me to be this, that his eyes (which are blue and rather prominent) remain entirely unmoved when he is smiling. He smiled and laughed a good deal during the conversation and once or twice he 'smiled all over his face', but while every other feature was involved in the change of expression his eyes remained entirely cold and unmoved, without a glimmer of geniality. If I had never known anything at all about him I would have said that he was a bitter and disappointed man. (He was, I should add, entirely pleasant and agreeable to me throughout.)

. . . . .

SIR JOSEPH NALL IN THE TRAIN

Sir Joseph Nall was a leading Manchester Unionist and MP for the Hulme division of Manchester, 1918–29 and 1931–45. This interview is the only one in the entire series with a backbencher—and a Die Hard at that.

I asked him about MacDonald, and he said he was personally by no means one of the 'MacDonald hunters'. He thought that Mac-Donald was not as bad as he was painted and that he was, at any rate in many things, a better Tory than Baldwin. He did not think that it had been sufficiently observed, but MacDonald had on several occasions let drop remarks, as on the subject of death duties, which were much more Tory than Socialistic in character. I said I had not noticed the death duties passage and asked whether MacDonald was critical of them. Nall replied that Mac-Donald was 'against them' and that he had said other things of a distinctly Tory trend.

As to India, he said that the Die-hards had no intention of being obstructive. Parliamentary obstruction was a dead policy and would not be revived. He did not suppose any important changes would be made in the Bill, but they would try to make some. I inquired about Churchill's position in the Party and put to him the suggestion that no Tory member would be willing to serve under Churchill as leader of the Party or of the Government. He said that was not the right way to put it; that if there were a big political crisis an individual became a leader or Prime Minister because by force of events or personality he was the man, or the best man, or the only man, for the position, and a crisis was conceivable in which Churchill by virtue of his brains and personality would take the foremost place, and would in that event be accepted by the Tory Party.

He did not think much of the idea of getting L G into the present Ministry. He did not see why they should want to do it. There was nothing really novel in L G's policy, and he was himself a spent force. Anyone could see, he said, that L G was no longer the man he used to be. Discussing personalities, he said that neither Simon nor Hoare was a leader with a grip on the House of Commons. They were both of them too judicial and cool headed, setting out the two sides of a subject, for and against, with great care and caution, and eventually deciding that, on the whole, one particular view seemed to be better than the other. Reverting to MacDonald, he said that largely he believed it to be a matter of health. The simple fact was that the man in his state of health could not tackle the job.

I had a long discussion with him on the Indian question. He would not admit that 'India' had had a large and growing measure of fiscal autonomy: everything, according to his argument, had been done by the Indian Government, and since 'India' had never exercised any measure of autonomy in tariffs it was not taking anything away from her if we now said that in future tariffs were to be so-and-so according to our discretion. He said, moreover, that if we were going to talk about 'India', India was the scores of millions of people who rarely figured in the discussions, and not the small politically-minded minority—'a couple of millions', he said contemptuously, to whom we were conceding everything. He saw no difficulty in applying the policy of the Die-hards if we were prepared to treat the vocal minority 'firmly'. Unfortunately no Viceroy was prepared to do this. Even Lord Reading had only arrested Gandhi when Lloyd and Zetland had gone to him and told him that unless he did they would resign, return to England and state the facts. Baldwin's mistake, he said, was to speak of and to treat the Indian politicians as though they were Europeans. I asked him whether it was not somewhat late to discover that they were not 'Europeans' when we had been treating them as such, and encouraging them to regard themselves as such, since 1862 or thereabouts. He quoted the French system with its Customs Union with the colonies against us, but he admitted that the French had from the beginning pursued one policy with regard to their colonies while we had pursued the opposite. He declared positively that a great deal of intimidation of people (civil servants, etc.) who were anti-White Paper was going on: what was happening, he said, was that these officials were being chosen out to be 'retired' or they did not get promotion.

Nall also expressed himself very strongly about Elliot's schemes.[1] He said it was repulsive to him as a Tory to read of farmers being fined for disobeying regulations for the disposal of their milk, etc. He thought that there was growing resentment, and very rightly, and that the time was coming when it would break out in a formidable manner. He said he disliked the whole business, and when I suggested to him that Elliot was elaborating in some ways what Addison had done, and that the Elliot policy was highly agreeable in many ways to the Labour party, his indignation increased.

Referring to the general position in Parliament, Nall said that members suffered under a 'dictatorship'—a dictatorship 'worse than existed in Germany or Russia!' The Government did not want to hear the views of private members at all: they merely wanted them to do what they were told and it was all neatly arranged under constitutional forms. The Labour party also, he said, had its dictatorship. The Labour members complained bitterly in private about the dictatorship of Lansbury,[2] who was worse in that respect than MacDonald had been. 'When Lansbury meets the Labour members in conference,' said Nall, 'he does not want or ask for their advice. Old George simply tells the lads where they get off.'

25 May 1935

SIR GEOFFREY KNOX AT DUNHAM MASSEY HALL

The treaty of Versailles put the district of the Saar under French administration for fifteen years to compensate France for the destruction of her coal mines by the Germans during the first world war. On 13 January 1935 a plebiscite in the Saar voted for return to Germany by an overwhelming majority. Sir Geoffrey Knox was head of the governing body of the Saar from 1932 to 1935.

Knox is a man of striking appearance and personality; steady 'penetrating' blue eyes, quiet and moderate in speech, extremely clear and firm in his views. He regards Germany as 'the enemy'. When he was asked whether he thought that the present mood of Germany went back to the Treaty of Versailles, he replied 'No,

1. Walter Elliot, minister of agriculture.
2. George Lansbury, leader of the Labour party, 1931–35.

to the battle of Leipzig.' He said that the character of Germany and the Germans must be regarded over a long period of time; that they have always appealed to force; that they have always conquered by isolating their enemies (the great war was their one failure); that they never accepted the verdict of the war; that they never truly disarmed; and that the main object of Germany at the present time is to detach England from France, because unless she can do this her plans are going to be very badly hampered.

Knox expressed gratitude to the MG for the support that it had given to him during the Saar business. He said that Voigt was head and shoulders above any other correspondent who was there.[1] He was the only man in his opinion who understood the Germans and the Saar situation. The Times man had been poor, though the Times had been served extremely well at the start of the Nazi regime by Ebbutt in Berlin. Latterly Ebbutt and the Berlin correspondence had declined for a variety of reasons. One was that the Times had shown itself the most credulous and gullible of English newspapers in respect of Hitler's policy. He was unable to conceive how any paper in this country could believe Hitler's protestations about his peaceful intentions when the whole efforts of the man and his régime in Germany were devoted to making the nation the obedient and efficient instrument of war. It was lamentable, he said, that people in this country had next to no understanding of the German character. No doubt a certain number of individual Germans liked the idea of peace, but the fundamental thing about the German was that he longed to be given, and was unhappy unless he was given, orders. Knox kept on repeating that the Germans do not possess the individual moral courage or independence of the Englishman and many other nationalities; they want to be told what to do, and whether what they are told to do is good or bad does not affect them; they will do it whatever it is and be content. He gave various instances to illustrate this docility. While he was in the Saar the leaders of the Churches came and told him that they had been ordered from Berlin to fly the Nazi flag over their churches. They wanted him to forbid it in order that they might telegraph back that they had been forbidden. He told them that it was no part of his duty to give them official instructions, and they then begged him to express a private opinion. He replied that his private opinion had no value, but he could not understand how

---

1. F A Voigt was the leading MG writer on German affairs.

religious associations like theirs could decently fly a heathen flag. They went away sorrowfully but immediately obeyed the orders from Berlin.

.   .   .   .   .

In discussion Knox declined to admit that the Treaty of Versailles had had anything substantial to do with the triumph of the Nazis, nor would he admit that the German Government had ever had any strong case for rearming. The truth was, he affirmed, that the German Government had always (after 1919 onwards) rearmed to a much greater extent than the rest of the world knew; the other Governments knew it and that was why they were reluctant to reduce their own armies during the Disarmament Conference. I suggested to him that at the present time the German Government was anxious to make some sort of a settlement with England and France in the West in order to keep its hands free in the East. He said of course it was true that Hitler used the alleged Communistic menace and the Russian Bolshevik menace as part of his propaganda, but in point of fact in his opinion the only thing that mattered was that Germany meant war within no very long time, and that she would make war in whatever direction suited her best when she was ready. He himself put the date at which things would be really dangerous at about July, 1937, and he said that his opinion of Hitler and his friends was such that he sincerely believed that a 'surprise attack' was a real possibility. He considered that the duty of the Press in general —if it would only do it, of which he knew there was very little prospect—was to waken up public opinion as to the true character of the German Government. He expressed great disapproval of the line taken by the Daily Herald, and as to the Times he said it was doing infinite harm, not so much here and in France as in the smaller countries of Central Europe, especially like Austria and Yugo-Slavia, because these peoples thought that it represented the British Government, and therefore that the British Government was proposing to yield to Germany as she became stronger and stronger and threatened and presented the world with 'accomplished facts'.

.   .   .   .   .

28 May 1935

2.30 P.M. SIR JOHN SIMON AT THE HOUSE OF COMMONS

Simon seemed to me to be wearied and gloomy as compared with the last occasion when I saw him. He began immediately on Italy and Abyssinia,[1] and it was evident that that was what he wanted to talk about much more than anything else. He was friendly and complimentary in his reference to Eden, but he was clearly anxious to explain what he and the Government in London had contributed to the compromise just reached at Geneva.

He began by asking 'What is your opinion of this Geneva business?' I replied 'Success up to a point, but we are obviously far from being out of the wood.' He said 'Yes, that is correct if, about which I am a little doubtful, we ought to call it a success.' We had gained certain points, such as the reference back to the League that was to come in August, and Mussolini had had to agree to that. They had had to put severe pressure on him, and his attitude was at any rate very different at the finish from what it was some weeks ago. He described what had happened at the extraordinary meeting of the Council which was held at Geneva just after Stresa. The 'little Abyssinian' had proposed that the Abyssinian question should be put on the agenda, which, of course, contained nothing but Germany, and he had made a powerful plea. The rest of the Council said nothing at all, the proposal being unprecedented. At last he (Simon) had suggested that an addition to the agenda could hardly be accepted, but that they should express the opinion that the two sides should get busy on negotiations and make some real progress before the ordinary meeting of the Council in May. This little speech of his, he said, was received in 'frozen silence' by the Council, who showed no sympathy at all, and the President, the Turk, had made a perfunctory remark and brushed the whole thing aside. That was all the support that he got for his good intentions. Afterwards he was given to understand that Mussolini had expressed the opinion that his intervention was decidedly 'mal vu', to which he had replied in effect that he could not help it if it was, and he thought that he had done the right thing.

.   .   .   .   .

1. Relations between Italy and Abyssinia were becoming increasingly tense. The League of Nations wrestled with the problem in vain.

He had sent for Signor Grandi, the Italian Ambassador in London, and told him exactly what in the opinion of the British Government the issue in principle was and what they thought about it. I could not distinguish what he said to Grandi from the argument which he was addressing to me, but it amounted to saying that at Stresa they had censured one Government for treaty-breaking and that they really could not condone the action of Italy if, immediately after Stresa, she was going to start treaty-breaking herself. This was, I gathered, the gist of the point that he had put to Grandi. He then said to me, 'If we had done this [condoned Italy's action], there is not a newspaper in the country that would not have attacked us. I should have found it impossible to defend the Government's action in the House, and if I had tried the House would not have listened to me.' Therefore he had wound up, he said, by telling Grandi that the League and the Covenant were the things we had to stick to in this country, and if the choice ultimately was found to lie between the League and Italy, it was by the League we would stand.

He then came on to the future. He said the situation was extremely dangerous. Mussolini was getting into a position from which he could not extricate himself without humiliation or, as an alternative, show a considerable success. It was only speculation, but he himself suggested two motives for Mussolini's policy. A new generation was growing up who no longer felt the appeal that Fascism always made at the beginning. Some sort of stimulus had to be given to them. The worst of these dictatorships was that they always had to be applying a fresh stimulus. The young men in Italy, who were only children when Mussolini marched on Rome, had to have something out of the common to get excited about. Secondly, he thought that Mussolini might be becoming dubious about his Austrian policy. He might be coming to see, as many other people were, that it was doubtful how long the Germans could really be kept out of Austria. He might be more dubious than he seems to be about the advantage of keeping large numbers of troops mobilised on the Austrian frontier, and it might be that if he foresaw disappointments in Austria he was preparing some sort of compensating coup to present to the Italian people for the purposes of prestige.

I suggested that although the prospects looked thoroughly black, Mussolini was a person who jumped about erratically in his policies and might conceivably reverse a policy that had gone a good long way where other more logical and determined men would not do so. He said he thought that was possible, as Musso-

lini had before now gone round about—he made vigorous gestures
with his hands—in the most extraordinary way. He was strongly
pro-Nazi and had treated France and England pretty badly in his
determination to support Hitler: now, after the Austrian affair
and conscription, he was showing himself more violently anti-
Hitler than anyone else—this had been made perfectly clear at
Stresa. Similarly in regard to Yugo-Slavia; after the death of
Alexander he had been extremely violent. Now he had sent a new
Ambassador to Belgrade to make the most effusive declarations of
friendship.

With regard to the future, Simon said that if Mussolini did
ultimately refuse to give way, an extremely serious situation would
arise, and I gathered that he meant, although he did not say so,
that the League could not be expected to put any such pressure on
Mussolini as would stop him in his course if he were determined
to go on.[1] He implied that the only thing which might stop
Mussolini were large economic concessions by Abyssinia. To this
I said 'And Abyssinia, I imagine, will refuse them?' He received
this in silence for a second or two, and then said something which
clearly indicated that he was doubtful whether Abyssinia would
refuse the concessions, and whether she ought to. I summed
up my general impressions of this part of the conversation as
follows:

(1) Italy will probably go on with her military preparations
and will not settle by arbitration by the end of August.

(2) It is possible that she might be bought off by economic
concessions from Abyssinia.

(3) Abyssinia would be well advised to make these concessions.

(4) I should expect England and France to advise her to make
them.

The latter points are inferences from the manner and tone rather
than from any words he used. He said, incidentally, that he knew
the two dictators pretty well, and Hitler struck him as the more
solid man of the two. Hitler knew his own mind and what he wanted, and was not likely to turn back. Possibly he knew only a limited
range of subjects, but these he had 'chewed over': he had 'masti-
cated them' and got them well settled in his mind. Mussolini was
a much more uncertain quantity.

Simon had taken up nearly the whole time in talking about
Italy, so that when he was informed that the German Ambassador

---

1. This was far from the resolute support for the League that Simon had implied
earlier.

O.T.R.—C

was waiting I had only time to ask a few questions about Germany and the air.

.   .   .   .   .

Simon asked me whether I had met the German Ambassador, and when I said no, he said he must introduce me. His Excellency came in, Simon introduced me, and the Ambassador was extremely polite. He said that not long ago he had met a member of the London staff of the MG, but could not recall his name. On the spur of the moment, without thinking, I suggested 'Voigt?' Immediately he rapped out emphatically 'No, I don't know *him.*' (Of course, he knows all about him!) I then remembered that Bone[1] had seen him, and supplied his name.

.   .   .   .   .

Simon then said 'The Manchester Guardian, your Excellency, is called the conscience of the country; it does us all good to have a purge sometimes.' Whether this was deliberate or not it seemed to have a distinct moral for the German Ambassador if he chose to think over it.

30 May 1935

L B NAMIER

L B Namier was professor of modern history at Manchester university and deeply versed in Eastern European affairs. He had many talks with Crozier, but this is the only one which has survived in the present collection. As this talk shows, Namier did not credit Hitler with any grandiose design of winning Lebensraum at Russia's expense. In his opinion, Hitler was out to create Greater Germany by bringing all Germans into the Reich. Then he would impose his will on the western Powers. Hence, in Namier's eyes alliance with Russia, if it could be obtained, was an unmixed blessing, bringing far more advantages to the western Powers than to Russia. As this talk also shows, Namier exaggerated both the will and the ability of the smaller European states to resist Germany. He was correct in believing that Austria would be Hitler's first acquisition, but none of Austria's neighbours resisted this, and Yugoslavia, as Crozier foretold, preferred the Germans in Austria to the Italians.

.   .   .   .   .

---

1. James Bone was London editor of the MG.

He began by saying that he could not understand why Russia was afraid of Germany. Undoubtedly she was, and he thought it was due to her extraordinary seclusion and ignorance of what went on in the rest of Europe. She had never got over the conviction that some of the other Powers were intending to attack her, and at the present time she thought it must be Germany. It was, in his opinion, incredible that Germany should attack Russia at all. Hitler, of course, denounced Russia most violently, but that was part of his propagandist stock-in-trade—anti-Communism, anti-Bolshevism and all the rest of them—but in point of fact how and why should Germany go to war with Russia?

I made the usual suggestion that Germany might strike a bargain with Poland, by which Germany should get the Corridor from Poland and Poland should acquire a large chunk of the Russian Ukraine as compensation. I inquired whether this was not the sort of policy that the Rosenbergs talked about, and he said yes, it was, but that did not make it less preposterous. Under no circumstances, he said, should Poland give up the Corridor— 'not a single village'—and for the good reason that the Corridor was infinitely more Polish than it was German. At one time the Germans in the Corridor had been 43% of the total population, and now they were only 10%. It was absurd to suppose that any Poles would ever surrender what was genuinely Polish territory, with Polish population, to Germany. Besides, the suggested compensation in the Russian Ukraine was no compensation at all. Had not the MG repeatedly demonstrated that the Ukrainians already in Poland, being completely disaffected, were a grave source of weakness to the Polish State? And was it common sense that any Polish statesman would be willing, let alone desire, to double or treble the number of disaffected Ukrainians? Poland, he said, had made her treaty with Germany because she hoped thereby to do something towards pushing Germany off in the direction of Austria and Yugoslavia, and it was there and nowhere else that the great danger lay.

It was true, Namier went on to say, that Germany would not abandon the idea of getting back the Corridor or part of it, but that would come later. There was not, in his opinion, a shadow of a doubt that Germany would in the first place burst out towards Austria, which meant also Czechoslovakia, because the Czechs would never let Austria become German without fighting, since they would infallibly be the next victim. Austria, there was no doubt, was dearest to Hitler's heart, it always had been so, and he remarked as a parallel that Pilsudski had been more devoted to the idea of acquiring Vilna, where he had been born, than to anything else. Namier said that in his opinion it was not conceivable that Austria should be absorbed by Germany without a European war. The point was that by the absorption Germany would come down to the frontiers of Hungary, and Hungary would immediately bestir herself energetically in order to secure revision of frontiers. The Magyars had only two ideas in life— rearmament and recovery of Hungary's lost territories: they were still a high-spirited and ambitious people and just about as ready to go to war as Prussians or Serbs. If, therefore, Germany's coming down to the Hungarian frontier had this affect, the Czechs, the Yugo-Slavs, the Roumanians—all of whom hold Hungarian territory—would go to war. Bulgaria, which had lost almost as much, would join in, and would be followed by Turkey and Greece. Then it would be seen who else would stop out. I put to him the suggestion frequently made, that the Yugo-Slavs would on the whole rather see the Germans than the Italians in Austria. He said that he did not believe that this was in the least true. The Yugo-Slavs hated the Italians, but they knew perfectly well that if Germany got hold of Austria they, the Yugo-Slavs, would be in danger of losing part of their newly-gained territories to Hungary. He predicted that the warm welcome just given to Goering's journey in Budapest and Sofia would be followed by signs of resentment in Belgrade.

On the German situation in general, he declared that Germany would, if necessary, go to war in support of union with Austria at the earliest appropriate moment. There would be no resistance by the German people to their Government, because the Germans only wanted to be told what to do and they would do it. He told a story about Breitscheid, to whom a party of people in London, Namier among them, had said that they could not understand why the whole German Social Democratic Movement had suddenly and utterly collapsed. Breitscheid said that the Socialist leaders had not anticipated that Hindenburg would put Hitler in power and therefore they had not had the requisite time 'to give orders to their followers'. As though, said Namier scornfully, a truly liberal democratic movement would have waited for 'orders' from Breitscheid.

·   ·   ·   ·   ·

Regarding Hitler, Namier refused to admit that he was or had shown himself anything of a statesman. I suggested to him that the Foreign Office people and those who went to Berlin had been greatly impressed by Hitler's intelligence, clearness of mind, etc. Namier was entirely scornful. Put a mediocrity, he said, in an imperial seat and he immediately impresses you enormously. Meet a man when he is dictator and you are pretty certain to think what a great figure he is. Phipps, he added, the British Ambassador in Berlin, had no opinion of Hitler. He said that Phipps had reported how Hitler in an ordinary interview bawled at him as though he would like to 'gobble him up'.

As to the coming conference about the independence of Austria, Namier said that if it were held, of which he was doubtful, nothing whatever would come of it. Hungary would agree to nothing, Germany would agree to nothing, and if she did her signature would be entirely valueless. Any signature by Hitler to any document was of no value whatever. He believed it to be established that when Roehm was murdered he had taken a room for Hitler, by arrangement with Hitler, in his own house or hotel for that Saturday, June 30, and then Hitler came down to carry out the calculated plot of arresting and murdering him. What was the value of any signature made by such a man?[1] As for the present governors of Austria, they were a 'lot of bounders' who had no ideas and no proposals. 'So,' I said, 'the bounders will hang on in power as long as they can? Austria will probably become more and more uneasy and so far as you can see the probability is that she will slip towards Germany and that she will either be absorbed or the neutral States will occupy her, and in any event it is likely to be war!' He said that this pretty correctly represented his view of what was coming.

Namier mentioned Lord Lothian and his views about Germany.[2] I inquired whether it was not true that Lothian appeared to accept everything that Hitler said. 'It is not quite that,' said Namier. 'To understand Lothian's views of Hitler you must remember all the time that Lothian is a most convinced and fervent Christian Scientist. He thinks that if he can construct a great international praying league to pray for Hitler, whatever evil there is in Hitler will speedily be dissipated.'

1. On 30 June 1934, when Hitler murdered Roehm and many others of his early associates, Namier visited me in the country. As his train drew into the station, he put his head out of the carriage window, waved his newspaper, and cried joyfully: 'The swine are killing each other! The swine are killing each other!'

2. Lord Lothian, formerly Philip Kerr, was a leading appeaser and later British ambassador at Washington, where he died in December 1940.

12 June 1935

11 A.M. DAVID LLOYD GEORGE AT THAMES HOUSE

Short account of the Council of Action for Peace and Reconstruction which Lloyd George set up with the support of Free Church leaders on 1 July.

LESLIE HORE-BELISHA

Leslie Hore-Belisha, formerly a Radical, became a Liberal National after the formation of the National government and minister of transport in June 1934. Being a great believer in publicity and also a former journalist, he was always ready to talk indiscreetly to Crozier or indeed to anyone else. He had a high opinion of himself and may be numbered among the future prime ministers with whose corpses the field of British politics is littered.

The National government was reconstructed on 7 June 1935. Baldwin became prime minister, and MacDonald lord president. Other changes are mentioned in the text. Hore-Belisha only became a cabinet minister in October 1936—a fact not obvious from the tone of his conversation.

The talk was mostly about Cabinet reconstruction. He declined to admit that Baldwin was, or would be, much better as a Premier than MacDonald. He said that at any rate MacDonald had made a good chairman in the Cabinet. He at all events announced decisions and conclusions. There was no voting, of course, in the Cabinet, but MacDonald was quite good when a certain stage in the discussion had been reached at saying: 'Very well then; the decision of the Cabinet is so and so', although it was possible that that decision might not be so much the Cabinet's as MacDonald's view of what he most wanted. Baldwin was not a man of action, did not like action, and would not be particularly friendly to a 'drive' or a programme of bold action from any quarter. He said that Ll G's description of Baldwin, as a man who stumbled over the truth and then went on unconcerned, was accurate. I asked whether if what happened to be a good programme of action was put to Baldwin he would not assist to shove it forward. He said 'No, when you have explained your great plans to him, he will begin to tell you about some most interesting little book that he has just been reading, and will get up and run over all the shelves in his room till he finds it. Then he will talk about it again and eventually part from you without having promised you any assistance, which in fact you will not get.' Said he had had this experience himself.

He criticised the reconstructed Government. He said that Baldwin, who was always talking about giving youth a chance, had done little or nothing to carry out his words. He had put

Eustace Percy into the Cabinet, but that was an afterthought, done because he was afraid of the discontent of the young Tories.[1] He ought to have put Duff Cooper into the War Office—an obvious appointment. Moreover, he owed Duff Cooper a great debt of gratitude.[2] D C had fought the Westminster by-election for him at the height of the Beaverbrook-Rothermere vendetta. By winning the by-election D C had scored a tremendous blow for Baldwin and actually saved him. 'But for Duff Cooper, Baldwin would not be Prime Minister today.' Also, there were wheels within wheels. Neville Chamberlain, at that time at the head of the Tory organisation, had advised Duff Cooper not to fight because defeat might injure his career. He had also said that the machine could not find the election expenses—he wanted, that is to say, to deter Duff Cooper from assisting Baldwin at that most critical stage of Baldwin's career, and now Baldwin had ignored Duff Cooper and put into the War Office Lord Halifax, who had wanted to retire, being much more interested in the country than in military pursuits.

Simon, he thought, had been 'done in'. There had been two main motives for the reconstruction movement among the discontented Tories—one was to get rid of Simon, and the other was to get Thomas out of the Dominions Office. They had only succeeded with Simon. Simon had resisted removal. They had started by saying 'Oh well, you will be Leader of the House and Lord President of the Council'—both of them great positions. Then Ramsay had declared that he would be Lord President and nothing else. So they had gone back to Simon and said 'We are sorry, but you cannot be Lord President, you must be Home Secretary,' and Simon, though very reluctantly, had agreed. Then they went to Thomas and said they wanted him to move. Thomas said yes, but not to any other office than Home Secretary. So they went back to Simon and said 'We are sorry, but we want you to give up the Home Office.' Simon had positively refused, and Thomas, to the discontent of the Tories, retained the Dominions Office. He thought there was bound to be another reconstruction

1. In the Baldwin government Lord Eustace Percy was minister without portfolio. He resigned in March 1936.

2. In March 1931 Duff Cooper ran as official Conservative candidate at a by-election at St George's, Westminster, against an Empire Crusade candidate backed by Beaverbrook and Rothermere. He won by 5,710 votes. If he had lost, Baldwin would have been driven to resign as Conservative leader and Neville Chamberlain would have succeeded him. The coolness between Chamberlain and Duff Cooper, alleged by Hore-Belisha, is therefore easy to understand. Duff Cooper became secretary for war in November 1935.

either immediately after the coming election or possibly just before the election took place.[1]

The trouble, he said, in all this Cabinet making was that 'claims' counted for so much. Merit was all right for the Bar and journalism; if a man did badly at the Bar he failed, while if he did badly in journalism he lost his job, but in politics 'claims' counted enormously. Lord Londonderry was an instance. He was a second-rate man, not capable at all and really ignorant, yet when they got him out of the Air Ministry he was made Lord Privy Seal.

As to Malcolm MacDonald, he was an able man, but it was a mistake to promote him into the Cabinet. Malcolm would have been wiser to take a smaller office and get into the Cabinet next time. Now everybody would say, and go on saying, that his inclusion in the Cabinet was just a piece of nepotism.[2]

The treatment of Eden was extraordinary.[3] He was obviously the man for the Foreign Office if Simon moved, but they had even taken away from him the great title of Lord Privy Seal and given him one of less importance, even if they did put him in the Cabinet. But to have both Eden and Hoare speaking for foreign affairs was the most remarkable stroke of all. It was most dangerous and he did not think it would work. How would they get on in the Cabinet with two equal Ministers for Foreign Affairs (on certain subjects) giving opinions to the Cabinet which might be diametrically opposed to each other? Such a thing had never been heard of. As for Hoare himself, it must be remembered that he was Baldwin's man:[4] he would never disagree with Baldwin and he would always support him faithfully in any tussle between rival ambitions in the Tory party. Neville Chamberlain was a formidable figure in the Tory party and had great support among the rank and file. Baldwin, therefore, naturally wanted as many loyal supporters as possible in the principal offices, and that was partly why Hoare was at the Foreign Office. (Also, of course, Halifax was a great personal friend of Baldwin's.)[5]

---

1. Though Thomas remained Dominions secretary in June 1935, he changed places with Malcolm MacDonald, the colonial secretary, in November.

2. Malcolm MacDonald may have owed his rise to being the son of his father, but his subsequent career was a good deal more distinguished than Hore-Belisha's.

3. Eden was appointed minister without portfolio for League of Nations affairs, while Hoare became foreign secretary. This was certainly an unusual arrangement.

4. Hoare may have been Baldwin's man but this did not do him much good when he was in trouble a few months later.

5. Both Hoare and Halifax managed to become great personal friends of Chamberlain's also once he was prime minister.

19 July 1935

9.30 A.M. LESLIE HORE-BELISHA AT HIS HOUSE

Lloyd George's Council of Action campaign had now begun. Though Lloyd George spent £400,000 on it from his political fund, it had no serious impact.

Hore-Belisha, as minister of transport, was naturally jealous of Lloyd George's proposal of a national road-building programme to relieve unemployment.

We had some talk about Lloyd George and his Council of Action Campaign. Hore-Belisha thought that Ll G had made a mistake in trying to work his campaign through the Free Churches. He gave an account of a visit that he had paid to Churt some time before the Council of Action business had been announced, and he said it was apparent then from Ll G's conversation that he was assuming the existence of a 'Nonconformist vote' of the old kind. He had talked a great deal of what had happened in the days of Gladstone (just as he did to me later) and seemed to think things had not changed. He thought that Ll G had made a considerable impression when he first came out with his new policy at Bangor[1] but that he had lost ground ever since. 'Besides,' he said, 'what is one to make of him? His speeches at and after Bangor, however much they may be called non-party, were intended to injure the Government, and then he goes and lets it be known that he would be willing to enter the Government.' He seemed to think that this was a bull point against Ll G. He referred also to Ll G's attempt to make capital out of the submarine question, which he thought had been not only a failure but a mistake. I asked him if he thought that Ll G's flair in tactics of politics was declining, and he said he thought that was an understatement and that the old skill had gone.

With regard to Ll G's actual programme, he said that those parts of it which concerned himself—that is to say roads and electricity—had been lifted bodily from his (H-B) plan. He had actually announced them at a dinner at Birmingham at which Ll G had been present, and they had been lifted pretty completely into the Ll G memorandum. He mentioned in particular the policy of making the main roads of the country a national concern and taking them out of the hands of the innumerable local authorities. As things stood it was impossible to make progress owing to the multiplicity of authorities. He had already put forward a scheme to the Cabinet for taking these roads under the Ministry of Transport. The scheme had not gone through, but

---

1. Lloyd George first announced his New Deal at Bangor on 13 January 1935.

that was partly owing to administrative difficulties concerned with the block grant system, and he was confident that he would get it through in time if he still continued at the Ministry of Transport.

·　　·　　·　　·　　·

11.30 A.M. SIR HERBERT SAMUEL, AT HIS HOUSE

Samuel began by talking about Lloyd George and the Council of Action. He did not seem to have any large expectations from the movement and he said that there was a whole lot of Liberal opinion knocking about which found no point of focus at the present time and he thought that the Councils of Action would bring together a certain amount of voting strength in the right direction. I asked him about the prospect of Council of Action or Ll G candidates, and he said that he thought there might be a few, but only a few: he did not seem to attach any importance to the suggestion of a number like 350.

He went on to refer to the Government position in the House of Commons. He said that the Liberal Parliamentary Party had had to do most of the work of critical opposition, and he mentioned that not only were the Labour people not very good at working-up and mastering subjects in order to tackle the Government but that for the most part they were singularly poor and unimpressive speakers. He mentioned one of them who, he said, was among the best in respect of capacity, but who was a woefully bad and monotonous speaker, merely wearying the House. The trouble was that the Liberals had to do too much speaking. He had had to make four substantial speeches during the last week, and Isaac Foot and Mander and one or two others had too many calls made on them.[1]

As for the Government, it was run by Neville Chamberlain. 'What he says goes. When he puts his foot down and says that something must be done, that decision settles it. Baldwin has plenty of good ideas and instincts but he will not fight for them.' He had made the best speeches on several subjects, as, for example, air, but in spite of the speeches the position was just as bad as it had ever been. It should not be forgotten that Neville Chamberlain was a great power in the Tory party. It was true, he believed, that Neville had said right from the first that he would not have

---

1. Isaac Foot and Geoffrey Mander were active Liberal MPs.

Ll G brought into the Government, and that had settled things.[1]

He had something to say about Italy and Abyssinia, but nothing particularly fresh. He had come to the conclusion that if Italy did attack Abyssinia the League on the whole would be better without her than with her, because if Italy made war with Abyssinia and remained within the League there would be very little to be said for the League at all.[2]

He made some reference to the press and said he had been delighted recently with various articles in the MG which maintained the old tradition of plain and powerful speaking. Twenty or thirty years ago, he said, there were a number of papers, and he mentioned the Times and the Telegraph, which wrote with power and grip. Nearly all that in his opinion had now disappeared and he was glad to think that the MG was an exception. He referred particularly to the Times as a paper which nowadays always seemed to be voicing someone else's opinion.

3 P.M. SIR ROBERT VANSITTART AT THE FOREIGN OFFICE

The Italians, as mentioned in the previous interview, were now preparing to attack Abyssinia. In April MacDonald, Simon, Flandin and Laval met Mussolini at Stresa. They set up 'the Stresa front' to resist any attempt to change the treaty settlement in Europe by force. The French, and Vansittart along with them, were anxious to preserve this anti-German combination. An Italian attack on Abyssinia threatened to disrupt it. In June Eden went to Rome with a proposal that Abyssinia should be induced to surrender her outlying territory to Italy in exchange for acquiring an outlet to the sea at Zeila in British Somaliland. Mussolini rejected the proposal. Vansittart was anxious to resurrect it, and it ultimately bore fruit in the Hoare-Laval plan.

I said I had come to ask him for the solution of the Abyssinian problem. He said he would be grateful to anyone on earth who could tell him that: he was not at all hopeful. All he could say was that efforts to stop the war would have to go on, and so far as we were concerned would go on right up to the last moment. There were still two or three months and he did not despair, though he had little hope.

---

1. The recent biography of Baldwin by Keith Middlemas and John Barnes claims that he was more active over rearmament than is usually made out. Samuel was however right in believing that Neville Chamberlain was largely responsible for keeping Lloyd George out of the government, a stand he took again in 1940.

2. Italy was now actively preparing for her invasion of Abyssinia which began on 3 October 1935. Samuel evidently expected League action on behalf of Abyssinia to be limited to the expulsion of Italy.

There was no special plan or proposal for compromise or settlement under consideration at the present moment. The British offer about Zeila was dead. He was entirely unrepentant about this offer, and from the way in which he said it I gathered that he was quite ready to claim some personal credit in the matter. He went on to say that the Zeila offer was good because it showed that we were really willing to do something positive to preserve the peace. It did not cost us a great deal but it cost us something, and speaking for himself he would have been perfectly willing, if Mussolini had showed any signs of considering the offer, to go still farther and to make larger concessions. But Mussolini had flatly refused to consider the idea at all. The whole thing had been extremely disappointing: the offer had annoyed the French and offended the Italians, and in addition all the reward the Government had got was that a lot of its own supporters had jumped on its back. He proceeded to talk of the prospects of the League bringing pressure on Italy. I mentioned France, and he said that not only France but the smaller Powers in the East, like the Little Entente, were against taking any sort of serious action against Italy. What the French said was 'For ten years you have been pestering us to make up our differences with Italy and at last we have done so; we have done it so successfully that there are now almost no troops on the Franco-Italian frontier, and if we have not actually got military alliances with Italy we have got a military understanding, such that we know we can pretty well rely on the help of each other's armies; and now with Germany arming and becoming steadily stronger and more dangerous, you ask us to destroy the new understanding with Italy and all that we gain from it. How do you think it is going to be done?'[1]

The smaller Powers, like the Little Entente, he went on to say, put their case rather differently. They said that no one could foretell the consequences if it came to putting on sanctions against Italy, and they had never contemplated the use of the powers of the League in the case of a country like Abyssinia. Show us the danger of violation of treaties and war in Europe, they said, and we will operate the Covenant all right against the aggressor, but

---

1. Vansittart states the French position correctly. For him the French objection was decisive. Other British statesmen, and especially Hoare the new foreign secretary, however drew the moral that France should be urged to support League action. If she did, the burden on Great Britain would not be severe. If she refused, she could be blamed for the failure of the League, and British public opinion would be satisfied. The smaller Powers, against Vansittart's expectation, proved loyal to the League and imposed sanctions against Italy.

we do not feel like doing it for the sake of a remote and backward country like Abyssinia. I made the obvious comment on these two cases—that France had made full use of the League and Covenant when it suited her in the recent breaking of the Peace Treaty by Germany and that if she was not now prepared to stand by the League in the case of a much worse moral offence then it was obvious that she was using the League simply for her own purposes: similarly that the position of the Little Entente as described by him was that the Covenant and collective security were not to come into operation until they felt that they and their individual interests were threatened. He said that he did not contest this point at all: he was merely attempting to state the case which in fact these people put forward as accurately as he could.

With regard to coming events at Geneva, his view was that things should be handled carefully and gradually. It might come to appointing a Commission and making an inquiry etc., but the important thing was not to take such steps as would drive Italy out of the League prematurely or give her an opportunity of walking out in dudgeon. If she went out war would follow at the earliest possible moment, and once war began it could not be stopped. As long as she did not go out there was always a chance —even if it was a poor one— of preventing the war. It was essential to keep the League going. If Italy went out it would greatly weaken the League. What was left must be held together with a view to building up again. He did not dispute the suggestion that if Italy made war and stopped in the League without anything being done against her there would be little virtue left in the League itself. He hinted that all one could hope for at the present time was a systematic attempt (which is clearly now going on) by France and England behind the scenes to get some sort of basis of settlement with Italy. He was rather strong on the point that countries like Abyssinia and Liberia ought never to have been admitted into the League.[1] He said that no country should be admitted until it had attained reasonably recognised standards in certain respects, and these Abyssinia never had attained. All the same, she being in the League, was an equal member and had to be treated as such. I mentioned the suggestion in the Times that the League should confer a mandate over Abyssinia on Italy, and asked whether there was anything behind that; any actual proposal from any quarter. He said that so far as he knew there was no

---

[1]. Ironically Abyssinia had been admitted to the League in 1925 at Italy's suggestion and against British opposition.

official proposal of that kind from any quarter whatever; it was a purely unofficial idea thrown out apparently for discussion. In any case it simply could not be carried out. No mandate over Abyssinia could be conferred unless she were first expelled from the League and such a thing was, of course, now inconceivable. In his view Abyssinia was the sort of country which would benefit a great deal from a mandate efficiently worked, and if she had not been in the League a mandate might easily have been very much to her interest. But the position being what it now was, and Abyssinia being under the Italian threat, all talk of mandates and expulsion was entirely unpractical.

He mentioned at the finish that he had been pleasantly impressed by Mussolini when he was at Stresa. Mussolini was quiet, reasonable, and not nearly as talkative as some of the other statesmen. He had been much disappointed in Mussolini's tactics and bombast since Stresa.

21 November 1935

11.45 A.M. IVAN MAISKY AT HARINGTON HOUSE

Maisky had been away from London for about three months. He explained that instead of holidaying in the South of Russia this time he had gone North. He had travelled the whole length of the newly made canal to the White Sea region and said that he had found very reasonable weather. Unfortunately on the way back from Russia he had been taken ill, and then taken ill again after his arrival in London.

Maisky began by talking about the extent of German rearmament. He said that he had stopped about a week in Berlin on the way back and both there and in Russia he had acquired a quantity of knowledge on the subject. The Germans were going ahead at a great pace. According to the much talked of 'timetable' they would not be ready for action until 1938; on the other hand, who was to say that they would choose to follow the time-table.[1] That doubt was, from the Russian point of view, one of the first results

---

1. The German 'timetable' remains difficult to gauge. Despite the contemporary alarms, German rearmament did not start seriously until 1936. By 1938, according to some authorities, Hitler may have believed that Germany was ready for minor actions as against Austria and Czechoslovakia. In April 1939 Hitler and Mussolini agreed that their two countries would not be ready for a major war until 1942 or 1943. The Russians, who expected to be attacked first, were naturally the most urgent in sounding the alarm.

of the Italian war. If the Italians became engaged up to the neck, what reason was there to suppose that the Germans might not take the opportunity to break out in Austria, or Czecho-slovakia?[1] If the latter, it was not necessary to assume that Poland would help the Germans; all that would be necessary would be for Poland to remain neutral and at the finish of the war she would get her reward by being allowed to swallow the particular piece of Czecho-slovakia which she coveted and claimed.[2] Maisky became amused, and said it was not necessary to conclude that the whole of Czecho-slovakia would be annexed: Germany would take a large part, Poland would take a part, and a wee bit might still be left as an independent Czecho-slovakia. He could not believe, he said, that if Italy were heavily weakened by the war France was going to fight Germany for the sake either of Austria or of Czecho-slovakia. He regarded the situation as very dangerous.

I asked him about Laval's overtures to Germany, and whether in his opinion anything was likely to come of them.[3] He said that nothing whatever could come of them unless France was prepared to sell her Eastern allies and leave Germany a free hand in the East, and how could France do that seeing that she had an actual treaty of alliance with Czecho-slovakia which bound her to come to the assistance of that country if she were attacked? We need not suppose that Germany would make an agreement with France on any other terms than the free hand in the East: why should she? That was the only thing that she wanted and the only thing for which she would make a definite agreement with the French.

He said that, of course, it was true that the position of France had been enormously changed and weakened by the coming of German rearmament. In the years following the war France had been predominant in Europe—herself armed to the teeth, herself fortified by Eastern alliances, Germany disarmed. Now her military superiority was cancelled by Germany and her alliances were no longer a stout reinforcement as they had been. All the same, in the Franco-German negotiations everything came back to the same point, that to be serious they had to mean that France would throw the Eastern countries to the German wolf.

· · · ·

1. Crozier wrongly spells Czechoslovakia with a hyphen. Until October 1938 Czechoslovakia was a unitary state, and the hyphen is correct only during the last six months of Czecho-Slovakia's existence.

2. The Poles had their eyes on Tešín which had been allotted to Czechoslovakia in 1920 and which in fact they seized in September 1938.

3. Laval was trying to secure the return of Germany to the League in order to escape from his difficulties over sanctions.

He pressed very strongly the point that to establish peace in Europe the most necessary thing was a close collaboration between England, France and Russia. He thought that if these three countries without formal alliances would stick together there was some chance of peace being preserved, but the Italian war had made things very uncertain. He was obviously much concerned to improve general relationships between this country and Russia. He mentioned that he was going to try to organise a visit of a League football team to Moscow, Leningrad and one or two other big cities. I said, 'Have you chosen your team?' and he laughed considerably and said 'Yes, Arsenal!' I said, 'Do you go to watch them?' and he said yes in a curious diffident manner, as if he was not sure whether an Ambassador, even a bolshevik, ought to be doing that.

4.45 P.M. SIR SAMUEL HOARE AT THE FOREIGN OFFICE

On 3 October 1935 Italian troops invaded Abyssinia. The League of Nations condemned Italy as an aggressor and imposed sanctions, banning all imports from Italy and cutting off credits to her. This programme of 'all sanctions short of war' enabled the National government to win the general election.

The Secretary of State's room is on the second floor of the Foreign Office, and three gold-braided officials were on duty outside it. The waiting-room is a large room, with enormous oil-paintings on the walls—George I, George II, Queen Caroline, Queen Victoria in middle age, and a smaller one of Matthew Prior; I did not understand exactly what Prior was doing there, but discovered from the inscription that he had been at Paris 'in an ambassadorial capacity'. On the table in the middle of the room there was only one paper, and that was the Morning Post: in addition there were two or three directories and the Times Atlas.

By way of starting the conversation, I said to Hoare, 'At any rate I am glad that the Government's majority[1] is so big that you can afford to do without. . . .'—'Winston Churchill,' he said, without letting me get any farther. 'I think you may take it as definite,' he added, 'though I have not got it from the horse's mouth, that he is not going to be in this Government; and you may also be assured that this Government is not going to move towards the diehards or towards the Right Wing. On the contrary I think it is going to move rather more towards the Left.'

---

1. The National government had now won the general election. Supporters of the National government 432; Labour 154; Liberals 20; Communist 1.

'Now, I will tell you,' he said, 'what is going to happen in foreign politics—in regard to Geneva and the League, I mean—we are going to go on as before, there is not going to be any change, in any way' . . . He could see nothing cheerful and no daylight anywhere. He just did not know what to think about the war; no one really knew how things were going there. The Italians kept on telling him about victories, and chiefs and tribes going over to them, but whether they were really getting on as well as they said he had no idea, nor, equally, whether the Abyssinians were doing badly or were yielding ground according to plan. There was nothing to be done at the moment but wait and see how things went at the war and how sanctions worked out. The position would be much clearer for us if the French were not so difficult; relations were on a better footing now, but still things were not all that could be desired.[1] There had been a lot of trouble at the time of the Notes exchanged in October. 'You mean those', I said, 'which were not published?' 'Yes,' he replied, 'and which will not be published.' It was very inadvisable that those notes should be published because 'they would have shown the French in so bad a light' and they would have put the French 'in the dock'. It was quite true that at the finish the French had promised us their unqualified support if we were attacked in the Mediterranean. 'And yet even now . . .' He said that unfortunately it still had to be assumed as a bare possibility that Mussolini, who was 'undoubtedly abnormal', might start on some 'mad dog' step against us, and then it might be found that the French were so completely divided into two sections (the pro-sanctions and the anti-sanctions) that the French Government would hardly dare to come to our assistance. He thought that the division of opinion in France was extremely serious. There were signs that another attack on this country was blowing up in the French press. I referred to the reports that some of the Paris papers were paid by Italy, and he said, rather drily, that he thought all of them were paid by someone. I then asked about the Notes which the French and British Governments are sending to Rome this week in reply to the Italian

---

1. The British government feared an Italian attack on their fleet in the Mediterranean and were prepared to contemplate this only if they were certain that they could have the use of French ports. Laval, the French foreign minister, would agree only if there had first been an attempt to conciliate Mussolini. Hence the discussions described on p. 60. The League had set up a committee of five to devise possible terms for a compromise. Great Britain and France had also been invited to suggest terms. Hoare was less than frank with Crozier over this. Vansittart was pressing strongly for agreement with Italy, and Sir Maurice Peterson of the foreign office was negotiating the details in Paris on Hoare's authority.

protest about sanctions, and he said 'Well, you will find that they are all right.' But he added that there had been some trouble about the French Note, that the French had tried to have it '50-50' (pleasant to the League and also pleasant to Mussolini) but that things had been made all right.

Hoare then went on to talk about the character of Laval. He said that he was a great opportunist, always extemporising and willing only to deal with each difficulty as it came up—'like Lloyd George'. It was no use to tell him that some policy which he was advocating would never get past the League if it was proposed in the course of days or weeks; all Laval cared about was to do what he wanted to do at the moment and to leave the consequences until eventually the moment came when they could not be evaded. Laval was a subtle and cunning person—'rather like a French peasant who was always thinking of getting the better of someone over the price of a chicken'. It would have been much simpler for us if we had had Briand to deal with.

With regard to the chances of settling the war, Hoare said that he had at present no hopes. Mussolini's terms were too far away from anything that either this country or the League could accept. He had sent Peterson, the head of the Abyssinian section of the Foreign Office, to Paris to see if they could devise some basis of a settlement that was worth consideration, but he had no hopes that anything would come of this. I inquired what sort of terms of settlement he himself now regarded as practicable—the Paris proposals or the plan of the Committee of Five, or what? He said the plan of the Committee of Five was in his opinion a reasonable basis; it was a League plan (as compared with the Paris proposals) and the Emperor of Abyssinia had actually agreed to it; he thought moreover, that if it were carried out honestly it would strengthen Abyssinia. It was a plan also which in some of its particulars permitted of variations. There was, however, a new difficulty, and that was the way in which the Italian army was occupying Abyssinian territory. The Italians were telling us, and would continue to tell us, that as they penetrated into Abyssinia the chiefs and the tribes were spontaneously declaring their anxiety to be rescued from Abyssinian oppression and, of course, said Hoare, there is some reason to think that a good many of those tribes have no affection for their Abyssinian masters.

We then came to sanctions and Laval's recent feelers towards Germany. As to sanctions, Hoare said that he had no doubt that when Parliament met the Government would be attacked from two sides, by those who would say that sanctions were ineffective and must be strengthened, and by those who would say that sanctions were so ineffective that they ought to be abandoned. He was going to say that sanctions were not ineffective and that they would be effective in the future even if their operation were somewhat slow, provided that the League Powers stood together. Italy's financial and economic position was weak and it was his opinion that the cutting off of her exports and the consequent drain on her money would before long be a serious thing for her. The process would, however, be irritating not only to Mussolini but also to the sanctionist States who would suffer loss. I asked him if he thought that these States would stick together, and he said yes, provided that the French remain constant, but if the French showed signs of weakening then he thought that a number the smaller States would very soon 'take cover'. I asked him if he thought that the appointment of Badoglio was a sign that Mussolini feared sanctions and felt that the campaign must be hurried on.[1] He was not prepared to say, he said, but was quite sure that the Italian Government was really apprehensive of the results of sanctions and that all the defiant shouting on the subject was a sign of this. As for Badoglio, he knew one thing—and this he had from the French General Staff—that when Badoglio attended the recent French manoeuvres he was holding up his hands in horror at the idea of the campaign.

.   .   .   .   .

Throughout the interview Hoare made on me a strong impression of straightforwardness, sincerity and largeness of view.

Attached to this interview is a note by John Russell Scott, the proprietor of the Manchester Guardian:

'Many thanks for the sight of these most interesting documents. It is particularly useful to know Hoare's mind. I have entertained high hopes of him ever since the India Act and everything you say confirms this. In view of Baldwin's age & known desire to get out of politics it is possible that the leadership may become vacant even during this Parliament & it is important therefore to do all one can to strengthen Hoare vis-à-vis Neville [Chamberlain].'

---

1. Badoglio, chief of the Italian general staff, had been sent out to take command in Abyssinia.

28 November 1935

11.00 A.M. SIR BOLTON EYRES-MONSELL AT THE ADMIRALTY

This interview with the first lord of the admiralty discussed the technical details and British programme for the forthcoming naval conference in 1936. Thanks to Japanese opposition to any agreement, the conference was never in fact held.

Sir Samuel Hoare did not live up to the high expectations which Crozier and Scott had placed on him. On 7 December, Peterson having prepared the way, he went to Paris and negotiated with Laval. The two men devised the Hoare-Laval plan. Italy would receive the fertile plains. The emperor of Abyssinia would retain his mountain kingdom and would receive a corridor through British Somaliland to the sea. The British cabinet approved the plan. Mussolini indicated his readiness to accept it. Once the League acquiesced, as it would, the plan could be imposed on the emperor. Hoare went off for a holiday in Switzerland, confident that he had solved the crisis. The plan appeared prematurely in the Paris press. British opinion was aroused. A storm blew against this betrayal of the League. Hoare was induced to take all the blame by a promise that he would be brought back into the government at the earliest possible moment. The government repudiated the Hoare-Laval plan. Their moral standing was restored.

That was all. The League did not impose any further sanctions, such as the oil sanction, on Italy. By May 1936 Abyssinia had been conquered. Two months earlier German troops entered the Rhineland. This end of the old order brought, or coincided with, a long break in Crozier's recordings.

2

Before the War, 1936–39

Crozier's interviews are disappointingly thin in this period—only one recorded visit to London in 1936, only one in 1937, and only two before the outbreak of war in 1939. Some accounts of interviews have disappeared, as noted at the relevant dates, but it is also clear that Crozier recorded less. No doubt he often went to London. Maybe he needed less briefing on such topics as the Spanish civil war; maybe he relied on his own staff, especially F A Voigt.

Even the records for 1938, though fuller, are disappointing to a latter-day reader. Looking back now, the year 1938 seems dominated by the Czech crisis which led up to the Munich conference. Crozier's interviews are a reminder, perhaps accidental, that this did not stand out so sharply at the time. There were other topics: the Spanish civil war which preoccupied the British Left far more than the Czech question did; the appeasement of Ireland, which concerned Crozier as editor of an old Home Rule paper; and the problems of Palestine, which concerned him as a deeply committed Zionist.

The interviews suggest a further adjustment of view. Many historians nowadays see in the prewar years the story of Hitler's deliberate march to war and world conquest. Austria, Munich, Prague and Danzig were so many milestones on the road. The only question for others was how to stop Hitler and when. Some contemporaries, including Vansittart and perhaps the British chiefs of staff, certainly took this view. Many did not or took it only with one part of their minds. Until the late summer of 1938 the Czech question was generally treated in terms of the Sudeten Germans rather than of Hitler. These German-speaking inhabitants of Czechoslovakia had grievances, widely accepted as genuine. If these grievances were met, the question would be settled. I do not think that this view was altogether mistaken. Whether Hitler was set on war or not, he needed material, and the Sudeten grievances provided it. An analogy with recent events in Northern Ireland is not out of place. The IRA want to end Northern Ireland and to set up a united Irish republic. But the IRA would get nowhere if the Roman Catholic minority in Northern Ireland did not feel, and with just cause, that it had been unfairly treated during the last fifty years. We may say now that the Sudeten Germans could never have been satisfied and that Hitler used their grievances as a pretext. This is the wisdom of hindsight. The men of the time thought, rightly or wrongly, that the settlement of Sudeten grievances was the only course to follow, and we err if we interpret their outlook in other terms.

15 July 1936

Hore-Belisha was still minister of transport and still not a member of the cabinet. Obviously he had lost all hope of promotion under Baldwin, though in fact he entered the cabinet in October, and had set his sights on Neville Chamberlain.

Baldwin gave signs during 1936 of being near a physical breakdown. In June he discussed his resignation with Neville Chamberlain and decided to put it off for a year. His condition grew worse during the summer, and he might well have resigned in the autumn if it had not been for the problem of king Edward VIII's relations with Mrs Simpson. This affair reinvigorated Baldwin. He conducted the king's abdication with impeccable skill and remained as prime minister until after the coronation of George VI in May 1937.

.　　.　　.　　.　　.

Much the most interesting things that he said concerned Baldwin and the coming change of Government. He said more than once, with great emphasis, that he was sure that Neville Chamberlain had already a firm agreement with Baldwin that Baldwin would resign during the recess and that he, Neville, would succeed him. Twice over he used the words 'I am convinced' that such an arrangement had been made, and he gave me the impression throughout that he either had his information, as he said, direct from someone in personal communication with Neville, or possibly directly from him himself. With regard to Neville's views on politics and personalities he said he had the information straight from someone who had been talking to Neville, but I should not be surprised if he himself were the person.

He put it that Baldwin admittedly was tired and anxious to give up the burden, and that his prestige and that of the Government had been continuously sinking. He said it was impossible to go on indefinitely with a Premier who had to be 'explained almost every week'. Moreover, Neville himself could not contemplate such a steady decline of the prestige of the Government without anxiety. He would not want to take over a declining concern; he had the strongest reason for desiring to succeed, if he was going to succeed, while the Government had a reasonably strong position. Therefore he (H-B) always came back to the same conclusion, which was that there would be a change in the premiership before the end of the recess.

He had a great deal to say about the nature of the changes that would be likely to follow if Neville became Prime Minister. The guiding principle, he thought, would be that 'passengers' and inefficients would be dropped and actual working achievement would be rewarded. It followed that Neville would not be greatly concerned to preserve the arithmetical proportionate strength of each section in the Coalition—Tories, Simonites, Labour. He would drop the useless and keep, or bring in, useful men, even if it involved altering the accepted proportions. This did not mean, of course, that he would drop the National Government idea. The election had been won on that basis and therefore that basis would be continued.

H-B seemed to be quite certain that Ramsay MacDonald would be dropped. Ramsay apparently came under the category of the 'passengers' and therefore on the pure ground of efficiency he would certainly be dropped. He was merely representing the National idea and contributed nothing in the way of work or achievement to the Ministry and therefore there would be no place for him in a hard-working Cabinet. Malcolm, on the other hand, would remain.

It appeared also that N C had certain dislikes. He apparently has no love for some of the younger and, as is commonly supposed, more enterprising Tories. Those who were mentioned as not being loved by him in this connection were Elliot, Eden, Ormsby-Gore and Duff Cooper (nothing, however, was said to indicate that N C would try to do without them but only that he had no love for them).[1] H-B went on to say that it was most important to remember about N C that he still retained a great deal of the Birmingham Radicalism of his father, Joseph. He was not only a Chamberlainite Protectionist but he was radically minded with regard to social and political affairs at home. H-B believed that this side of his character would come out strongly when he was in the saddle as Premier and that a good many Tories would not like it when they discovered it. He said that he himself in his projects at the Ministry of Transport had not only had strong support from Neville when dealing with rights of property, etc. but could simply not have got some of his proposals through the Cabinet (he instanced property rights in the Ribbon Development Bill) had not Neville backed him up.

I got the impression as a whole that H-B was looking forward to Neville's Premiership and that he thought that a comparatively

---

1. Walter Elliot continued in office throughout Chamberlain's government. Eden, though remaining at first as foreign secretary, was got rid of by Chamberlain in February 1938. Ormsby-Gore, colonial secretary, went in May 1938; Duff Cooper, first lord of the admiralty, in October 1938, not altogether of his own volition.

good time might be coming under such a Premier for Ministers with comparatively liberal and radical ideas of policy. He also laid some stress on the advantage of having a Premier with a mind of his own who wanted to get things done. And when I made some reference to Neville's gift for indiscretions and not seeing the effect which his words might have on the public, he agreed that that was so, but reverted to his clearness of mind and purpose.

I asked H-B about Austen Chamberlain and in particular why, without any preliminary sign that I knew of, he had made his ferocious onslaught in the House on Baldwin. He said he believed the story was as follows:—At the time of the Hoare-Laval fiasco Baldwin had really made an appeal to Austen Chamberlain to come to the rescue of the Government; a very serious revolt was brewing among the Tories, apart altogether from the Opposition and the League people. Austen had responded, had held his hand, had exercised a restraining influence and in general had something substantial to do with 'saving the Government', and probably thought that he had done most of that himself. At any rate the Government was saved, Hoare resigned, and Austen expected the Foreign Secretaryship. Instead of that Baldwin sent for him and explained to him in effect that he was too old a man for the job. This Austen had bitterly resented and probably it accounted in part at least for the unexpected and ferocious attack in the House.[1]

16 July 1936

LORD ZETLAND AT THE INDIA OFFICE

The Marquis of Zetland was secretary of state for India from 1935 to 1940. He had little impact on events.

The omitted passages cover political developments in India and the problem of Palestine. Crozier concluded that Zetland 'would be firmly on the side of the Arabs'.

He is a not very impressive figure, does a good deal of laughing, and almost giggling, during the conversation, and gives one the impression, rather like his books, of being goodish but something of a lightweight. This was, however, only my first conversation with him. It rather gave me the feeling that a friend of mine who

---

1. Austen Chamberlain criticised the government over rearmament solely because he was dissatisfied at the delays. The story of how Baldwin cheated him over the foreign office at the time of the Hoare-Laval plan is however correct. Or maybe he cheated himself. At any rate he complained of Baldwin: 'He told me I was ga-ga'—which he was.

had known him for a long time was pretty accurate when he said
to me sometime ago, after Zetland's appointment; 'Zetland? Oh
there is no harm in Zetland, no harm at all.'

16 December 1937

10.30 A.M. LESLIE HORE-BELISHA AT 16 STAFFORD PLACE

Hore-Belisha became secretary for war in May 1937. He was anxious to
modernise the war office. In December 1937 he pushed out Field-Marshal
Sir Claud Deverell, the CIGS, and General Sir Harry Knox, the adjutant
general. Major-General Sir Alexander Knox MP who made a fuss about this
in the house of commons was Sir Harry Knox's brother. General Lord Gort
became CIGS.

'X' is presumably Deverell, and 'Y' presumably Knox.

He spoke of the recent resignations, expressed great pleasure at
the good press he had had and thanked the MG again; he said
that he thought there had been only two really critical articles and
he could not remember where they had appeared. I told him that
I was astonished that General Knox, MP should have stated in
the House of Commons what had been so carefully concealed
under the kindly words of the official report about 'resignations'
(Knox had asked whether it were not the fact that the resigning
Generals had only been given two hours' notice). He said it was
surprising and that Winston Churchill had afterwards said to him
'Knox has torn away the fig-leaf which you had so carefully
provided.' David Kirkwood had come up to him and said 'This
has made you an idol of the Clyde.' I told him he could take it
from me that public opinion would support him in almost anything that he could do at the War Office in the name of efficiency;
that public opinion ever since the Boer War (so far as modern
memories went) regarded the War Office as a place of woodenness
and conservatism and would heartily support him if he could
remove the prospect that it would go into the next war as slow
and hidebound as it was in the last (witness the Tank).

He talked about 'X' and said when he had asked him to draw
up a memorandum organising the army on a Home and Empire
basis, cutting out the continental war basis, he had composed such
a scheme as made out the desired basis to be impossible. As to 'Y',
he said that he had attributed the whole of the recent increase in
recruiting to the lowering of the medical standard, although the
figures plainly showed that the whole increase was about 2,500
and the increase due to the lowering of standards only 800. 'Why,'

he had asked, 'do you attribute the whole of this increase to this cause only; it simply is not true.' 'Y' had replied that it was necessary to do this in order not to let the idea get about that recruiting was really improving; it was necessary to show every year that the position was as bad as ever.

He spoke of Gort and said that he would do well. He was not a first-class brain, but he was co-operative and open to ideas. Also he was a man of private means and this was not unimportant, because he found that soldiers who had to be thinking about their pay, their future, their pensions and so on had not got the courageous and independent mind that was needed; if they had means of their own they cared for nobody and did not think of hanging on to office.

.   .   .   .   .

With regard to ships being sent to the Far East in view of Japanese outrages in the Yangtse etc., he said that we should of course send if USA sent. I said what would we do if the Japs went on 'outraging' and USA would not do anything? I said that in that case, in view of Italy etc., we could *not* send ships. 'But we must!' he said (i.e. cannot let ourselves be blotted out in the Far East). (Contrast this with what N Chamberlain said to me;[1] it shows the division in the Cabinet.)

3.30 P.M. SIR ARCHIBALD SINCLAIR AT THE HOUSE OF COMMONS

Sir Archibald Sinclair became leader of the Liberal party after the general election of 1935 when Sir Herbert Samuel lost his seat and went to the house of lords.

The admiralty were anxious to establish a 'two-ocean' navy (i.e. one fleet in European waters and one in the Far East) and in 1939 claimed to have accomplished this.

He was late, having just come from a luncheon party with Eden[2] at which the subject of possible naval reinforcement for the Far East had been discussed. He mentioned the same point that others had made to me, namely that as Italy's two modern battleships were still under construction and the German pocket battleships were not regarded as highly formidable, we were in a position to

---

1. See Crozier's interview with Chamberlain on the following day.
2. Anthony Eden was foreign secretary, Dec. 1935–Feb. 1938.

send a pretty considerable force to the Far East if we desired to. The question of British interests as against League or general interests was raised and he said that he approved of the ships being sent to the Far East, but was sorry that we were going to send them if it were for the sake of purely British interests instead of the more general interests as might have been the case.

5 P.M. J W DULANTY AT HIS LONDON OFFICE

John Whelan Dulanty was Irish high commissioner from 1930 to 1950. He was a windbag of a man who liked imparting as strict secrets information that was known to everybody.

This interview merely summarises the topics which de Valera proposed to discuss with the British government. The Anglo-Irish meetings began on 17 January 1938. Details of these negotiations are given in the biography of de Valera by the Earl of Longford and Thomas P O'Neill (1970).

17 December 1937

11.30 A.M. NEVILLE CHAMBERLAIN AT 10 DOWNING STREET

Chamberlain's method of inviting precise questions did not encourage conversation, and Crozier did not meet him again. According to the records, Chamberlain doubted whether any effective co-operation could be obtained from the United States in the Far East.

The Premier struck me at once as a very practical businesslike person. He began by saying that if I would put the points which most interested me into a few questions he would do his best to answer them.

I began by saying that I was much interested in the question of Anglo-American co-operation, both in respect of trade agreement and of the Far East, and how was he getting on. He said 'Very well. The trade agreement talks were making progress' and that I could be assured that the Government attached the greatest importance to securing agreement, and meant to get it. I said something about the political side of it and he replied that although no doubt the making of the agreement would be important politically, what he would emphasise was that serious damage would now be done if the agreement did not come off. 'We must have it', he said with considerable energy. I asked him how the dominions were regarding it and said that I had been told by an Australian, who knew some of the Australian Ministers, that it would be a very good thing if for once the Downing Street Government were not diffident about giving a lead but actually put pressure on the Australians to co-operate in a positive way in helping on the agreement. 'They are getting it all right', he said, 'they are certainly getting it.'

He then spoke of the Far East. I made some reference to the unfortunate events of 1931–2, when Sir John Simon was supposed to have rebuffed Stimson's offers of co-operation. Chamberlain replied with some energy that the whole American story as told by Stimson did a great injustice to Simon, who had been quite willing to co-operate (a few weeks before Eden had used the same sort of language to me). He said he had read the whole file of documents relating to that episode and he could find no basis whatever for the charge against Simon. He believed that it arose out of certain telephone conversations between Stimson and Simon —which is the fact—and that personally he would take care not to conduct any important negotiations of this kind again by telephone.

Chamberlain went on to talk of the possibilities of 'parallel action' in the Far East and said that he thought it possible that the Americans might be willing to do something, and that if they were willing to move ships he would be willing to send out ships 'like a shot', but, if not, then no. He referred also to the episode of the sinking of the PANAY on the Yangtse and its effect on American opinion.

1 March 1938

5.15 P.M. J W DULANTY AT HIS OFFICE

Further details of the Anglo-Irish negotiations which had run into difficulties over partition. They were resumed on 3 March.

6.30 P.M. SIR ROBERT VANSITTART AT THE FOREIGN OFFICE

Vansittart was now Chief Diplomatic Adviser, a post to which Eden had consigned him at the beginning of the year. His previous conversation with Crozier referred to in the opening sentence and presumably on or about 4 February, has not survived.

On 4 February, at the last meeting of the German cabinet held during the Third Reich, Hitler made a clean sweep of the surviving non-Nazis in high places. Blomberg, supreme commander of the armed forces and war minister, was discredited by his marriage to a woman of bad character; Fritsch, the commander in chief of the army, by trumped-up allegations of homosexuality. Both were dismissed. Hitler himself took over Blomberg's offices; a tame soldier, Brauchitsch, became commander in chief of the army. At the same time Neurath was succeeded as foreign minister by Ribbentrop, Hitler's dependent. Himmler, head of the SS, did not advance his position and does not seem to have exercised a decisive influence on foreign policy at this time. Contrary to Vansittart's view, the upheaval was not directly concerned with foreign affairs. According to some authorities, Hitler may have decided on a more active foreign policy in the autumn of 1937, but the only dispute was over the rate of rearmament and even this was unclear. Hitler it seems, simply took advantage of Blomberg's marriage to get rid of dead weight.

On 12 February Schuschnigg, the Austrian chancellor, visited Hitler at Berchtesgaden. He intended to protest against Nazi activities in Austria. Hitler got his blow in first. He complained against the treatment of the Austrian Nazis, and Schuschnigg was compelled to make considerable concessions. On 20 February Hitler addressed the Reichstag and was able to use the agreement with Schuschnigg as a diversion from his dismissal of the conservative ministers and generals.

Mussolini had earlier acted as the protector of Austria. He now recognised that he was too weak to do so any longer. Neville Chamberlain however hoped that Hitler might be deterred by the prospect of Anglo-Italian reconciliation. He insisted on opening conversations with Italy, thus provoking the resignation of Eden, the foreign secretary. Hitler was not impressed by these manoeuvres.

Mussolini's policy of co-operation with Germany ultimately brought Italy and himself to disaster. At the time it seemed the safer course. If he opposed Hitler, Italy would have to stand in the front line. By going with Hitler he could make easy gains in the Mediterranean, as almost happened in the summer of 1940.

I reminded him that when I had seen him last the Hitler crisis, supposed to be over Blomberg and the army officers, was in full swing and that he had told me that in his opinion the crisis was only primarily concerned with the army and had really to do with a forward policy in Austria, if not perhaps also with Spain.

He now said that in his opinion there had undoubtedly been some opposition in the higher ranks of the army over Hitler's intention to go ahead in Austria and he had swept this opposition out of existence. The whole affair had, however, created doubt and anxiety in Germany, and Hitler intended to have something positive to show his people; he had promised to speak in the Reichstag and this had had to be postponed. He needed something therefore from the point of view of prestige for his speech, hence perhaps the choice of this moment for the coup at Berchtesgaden. I asked him if he thought the purge of army generals, etc. would in any way weaken the German army, and he said for the moment that it would to a certain extent, but that this would soon pass away.

He then went on to discuss Mussolini's part. He said that for some time he had not been able to make up his mind whether Mussolini had been informed of the new attack on Austria or not. He had, however, now come entirely to the conclusion—and he

added with emphasis that there was a certain amount of knowledge
behind this—that Mussolini had been told nothing at all, that the
stroke must have come to him as a most unpleasant surprise and
that in fact he had received 'a violent kick in the pants.' It must
not be supposed, however, that Mussolini would be able in any
way to weaken or retire from the axis; he must stick to the axis
as long as he had no friends in the Mediterranean and he dare not
do anything to weaken it until it was entirely certain that he was
free in the Mediterranean from his present embarrassments. He
was quite sure that the Berchtesgaden proceedings had in fact
greatly quickened Mussolini's desire for conversations. [Note that
a week later the Polish Ambassador told me that he took the same
view, only that he was still more emphatic; he said that Mussolini
had eagerly desired the conversations ever since Neville Chamberlain became Prime Minister and had desired them even more
urgently after Berchtesgaden.] He went on to say that in his heart
Mussolini must desire to be in a position to put a brake on the axis;
it might very well be that he was already too late. In that case he
was completely 'done' so far as Austria, and indeed Italian ambitions in Continental Europe, were concerned. I suggested that if
Mussolini were willing to sacrifice Austria he must be hoping to
recoup himself on a great scale in the Mediterranean, otherwise
he would have lost the game everywhere. V replied that in his
opinion there was no possibility of Mussolini being able to to do
this; he seemed to think that that game was up. [Franco's advance
towards the sea followed a week later.] I said that supposing
Mussolini did get out of Spain as a condition of the settlement with
us, was Germany likely to clear out; she hoped for raw materials,
etc. and to provide a third hostile frontier for France. He said
that these were strong points and that he was not at all sure that
Germany would go out.

Referring in general to Mussolini's policy, he said that he
thought M had made a great mess of things. After sanctions he
had gone over to Germany in a fit of pique, perhaps thought that
he could hold Hitler in and that the attack on Austria would be a
gradual affair. Moreover, if Mussolini now made an agreement
with England and France, it was quite possible that Hitler might
strike in Austria lest Mussolini should try to hamper him, as by
giving him strong hints that he must go slow.

On the question of the changes in Germany V said that the
growing importance of Himmler and Ribbentrop was a thoroughly
bad sign. Ribbentrop, he kept on repeating, was a dangerous man
because thoroughly ignorant—'He knows nothing, he knows

nothing'—'and Himmler,' he said, 'belongs to the very worst and most violent section of the Left Wing of the Nazi Party.' With such men in power only the worst was to be expected.

11 March 1938

10.00 A.M. LESLIE HORE-BELISHA AT HIS HOME

Hore-Belisha had introduced the army estimates the night before. He ran over his proposed reforms and said: 'The army would not be called upon again for duty on the Continent on a national scale.'

1.00 P.M. DR CHAIM WEIZMANN AT THE CARLTON GRILL

Weizmann who was leader of the Zionist movement had discussed Palestine with Chamberlain and other ministers. Halifax had just become foreign secretary, and Weizmann said: 'If Halifax knows no more about the other questions of foreign policy than he knows about Palestine and the Near East, God help this poor country.'

3.30 P.M. SIR ROBERT VANSITTART AT THE FOREIGN OFFICE

On 8 March Schuschnigg defied Hitler by announcing a plebiscite on the question of Austrian independence. On 11 March Hitler's emissaries delivered an ultimatum, demanding that the plebiscite be postponed for three weeks. Schuschnigg agreed after some hesitation and resigned in the course of the afternoon. However German forces, though not prepared for action, crossed the Austrian frontier at dawn on 12 March. Austria was incorporated in Germany on 13 March, and a plebiscite approved this on 10 April (99.08% in Greater Germany, 99.75% in the former Austria).

I had not expected to see him, but as an appointment was post-poned I called at the Foreign Office on chance and he said he would like to see me.

He was quite different from the man I had seen on various other occasions. He said wearily 'Well, we are face to face at last with the new Germany', and then sat down and relapsed into silence. I should mention that the evening paper bills up to that moment had said only 'Germany Moves Troops' and they contained nothing more than reports of the gathering of troops along the Bavarian-Austrian frontier. Vansittart was obviously gloomy, depressed and also bitter. He said that the methods and intentions of Hitler were now at last openly disclosed and he hoped that people (whom he did not name) would now at least pay some attention to what he had all along been telling them about the mentality of the Nazis. 'I know the Nazis well', he said, and went on to say that they had only one method of action, which Hitler had now made use of against Austria, and that was ultimatum backed by force and, 'mark my words', he added, 'one of these ultimatums will be coming our way sometime'.

.   .   .   .   .

We again went over the ground about Italy and Austria and he repeated his view that Italy had at bottom suffered a great defeat and that Mussolini was anxious for the conversations with England to some extent because of the mess into which the axis had got him. He was sure that Mussolini would not be able to obtain large compensation in the Mediterranean, but I think that what he meant was not that Mussolini might not try to obtain it, but that we should not let him. [I do not know what he would have said to the Chamberlain point of view that Franco, if conqueror, will not be guided by Italian and German influence; he certainly does not himself hold that view at all, as he told me on an earlier occasion that he regarded the Franco threat through Italy and Germany as serious and that it was of no use to say that in two or three years Franco would come round to our side; because it was just those two or three years which were likely to be decisive. I think his view undoubtedly was that if the Franco threat seemed likely to develop in that way we should have to tackle it decisively, whereas Chamberlain's idea seems to be to deny that there is going to be a threat at all.][1]

There being nothing in the papers except movements of troops, I asked him whether there was likely to be pressure behind it— something in the nature of an ultimatum—and he said that undoubtedly that was the effect and that Hitler was really striking at last. As I was leaving he repeated his view about the Hitler method and in particular that the time would come when we would receive one of the ultimatums.[2]

---

1. Germany and Italy both assisted Franco throughout the Spanish civil war. Presumably they expected to profit from this. As things turned out, Franco remained neutral, except against Soviet Russia, during the second world war.

2. Curiously enough Vansittart's prophecy was not fulfilled. The only ultimatum exchanged between Great Britain and Germany was the British ultimatum to Germany of 3 September 1939 which preceded the outbreak of war.

LATE AFTERNOON. TELEPHONE CONVERSATION WITH J W DULANTY

Details of the Anglo-Irish negotiations which had reached deadlock.

12 March 1938

10.30 A.M. COUNT EDWARD RACZYNSKI AT THE POLISH EMBASSY

Count Edward Raczynski was Polish ambassador in London from 1934 to 1945. Crozier and he attempted to listen to the broadcast of Hitler's proclamation to the German nation. 'The crackling and roaring were so terrific that he soon turned it off again.'

12 April 1938

The following interviews have been lost:
4.30 P.M. SIR ROBERT VANSITTART.
5.45 P.M. J W DULANTY.

22 April 1938

4.00 P.M. SEÑOR AZCÁRATE Y FLÓREZ AT THE SPANISH EMBASSY

Azcárate was Spanish ambassador from 1936 to 1939. 'He was fairly cheerful.'

5.15 P.M. J W DULANTY AT HIS OFFICE

Details of the Anglo-Irish agreement which was signed on 25 April 1938.

·　·　·　·　·

Malcolm MacDonald[1] told him that he could have done nothing however hard he had tried unless Neville Chamberlain had determined to give in all through. De Valera had been good too. M M had done magnificently. Inskip had helped. Simon not so useful, but that might be his manner.

26 May 1938

AT BREAKFAST. LESLIE HORE-BELISHA

He was much worried on the telephone and said people had been

---

1. Commonwealth secretary.

O.T.R.—D

ringing up since 8 o'clock. I could not but hear that one of the subjects was the large brick dropped by Col. Kerr, the Liberal National Whip, with regards to the Jews in his speech the previous night. It was obvious that trouble was brewing and I heard afterwards (from Neville Laski) that H-B had taken a prominent part in the discussions in the matter.[1]

.　.　.　.　.

I mentioned to him that there were all kinds of statements appearing, as in the Times, to the effect that there had been no serious movement of troops on the Czech frontier on the previous Thursday and Friday, and therefore no genuine ground for international crisis. He said that certainly there had been troop movements and if there had not been something serious why did the Czechs mobilise so suddenly?[2]

11.30 A.M. JOSEPH KENNEDY AT THE AMERICAN EMBASSY

Joseph Kennedy was American ambassador from 1936 to 1941. He is usually supposed to have favoured the appeasers. In this interview he complained of the inadequate reporting of United States affairs in the British press. He also foretold, correctly, that Roosevelt would be a candidate at the Presidential election in 1940.

22 June 1938

JAN MASARYK

At this time, Crozier was noting his interlocutors as A, B, C etc. A was Jan Masaryk, and this interview was therefore the first of the day. Masaryk was Czechoslovak minister in London, 1925–38.

---

1. Lieutenant-Colonel Kerr told the Scottish Liberal National association at Glasgow that there were intrigues, inspired by the Communists, to oust the National government. 'He regretted to say that the bulk of the people working in that direction were of the Jewish race. Their policy was to build up the League of Nations really to fight those outside the League.' In a letter to The Times on 28 May Kerr explained that he was merely attacking the idea of Liberals working with Labour in a popular front and that many of his best friends were Jews.

2. On 21 May the Czechs mobilised on an alarm that German forces were moving towards the Czechoslovak frontier. Despite Hore-Belisha's remark, it appears from the German records that there were no German troop movements. The story was probably a plant, perhaps by British intelligence officers, with the hope of deterring Hitler. The effect was quite the opposite.

Konrad Henlein was the leader of the Sudeten German nationalist party. In May he visited London and made a favourable impression on, among others, Churchill, Sinclair, Vansittart and, it seems, Masaryk. Later writers have usually dismissed him as a mere stooge of Hitler's, telling lies in London. Keith Robbins has recently argued (Historical Journal, xii, 674–97) that Henlein was trying to follow an independent course and genuinely wanted autonomy for the Sudeten Germans.

I asked A whether the discussions between the Czech Govt. and the Henlein party were likely to come to a settlement. He said that they certainly *should,* there was no doubt about that. The Czech Govt. *was* willing to concede what Henlein wanted, if it were only Henlein that were concerned. He had told Henlein so in London. He had talked to him for two hours in the room where we were and there was nothing in Henlein's demands as put forward there which could not be granted by the Czech Govt. Of course, the German Govt might spike the chances of a settlement, and Henlein had extremists of his own to consider. [It was obvious that Henlein had talked a lot about his 'extremists', but A certainly believes that Henlein was himself comparatively moderate.]

A thought that Germany might allow Henlein to make a settlement though 'I don't say that it will be permanent!' But Germany had, for the time, learned a lesson. She had learned that she could not overbear Czecho-Slovakia without a war—that Cz-Sl would fight instantly if she were threatened with force. It was the Czech mobilisation and what France had said and what Britain had said which had taught Hitler a lesson and had made it probable, he thought, that Hitler would not take violent measures in the near future. He was obviously extremely pleased with the events of the May 21 week-end and, above all, with the action taken by Britain. I asked about German troop movements on the Czech frontier (which the Germans had angrily denied) and inquired had there really been any of any consequence. 'Yes, there had,' he said, 'and don't forget,' he added, 'that we, the Czechs, heard of these movements *first from your people!*'[1]

A proceeded to talk with great vigour about Ribbentrop and his interviews with diplomatists at the week-end of May 21. There had been a violent scene between R and Henderson, the British Ambassador in Berlin. He had asked R whether the German Govt. really meant to do anything about Czecho-Slovakia that would bring the whole British Empire with all its resources, etc., etc. into the field. R replied contemptuously 'Ramshackle Empire

1. See the interview of 26 May with Hore-Belisha.

talk that is!' and H had retorted with great heat.[1] R had talked most offensively to the poor little Czech Minister in Berlin. 'Germany', he said, 'had not threatened and was not proposing to attack Cz Slovakia, but if the Czechs did not take care, they would destroy Prague and everybody in it.'[2] I inquired about R's character, mentioning some of the things I had heard about him, and he said that he was a dreadful creature. 'I've sat next to him continually on the Non-Intervention Committee—I must have spent 300 hours sitting next to him—and he's ignorant, overbearing, violent and reckless.'

He was cheerful about Italy and said that 'Italy will never fight alongside Germany in a European war—never!'

He told me an extraordinary story. Halifax, he said, had actually asked Lothian to write to his friends in Germany telling them that Britain had, after all, not meant much at the crisis of May 21; they must not interpret it in an unfriendly way at all! Lothian had refused—(A was immensely jubilant and amused over this)—and had replied that it would be futile to do any such thing—'Lothian, mind you, Lothian!'

A is an extraordinarily vivid personality, dramatic in words and gestures, speaking English more fluently and easily than any foreign diplomatist I have met, and using violent expletives with great neatness and facility. He asked me to come and see him again whenever I could.

SIR ROBERT VANSITTART (B)

I asked B whether there was a good chance of settlement between the Czech Government and the Henlein Germans. He said that there certainly *could* be a settlement, but Beneš *must hurry*; he was too slow and thought he had more time to spare than he really had. Hitler and Co did not want a settlement and would prevent one if they could. Why did not the press point out more clearly what was the German game? The last thing Hitler wanted was a good, firm settlement in Cz-Sl.

The Anglo-Italian Agreement looked like being a failure. He

---

1. No such remark by Ribbentrop appears in British Diplomatic Documents. Masaryk, like Beneš, had a vivid imagination.

2. Crozier added a note in pencil: Raczynski, Polish Minister in London, said to me about Dirksen, the German Ambassador:—'He says the most appalling things in the calmest, gentlest manner. He said to me about the Czechs "Count, if they go on the present way [he was speaking of their 'provocations'], we shall have to take action".'

had thought that the experiment was worth making and that the Agreement might to some extent 'loosen the Axis'. But there was no sign of that yet. Mussolini in his Genoa speech had shown the utmost hostility towards France and that was still maintained; he showed no sign of renewing the conversations with France!

No one was pointing out—and it was lamentable—what were the objects of German-Italian policy. They were:

(1) to drive Russia out of Europe politically.

(2) to divide England and France.

What greater victory could they desire than to get rid of Russia and to have England and France divided? They were aiming at these two things all the time. They aimed at smashing the Cz-Russian alliance and the Franco-Russian alliance. Germany would have no Czech settlement, if she could help it, that left the Czech-Russian alliance intact. And Italy aimed at driving a wedge between England and France—that was what she had been after ever since the Anglo-Italian agreement was made.

For us to help to push Russia out of Europe would be 'fatal'. I said that though I had no desire to mention names I thought that that was the Prime Minister's policy. I quoted what he had said during the Eden debate and asked B if he had seen Sinclair's quotation from a Canadian article which said the British policy aimed at a Four-Power Pact with Russia left out (until she 'behaved') and that all this was attributed to Chamberlain! He had not seen this at all, so I showed it to him in the Times of the day. He read it with some excitement and said that, if it represented the views of N C, it was 'very serious'.[1] He said that he entirely disapproved of the Four-Power Pact idea and most strongly of any idea of excluding Soviet Russia. [It was clear to me that in certain directions he was entirely out of sympathy with Government policy; he believes, for instance, that Italy and Germany mean to stop in Spain and that the German threat from Spain is most serious—he regards it as a sort of encircling movement directed against England from Holland down to Gibraltar.]

As to Spain, he said that 'people' told him that Franco could not hold out against our influence and that all would be well 'in, say, ten years'. Maybe, he said, 'but I'm not concerned about ten years, what I want to know is what is going to happen in the next year or two.'

He seemed to me to have little hope of stopping the dictator-

---

1. Crozier was evidently better informed than Vansittart about Chamberlain's policy.

ships now that the Axis was, as he thought, stronger than ever after the Anglo-Italian Agreement and Hitler's visit to Rome. He agreed that Mussolini's attack on France must have been caused by annoyance over the Spanish Government's renewed resistance, but it had persisted, and was still persisting although France, to please Musso, had closed the Pyrenees frontier. If the Anglo-Italian Agreement was to have any good results (from our point of view) you expected to see *some* fruits in, say, 2 or three or four months, but there were no fruits at all in the broad European field.

He added that he thought that if we were to impress the Dictators at all there would have to be some form of 'national service' in this country. Nothing less would make them believe that we were in earnest and could resist them.

He said that as to Germany, the Austrian coup and threats about Czech-Sl. had made 'some people' think rather more of him; he had been telling them the truth for years and now they were a little more ready to listen. Some of the credulous were beginning to think a little more sensibly—Londonderry and Geoffrey Dawson. I added Lothian [because A had told me about Lothian—see 'A' notes.]

.   .   .   .   .

I told B that I believed the British Govt policy about Cz-Sl to be ultimately this:
 (1) that the Sudeten Germans should have cantonal Autonomy
 (2) that Cz-Sl should be 'neutralised' (that is, should drop her Russian and French treaties) and that her neutrality should be guaranteed (by Germany, France, Britain, Italy).

He said—'by Germany! and if she violates it, who then will vindicate her neutrality! She will have lost her two alliances and have to depend on a nebulous and more general guarantee!' He obviously thought nothing of it. When I told him that I believed that it was the Government's policy (it *is* Halifax's, as I know from other sources) he said he had never heard it avowed (that is true enough, no doubt) and that he could hardly believe it. He seemed to be puzzled and fell very silent about it (I did not mention Halifax by name).[1]

---

1. There is nothing in the official records to confirm Crozier's statement, but of course Halifax did not reveal his intentions in the official records. At all events, this was how it worked out—a German guarantee of Czechoslovakia against Germany.

C. J W DULANTY

The opening remarks were on the Irish elections.

He went on to talk about the British Government and discussed the question of who might be likely to be the next Prime Minister in view of Chamberlain's age. He thought that Malcolm Mac-Donald, of whom he has the highest opinion owing to his conduct of the Irish business, and Eden were the coming men, but, of course, they were too young to succeed Chamberlain and therefore an interim Premier would have to be found. He did not, however, seem to have any more positive ideas than anyone else that one meets in London.[1]

11 July 1938

SEÑOR AZCÁRATE Y FLÓREZ

Discussion of the non-intervention committee and its futilities.

12 July 1938

11.45 A.M. JAWAHARLAL NEHRU AT ORMOND HOUSE

Nehru was Gandhi's principal lieutenant in the Congress party and subsequently prime minister of India.

·   ·   ·   ·   ·

He said that Gandhi's idea was that the Indian Government might have certain reserved powers, but it should have them in theory only and not exercise them. I said that apparently the idea was that these powers should suffer atrophy before they had come into existence and that, if so, India was trying to produce a state of things in a year or two which, so far as certain powers of the Crown were concerned, in this country had taken us hundreds of years. He said, well, that was Gandhi's idea, though it was not his, and

---

1. Neville Chamberlain was rising seventy. His successor would have to be a Conservative. This ruled out Malcolm MacDonald who was National Labour. Chamberlain's own favourite at this time was probably Hoare. In May 1940, when he had to decide, circumstances had changed and, though he preferred Halifax, he had to recommend Churchill.

the argument was that if you wanted to get rid of the reserved powers of the British Government in practice and could not get rid of them legally, you should allow them to exist in theory but that they should not be practised. . . .

12.30 P.M. MALCOLM MACDONALD AT THE COLONIAL OFFICE

MacDonald had moved to the colonial office in May. Situation in Palestine: 'It seemed pretty clear that the Foreign Office and the India Office, who together brought about the recent wobbling of the Government on partition, were still using their influence with MacDonald.'

3.00 P.M. LORD HALIFAX

This was Crozier's only meeting with Halifax, who had become foreign secretary in February. The tone of the interview explains why it was not repeated.

Halifax began by referring pleasantly to the critical articles that had appeared in the MG. I said modestly that I was glad to think that he read the MG sometimes. He replied 'Oh, much more than sometimes. I read the Yorkshire Post out of territorial loyalty, but I read the Manchester Guardian in any case." He went on to say that the Yorkshire Post had been very critical of the Government's foreign policy, and I said yes they had had a great many leading articles on that subject and that since Eden's resignation their opposition had been persistent. Just as I said 'persistent', he said 'violent' and then added 'Yes, persistent would be a fairer word.'

I told him that my chief desire was to know what he thought about Spain, the agreement with Italy, Mussolini's policy and the Axis. I would like to know what he thought of the prospects of the plan for withdrawal of volunteers which had been published on the previous evening. He said that he was hopeful, but could not conceal the fact that there were any number of opportunities for procrastination and I got the distinct impression that he was in fact doubtful whether the plan would ever come to anything. He said 'There is another possibility which I would like to put to you. What do you yourself think? What would you say to the British Government formally proposing a truce?' And then he added 'supposing the obstacles in the way of the withdrawal plan appeared to be very great.' He said that he thought the truce proposal might be worth while even if it was pretty certain to be

rejected. I said that I thought it was certain to be rejected if put
forward, because Franco believed himself to be within reach of
victory. Mussolini still apparently intended that Franco should
win outright and the Spanish Government would refuse to look
at a truce until the Italians and Germans had left Spain. He said
that that might be so, but that both the Catalans and the Basques
desired peace and it was not impossible that they would put a
great deal of pressure on the Government to get it.

I raised the question of the whole non-intervention policy. He
said that he had never thought that that policy would keep
Italians and Germans wholly out of Spain. He recalled a conversation that he had had with Eden before the policy had started.
He had said 'Let's be honest with ourselves about this; it cannot
possibly succeed 100% (in keeping Germans and Italians out of
Spain), but even if it succeeds 70 or 80% that will be worth
achieving.' I said that for my part I could not see that the sacrifice
of the legal and natural rights of the Spanish Government had
ever been justified, and he talked a good deal about this, saying
in effect that if it were so they aimed at the greater good of preserv-
ing the peace of Europe, etc. I said that I could not see that the
Government had got much for its sacrifice of the plain rights of
the Spanish Government; the Government certainly could not
prove that if it allowed the Spanish Government to buy arms that
would have led to war. That was only one opinion against another.
Moreover, it seemed to me unproven that we had got anything
substantial for our Italian Agreement, which was the final sacrifice
of Spanish rights. I said that I assumed that he had made the
Italian Agreement for the purpose of loosening the Axis and enabling Mussolini to build up a counterpoise which he could use
against Hitler (I put this fairly bluntly, because Voigt had told
me that Halifax had been going about saying that they had had
no intention of loosening the Axis, while Chamberlain had been
saying that that was the whole purpose of the Italian Agreement).
Halifax did not make the slightest attempt to contradict or correct
me on this, but observed very mildly 'Well at any rate we have
got as a result of the agreement the withdrawal of troops from
Libya and the cessation of anti-British propaganda, and I do not
think that these things are negligible.'

I returned to the question of 'loosening the Axis' and said that
I supposed it was generally accepted that in that field the Italian
Agreement was not much use unless there were an Italian-French
Agreement also; that Mussolini after his Genoa speech had broken
off the conversations with France and had never renewed them;

that France had recently closed her Spanish frontier in the hope that Mussolini would relent and that in fact he had not shown the slightest signs of relenting. Halifax said in reply that he admitted that Mussolini's present policy puzzled him, but he thought that Mussolini had been much irritated on finding that the Spanish war was not over and on coming to the conclusion that the French were bolstering up the Spanish Government. I said that many people had accepted that view at the time of the Genoa speech but that was now a long time ago and it was very hard to believe that Mussolini's actions could still be accounted for by a fit of irritation. He replied that he was much puzzled but he thought that perhaps the irritation still lasted and still accounted for Mussolini's policy.

.   .   .   .   .

Halifax made one rather dramatic reference to events in Spain. He said that Lord Cecil had taken to see him in the House of Lords a young Englishman who had been fighting for the Spanish Government and that this man, describing the scenes that he had witnessed in Spain, including the effects of indiscriminate bombing, had declared that they made him feel 'ashamed to be an Englishman.' 'I replied,' said he, 'that these things made me also feel ashamed to be an Englishman, but it was the events in China more than those in Spain which made me feel this, because at any rate in Spain it was a civil war that was raging whereas in China they were suffering from the entirely unprovoked attack of the Japanese.'

4.30 P.M. DR QUO TAI-CHI

Dr Quo was Chinese ambassador in London. China and Japan had been in a state of undeclared war since the previous year. Dr Quo was hopeful that China would get a loan from the British government. Crozier noted: 'He is always too hopeful.' So it proved about the loan.

11 August 1938

3.30 P.M. SIR ROBERT VANSITTART

Things were not promising; he was afraid that serious trouble was coming to Central Europe in the near future. His opinion was that the German Government did not intend that the Sudetens should agree to any solution propounded by the Czechs. In particular he was much perturbed by the recent and present labour mobilisation designed to complete the western fortifications of Germany. There was no doubt about this. It amounted to a serious dislocation of the national life and why should Hitler go to this extreme except for some grave end? He meant to have the western defences finished by an early date. No one dreamed of attacking him, certainly not France. Therefore he must mean to do something that might put Germany in danger of attack from France and this could only mean violence against Czecho-slovakia. Some people said that Hitler was doing all this in order to *intimidate* the Czechs, France and anyone else, but his opinion was that something much less formidable than this great and hurried effort would have been ample if the aim was only to 'intimidate'. He 'had a hunch' that something more extreme—the use of violence, the only thing they understood—must be intended, and in all probability before long.

He suggested the following sort of programme on the part of Hitler:—

(1) The Sudetens reject each offer of the Czechs and demand more and more.

(2) They press their demands to a point that the Czechs cannot concede and then break off negotiations altogether.

(3) The Sudeten Germans are discovered to be persecuted more than ever on the breach between the two parties and

(4) The Germans invade, in order to rescue their brethren.[1]

I asked what he thought, on this view, Hitler and Co meant to do about Czecho-slovakia if they invaded. Would they annex the Sudeten regions, leave Teschen to Poland, etc. and leave the Czech part (Bohemia, etc.) as a mutilated Czech State?

He said Oh no, he had no doubt in his own mind that Germany would annex the lot. She would destroy the Czech State and incorporate it in the Reich. She was out for the great drive to the East (the Drang nach Osten). When she had Czecho-slovakia all else would fall to her. In his view she was out for nothing less than Weltmacht, world power [a theory which means that her ultimate enemy is England]. All the professions about poor persecuted Czechs were deceptions, means to an end, etc.

---

1. Vansittart's forecast was correct except on the last item which was threatened but, owing to Chamberlain's visit to Hitler, not executed.

I asked whether Poland and Yugo-slavia might come to Czecho-slovakia's aid. He thought it possible but unlikely. Beck, of Poland, was pro-German, though the Poles ought to know that 'Poland's turn would come.' There were 1,500,000 Germans in Poland. We heard nothing about their grievances now but should hear about them in due course. As to Yugo-slavia; he feared that Stoyadino-vitch, the Premier, was rather heavily inclined to Germany, though the people were not so much of his view.[1]

I asked about Italy. He said that Musso was as much as ever bound to the Axis. He would do nothing to restore good relations with France, who had kept their frontier 'sealed hermetically' since June and had got nothing for it.

Then Russia. He talked about the row with Japan and I said something of what Masaryk had said to me (mentioning no names) about Russia's 'firmness'. I said that our constant surrenders in Spain to Franco must have made the worst impression on Germany and Italy, making them believe that under no circumstances would we do anything to resist them. He agreed to this. He said that Germany and Italy believed the democracies were senile, weak and irresolute. Hitler and his lieutenants probably did not believe that Britain would oppose them now in any event. I suggested that Nyon and May 21 had made an impression on them that they could afford to neglect us.[2] He said that was so. May 21 had made a deep impression at the time but he thought it had largely been 'effaced'; every fresh surrender in Spain had deep-ened the 'effacement'. He doubted whether there was now a single adviser to tell Hitler that he might soon be fighting a European war. They—especially Himmler—were absolutely reckless people to whom ordinary natural calculations could not be applied. They were the sort of men who would sweep aside contemptuously any idea that France and Gt Britain could or would resist them. They (and Hitler) were not ordinary rational beings—this must never be forgotten.

·   ·   ·   ·   ·

1. Poland took advantage of the German threats against Czechoslovakia to acquire Těšín. Yugoslavia did nothing. Stoyadinovic was overthrown by the Yugoslav up-rising of March 1941.

2. At the Nyon conference in September 1937 the British and French governments agreed to set up naval patrols against the 'unidentified' (actually Italian) submarines which were attacking ships taking munitions to the Spanish government. The attacks at once ceased. On 21 May 1938 there was a Czechoslovak mobilisation against a supposed threat of German aggression. The British government undid the effect of this by apologising to Hitler for the Czech behaviour.

He ended on the same note, that he regarded the next four weeks with great anxiety. He thought the Runciman mission was a good idea. It would test the German sincerity about a settlement and perhaps make it more difficult for the Germans to break out, but he did not seem particularly confident about this.[1]

．　　．　　．　　．　　．

He also referred to the press, which in general, he said, was by its 'optimism' misleading the people. The people would 'have a rough shock soon' he feared. He got up and pointed to a column in the Times today, which said that the spirit of the FO was one of 'cautious optimism'. He did not know where they got that from, but it did not represent anything that he knew of the FO.

5.30 P.M. JAN MASARYK

Masaryk has now become B, presumably because Vansittart in the previous interview ranked as A. The Nyon conference, the Runciman mission, and the Czechoslovak mobilisation of 21 May, referred to in this interview, are described in the preceding interview with Vansittart.

He had no holiday except an occasional day or two off. He was hoping to get away to see Eden and Halifax in Yorkshire shortly, otherwise he must remain on guard. He was now very anxious about the position. I reminded him when he last saw me[2] that he had been reasonably cheerful and thought that there might quite well be a 'solution' of the Czech-German problem, though it might not be a permanent one. He said yes, but he was not now anything like so confident. Many things disquieted him greatly; he mentioned, of course, the labour mobilisation to complete the German defences in the West.

He referred to Runciman's mission. It was entirely Chamberlain's idea, no one else's. The FO knew nothing about it until N C told them what he had arranged and instructed them to tell Bonnet and Daladier,[3] from whom he himself got the news. It was sheer nonsense that he himself had suggested it. He approved of

---

1. Lord Runciman had been sent to Czechoslovakia in order to devise an agreement between the Czechoslovak government and the Sudeten Germans. He did not succeed.
2. See the interview of 22 June.
3. Respectively French foreign minister and premier.

the mission, thought it would help and that long discussions in Prague would make it more difficult for the Germans to resort to violence. Runciman knew something about the problem, he was a cool-headed man and he was—fortunately, he thought—a lazy man.

He had been on the telephone with XYZ[1] who also approved of the R mission and thought that things were going moderately well, but, of course, no one knew exactly what Hitler was intending. His information was that of late Hitler had become moody, irritable and silent. For some time now he had seen scarcely anyone to speak to and, having sent W[2] to London to report to him, had not seen him after his return. He thought this present mood of his was most dangerous and, of course, nothing was to be hoped from the Goering-Himmler lot.[3]

Then he said that a man whom he had not met for some time had invited himself to tea yesterday and had broached the question whether Cz-Sl would not give up her Russian alliance! He had replied 'What then will you give me in exchange?' If he could get neutrality sincerely guaranteed by 'all the Powers of Europe' there might be something to be said for it, but if it was to be guaranteed mainly by Germany, with Russia left out—he was very derisive. (He thought it likely that this man had really come from Chamberlain 'to sound him'.) I asked him what he thought Chamberlain's European policy was, and he said he doubted whether he had one—'except no doubt, a 4-Power Pact'. I reminded him of the things Chamberlain had said which indicated that Russia was to be left out, and he said 'Chamberlain doesn't like to think about Russia. He wants to leave her out of consideration. I was told that recently at No 10 someone said "of course we can't leave Russia out" and N C rejoined "Well, you might leave her out this afternoon anyway." He was told that Stalin had said that he didn't mind N C being anti-Russian but he wished that he had a clear policy that could be understood. B added that he didn't pretend himself to understand what the policy was. He clearly, however, thought that this idea of pushing Russia out of Czecho-Slovakia was part of it (and in this he is almost certainly right). XYZ had assured him that Russia would fight for Czecho-

---

1. Note by Crozier: Beneš (president of Czechoslovakia).

2. Captain Wiedemann, Hitler's company commander in the first world war and now his personal adjutant, was in London on 18 July.

3. It was commonly, though mistakenly, believed at the time that Goering was an extremist and that Himmler had a powerful influence on Hitler's foreign policy.

Sl if need be.[1] I asked him if he thought that the Russian Army had been badly weakened by the purge and mentioned that the French thought so. He said 'So do your people too', and he added that a Czech general and Czech inquirers in Russia itself disagreed and thought that the army was very formidable. He said 'You see, the Russian army is mostly peasants and they fight well. It does not matter to them who leads them. Not long ago they knew of "Papa Tsar"—and crossed themselves at the bare mention of him, and now they hear of "Papa Stalin" and cross themselves just the same—it is all one to them.' It would make a great difference what Hitler thought about Russia and about the chances of Britain's joining in. Britain had done a good stroke on May 21 by making some of these Germans believe that she would be drawn in, and what was needed was something more now to confirm the impression, which had become weaker with time.

There were, he said, three things in the present situation which alarmed him. One was the immense military activity going on in Germany and especially the apparent determination to complete the lines of fortifications at the earliest possible moment. The second point was the incessant campaign that was carried on in the German press against Czecho-Slovakia. It seemed clear that they were determined not to let her alone and to keep alive the charges of 'provocation' that they were always making against her. The third thing, to which he attached great importance, was what he thought to be the increase everywhere of international tension. Spain, the Far East, the trouble between Russia and Japan, the depreciation on the stock exchanges, the anxiety about the pound, the dollar, the kroner, the pengo and every other currency—on all sides there seemed to be a mounting up of tension which he was afraid would end in an explosion. If in the future this general tension seemed in any way to be abating he would think it a most promising sign. He mentioned incidentally that if it came to war he would himself 'fight for Holy Bohemia to the last drop of my blood'.

He mentioned as a small matter of interest that it was in Runciman's house in London that the famous Masaryk, his father, had delivered his first speech when he went on his world campaign

1. By the Czechoslovak-Soviet pact of 1935, Soviet Russia was committed to supporting Czechoslovakia against aggression if France did so first. President Beneš deliberately refrained from asking the Russians whether they would fight for Czechoslovakia even if France did not. No one knows whether they would have done so. Also no one knows whether the Soviet army had been seriously weakened by the purge of generals which Stalin conducted at this time.

on behalf of an independent Czech State during the war (this visit was in 1916). He said that Runciman's house had not been chosen because Runciman was known to be pro-Czech, but because it had a bigger room than any other available.

I had suggested to him that if it was true that the German leaders had begun to forget the impression produced by such things as the Nyon Conference and our firm words of May 21 it would be a good thing if something further could be done to renew the wholesome impression that had been made—if the Germans again felt that there was a risk of a terrible European war, with us in it, they might be more reasonable about Czecho-Slovakia. As I was leaving he said that he had been wondering whether anything of the kind could be done and as he was shortly going to see 'the big man' he would try to impress on him the desirability of some such move.

Crozier's interviews contain nothing about the crisis of September 1938. When they resume, the Munich conference had been held. Czechoslovakia had lost her Sudeten territories and had abandoned her alliances with France and Soviet Russia. Six months of uneasy peace followed.

8 December 1938

5.00 P.M. SIR SAMUEL HOARE

Hoare was now home secretary and also one of Chamberlain's closest advisers on foreign policy. Clearly his enlightened administration of the home office led Crozier to forgive his earlier lapse over the Hoare-Laval plan.

PENAL REFORM

Prospects were good; they would amend in Committee but there would be no great conflicts. Flogging—opinion divided. When in Lords there would be danger from a few. The Government would mobilise opinion. He had no sentiments if what he wanted was threatened. He would get together with Labour.[1]

OFFICIAL SECRETS ACT

He would do his best to put his assurances into a bill, but it was not easy. Hewart had been very contradictory in his speeches in the Commons. The Government must have powers beyond mere spying, but clause 6 was the real trouble. He meant his assurances absolutely and no one would get behind them. It was suggested

---

1. Hoare was promoting the Criminal Justice bill, a highly liberal measure. Its most controversial clause ended judicial flogging. For this and other reasons the bill had not become law by the outbreak of war, when it lapsed. An almost identical bill was passed nine years later.

that another legal tribunal—not the Attorney-General—should decide about police inquiries under clause 6.[1]

ITALY

He did not think Mussolini *meant* Tunis very seriously. Might be trying to get something in Spain, or minority rights in Tunis. Mussolini was really full of fears about war. *Moral* in Italy was not good. The Mediterranean was, to us, the best part of the situation. They (the Govt. and the naval people) did not anticipate much danger from the Italians. Spain had an open coast and so had Italy. I said yes, but asked about air-force? He did not think a great deal of that. We and France would be all right so far as Mussolini and the Mediterranean were concerned.

But I said X^2 very weak in air. Yes, it was, and not greatly better yet. I used Werth's article and said *80* planes were predicted by October-November, but may be too big. Yes, it was too big. France was sending over a Commission in regard to organisation.

SPAIN

His ultimate answer was that the Spaniards would pitch out the foreigners—he was sure of it. They would never be able to stop. I said would not Franco need men and quoted history. He said that Spain would all be at each other's throats if and when Franco won. I said 'Yes, but isn't that why Franco would need his foreign Allies?' He said he thought No, national feeling would drive them out.

What would Chamberlain do at Rome?[3] He thought he would try to get Italy closer to France. He would try to end the war. We would go for mediation? Yes, we would if we could. Did we not assume that Franco must win? No, not altogether. We must try to get an end to the war and perhaps it might be by mediation. Mussolini was not as strong as he professed to be. He was, probably, shouting to keep up his courage.

GERMANY

Things not very good but very mysterious. There had not been

---

1. A journalist in Manchester published a document marked Confidential that had been circulated to the local police, and refused to reveal his source. For this he was convicted under the Official Secrets Act of 1920. Sir Gordon Hewart, when introducing that bill as attorney general, had stated that it would apply only to espionage. Now Lord Hewart, as lord chief justice, confirmed the journalist's conviction. The best comment on Hewart is Low's drawing of him.

2. Presumably France. Alexander Werth was MG correspondent in Paris.

3. Chamberlain and Halifax visited Rome from 11 to 15 January 1939. Though they did not succeed in getting Mussolini to moderate Hitler, they seem to have given him a fright, and from this time he was anxious to keep Italy out of a European war.

much row lately over our Jewish attitude, and not much about
Hudson's truculent speech either. Goering was talking a lot and
was not marching with Goebbels–Himmler in their anti-Jewish
ferocity. Hitler was 'strangely silent'—his information was that
Hitler did not want war. He thought that there was no doubt
there was considerable 'disunion' now among the Nazi leaders.
Goering did not get on well with Ribbentrop.

ARMS

I asked about ca' canny on arms. He replied (1) that it was
untrue that we were going slow in any way in order not to irritate
Hitler; (2) neither the fighter–bomber decision nor the Ministry
of Supply decision meant anything of the kind. The Ministry of
Supply would, for a good many months, reduce, not accelerate
production. The increase in fighters was largely caused by the
lines of development of our anti-aircraft defences.[1] I could ask
Kingsley Wood—he would tell me that, if the appeasement policy
did not exist at all, we could not do more at present in respect of
air force than we were doing at this moment. He suggested that
Chamberlain and his policy would not slow-down the programme
at all in any respect.

SPAIN

The British Government were sticky [?sticking], and would
stick to the Non-Intervention Committee's programme in respect
of belligerent rights; they had no intention of giving way on that
point. He did not think Mussolini was sending more planes to
Spain in order to bomb the Government into submission. Our
Government intended to watch Italy on this point. If she sent
more troops, etc. it would be a direct violation of the Agreement
with us and we should keep a close watch on her. I urged as bluntly
as I could that Spain was a great danger to us should there be
another 'crisis' with Italy and Germany still there and that we
ought to get them out. He said he agreed, but he would not go
beyond the point that Italy must not send more forces there and
that N C would, at Rome, try to 'bring the war to an end'. He

---

1. Chamberlain resisted the demand for a ministry of supply, possibly for the reason
that Hoare gives, possibly for other reasons. The government had recently given
priority to the production of fighter aircraft. This provoked an outcry, particularly
from Trenchard, the great advocate of strategic bombing, that the government, by
putting bomber aircraft second, were abandoning the offensive spirit. In fact the
government had been swayed by the pleadings of Dowding, chief of fighter command.
No doubt it also weighed with them that, fighters being easier and less expensive to
produce than bombers, the more rapid increase in numbers of aircraft impressed the
public.

said that the war in Spain was going to be on another twelve months or more anyway.[1]

6.00 P.M. SEÑOR AZCÁRATE Y FLÓREZ

He thought that opinion was a little healthier towards the Spanish Government.

He was afraid of the British Government in respect of belligerent rights. I said the Government seemed to be pretty firm at present in sticking to the N-I Comm's plan. He said yes, but suppose the Committee crumbled, as some of the countries said that anyhow it was no use—and so Germany and Italy would demand—all over again. Two points should be held to:

(1) The N-I C's plan of only giving belligerent rights on strict conditions.

(2) If the N-I C's plan were jacked up and anyone, like the British and French Governments, franked belligerent rights, then obviously the Spanish Government must have the ordinary belligerent rights of buying war material freely. You must be logical; you can't give Franco the right to search for war material if you deny the other Government the right to buy it!

Food was not so bad. It would not get the Government down. A lot of help was being given from GB and USA. They were badly punished but would survive. The Ebro offensive had been a severe blow to Franco, but he was preparing a new offensive, though one could not say where he would strike. Franco had an enormous advantage in material. Whenever he opened an offensive he would penetrate a certain distance and then, after a few days, the offensive would peter out. The Republican Army would remain. He would not win unless he destroyed that. Even if only one province remained in the Government's hands, the army would remain and until it was destroyed Franco could not win.

He insisted that the Republican Government represented *all* Spain, Franco only part of it. Negrin, the Premier, had said that food supplies should be used to help *all* needy Spaniards, including those in Franco Spain. They were all *Spaniards*, but Franco regarded only those in his own territories as Spaniards and the rest as enemies. Negrin's spirit would win in the end.

He feared Chamberlain's visit to Rome and thought Chamber-

---

1. The Spanish civil war ended on 30 March 1939. Hoare was never good with his timing.

lain would surrender something more (especially in respect of belligerent rights).

. . . . .

WEST PERTH

He was very curious about the by-election and asked me many questions about the Liberal candidate, the importance of the Liberal vote if she withdrew, and the significance of the result with regard to the Spanish crisis in this country if the Duchess won.[1]

9 February 1939

3.00 P.M. SIR KINGSLEY WOOD

Sir Kingsley Wood, referred to here as A, had been secretary for air since May 1938. He is generally held to have been more successful in staving off criticism in the house of commons than in producing aircraft.

A said that the position with regard to aircraft production was not only much better, but better than he was able to say in public. He was much easier in his mind than he was at the time of Munich; if there was another six months' respite he would be easier still and if we got through to the end of the year he would be feeling quite confident. If, however, he said publicly that the position was as much better as it really was, it would be notifying Hitler to attack us or at any rate notifying Goering and similar people to announce that they must have a great new rearmament programme in order to protect themselves from us.

I asked him about the likelihood of a crisis being provoked in the near future by Italy. He said he did not think it was likely as, if Mussolini were intending to provoke a first-class crisis with France, we should expect to find certain movements taking place in the Italian Air Force and in point of fact such movements were not taking place at all. I asked him if it were true that Italian aircraft production had passed its peak, and he said that was the fact. There was no doubt that the Italian Air Force had been considerably stronger some months ago than it was now. Partly that was a matter of production and partly also, he said, 'Mussolini must have been keeping an average of three or four hundred planes in Spain—and not all of them have returned.'

---

1. The duchess of Atholl, a Conservative MP, resigned her seat in order to fight a by-election against Chamberlain's foreign policy. She lost by 1,313 votes.

He spoke of a possible German attack on London. He said that he thought there was a tendency to exaggerate the number of planes the Germans could send against London at the beginning of a war. She had long stretches of frontiers which under the most favourable circumstances she would be compelled to guard, and also one must remember that a considerable proportion of her aeroplanes was scheduled to act with the army and it might be taken for certain that the army authorities would fight very hard to prevent these forces from being taken from them to bomb London or anywhere else.

.   .   .   .   .

A spoke also of the manufacture and production in this country with great confidence and said that the development of the new factories was going on at a remarkable rate. I asked him about reports that German factories were working 24 hours a day in three shifts and he said that that was not the case, although the Germans desired that it should be thought to be so. He said that they were very skilful in getting people over to see their factories and then go back and spread reports about their terrific skill and efficiency.

4.45 P.M. SIR ROBERT VANSITTART (B) AT THE FOREIGN OFFICE

B spoke of what was likely to happen in the near future. He predicted that March would be a very dangerous month and that Germany would not be quiet. It was just possible that the crisis would arise in the West through Mussolini pushing his demands against France. The most likely thing to stave that off was action by Britain to convince Mussolini that if he attacked France we should be in France against him. Mussolini would be hard to convince of this. Chamberlain's assertion of our solidarity with France the week before had been excellent. It was not, however, enough. The same assertion must be repeated, and repeated more emphatically. His own view was that assertions even if repeated would not be sufficient and that we ought to take some definite action, such as moving troops or aeroplanes, the meaning of which would be perfectly understood by Mussolini. It was doubtful at that moment whether after the Rome visit, the Italian Agreement, and so on, Mussolini really did understand; but he thought that it could be done.

B went on to say, however, that he doubted whether the crisis would arise in the West. His view was that Hitler meant to strike south-eastwards before long; that was to say that Rumania was his object.[1] If he got Rumania the road was open to him towards Turkey and everything that went with control of Turkey. His view was that such a drive towards Rumania should be opposed (he did not say how) and he was afraid that since public opinion would not see the great danger involved it would go unopposed. Germany would, of course, be strengthening her resources enormously; she would turn back with greatly increased power against the west and she would be much more immune to a blockade; he agreed that she was very far indeed from being immune at the present time. He was throughout entirely confident that Hitler had no intention of resting or allowing things to settle down, and also expressed surprise at those who accepted too readily the assurances of Mussolini.

10 February 1939

MIDDAY. SIR ARCHIBALD SINCLAIR AT THORNEY COURT

He had been speaking the day before at the Yorkshire by-election at which Aline Mackinnon was Liberal candidate: said she was putting up a very good fight.[2] He went on to talk of the Cripps movement.[3] In many ways he approved of it, but said he had been wanting to stand out for some minimum Liberal terms, above all Electoral Reform. (The rest of the conversation was taken up with foreign policy, Chamberlain's visit to Rome and his extraordinary belief in the assurances of the dictators.)

3.30 P.M. LORD STANHOPE

Viscount Stanhope was first lord of the admiralty from October 1938 to the outbreak of war. Most of the talk was about aircraft carriers. Crozier noted at the end: 'He gave me the impression that if war should come we calculated that we could and would give Mussolini a great deal to think about.'

---

1. On 16 March an alarm that Hitler was about to move into Romania led the British government to guarantee Poland, and this in turn led to the second world war. The alarm about Romania was without foundation. It was believed because, as Vansittart's remarks show, people had been expecting it for so long.

2. At the Holderness by-election polling took place on 15 February 1939. Though Aline Mackinnon increased her vote by eight hundred, the Conservative candidate was returned.

3. Sir Stafford Cripps was advocating a Popular Front of Liberal and Labour against Chamberlain's government. His reward was to be expelled from the Labour party.

6.00 P.M. J W DULANTY

Dulanty said that some weeks before they had had somewhat of a shock when they were told that the Government took a most gloomy view of the situation and even feared that a direct attack might be made on Holland.[1] This had surprised them as there was nothing in what they had recently been told to justify any such account of the immediate situation. They had, of course, sent out their reports, but they had had a meeting and had decided to ask the FO for a more extended 'appreciation' of the whole situation, which they thought would put the previous alarming statement in its right perspective.

On 15 March the Germans occupied Prague and ended even the nominal independence of Czecho-slovakia. This began a new, and as it proved final, period of tension. Crozier was in London immediately afterwards. Unfortunately the accounts of his interviews have been lost. The interviews were, according to his list of engagements:

16 March 1939

SEÑOR AZCÁRATE Y FLÓREZ

3.30 P.M. SIR ROBERT VANSITTART

5.30 P.M. DR QUO

17 March 1939

10.00 A.M. LESLIE HORE-BELISHA

11.00 A.M. M. CORBIN, FRENCH AMBASSADOR

The British government made some feeble attempt to organise a coalition against further German aggression. This broke down on the Polish refusal to be associated with Soviet Russia. On 31 March the British government gave a guarantee to Poland. A fortnight later, alarmed by Mussolini's occupation of Albania, the British government extended the guarantee to Greece and Romania. Thereafter they made still feebler, and by no means sincere, attempts to secure some sort of Soviet co-operation. Crozier paid three visits to London during this time. Only one interview has survived.

---

1. The story about the British government's alarm over Holland is correct. According to the German records, the alarm was entirely unfounded. Maybe members of the so-called German resistance were trying to stir up the British government, or possibly the British intelligence services credited Hitler with precise plans for the future that he did not have.

'They' are presumably the Dominions high commissioners.

13 April 1939

He said that he thought it was just possible that the coalition now being formed might deter Hitler and Mussolini from further attack.[1] He would not put it higher than that; the question was whether it was not now too late. Two years ago a coalition might have been formed which would certainly have preserved peace; even one year ago, after Austria, it would have been comparatively easy. Everything must be done now to organise the coalition rapidly and it might be that it was not too late, but one could not say. The Dictators were undoubtedly convinced of the decadence of the Democracies and would be slow to believe that the Democracies had either the will or the means to resist them. This was the great danger.

He spoke of Russia and of the difficulties made by the Poles. He said that Russia could not be left out and that the main thing was to make it plain with great frankness to Russia that we wanted and invited her co-operation and we should then ask her what she was prepared to do to help in the coalition. He said that the same thing might have been done last year, before Munich. The French, who had their alliance with Czecho-Slovakia and also their alliance with Russia, should have gone to Russia and asked her plainly what she was prepared to do to assist the Czechs if Hitler attacked them, but instead of that Russia was kept at arm's length the whole time. It might not be possible, or even desirable, in view of the difficulties raised by Poland and Rumania to have a complete alliance with Russia, but it was necessary to do something and to do it quickly in order to bring her and her assistance into the coalition. He agreed that there was great distrust by Russia of this country and its policy, but said that since now we had reversed the policy of appeasement our aim was to convince the Russians that we were sincere, and he thought that the Russians for their part ought not to harp too much on the past grounds for their suspicion. Everyone knew that there had been important people in this country who would have been glad to see Russia involved with Germany while we looked on, but most of these people had been converted or were not now important and he thought that an agreement with Russia ought to be quite possible. He said also that the negotiations between Poland and Rumania and the

---

1. This was the day on which British guarantees were given to Greece and Romania. The deterrent effect of this action was slight.

negotiations between us and Poland were not going ahead as fast as they ought to.

Speaking of Ministers, he said that Samuel Hoare was perfectly sound on the question of bringing Russia in. I had reminded him of the many utterances by which Chamberlain appeared to have shown that he at any rate had little use for Russia except under compulsion.

While we were talking Chamberlain was making his speech in the House of Commons and he asked his secretary to bring in the summary of the speech as soon as it came over the tape. When he received it he commented that it was 'not so bad' and in particular declared his pleasure that the Government had given a pledge to Rumania as well as to Greece. He said that the pledge to Rumania had been uncertain, and it was apparent that it must have been decided on only at that morning's Cabinet meeting and that he himself had not up to that moment heard that Rumania had been included.[1]

The accounts of the following interviews have been lost:

14 April 1939

4.00 P.M. COUNT RACZYNSKI

5.50 P.M. J W DULANTY

11 May 1939

4.00 P.M. SIR ROBERT VANSITTART

12 May 1939

11.30 A.M. SIR KINGSLEY WOOD

4.00 P.M. COUNT RACZYNSKI

5.30 P.M. J W DULANTY

16 June 1939

2.30 P.M. SIR KINGSLEY WOOD

---

1. Vansittart was no longer invited to the meetings of the foreign policy committee of the cabinet, even though he had the title of chief diplomatic adviser.

3.30 P.M. SIR ROBERT VANSITTART

5.00 P.M. COUNT RACZYNSKI

17 June 1939

11.00 A.M. BJÖRN PRYTZ, SWEDISH MINISTER

On 1 September 1939 German troops invaded Poland. On 3 September Great Britain and France declared war on Germany.

3

The Phoney War
October 1939–May 1940

With the outbreak of war Crozier's interviews become more frequent and also wider in range. He went to London once a month from October 1939 to May 1940—the longest continuous run in the records and one that coincides neatly with the phoney war. These were the months of war without fighting except at sea. Poland had been conquered, and her allies had done nothing to help her. In November Great Britain and France braced themselves against a German offensive on the western front. It did not come. At the end of November Soviet Russia attacked Finland. The allies debated whether to help Finland and how they could do it. After three months of confusion and delay they nerved themselves to action and were then forestalled by Finland's surrender. The enterprise was abandoned, a most fortunate occurrence. On 8 April 1940 the Germans invaded Denmark and Norway. At last there was some fighting even if on a small scale. The real war began only on 10 May 1940.

Though nothing was done, much was discussed. Was Soviet Russia, after the Nazi-Soviet pact, an ally of Germany's? Was a German offensive imminent? Alternatively, was Germany already cracking under pressure of the British blockade? Would Sweden aid Finland? What would her attitude be if the allies did so? On a more practical level, was Chamberlain's war cabinet an effective instrument for conducting the war?

Crozier was interested in all these questions. He added the Danish and Swedish ministers to the list of those whom he saw regularly. Churchill welcomed him and was always ready to talk at length. The war enhanced Crozier's standing. The Times was discredited by its support of appeasement. The Manchester Guardian, which had preached resistance, was on the way to becoming the organ of a rival and, as it proved, victorious establishment. These strange months of suspense are now largely forgotten, and this makes Crozier's records the more precious.

13 October 1939

3.15 P.M. SIR ROBERT VANSITTART AT THE FOREIGN OFFICE

Soviet Russia occupied the eastern territories of Poland after Germany's victory and compelled Estonia, Latvia, and Lithuania to accept Soviet garrisons. The Soviet government also supported Hitler's 'peace offensive'.

I began by asking what he thought about Germany and Russia. He said that Hitler was paying a very high price indeed for Stalin's neutrality and support. Stalin was wringing all the advantage that he possibly could out ot Germany's involvement in the West. In the military sense Russia was a 'fake'; her army and its equipment were nothing very grand; her air-force was part good and part not, and her general internal condition was not strong. Germany, if she had to deal single-handed with Russia, could and would 'roll her up like a carpet'. Germany's hands were tied in the West; Ribbentrop was a stupid negotiator and Germany, he believed, was having to concede more than she liked. He was, as always, contemptuous of Ribbentrop; he described him as an ignorant donkey, a bone-head, as the Americans call it—'all bone above here,' he said, graphically clutching his ears—and he thought that although the division of Poland had been deliberately agreed upon between Ribbentrop and Stalin that was not so true about the Baltic States. There might have been some more general agreement about that, but he thought that the actual steps which Russia had taken had not been agreed on in advance and that Stalin had exploited his chance successfully in Hitler's own manner. I suggested that Russia's primary aim was to secure the approaches to Leningrad and to make herself impregnable in the Eastern Baltic. He said no doubt that was so, but all the same Russia's establishing herself in the Eastern Baltic, on the coasts and in the Baltic States, was a formidable event for Germany, and he repeated that if Germany's hands were free she would very quickly throw Russia out.

I asked him whether he thought that Russia, having secured her centre by taking Eastern Poland and her right flank through the Baltic and the Baltic States, would next develop claims in conjunction with Germany in South-Eastern Europe and towards the Black Sea. He replied that it was quite impossible to say; the Russians kept their secrets well and we should not know what either or both of these powers intended until they began to carry out their intentions. I referred to Turkey, and he said that no doubt the Turks desired to stand loyally by their engagements to us and France, but he agreed that Turkey was in a very delicate position when faced by an active aggressive Russia and she must needs go carefully.

I asked whether he thought that Russia, if Germany stood in need of it, would give her military assistance, and he was disposed to think not. His point was that at any rate Stalin was unlikely to assist Hitler to a substantial victory over England and France, because if he did he knew what the consequences would be; namely that Hitler would turn East again and roll Russia up 'Like a carpet.' [This is, of course, very different from the opinion of Voigt, who thinks that the two Powers have made a deep and extensive agreement for aggrandisement which will last for a long time.][1] Even if Russia should give military aid to Germany he did not seem to be much disquieted by the prospect. She might furnish things like submarines and aircraft, but he did not apparently attach tremendous value to their aid. As for a threat to India, Russia would have to go a long way before she could make much of that. He thought, however, that Russia would furnish Germany so far as she could with supplies of various kinds, but only in order to keep the war going and to secure that Germany should come out weaker at the end.

Something was said about the question whether it was ever practicable for us to have got Russia in on our side. He said that there was one point at which he thought that it would have been practicable, namely in April, immediately after we gave the guarantee to Poland. He thought that then if we had gone straight to Russia with an invitation we might have got her in, but he added that it was to be remembered that we had to meet great obstacles; Poland did not want Russia in, nor did Rumania; and the Baltic States were very sticky about anything being done which involved them. They knew pretty clearly now, he said, what Stalin's real intentions were about them.

We then turned to Italy, Spain and Japan. He said that the Russo-German pact had done us something of a good turn with Italy. It was, however, better not to say much publicly but to allow the situation to develop by itself. In his opinion Italy had been sincerely anti-Bolshevist though, of course, that was not her only motive in fighting the Spanish war. Both Italy and the Franco Spaniards felt that they were fighting against the penetration of Moscow and thought they had a sincerely convinced ally in this respect in Germany. Italy was distinctly troubled about the complete abandonment by Germany of this position.[2] He thought the articles in Balbo's paper, attacking Russia violently, could be taken as one sign of Italy's discomfiture. He was not prepared to say how far it would go or what results it would have. Italy was also concerned by the sight of Soviet Russia looming up in this

---

1. Voigt believed that Nazi Germany and Soviet Russia were allies in an anti-Christian crusade. See his book, Unto Caesar.

2. In fact Italy played for a Russo-Italian entente to contain Germany both now and later in 1940. However, Mussolini took fright when Hitler stamped his foot.

formidable way over South-Eastern Europe and the Balkans. I put in a question about the Pope. He said that clearly the Pope could not be pleased about the disruption of a country of 20 million good Catholics by the Bolshevics and the Nazis, but he thought that he was an extremely cautious person, more cautious even than his predecessor, and he was not expecting anything from him. I inquired whether if Mussolini became more and more disgruntled about Russia and Germany the Pope might become a little more outspoken, but he did not seem to have any confidence about that either.

Germany had done us a good turn also with the Japanese. The Japanese were genuinely fearful of Communism both in China and in Japan itself and they found it difficult to understand or to forgive Germany's reversal of policy. It was natural that when Japan recently made a truce with Russia in Mongolia everyone should wonder whether a Russo-Japanese Agreement was coming. He doubted whether this was likely, though you could never be quite sure, but after all Russia was the one Power that Japan feared, or had cause to fear, and she did not like being, as it seemed to her, let down.

I said that on all this it did not seem that we had ground to fear an alliance of the four Great Powers—Germany, Russia, Italy and Japan—against us, at any rate as things were going, and he shook his head emphatically and said he did not think that combination was in prospect at present. A reference was also made to the United States and the possibility that she might at some stage or other give active assistance to our side. He laughed and conveyed the impression that no one must predict anything at any time about the United States. I mentioned the dispatch of a considerable American Squadron to Hawaii and he said it was, of course, a 'gesture'.

We then touched on peace activities in this country, the proposals for a conference and so on. I asked him what his impression was of these things. He said he did not attach very great importance to the move from the Left and the Pacifist side; he did not think that it was likely to come to anything dangerous. What he feared was that there might eventually be a move from the Tory Right, including people like the Astors and Montagu Norman, to save Germany from Bolshevism. He said it was necessary to remember that since 1931 we had not only had a Tory Government in this country, but a Government in which the Tories of the Right had from time to time had great influence. He thought that if Germany appeared to be moving to the Left these Tories

might engineer and support a movement to save her from Bolshevism, and he added that if that time came no doubt the Times
would be active in the same cause.

We then referred to Ll G's recent move, and he said that Ll G
was all wrong about Russia.[1] He went on, 'I wish that Ll G would
occasionally see some other diplomatist in London than Maisky.
Apparently Maisky is the only diplomat he sees. Of course Maisky
is a very nice little man and my wife and I have liked him and
Madam Maisky for years. But the trouble about Maisky is that he
knows nothing about Russia. He knows a lot about England, a very
great deal, but then I know a lot about England myself and I do
not want to hear about England from a foreigner. I want to learn
from him about his country, his people and his statesmen, but
when you want to hear from Maisky what and how they are thinking and intending in Moscow, he knows nothing about it—
nothing, nothing!'

We finished up by talking about German intentions in the West.
He thought that we would very soon now be having a German
attack of some sort. It might be on land, and also certainly was
going to be in the air; it might be directed against England or
against France, but not, he thought, against both, unless it was a
terrific air attack in conjunction with a land offensive from the
direction of the Siegfried Line. Whichever it was he thought that
Hitler was probably intending to use poison gas and that the
German wireless announcement that we had supplied poison gas
to Poland was intended to provide the pretext.

Referring finally to the idea of an armistice and a conference,
he said that in this war this country had been given a last chance
to defeat Germany and secure its own safety. If it did not take that
chance and fight the business out it was, in his opinion, lost. This
country was very slow to be roused and very slow to realise its
danger. It had had the most extraordinary good fortune in being
given by Germany successive warnings of what was to come. The
seizure of Austria was a warning; the seizure of Czechoslovakia
was another; the attack on Poland was a third. Each of these
things had given us both a warning and a respite, a little time in
which to prepare to resist, and this had so far saved us. There
would be no more warnings, no more respites. If we went into an
armistice and a conference with Hitler we should lose and then

---

1. Lloyd George was advocating a peace conference at which the neutral Powers—
Italy, Soviet Russia, and the United States—would impose tolerable terms. He was
also declaring that Russia could still be won as an ally.

the final assault, the Blitzkrieg, would be upon us and we should lose everything. Whereas now we could still win.

Postscript: One or two small points which I find I have omitted:
   (1) He described Russia to me as 'a sort of Carnera'—a great man-mass, but not a formidable fighter when it came to the test.
   (2) He thought that the Polish armies if properly handled could have prolonged the campaign for several months.

4.15 P.M. WINSTON CHURCHILL AT THE ADMIRALTY

Churchill was first lord of the admiralty from the outbreak of war on 3 September 1939 until 10 May 1940 when he became prime minister. He was a member of the war cabinet. This was Crozier's first meeting with him. Brendan Bracken was Churchill's faithful follower and now his parliamentary private secretary.

I had to wait a few minutes and was shown into the room of Brendan Bracken, MP, who is, I think, a private secretary to the First Lord. It was a big room, with Bracken's desk and chair at the far side, near a window looking on the Horse Guards Parade, and furnished with three or four chairs set round the walls. I sat on one of these and waited and after a few minutes Bracken got up and disappeared. Two or three minutes later a general of some sort was shown into the room; he also had come to see the First Lord. He must have been a very distinguished person as he wore a large number of ribbons. He took a look round at the ordinary chairs against the walls and then strode across the room, pulled out Bracken's chair from Bracken's desk and seated himself in it with great decision.

Churchill close to, looked a good deal older than I had expected and spoke in a very quiet and rather weary voice. He being First Lord, I asked him first about the naval business—whether he was satisfied with our reply to German submarines and German aircraft. He replied that he certainly was so far as we had gone. The new method of hunting submarines was 'extremely successful' and so far as we had experience of attack from the air—he was speaking, of course, a few days after the attack on our squadron in the North Sea—we had every ground for encouragement. The Germans had sent out 18 planes to attack our squadron and they had lost six. It was to be noted that the Germans had flown out nearly 500 miles from their bases. They had started bombing at 10,000 feet and our anti-aircraft fire had driven them up to 20,000, which accounted for their aim being so inaccurate. We then talked a little about the future and I was impressed by the extreme sobriety and caution of his views. He thought that a big German attack was shortly coming in the West and it might very well be on the fleet and certainly also on our ports and naval bases. I mentioned that a few weeks ago a German newspaper had declared that they would send three thousand bombers to attack our naval bases. He smiled, and said 'Well, they can't send that many, but they might send 500—in waves, I mean—and if they do, well then we shall see what happens. We don't know; no one can know.' He was more impressive on this matter than if he had professed complete confidence of the results of any such attacks.

We then got on to the general situation. I was particularly anxious to know what he thought, because Voigt had reported to me on what he described as 'fairly good authority' that Churchill was doubtful as to whether we ought to go on with the war. This report was entirely untrue. He was very emphatic that any conference at the present time which would be accompanied by an armistice or a truce would mean defeat and disaster for us. He referred to Lloyd George's intervention and said 'I do not know what George is thinking about. For God's sake no weakness now; it would mean our total absolute defeat.'

We spoke of the blockade and he said that the Scandinavians were at present pretty well scared by the German submarine and other attack and were afraid for the moment to send their ships to us. That would pass, of course. We were making convoys as safe as possible by conducting ships along our coasts (this was shown by the attack on the convoy near the Humber shortly afterwards) but it had to be remembered that convoys presented generally a bigger target, and no doubt some damage would be suffered. Then I mentioned Russia and he took the view that Russia had put a spoke in Germany's wheel in respect of South-east Europe. He said that in his opinion Russia had stopped the German Drang nach Osten (this is the opposite of the Voigt view, which thinks that Russia and Germany are in connivance about exploiting countries like Rumania) and that Germany will not be allowed by Russia to push down towards the west side of the Black Sea.

10 November 1939

3.30 P.M. SIR ROBERT VANSITTART AT THE FOREIGN OFFICE

He said that the advance of Russia was going as predicted. She and Germany were hand in glove and anyone who believed anything else was the victim of wishful thinking. Russia would certainly give every possible help to Germany except actual warlike measures, and it was not certain that she would not contribute those also. He did not, however, believe that the contribution would be very serious. Russia was most likely to contribute submarines, as they were not easily detected. He did not think she would supply aircraft, as she could not spare them. The truth was that only a small proportion of her Air Force was good; the great bulk of it was poor. Also, he felt pretty certain that Hitler would not like to have Russian air bases in Germany.

With regard to Finland; he did not think that Russia would actually attack Finland.[1] He thought that she would put increasing moral pressure on the Finns. What about South-east Europe then? Would Russia go ahead there? He said that she would certainly like to seize Bessarabia but that she would desire to do it while Germany's hands were completely tied.[2] If Germany objected to Russia attacking Rumania and had even 'a few divisions' in that quarter, Russia would not dare to make herself unpleasant.

He was fairly certain that Hitler meant to attack Holland in order to make a great air attack on Britain. The position of Belgium was dubious. It was impossible to say what she would do, but he feared that her Government was pursuing a two-sided policy and was going to prefer a temporary gain to permanent advantage. If Holland were attacked and Belgium did not intervene then either she would be attacked herself or she would become a vassal State. Here he made certain references to the King of the Belgians.[3]

If Holland were attacked we should, of course, rigorously blockade its coasts, which would be bad for Germany. Germany sent out the greater part of her exports through Holland and we would put a stop to all that. This would certainly be a serious blow to Germany and he imagined that some of the ruling people in Germany might be opposed to invasion of Holland for that reason. I asked him whether he thought that there was any agree-

---

1. Soviet Russia attacked Finland on 30 November 1939.

2. Soviet Russia occupied Bessarabia on 28 June 1940 while the German armies were still occupied in the west.

3. Hitler had fixed an offensive through Belgium, repeating the Schlieffen plan of 1914, for 12 November 1939. This offensive was repeatedly postponed (no less than twenty-nine times), because of unfavourable weather conditions, delay in operational planning, and the opposition of the High Command. Holland was included in the offensive plans only on 24 February 1940, when the main weight of the German attack had shifted from the right wing to the centre.

ment between Holland and Belgium to act together. He replied that he would like to think so, but there was no proof of such a thing at all. Of course, Hitler might very well have threatened both Holland and Belgium that they would suffer heavily for it if such a thing either existed or should come about. He was discouraging about Holland's prospects if she should be invaded; in particular she had no Air-Force. I inquired as to his view of the moral results of an invasion of Holland. Would it not have important effects in the United States? He said that moral effects would be of no use at all. Nothing would be of use except intervention and he was sure that the United States would keep quiet and do nothing. It would declare it had no good reasons for doing anything. It would say that it could not take action as long as a bad man like Chamberlain was in power, or as long as it was uncertain of the purity of our war aims. The small countries could do nothing whatever to help us in the struggle; never in history had they been so completely 'terrorised' as they were now, and so far as they were concerned the moral shock that would be produced by the invasion of Holland would have no effect at all.

As to Italy, the best thing was to leave the situation there alone—'let it brew'. Italy, he thought, would probably remain neutral as at present 'provided, of course, that we do not suffer reverses'.

As to the war in the air, we were certainly better than the Germans in equipment and in training, but so far the conflict had been only on a small scale. The big thing was still to come and about that 'we do not know'. Certainly the Germans had at present a great superiority in numbers.

When I left him, he asked when I was likely to be coming up again. I said that I hoped in about three weeks. He replied 'I am afraid you will find communications much more difficult!' [He was certainly on this day pretty well convinced that Holland was to be attacked immediately and that the Blitzkrieg was upon us. Many other people, of course, held the same view, and some asserted that the invasion of Holland was timed for that same night (Nov. 10 to 11) but that something occurred at the last moment to make Hitler change his plans. The most plausible explanation is that Hitler had received (1) a declaration from Italy and Spain that they were strongly interested in the independence of Holland; (2) a much stronger declaration to the same effect from the United States; and (3) a formal intimation from Belgium that if Holland were invaded she would go to her assistance. Voigt has since said that all these three declarations were actually made.][1]

4.30 P.M. SIR SAMUEL HOARE AT TREASURY CHAMBERS

On the outbreak of war Hoare became lord privy seal and a member of the war cabinet. He and Hankey, minister without portfolio, were the only members of the war cabinet without departmental duties.

He began by saying that he thought the German offensive on the Western Front was now coming off.[2] It had been regarded by the French General Staff as certain in mid-October, but it never began and he was of opinion that the German Generals had probably vetoed it. He said that Gamelin[3] himself had confidently expected the attack at that time; then it was thought with equal confidence that the attack was coming on Holland, and that seemed the most likely event at that moment. It was so likely that if it did not come off we could assume that there had again been some powerful intervention against it; he himself thought that it was coming, but it was quite possible that just as in mid-October there had been a tug of war which resulted in the calling off of the attack, so a tug of war might be going on at that moment about the desirability of invading Holland. If the attack did come off, he thought that the Dutch resistance—here he shrugged his shoulders—'might last one or two days'. He thought that the Germans might drop men from parachutes and that in Holland, where they could come down behind the water defences, this might be serious. [I thought this wholly dubious.[4]] If they overran Holland the Germans would, of course, make a great onslaught on Britain. I inquired about the Belgians and he said that they were 'very reticent' and would not say what they intended to do. 'The French were very cross about this.'

As to the future of Germany, his information was that Hitler was going to bolshevise the country 'good and hard'; in fact he was now doing it. The officers might dislike the prospect, but he thought that the German people would not mind. In further reference to the Western Front, he said that, of course, if Belgium remained neutral when Holland was invaded we obviously could not attack through Belgium. What, then, could we do? Con-

---

1. None of these three alleged declarations appears in the German Diplomatic Documents. The offensive was postponed purely for technical reasons.
2. See the preceding interview with Vansittart.
3. Allied commander-in-chief.
4. Subsequently deleted by Crozier.

ceivably we and the French could launch great bombing raids on military objectives, including munition works, etc. in Germany. There was, however, a certain objection to such a policy on the French side (the nature of which he then proceeded to discuss).

Some further points:

(1) The sending to this country of Bastianini as Italian Ambassador was significant; Bastianini was very pro-British.

(2) We talked of the moral effect of a German invasion of Holland. He thought that it would have a great moral effect in the United States, but that this in our present circumstances would not help us. The Americans, he thought, would do nothing in the way of active military support for us. He did not, however, believe that in the last resort, if Britain and France seemed 'to be going down altogether' the United States would stay out.

(3) He was of opinion himself that the bomb explosion at Munich was a genuine plot against Hitler.[1]

6.30 P.M. J W DULANTY

We began by talking about Ireland. He referred to the discussion in the Dail of the hunger-strikers, that is the IRA people whom the De Valera Government had imprisoned. He said that the Government could do no other than what it was doing, but the results might be very unfortunate. The Irish more than any other people were apt to make martyrs. When Birrell had been thinking of imprisoning Carson, John Redmond had protested on the ground that if such a thing were done Carson would become an Irish hero.

.   .   .   .   .

He spoke of Halifax and described him as a 'fine Christian gentleman'. He gave an instance of Halifax maintaining a very fine and dignified spirit under attack. He referred also to the last few days before the war and said that he thought we might have

---

1. On 8 November 1939 Hitler made his annual appearance at the beer cellar in Munich from which he had launched the putsch of 1923. Shortly after he left, a bomb exploded and killed several Nazi party members. The bomb had been placed by Georg Elser, a carpenter. Goebbels alleged that Elser was a British agent. The British alleged in return that the bomb was a Gestapo plant. According to the latest research, both allegations were unfounded. Elser was a genuine anti-Nazi and a lone operator who would have succeeded if Hitler by chance had not left the cellar early.

put more pressure on Poland during the negotiations in order to make Hitler's position as difficult as possible.[1]

We then talked of Russia and Germany. He doubted whether Maisky was really well informed about Moscow's intentions. He said that at the Non-Intervention Committee most of the Ministers spoke up bluntly for themselves: Ribbentrop certainly did; he spoke abruptly and in an overbearing manner. Grandi, if some new point came up, would meditate over it quietly, but Ribbentrop jumped into the attack at once; he was of a very different type from the two other representatives of the German Embassy, Bismarck and Waermann. He added that Ribbentrop had spent so much time in Canada that he spoke with a 'burr'. Maisky, he said, when at the N I Committee, frequently seemed to be reluctant to speak off his own bat. Unlike the other representatives, he constantly consulted his lieutenant 'C', who sat behind him and advised him. This 'C', he thought, was the real power and was also, he added, 'well in' with the OGPU.

.   .   .   .   .

11 November 1939

11.30 A.M. BJÖRN PRYTZ AT 27 PORTLAND PLACE

Björn Prytz was Swedish minister in London from 1938 to 1947. Being fearful that Sweden might be involved, he was naturally anxious that the war should come to an end.

Russia, he said, was in the first place trying to make herself secure against any possible future enemy, but he thought that to some extent there was also aggrandisement in Stalin's doings. The 'Peter the Great view' was not, however, in itself sufficient.

Whether Sweden would go to war if Finland were attacked by Russia he could not say, but there was no doubt at all that the Swedes were very much stirred up by the prospect. He himself thought that Finland would not be attacked; Stalin was not as crude as all that; Stalin would accept whatever Finland offered to surrender but would remain dissatisfied and would show it. He would keep up every kind of pressure and then in a few months, if the circumstances were good, he would present his demands once more to Finland and would press them.

He went on to say—with a laugh—that a rather awkward

---

1. Halifax did his best to make the Poles compromise.

situation would arise if Russia's advance in the Baltic went too far for Germany and Germany began to oppose her, for in that case Sweden would certainly be on Germany's side and against Russia. Sweden was, of course, more anti-Russian than she was anti-German; so in 1914 to 1918 Sweden was anti-Russian and pro-German, and therefore to some extent anti-Allies. In the same way Sweden was at the present time pro-British because she was anti-Russian. It should be remembered that for Sweden Russia was 'always the enemy'.

Russia was really an Asiatic Power. She certainly wanted to secure the approaches to her country in the west, but his view was that 'these people are Asiatic in their thought and minds'.

Contemplating the present position and that to come after the war, he said that the good days of the small countries had come to an end. Those were the days from 1919 to 1939, when they had a voice and it counted. Whatever the future after the war, even if Germany were beaten, he thought they would have to surrender some of their liberty. There would have to be, and would be, a 'big policeman' and he thought that it would be those that had the power that had the complete freedom.

He hoped that Britain would recognise that she really was part of Europe and that she could not jump in and out as she pleased. ——[1] had said to him recently 'We guaranteed Poland and Rumania, but we never guaranteed you (the Scandinavian Powers) and, to be frank, we can't help you at all.' That was all very well, but if we could do things like guaranteeing those two countries, away in the East, we could, and should, join ourselves firmly to Europe and recognise that that was our destiny. We ought to let the British Empire develop 'on its own'; thus Canada really belonged to America. He did not say that the Dominions need actually split off from us, but they ought not to be allowed to detach Britain from her proper place in influencing the destinies of Europe.

He also said that, if Germany were beaten, there still remained one obstacle to the liberty and happiness of certain of the small countries. This was Russia! I said, but would Russia dare to 'terrorise' Sweden and other peoples if Germany lost the war? He said not if those small peoples had the big ones, Britain and France, behind them, but otherwise yes! Russia, he thought, had no great *offensive* capacity, though she was difficult to beat. Stalin would get what he could without a war. He would renew his pressure on Turkey when he had a good opportunity.

---

1. Unidentifiable. Perhaps Halifax.

All the small countries wanted peace now if it could be got; they all feared that if war went on they would one by one be dragged in and they were all steadily becoming poorer and poorer; the war was exhausting them. They thought that if they could get peace, there would be a respite and that then 'something might happen' to save them.

The best the small countries could hope for in the future was that the big, strong Powers would be liberal-minded towards their small neighbours and towards world problems.

14 December 1939

5.15 P.M. COUNT REVENTLOW

Count Eduard Reventlow was Danish minister in London from 1938 to 1947. Like Prytz, and with even more reason, he was anxious that the war should come to an end. On 30 November Soviet troops invaded Finland. The Finns put up a stubborn and, for a time, successful resistance.

For all the small States round the Baltic the situation was now dangerous.

I asked if in his view Russia was likely to stop when she had overcome Finland. He said that if Finland had yielded to the Russian demands Russia might have stopped, at any rate for the time, but he thought that now she was definitely 'on the move'. She was unlikely to stop. Norway was, after Finland, first in the danger zone and she would be in real danger—in the northern part of her territory. I asked if he meant that Russia would come across from the Petsamo region towards Tromsö and he said it was something more important than that. It was extremely likely that Russia would covet Narvik, which was much farther south than Tromsö. The importance of Narvik was two-fold:

(1) it was the terminus of the railway which carried a large part of the Swedish iron-ore to Antwerp;
(2) it faced towards the open Atlantic and would fulfil Russia's perpetual urge to get to the open seas.

He seemed to attribute as much importance to (1) as to (2). Note, he added, that this ambition to get Narvik involved, to say the least, a threat to the Swedish railway.[1]

I then asked about Germany's attitude towards Russia's move against Finland and towards Sweden. He was very interesting about this. He said that Germany *would not interfere* with what

---

1. The British, not the Russians, had their eyes on Narvik.

Russia was doing and that he believed that anyhow she *could not*. He repeated this several times and conveyed plainly that Germany was now *in no position to* resist Russia. But this, he added, did no good whatever to us and France in this war. It merely meant that, in order to carry on the war against us, Germany must accept almost anything that Russia might now do. Hence, he said, the extraordinary reaction of Germany to Russia's attack on Finland and threat to Sweden—so far from resenting it and threatening Russia she was found to be attacking Sweden and backing up Russia. He said that as soon as he read that Germany was taking up this attitude he knew exactly what had happened—Germany was to a large extent now the prisoner of Russia.

I said that surely, if Germany had to watch all this happening and possibly both Norway and Sweden threatened or injured by Russia, the position of Denmark itself was dangerous, for would not Germany be driven to make sure of the exits from and entrances to the Baltic? He said that that was indeed the danger and there was the greatest anxiety in Denmark over the outcome. If Russia got to the Norwegian coast at Narvik or elsewhere Germany would insist on getting 'compensation' that could only mean trouble for Denmark. He admitted, however, the bare possibility that if Sweden were involved in a war with Russia, Germany might herself attack Sweden, but he thought that even that would be in collusion with, not in opposition to, Russia. On all this subject he was completely pessimistic.

He said that he understood, of course, Britain's preoccupation with the war against Germany; that was inevitable, but he wished that in this country we estimated more accurately and understood more vividly the overwhelming importance of Russia being 'on the move'. We suffered in this matter from our insular position, but to all Continentals it was the great new overpowering fact.

When the war was all over, even if Sweden survived, Russia would never forget that Sweden had attacked her *before she was threatened*. That was a terrible prospect for Sweden to face. Sweden would still be there and Russia would still be there—and Sweden would pay for her action. I said that on his showing, either Sweden and Norway would stand out and probably be squeezed or attacked by Russia afterwards, piecemeal, or they would go in piecemeal and be lost; I added that some authorities held that Sweden and Norway together might help Finland actually to defeat Russia. He did not believe it unless they were helped from outside (and who would help them?) and, besides, Germany would quite possibly join in against them.

Then he spoke of the south-east of Europe. Germany's road to the East, he said, *is* stopped there. There is no doubt of that. Therefore he held that Germany would have only two alternatives—either she would have to be friends with Britain or France or she would have to be continually at war with them.

He wished he could see any chance of an early peace. In his view, if this war was fought to a finish, if we went on until Germany 'crumbled' and collapsed, there would be Bolshevism throughout Europe. Germany would go Bolshevistic and Russia and Germany together would be so vast a centre of infection that it would inevitably spread. There would be 'chaos' throughout the Continent. I said something of British refusal to be frightened by this sort of fear, and he said that we did not appreciate what Bolshevism meant to the Continental States; it might not come here, but he thought it might very well come to France, whose internal condition was none too stable. No doubt British people were prepared to hold out, if necessary, for 15 years, but what would the state of western civilisation be at the finish?

Did I think that Chamberlain would in the near future be able, even if he wanted to, to make a negotiated peace with Germany? He said that there were lots of people in Germany who wanted peace; he thought—and he spoke confidently—that it might soon be possible to get from Germany a peace that meant an independent Bohemia-Moravia and part of Poland restored. If Britain could get some satisfactory sort of security or guarantee for the future, would peace be possible? I asked what were the 'guarantees', etc. to be that we could trust, and he had no answer to this except that he thought Germany might renew the naval limitation pact and that the German people *must* be left to deal with Hitlerism. He said that in 1914–18 we were 'out' to get rid of the Kaiser and now we were 'out' to get rid of Hitler. If it meant years of disastrous war we should look for some means of making a peace and leaving the German people to deal with Hitler and his colleagues. (On the question of our navy, he was all for its being 'on top', even if the neutrals were at present suffering.) One other element of 'security' that he mentioned was that if Germany got out of this war she would be too weak, in view of the Russian expansion, to make war on us and France again [R V[1] would laugh at this argument].

He returned several times later to the necessity of getting peace 'before the moral of the German army completely crumbled'. It

---

1. Vansittart.

was not possible now, but when it was plain that the crumbling process in Germany and in its army was beginning, then was the time for Britain and France to show themselves willing to make peace. 'This is the only hope.' Otherwise, Bolshevism in Germany that spreads into 'chaos'.

15 December 1939

11.30 A.M. BJÖRN PRYTZ

He spoke of the invasion of Finland. He doubted whether Russia would stop at Finland. 'My Norwegian colleague [in London] does not believe that Russia will go on to demand a footing on the north Norwegian coast, but I am not so sure.' I asked what would happen if Russia made demands on either Norway or Sweden. He said without hestitation that there was no doubt whatever; they would make 'common cause' against her. Sweden would almost certainly have taken action over Finland if it were not that they had to fear Germany. They simply did not know what Germany would do if Sweden went to Finland's aid. They had done all they could to find out and it was impossible. Certain quarters around Goering told them that they could go ahead without anxiety, but when they made inquiry 'in certain other quarters' they got a different sort of answer, and so they were hamstrung.

Sweden was doing a fair amount for Finland. A good many men and a lot of munitions were going over the Frontier and no doubt there were also some officers who (being released from the Swedish Army) were volunteering for service with Finland. The method was à la Spain (no 'war' and no 'intervention'). Public opinion in Sweden was ahead of the Government, but the Government had to beware of Germany lest she should invade southern Sweden and make sure of the Western Baltic.

.   .   .   .   .

He realised that we (the British) could not do much owing to our preoccupation with Germany. All the same, if events brought us in (but it would have to be soon) we could greatly help by stopping the Russian sea operations (landing of troops, etc.) in the Petsamo region, and that would be very important. He did not see how we could hope to intervene in the Baltic and interfere with Russia or Germany there. He did not himself think that

Stalin would like the idea of being involved in a war with a big Power, but one could not speak with confidence; he had not himself thought that Stalin would attack Finland as he had done.

He spoke of the effects in other countries of Russia's attack on Finland and said that for a moment, when indignation was so intense and world-wide, he had hoped that there might be formed a Holy Alliance against Russia—Britain, France, Italy and Japan. But that moment soon passed. He hoped now that, while indignation was still strong, the other countries, including the USA, would do a lot to help Finland, but everything depended on the indignation lasting. In September we had heard a lot about Poland, but whoever heard of Poland now!

He had something to say regarding the question of a long or a short war. Germany would no doubt be hit by the blockade, but she had various sources of supply on her northern and eastern frontiers (and this was one reason why she would not be well pleased if Russia were involved in a lengthy war) and also she was hoping to buy war materials all the time. But his belief was something different from these calculations. He believed that the German leaders, and especially, he thought, the Generals, were firmly confident that they were going to win this war and they did not envisage it as a short war either. There were 'some very clever people' in Germany thinking about this war and he was not at all certain that they do not actually desire a long war. He thought that they believed that totalitarian Germany could not 'live beside' a Britain and a France with a 'free economy', that Britain and France if defeated or forced to a stalemate would be compelled to abandon their 'free economy' and that if they were exhausted to that extent the result could only be a German victory. He thought that they reckoned that an exhausted Britain and an exhausted France would be likely to fall more or less under the influence of totalitarian ideas and that this idea was at the back of the minds of the most far-seeing among them. I suggested that there was a considerable way to go yet before he would see this come about in England, and he said that at any rate it was not so far to go in France and whatever happened in France must have a great influence on us here.

1.30 P.M. LESLIE HORE-BELISHA

He was suffering from a slight chill and was a little melancholy.

.   .   .   .   .

He expressed anxiety that a greater effort should be made in respect of munitions production.

.   .   .   .   .

There ought to be a national campaign in order to compel a great national effort towards the maximum output of munitions. I said that the country did not appear to be getting any strong lead in this direction from the source whence it ought to come, which was obviously the Government, and that in any event the PM was about the last person who was likely to 'raise steam' in this direction; it was surely one of his deficiencies that he was a rather cold, unimaginative, man who was not given to lead great national campaigns on behalf of great national efforts. He said well, anyway, where are we going to get a better PM? If it were not Chamberlain, who was it going to be? He at any rate could see no one who would be an improvement.

Reverting to the air weapon, he said that he had never at anytime himself believed that the Germans would make a great bombing attack on this country; no doubt they did not relish the prospect of suffering the same sort of thing themselves, but apart from that he believed that they kept their eye fixed firmly on the main objective of smashing the Allied Armies in France and that they would keep their Air Force more or less intact for the purpose of operating with their army in the great offensive when they let it loose.

.   .   .   .   .

I asked him about the War Cabinet and elicited his views about the present Cabinet of nine, including five or six departmental chiefs, and the alternative of a small Cabinet of four or five members not charged with departmental duties. He said that he did not believe in the very small Cabinet. He thought that the present one functioned very well; he said he was sure it was a good thing to have the departmental ministers there since, for one thing, they knew their jobs and were more in touch with the realities of the situation than people who had not a definite job to do. I said surely there must be some very important problems which the departmental ministers had not time to study and that it must be a good thing to have one or two ministers like Hoare and Hankey who could analyse the pros and cons of any particular course, sit back and think about them, and then lay the situation before the Cabinet, perhaps with recommendations as to what should be done. Had he not observed that this was indeed the function and the value of the non-departmental members of the War Cabinet? He replied drily, No he had not observed it. I pressed him on the point and said I could not understand how the services ministers, who must be occupied all day long with their own particular jobs, could find the time to worry out the major problems of the war which did not concern their departments. He repeated that he thought their intimate acquaintance with their jobs, which were tied up with the jobs of the other ministers also, compensated for any difficulties of the kind I mentioned. He was not for reducing the Cabinet, nor for excluding departmental ministers, nor for including any more who were non-departmental.

3.30 P.M. SIR ROBERT VANSITTART AT THE FOREIGN OFFICE

He began by talking about the people who were making peace manoeuvres of all kinds . . . He said that the worthy Noel Buxton had been to see him. He came ostensibly for some other purpose, but after a short time he worked round to peace and suggested to Vansittart that we ought to go in for peace overtures and a peace conference. I asked him what reasons he could produce for this and he produced none that I could understand. I said to him 'I will tell you my view. We went to war in order to restrain one bandit and I cannot see that we ought to make peace because he has been joined by another.'

He talked about Russia. He said that Russia always had been, and remained, inefficient. She had never won any war in recent times. In Manchuria in 1903–4 she had far greater numbers than the Japanese and was heavily beaten. In the Great War, 1914–18, she had really only been an active combatant for the first six months and after that she was done. She never had been able to wage an offensive war in modern times with any success, though her men were good on the defensive. As for the prospect of her actually coming into the war against us 'I'm not very much afraid of her if she does.' He said that he did not think enough attention was paid to one most important fact. He thought that it ought to be rubbed in, and if it was it would certainly impress the neutrals. This was that, although Russia was acting villainously, the real villain of the piece was Germany. It was Germany that had let Russia loose. It was only because Germany was conniving that Russia dare invade Finland. Germany was letting Russia do pretty much what she chose, because Germany thought that she could win the war, and if she did win the war she would make Russia do anything she wanted. Russia had had a 'nuisance value' for Germany, but she was not in the least capable of putting up any resistance so soon as Germany had her hands free to deal with her.

We talked about Italy. He said again that the best thing to do about Italy was to leave her alone. Things looked quite healthy there, since Italy was clearly disapproving of the Russo-German Pact and did not like the emergence of Russia in the Balkans. He thought it was still just conceivable that Mussolini, if the military signs looked favourable, might try to take Italy into the war alongside Germany and against us. But he wondered whether now it might be possible for him to do it. Popular feeling would be against him and also some other influences; for instance, there was no doubt where the Italian Royal Family stood in this matter.

He referred to German tactics in the west and said that he had certainly been pretty confident that Hitler was going to invade Holland. That danger had passed over for the time, but he still thought that an attack in that quarter was extremely probable. The small countries were all of them alarmed about Germany and it was important that we should hold our own and be successful on the sea in order to make them understand that they could rely on us. He did not like the successes that the Germans were winning with their mines; our losses were 'too many' and he gave an emphatic shake of the head.

4.15 P.M. SIR KINGSLEY WOOD

Strength of the RAF. 'We had doubled our production since February and we would double our present production within the next twelve months.'

16 December 1939

11.00 A.M. COUNT RACZYNSKI

Terrible conditions in Poland under the German and Russian occupations.

8 January 1940

NEVILLE AND NATHAN LASKI AT THE MIDLAND HOTEL, MANCHESTER

This is one of the few conversations in Manchester that Crozier reported. Neville Laski was president of the Jewish Board of Deputies in London. His father Nathan was a prominent Manchester Jew. Neville did most of the talking.

I said that I thought Chamberlain did not see Vansittart now.

N L said 'No, he does not; V told me so himself. Recently he was thinking of resigning as he has next to nothing to do, but he finally decided to stay on.'

I said that I had never understood why Anthony Eden, who was in general agreement with Vansittart's policy, should have agreed to making him Chief Diplomatic Adviser, which really meant kicking him upstairs. It was done while Eden was Foreign Secretary. N L said that Vansittart had come to the conclusion that Eden was not only second-rate but also a dirty dog.

. . . . .

The old man, when we were talking of Hore-Belisha, said that he was glad of it,[1] not from the national but from the Jewish point of view. It was all right as long as things were going well, but if things began to go wrong with the army Hore-Belisha would have been blamed and the Jews would have been made the scapegoat.

We spoke of Neville Chamberlain and they both of them complained that neither Chamberlain nor Ramsay MacDonald had ever expressed a word of sympathy for the Jews in Germany. N said that even on a purely private occasion when he had gone on a deputation to N C with Lionel Rothschild and other leading Jews, N C had not uttered a single word of sympathy with the persecuted Jews. That seemed to him extraordinary since nothing of it would have been published.

. . . . .

He expressed the greatest contempt for the brains of the people of the Ministry of Information. The Board had offered to the Ministry a magnificent file of cuttings dealing with Germany since the Nazis came into power in 1933. The bigwigs in the Ministry had inquired about the details and turned the proposal down. It had then been discovered that it had a department of eight persons exclusively occupied in compiling a similar file from 1933 onwards. He said that the existing Jewish file was complete and perfect and the Ministry of Information were employing eight people to do something which could never be half as good.

---

1. Hore-Belisha was dismissed from the war office on 4 January 1940. See the interview with him on 20 January.

Referring to Sir J S[1] he said that anyone whom he nominated as a Bencher in the Inner Temple was certain to be defeated. A most excellent candidate had been defeated because he was J S's nominee.

18 January 1940

4.30 P.M. WINSTON CHURCHILL AT THE ADMIRALTY

I told him that it was not originally proposed to broadcast his Manchester meeting, but that there had been a protest and now it would be broadcast.[2] He was anxious to know whether it was his speech in particular that was to be omitted or whether no Minister's speech was being broadcast. (The rule was, of course, general.)

German submarines were not doing much damage at the moment. There were not many of them about and the Germans were not building more than we had destroyed. When recently in the House he had given an estimate of German construction he had made it a little excessive deliberately. As to mines, he thought that we had 'taken their measure', but it was best not to say so because the Germans would then 'think of something else'. He insisted that we had got a good control of the seas and that convoys were working well. The neutrals ought of course, to join these convoys, but they were 'all in a state of nerves' because of German threats. Nevertheless, he said, 'before long we shall get the sea under such control as we have never had before'. He struck me on this occasion, as on others, as being confident without boasting.

He referred to munitions and said that we were now where we were in 1916, but we must get as rapidly as possible to 1918. He jumped up and took me to a graph hanging on the wall. It had been presented to him when he left the Ministry of Munitions and showed the striking rise in supplies. He claimed no credit, which he said was all due to Lloyd George, and we must now, he said, get thousands of women into munitions and do it quickly. The war effort must be intensified.

We then spoke of the German flank in the Baltic. It was quite true that we needed a flank to strike at, but, he said, 'take note that if we are involved in war in the Baltic the Germans have a vast air-force based on land which we have never had to reckon

---

1. Sir John Simon.
2. Churchill spoke in the Free Trade Hall, Manchester, on 27 January 1940.

with in our history before'. There would be great difficulties there for the fleet and—here he made a grimace—it was difficult anyhow for the fleet to find secure bases in these days. However, before long the ships would have much greater air power behind them or with them and then—here he visibly licked his lips—we should see.

No, he did not want Russia in the war; nevertheless events might bring Russia in. I reminded him of what the French Ambassador (Coulondre) had said—that Hitler's ultimate object was to get hold of the man-power and resources of Russia. Yes, he said, that should be kept in mind, but it would be no short job if Germany entered on it. It was quite true that it was most important to find the German flank, but alas! we had not the initiative and we were compelled to await events. Our chance might come via Holland and Belgium, or via the Balkans, or via the Baltic. I asked him whether we could assume that it would come at all. He said that he believed on the whole that it would come and that the Germans could not wait and wait indefinitely. It was true that the Germans were blockading us as we them. But we were punishing them severely, and the ban on German exports, he was convinced, would be a big thing. No sooner had it been announced than the neutrals were saying to Germany 'Sorry, we can't take your stuff.'

I raised the question of a smaller War Cabinet. I said it was no question of personalities, but I wanted to ask him some questions. I asked whether Departmental Ministers ought really to be in the War Cabinet. He said yes, he believed they should. They carried more weight. For instance, he had the British fleet behind him and—here he grinned broadly—'they are a bit afraid of the British fleet'. I said, could a Departmental Minister think of all the other immensely important problems that had to be settled; and—here he grinned again—he said he thought that he himself could do it. He did not believe in the school which advocated 'sit back and think' Ministers. They had not enough to do and besides they carried no authority. I said what about Lloyd George's War Cabinet in 1916–18? Oh, he said, that was all devised in order to enable Lloyd George to run the war himself; he did everything and the rest of the War Cabinet did not count. Well, I said, should there not be one Minister of Defence in the War Cabinet instead of all the Service Ministers and the Minister of co-ordination? He replied very grimly that, if so, that meant that the present Minister of Co-ordination would be in the War Cabinet and he himself would be out; not that he minded, because he wanted his own job, which was at the Admiralty. I said why should the Minister of Co-ordination particularly be put into the War Cabinet; after all, the whole thing was only a stop-gap when Baldwin put Inskip in. Yes, he replied, 'and he did it in order to keep me out!' And he then went on to speak bitterly of Baldwin's blunders about the German Air-Force and more bitterly still about Baldwin's lack of courage to tell the people about the necessity for rearmament lest he should lose an election. He was highly emphatic about this. The only person without a portfolio who should be in the War Cabinet was the Prime Minister; he had no job but every job was his. 'But you go on,' he said, 'and argue for a small Cabinet if you believe in it, though personally I stick to it that Departmental Ministers should be included.'[1]

As I was leaving he said 'Take a firm line, tell them what sacrifices the Government expects of the country, and set the appeal high. Tell them what the Germans are doing', and, he said, 'Yes, but we must tell them what the French are doing too!'

5.00 P.M. BRENDAN BRACKEN AT THE ADMIRALTY

B B talked to me when I was leaving. He said he had always liked the MG and its critical vein. Only two papers were really important with regard to the war, because they were prepared to be critical—the Times and the MG. But not the DT, because Camrose was on too close personal terms with the Premier. Proprietors of newspapers never ought to be on good official terms with Ministers and never ought to accept a title from the Government till they were retiring from business or reached an age like that at which C P Scott got the OM. I said 'He never got it', and B B replied 'Well, he ought to have done.'

He went on 'You know, of course, that Chamberlain hates criticism; he can't stand it; he gets hurt and angry at the sound of it. You know Arthur Mann of the Yorkshire Post was on very good terms with Baldwin, and when Baldwin resigned it was arranged that Mann should sometimes see Chamberlain. Then the YP began to criticise Chamberlain, and Mann, going to see him one day, began by saying, 'I am afraid that some of the things we have been saying in the Yorkshire Post must have been disagreeable to you." To which Chamberlain replied with extreme brusqueness "I never read your paper".'

As B B let me out of a side door, he said 'If you want anything

---

1. Churchill did not retain the three service ministers in the war cabinet when he himself became prime minister.

done by this Government you have got to push, and push and push!'

5.45 P.M. J W DULANTY

IRA receiving money from American sources.

19 January 1940

3.30 P.M. SIR ROBERT VANSITTART AT THE FOREIGN OFFICE

I asked him about the renewed threats to Holland and Belgium. Was it bluff or part of the war of nerves, or an attempt to find out what were the reactions? He thought it was none of these things, but a real intention on Hitler's part to invade. Just as Hitler had 'pulled his punch' on November 11, possibly owing to the opposition of the generals, so he had now done it again. But why? He thought it was probably owing to the 'indecisions of a lunatic'. He had been unable finally to make up his mind to send half a million men, or a million men, to their deaths on a gamble. He thought that Hitler did not know whether to make 'the great gamble' or not. Hitherto, partly through our folly, he had always gambled and guessed right. He was like a man who guessed right time after time at baccarat till it was almost a miracle, but would he make the venture yet again? It might win the war, but if he lost the gamble he might go downhill very quickly. He thought it quite likely that the Germans would not stand for the war if they received really heavy blows.[1]

Was it true that Goering and Ribbentrop were at loggerheads? One should not believe it for a moment. That might well come eventually, but there was no reason to think that it would come now. Also it was 'rot' to suppose that Goering was a 'moderate' but it was even possible that 'the fat heads' in this country might welcome Goering as ruler of Germany instead of Hitler or the generals; and the generals would be no better either; indeed, they might be worse, being more tenacious in their purpose than Hitler.

The Finns, he said, were undoubtedly in danger. He did not

---

1. Hitler had again fixed the day for the offensive in the west: 17 January 1940. On 10 January a German officer, carrying detailed plans of the offensive, made a forced landing in Belgium and failed to destroy the plans effectively. The Belgians took military precautions and allied troops moved up to the Belgian frontier. These steps, reinforced by the bad weather, led Hitler to postpone the offensive once more. On 10 May Hitler gambled successfully.

himself think it 'Very profitable' that Germany would attack Sweden, but it had to be reckoned with as a possibility. Germany might invade in order to get control of the iron ore mines and to secure Baltic bases. It had to be remembered also that Germany had always fought her wars on the soil of other people. In his opinion the great fault in 1918 had been to make the armistice at all. Unfortunately he had no influence himself at that time, but he had said then and he said now that they were well and truly beaten. Whereas now 'they all, yes *all*' believe that they lost the war only because of the Jews and the Socialists and so they were willing to try again. It was a fatal mistake that the allies had made. He thought that Hitler would very likely attack Holland or Belgium about the end of February or the beginning of March. It was much more likely that Hitler would attack Holland and Belgium than the Balkans because the gains there would be infinitely greater—he could get at England with bombers protected by fighters, and an attack on England was his great ambition. Would Holland and Belgium stand together if one of them was attacked? He thought they probably would. The position in that respect was pretty satisfactory.

We needed a much greater national effort in this country. We must have more men called up. The French were grumbling because they were taking men up to 45 years of age, who on going home found women and children working on the land, while we had called up no one over 23. Some of the French pressmen who had been in this country had even suggested that we ought to send over quantities of men untrained in order to make a show, but he did not favour this. People here simply did not understand the urgency of the need for a greater effort. In his opinion we ought to have a Coalition Government, but that apparently was impossible since Labour would not go in.

He referred to America in respect of Finland. The American attitude was thoroughly bad, because they had professed a special affection for Finland and could do a lot to help her. The papers that morning were saying that Senator Borah was very ill, and he was glad of it and hoped that he would die because he had done so much mischief to the right causes. Of course, it had to be remembered that 'politics' were preventing the United States from doing what they should.

5.00 P.M. COUNT REVENTLOW AT THE DANISH LEGATION

Of the Poles he said that they were 'cocky and vain-glorious';

also they had been badly led. Their disaster was that the Germans took them by surprise with air attacks on the first night and did enormous damage with bombing.

He said a curious thing about the Finns. He said there were a whole lot of them scattered over Northern Russia and some of them had talked about creating a 'Finnish Empire' at Russia's expense. I said surely they were just silly and that no one could take them seriously, not so seriously, for instance, as the way in which some Poles had bragged during 1939 that they would revive the great Polish Kingdom. He said that it was silly, but it was also unfortunate because it provided Stalin and his friends with a pretext for saying that the Finns threatened them. Actually he said that the Finns had been surprised by the attack. During the negotiations in Moscow they had got the impression that Stalin rather liked them and they never expected war. He thought that in point of fact Stalin for his part had not expected resistance but now he could not retreat because he had recognised Kuusinen[1] as the true Government of Finland and he could not possibly abandon it. He himself thought that this Government was the 'limit of wickedness' since it had absolutely no support in Finland and it was the 'end of everything' if a Government like Russia could set up and recognise a Government which had no support in a neighbouring country and then say they had backed this spurious body in order to liberate the people of the country attacked. He referred to the White Terror in Finland, but he said the worst Terror of all was the Red Terror which preceded it. It was as wicked as the Red Terror of Bela Kun in Hungary.

We spoke of Sweden, and he expressed the opinion that Germany would not invade Sweden, provided that Sweden remained neutral. In any case Finland would gain little if Sweden went to war to help her, because the moment that Sweden did so she would fear that Germany was about to attack and she would devote all her efforts to pure self-defence. He assumed that if Norway and Sweden were attacked by Germany we would go to their aid, but it was very undesirable that we should send British troops otherwise, because if we did Germany would certainly proceed to attack.

He mentioned that Denmark was sending a lot of help to Finland, but the least said about it the better. Also the less said about Swedish help to Finland the better. Also the less said about

1. Kuusinen, Finnish Communist leader, long-time exile in Russia, headed a puppet Finnish government during the Soviet-Finnish war.

Germany possibly attacking Sweden the better. All such state-ments made things more difficult and increased the danger and he disliked seeing anything of the kind.

He turned the conversation to domestic politics: the position of Labour and of the Liberal party. He asked what were the prospects of a new Government and who was likely to be the new Premier. I said that people spoke either of Halifax or of Churchill, and he said that Halifax would be much the better because he would be more likely to make peace. Churchill would be a bad premier from that point of view.

.   .   .   .   .

F A VOIGT

We talked of Vansittart and the fact that Chamberlain no longer consulted him. Voigt said the neglect was complete. Then he said 'Vansittart on one occasion made a great howler and Chamberlain has never forgotten it.' Just before Munich Vansittart advised the Government that France would certainly fight if Czecho-slovakia was threatened. He did this because he was convinced that France *must* fight and dare not, could not, do anything else. But he was wrong and when the French Ministers came to London anxious beyond words to avoid war, and to do almost anything to avoid it, Vansittart's misconception was exposed.

20 January 1940

9.30 A.M. LESLIE HORE-BELISHA AT 16 STAFFORD PLACE

Hore-Belisha was dismissed from the war office on 4 January 1940. The generals had taken against him from the first, and the incident of 24 November 1939, described in the second footnote on p. 131, finished him. The king, Lord Gort, c-in-c in France, and Ironside, CIGS, combined to get him out. Though he continued to dream of a return to high office, all he ever achieved was to be minister of social insurance in Churchill's caretaker government, and not in the cabinet at that.

Crozier attached exaggerated importance to him or perhaps merely found his conversation and behaviour entertaining. The entire interview was recorded in Mrs Crozier's handwriting—an indication of the value Crozier placed on it.

He said he had had thousands of letters about his dismissal. There were sacks and sacks. Many letters not yet even opened and he didn't know when they would be. He had had extraordinary nice letters from people in the army, including one from all the officers of a certain RASC unit. He was getting all kinds of offers to write or speak. He was offered £7,000 for a six weeks' lecture tour in the USA but he didn't want to take American money anyhow. He was also offered £2,000 for four articles but he wasn't accepting it. He had to make a living, though, which was a great nuisance, but he had no idea yet what he was going to do. At the moment he was enjoying his freedom from responsibility and he felt rather happy.

Then he spoke of his fall from office, 'Well, now I'll tell you all about it. I had no idea it was coming; it was a great surprise to me. As a matter of fact I had been on very good terms indeed with the Prime Minister lately and somewhere about Xmas he had said some pleasant things to me about the work I was doing at the War Office. He had been congratulatory, "almost affectionate". During the week before the event I had been at all kinds of meetings and Cabinets with him and there had not been the slightest evidence that he was dissatisfied about things or that he was contemplating any change.

'On the morning before the dismissal while we were in the Cabinet a note was passed to me saying that the Prime Minister would like to see me at 3.15 in the afternoon. As the Cabinet ended rather sooner than usual I went up to him and said "Would you like to see me now?" and he looked up at the clock and said "There's no time now; it had better be this afternoon. I've a proposal to make to you".

'So I went in the afternoon, with not the faintest inkling that anything was wrong. He said "Leslie, I want to make a change. I want you to leave the War Office. There's nothing at all against you. In fact, you've done a fine work there and your name will live in history".

(Hore-Belisha pronounced this phrase with great emphasis.)

' "But there's prejudice against you".' (This with emphasis, too.)

I said to Hore-Belisha 'He used the word "prejudice", did he?' and he answered—'he said, "There's prejudice against you".'

Then Hore-Belisha went on: 'I said "Can you give me some details?" and he said "No, but it exists." I asked what it was based on and he replied "Oh, some complaints of rudeness to Generals." I said "Can you give me some instances?" and he said "No, I can't, it's some time ago and I can't give any details" and then he said "I want to offer you the Board of Trade, of course you'll accept?"

'I said "Well, I'm not so sure about that" and he replied "But that's incredible. You must. You're an ambitious man and you can't just go out like that." I said "Yes, I know I'm an ambitious man; so are we all, but that doesn't settle it. Even if you offered me the Foreign Office or the Exchequer I doubt whether I would take it now anyhow. I have my job and I don't want to lose it."

'Then he went on "You had far better give up the War Office. You won't be able to stop there—They'll get you out some day!".'

(When I saw Hore-Belisha a month or so later I asked him to confirm that the words 'They'll get you out some day' had actually been used to him at this interview and he said that they had.)

Hore-Belisha went on ' "No", I said to him, "I don't see how I can accept. Because, the same reasons which have led to my losing this office might equally cause me to lose the other that you offer me."

'He pressed me for an answer and I said "Well, why this urgency? Why is it so pressing?" and he replied that other changes were involved. I said that I must have "time to think it over", and he said "Well, how much time do you want?" I said to him "Well, if you insist on an answer you can have it now and I know what it will be, but I don't know what the hurry is about. I will give you an answer at 10 o'clock tomorrow morning if that will do." I told him I couldn't answer before because I had an Army Council, and this and that to do, and I didn't propose to think about it till the end of the day. I went away and continued as usual with committees and councils. I never had any doubt what my answer was going to be. I did the day's job as usual and at 10 o'clock next morning I went round to No 10 and told him I declined.

'He said he was very sorry and also that it was very awkward for him, as he would now have to find another President of the Board in a few hours.

'I said to him "Well, I suppose I shall now have to write you a letter." He agreed, and I went away and wrote a letter and took it to him. He read it and said, Would I mind adding a sentence or two about there being no difference between us about policy, and I said "Not at all" and added them. Then he said to me "Now I must write to you, but what am I to say?" and it struck me at the time as very funny that having thrown me out of office he should be asking me what account of it he had better give to the public. I said "Oh, you'd better say so and so", which he thereupon did.'

I asked what effect all this had on the other members of the Cabinet.

He replied that as soon as it was known he was going he had

received a letter from a number of them asking him to reconsider his decision. Samuel Hoare had been particularly decent to him. Kingsley Wood had come running after him and had taken him by the arm and said 'But, Leslie, this is terrible. If this sort of thing can happen to you it can happen equally to me', and so, said H B, 'it can!'

I said that there had already been a rumour that Kingsley Wood might be in danger and he asked me rather urgently where I had seen this. I told him in the News Chronicle and suggested that the rumour might arise from Kingsley Wood having spoken as he had done in this matter. I asked what, anyway, was wrong with K Wood that he should be sacked, if he was, and he replied that he was an excellent organiser but that he was not too well liked by certain people; he rather suggested that K Wood was too much of a man of the common people to be popular with the high Tory-military people.[1]

Then I asked about Sir John Simon. 'Oh yes', he said, 'John sent me a letter. It was something like this—"Dear Leslie, I'm so sorry you're going and I hope you will soon be back. You will do me the justice to admit that at the Treasury I had always done my best to support your reforms. Yrs. J S"'

'To this', he said, 'I replied as follows—

' "Dear John. I am glad you are sorry I am going. I hope Lady Simon is better. Yrs. Leslie".'

At the meeting of the Liberal National party to consider his going John had spoken and again had made a strong point of the support which, as chancellor, he had always given H B. 'When I replied I said that Sir John Simon had only anticipated my intention when he paid his tribute to the support that he at the Treasury had given my plans.' It was plain that he thought that one or two of his principal colleagues in the Cabinet knew of what Chamberlain intended to do and could have prevented or at least obstructed it.

After the speeches on his resignation in Parliament Lloyd George had taken him to his room. Lloyd George had described his dismissal as 'Contemptible'. He (L G) considered that it was, in fact, a triumph of the military over the civilians. Also, he thought that Churchill was partly to blame for what had happened. 'But why', said H B, 'should Churchill have done anything against me, if he did?' 'Oh, well', said L G, 'he would not be sorry

---

1. Perhaps this explains why Wood, secretary for air, and Hoare, lord privy seal, changed places in April. Perhaps it also explains why on 10 May Wood, formerly Chamberlain's most loyal supporter, was the first to insist that Chamberlain must go.

to see you out of his way, would he, on the road to the Premiership?'

Well but, I said, wasn't Churchill in France while the thing was being decided? 'Yes', replied H B, 'he was; he was there watching a conferment of honours by Gamelin on Gort and Ironside which, incidentally, I had recommended—but he knew, he must have known, what was happening here in London and he could have been here to resist it had he chosen.'[1]

With regard to Churchill, as with Simon, he spoke with obvious feeling.

I then said that he had told me the real cause of his dismissal, but I thought he might like to know some of the reports on the subject that were going about. I knew of four or five. He said he certainly would.

The first, I said, and a frequent one, was that he had rebuked senior officers, colonels and such in the presence of subalterns. He said it was nonsense; there was just no truth in it.[2]

A second, I said, was that he and Gort and possibly Ironside had quarrelled. He said it was untrue if anything more was meant than the differences of opinion which there must necessarily be between the people at the top. It was quite true that he had made proposals which Gort and Ironside had not been able to accept.

For instance, he held that the thing to do on the West was to make an extension of the Maginot line along the Belgian frontier as 'impregnable' as possible in order that it might be held with as few troops as possible and therefore that troops should be relieved for service elsewhere. He would have set a great firm of contractors, like McAlpines, on the job of constructing such a line of fortifications, but the military chiefs would not have it. He wanted not only to set painters to work on the war but official historians also while it continued, but that too was rejected. 'But you will see' he said 'that if anyone was to complain of those differences it should have been me, because I was defeated and not the generals.' As to Ironside, he said that he was an 'Intriguer' and that Chamberlain, only a few weeks ago, had used that word about him.

I said that another report was that he had announced that all

---

1. Beaverbrook telephoned to Churchill on Hore-Belisha's behalf, appealing to him to intervene. Churchill refused angrily. Maybe he felt his own position to be too uncertain. More probably he was on the side of the generals.

2. On 24 November 1939 Hore-Belisha summoned Major-General Pakenham-Walsh, Gort's chief engineer, to the army council, when the adjutant-general was the only military member present, and instructed him to inform Gort that the war cabinet were gravely perturbed by the reported weakness of the British sector. This incident led directly to Hore-Belisha's dismissal. J R Colville, Man of Valour, 160.

soldiers were to have Xmas leave without consulting GHQ in France, at which he only laughed, and that he was said to have announced in Parliament the unity of the Anglo-French command, also without consulting the military chiefs. 'Well', he said, not denying it, 'I thought that everyone knew, or assumed, that there must be unity of command, it never occurred to me that there would be any doubt about it.'

When I said that I thought that, even if he had gone, his reforms would last he said 'I am not so sure of that. One of the last documents that I saw before I left the office was a memorandum of a military criticism of the system of promotion from the ranks which I had instituted.' He then went on to say that the root-cause of the hostility to him was the offence he had given to the military and high social castes.

'They resented my appointment to the War Office—a Jew and an ordinary person not of their own caste. They bitterly resented my overthrowing the military chiefs on the Army Council and they also resented the democratic reforms which followed. When I dealt with the Army Council, Fabian Ware (former editor of the Morning Post who became a general in the war) came to see me. He told me that "they" would never forgive me. He said that "they" would eventually get me out of office. They would not disclose their real reasons but they would fabricate them; they would accuse me of going with women, or of drinking or of any other accusation but the real one, but "get you out in time they will". And now it has all come true and they have got me out.'

He then said 'The trouble is that they turn everything to do with me into a personal issue. When other men are criticised it is a matter of the issue involved but when I am supposed to do any-anything wrong they at once make it personal to me. It is always that way in my case.'

He then went on to speak of the Cabinet. Hankey and Chatfield[1] were weak spots. Chatfield contributed nothing; Hankey had a prodigious memory and was a 'super-secretary' and nothing more. Both of them depended on Chamberlain; they had no party and therefore no authority behind them and in consequence were Chamberlain's faithful supporters. The Labour Party had behaved stupidly. In the debate on his resignation Attlee could have raised the issue of Civilians against Military men but he had

---

1. Hankey was minister without portfolio, and Chatfield minister for the coordination of defence. Both were members of the war cabinet.

preferred to talk nonsense about the dangers of a press dictatorship.

As for himself, he was going to try to devise a policy which he hoped would appeal to all Liberals—the independent Liberals as well as the Liberal Nationals. He believed that the prevailing sentiment of the country was liberal and he could appeal to it. He hoped to advocate an advanced social policy and he asked me to send him something interesting bearing on this subject that I thought he ought to see.

He mentioned that when news of his going was known in France the French government had immediately got busy and asked the British Government for an assurance that the change did not mean any change in British military policy. The French Government had also—and this annoyed him—used the censorship to prevent Paris newspapers from commenting on his dismissal in any way that might annoy the British Government.

11.00 A.M. DR QUO

Hopeful about China's prospects against Japan.

12 NOON. BJÖRN PRYTZ

Sweden helping Finland 'unofficially.'

Britain must help also, but she too must do it unofficially. No troops must be sent across Norway or Sweden. . . .

He had been talking to Halifax, and Halifax had seemed to suggest that Sweden ought to do more for Finland. He had said to him 'You seem to me to regard us in respect of Finland as in 1938 we regarded you in respect of Czechoslovakia, except that we have no responsibility for what is happening to Finland.' (He was pleased with himself about this.)

15 February 1940

4.00 P.M. MALCOLM MACDONALD AT THE COLONIAL OFFICE

Plans for colonial development.

. . . I raised the question of the Small War Cabinet without Departmental Ministers. He said that he himself had rather favoured this, but he could tell me what Chamberlain's view was after some months of war. It was that the Services Ministers in a War Cabinet were 'indispensable'.

6.00 P.M. SIR SAMUEL HOARE AT THE HOUSE OF COMMONS

He was to speak at Nottingham on the next day in the Cabinet Ministers' series, and told me what he was proposing to say. In particular, he would try to undo the mischief done by Simon who, in an otherwise excellent speech, had seemed to put a stopper on rises in wages—which had caused a most unfortunate impression. I said it was a pity that the BBC cut off these speeches immediately the speaker sat down, as there was no sound of applause and it sounded—at home and abroad—as though the speech had fallen flat, especially if there had been interruptions. He rang his bell and his secretary came in. 'Oh', he said, 'just ring up Ogilvie[1] at the BBC, will you, and ask him to keep the broadcast on just for a minute or two to-morrow after I've finished; Mr. Crozier says that they cut one off and it sounds as though the speech had fallen very flat.' [I heard the secretary in the next room talking to the BBC and from the next day onwards they gave a bit of the applause! So easily is it done when Authority wants it.]

About Finland—Sweden was very timid and Norway was worse. They would not let men go in except in twos and threes. He would 'take a great risk' to help the Finns. We were sending in a lot of stuff, including aeroplanes that we could ill spare. The railway transport was very bad and we had even to send people to speed things up. He thought that it would make a very bad impression if Finland fell and, on the other hand, if Norway and Sweden would only stand with us it would be an enormous *moral* gain to the Allies. They were, however, too scared of Germany.

He mentioned the Turks and said they now seemed quite sound and good, but they were getting an awful lot of money out of us. He thought the economic effort in this country was going better and it was going to go better still. We were doing much more in munitions production than most people knew and there was going to be an enormous increase by 1941.

On the question of an Economic Minister in the Cabinet, he said that it must be remembered that the Chancellor of the Exchequer came into everything and was a most intimate and important part of the economic effort.

---

1. F W Ogilvie, director general of the BBC, 1938–42.

16 February 1940

9.00 A.M. LESLIE HORE-BELISHA AT 16 STAFFORD PLACE

In Mrs. Crozier's handwriting.

There was a French paper lying on the table when he came into the room—the Paris Soir.

'Is this the French paper that prints your weekly article?' I said.

'Yes, exactly the same articles as are appearing in the News of the World.' He was in high spirits and began to sing a French song 'La Guerre! La Guerre!' His articles, he said, were syndicated by the agency 'Co-operation' which was run by Herr Rivisz. Did I by any chance know Herr Rivisz? I said I did, and was it Rivisz who had persuaded him to go into the News of the World? No, on the contrary, that was about the only Sunday paper which Rivisz had *not* discussed with him. Rivisz had proposed the Sunday Times to him, but that was no good; that was not 'reaching the people'. He wanted to 'reach the people who will remake the world after the war'.

'Well,' I said 'why not have gone into the Sunday Pictorial if you want a big circulation?' Because, he answered, the circulation of the Sunday Pictorial was a million and a half. Now the circulation of the News of the World was actually 4,600,000, which meant that it reached about 16,000,000 people. That was his reason for choosing that paper and no other—he would reach the people.

The telephone rang. 'My secretary!' He spoke into the phone 'Yes, of course, we must send Astor a telegram at once. What shall we say? "Your telegram just received. Much regret was unable to greet these naval heroes"? Will that do? Wait a minute, say "great naval heroes"—leave out "these"—yes, that's better, "unable greet naval heroes".' These were the crew of the Exeter.[1]

'There was some trouble about my first article', he said. 'The French censorship held it up altogether for seven hours. I said eventually that if they didn't release it I would withdraw it altogether and publish the facts. Then they let it through. The French won't let anything out, if they can help it, that the British Government might not like.

'Now about the News of the World. I know how it's regarded. I had an officer lunching here the other day and he told me that I had lots of friends in the War Office but that I was losing them by going into this paper with my articles.'

---

1. Homecoming after the sinking of the Graf Spee.

The telephone rang. 'Oh, is that you, Susan my dear? How are you, sweetheart? Well, I hope? What's that? You like my articles but you wish I hadn't gone into News of the World? You don't understand, my dear. We mustn't be so respectable.' He said to me 'The oligarchs must always be respectable. Well, I make the News of the World respectable by my articles!'

(The name was not really Susan, it was a well known woman politician. And these epithets ['My dear', 'Sweetheart' etc.,] mean nothing. He has the stage convention of using them to all and sundry.)

I said 'I see that according to the advertisement your next Sunday's article is to be "the boldest of the War"?' 'And so it will be', he said. 'It's all about Finland and the duty of Norway and Sweden to assist them under the Covenant. And our duty too! We've heard much too little of the Covenant in respect of Finland. Well, now we're going to hear about it. I've explained exactly what we can and ought to do under the Covenant, and no covering anything up?'

The telephone rang. 'Oh, is that you, Herr Doktor? How are you this morning, Herr Doktor?' (To me) 'It's Rivisz; he's come on about my article.' 'Yes, Herr Doktor?—There are some points in the article you want to raise? Right, tell me what they are. Those figures about Germany's imports of iron ore from Sweden? Yes, I know; yes, I think they're all right. I'll verify them now.' To his man—'Bring me that Bulletin of the Institute of International Affairs that you'll find on top of a pile of books on my desk.

'Now then, Herr Doktor! Yes, I think those figures are all right. You're not sure whether 10,000,000 tons will prove to be exact—it might be more or less? What shall we say then? I'll ask Mr Crozier—you know him—he's here now. Mr Crozier says, "say about 10,000,000 tons" and then we're safe anyhow whichever way the figure goes. Is that all, Herr Doktor? Right, right, ring me up again if you've anything else.

'The Herr Doktor was anxious he said, lest a single figure should go wrong—a very watchful man!

'Now about Finland. I'm pointing out that under Article 16 of the Covenant Norway and Sweden are *bound* to let allied troops through.'

'But', I said, 'I don't think they will, that would mean war with Germany and they are determined to avoid war with Germany at all costs.'

'But they have no option in this matter', he said. 'They are bound under Article 16. And the allies should therefore send a force to Finland's aid.'

'Oh come!' I said. 'What if they should resist? It sounds as though you were saying that if they resist by force nevertheless we must go in through their countries—that is, make war on them and that's incredible.'

'But, of course, my dear Crozier, it would not come to that. When they found we meant business and were persisting they would give way and let us in. We shouldn't have to force our way through. This is no question of attacking Belgium.' It was, he insisted, a duty to help Finland via the covenant of the League and it was the duty of Norway and Sweden to assist us;[1] therefore we must go in. At the same time it was not a question only of helping Finland. We must get the Gallivare iron ore mines and prevent the iron ore from getting to Germany, which would be a most serious blow to her because half of her imports of iron ore are now already cut off by the Allies and Sweden was now her only large surviving large source of supply.[2]

When I took my leave he was still in high spirits and said that he had seldom felt so happy. The burden of responsibility had gone.

'My position is good, I have my public, and if trouble comes and there is use for me, I shall be there. I shall be stronger, I think, than I was before.' He began to sing again. 'La Guerre! La Guerre!' 'If you see anything that you think I ought to read, you'll send it to me won't you? La Guerre! La Guerre!'

11.45 A.M. SIR ARCHIBALD SINCLAIR

He was a few minutes late in arriving, as he had been introducing to the War Minister a deputation of Highlanders who were pleading for the retention of the kilt. It was, he said, a most impressive affair.

He said that the appointment of an Economic Minister to the War Cabinet must come and in his opinion it was badly needed. I mentioned Sir Andrew Duncan's name and he said he thought he was a possibility as he was well spoken of in every quarter. There was, however, a 'solid group' in opposition to the idea; it consisted of Chamberlain, Simon and Sir Horace Wilson. Simon was determined to hold on to power; Chamberlain was thoroughly

1. Sweden and Norway did not take this view.
2. Hore-Belisha was only expressing in exaggerated form nonsensical views that were held by members of the British cabinet.

self-satisfied and Wilson was now an immense power behind the throne in all directions. Wilson was specially active with regard to appointments and promotions and he had reason to believe that he was keeping out people who had been opposed to Chamberlain's Munich policy. He thought that we might hear more on this point before long and he would keep me informed.

When we began to talk about the question of a smaller Cabinet, he said that he would tell me the inner history of the formation of the present Cabinet at the beginning of September. Actually Chamberlain was not then opposed to the idea of a small Cabinet; until 2 p.m. on the Sunday, the day when war was declared, the Inner Cabinet was to consist of six people only, and these were to be Chamberlain, John Simon, Hankey, Chatfield, Halifax, and Winston Churchill without a department; Samuel Hoare was not at this stage included. Before 2 p.m. the Chief Tory Whip (Margesson) had told the Labour leaders that this was to be the Government and that it would be announced in this form about 5 p.m. When the announcement was actually made at five it was found that the War Cabinet consisted of nine members including all the service Ministers. The Labour men to whom Margesson had spoken reproached him for misleading them and said it was rather awkward for them. Margesson replied that the reason for the change was that Churchill, if he were in the War Cabinet without a department to occupy him, would be 'too dangerous'. Further, when this plan of a small Cabinet, which would not include the service Ministers, had been mentioned Hore-Belisha had described it as a 'rotten' plan, saying that what would happen would be that the Cabinet would summon the Chiefs of Staff, who would be 'undermining' their Ministers.[1]

Sinclair went on to express his own opinion that it was quite impossible for any one of the service Ministers to do his own job with its immense responsibilities and at the same time to think of the all-important other questions that had to be decided. [He mentioned here that Churchill was convinced that the present Germany is by no means the Germany of 1914.]

·   ·   ·   ·   ·

3.30 P.M. SIR ROBERT VANSITTART AT THE FOREIGN OFFICE

It was expected that his play would be produced the following

---

1. This is more or less what happened.

Tuesday. He said it was 90% entertainment and 10% 'moral'. Nothing serious could be got in except by way of something like 90% entertainment. [The play never came off—it was indefinitely postponed.]

Finland was in danger; manpower was now the difficulty. The northern neutrals were 'rabbits', they thought only of the immediate future and were incapable of taking a long view. He doubted whether Germany would attack them except under great provocation. He thought that Germany would not 'move' if we and France sent in 30,000 or 40,000 men, provided they were 'camouflaged' to look like volunteers. Norway was worse than Sweden. The distances would be long for a German invading army and its job would be far from easy.

He was very angry about the treatment of the Poles by Germany. The Gestapo and similar people who were murdering all the Poles 'must be executed' when we had won the war. It was not a question of 'Hang the Kaiser' or of hanging Hitler and Goering. We must get hold of these Gestapo people and hang *them*. Such a thing had never been seen in history as was going on in Poland. There was a great class of German 'massacreurs' at work and 'they must be wiped out'. Never, never, must we trust Hitler and his crowd any more. There was no 'other Germany' now; it did not exist except perhaps for a mere 10% of the people—and quite impotent anyhow.

His general view was depressing. We could not help Finland unless Norway and Sweden made it possible. Everything turned on that. We had not the initiative anywhere. The general effort in this country was quite inadequate. Parliament was doing its job badly. The 'gag' prevented criticism. The Whip Margesson[1] had developed the gag to a further point than anyone ever. Nothing was to be hoped from the present Government. It had taken twelve months to get a decent Ministry of Supply—and then we got Burgin!

He disliked the Sumner Welles[2] mission and feared that harm would come out of it. He suspected the 'peace moves' ideas of the USA and feared lest some sort of plan for a compromise peace— which would be fatal—would emerge. It was largely American 'Politics' and he disliked and feared it.

---

1. Chief Conservative Whip.
2. Sumner Welles was touring Europe on Roosevelt's behalf.

4.30 P.M. LORD ZETLAND AT THE INDIA OFFICE

Attitude of the Congress party.

5.45 P.M. J W DULANTY

Hanging of two IRA men at Coventry. 'It was noticeable that although Eire is officially and strongly neutral he every now and then slipped into saying "we" and "us" when speaking of the Allies.'

17 February 1940

11.30 A.M. BJÖRN PRYTZ

.   .   .   .   .

Personally he would like to see all the neutrals come in on our side, but how could it be expected of the small countries when they saw the attitude of Russia and Italy! Besides, someone was going to suffer *first*. Britain and France had never rescued any neutral, e.g. Czechoslovakia. I said that the end of the great war had settled everything. Belgium, Serbia and Rumania had been restored. He said yes, quite true, nevertheless some small neutral —Holland or Sweden—was going to be smashed if they stood up to Germany. Poland was 'an example' to them. It was a deliberate example. What Germany was doing in Poland was horrible beyond words and it was intended to show small neutrals what was in store for them if Germany set about them.

He believed that we could stick it out, but how long was it going to be? He thought that the Allied strength would be very much greater in 1941 and that Germany by then would be losing some of her advantage. If war spread to the south he thought Germany would lose seriously by the stoppage of her supplies of oil from the Baku fields. We lived from day to day and no one could say what changes there would be. Sweden was arming in every possible way as fast as she could because the future was for her obscure and she must be ready to defend herself.

28 March 1940

3.15 P.M. SIR ROBERT VANSITTART AT THE FOREIGN OFFICE

Well, he said, things had been going a good deal worse since he saw me last (6 weeks ago). The Finns had 'gone'[1] and Russia was, on the whole, the stronger for her success, and it had better be taken that Russia and Germany were still hand in glove and working together. But on the question of the Allied expedition to Finland he was bound to say that he thought the Government had a strong case. That was made impossible by the attitude of Norway and Sweden.

He did not think that much was said about a peace plan at the Brenner.[2] He thought it possible that Mussolini had wondered whether Hitler had anything useful to say about a peace plan, and that Hitler had not, and that in consequence Hitler had talked a good deal about the Balkans—possibly what he had in mind was a division of profits in the Balkans between the three of them—Germany, Russia and Italy. But what it amounted to no one could say. It was not altogether easy for these three to reconcile their interests. For instance, here was Italy obviously dealing with Hungary as her best friend and making arrangements with her, but, on the other hand, Germany's road to exploitation in the Balkans also obviously lay through Hungary, if anywhere; that is to say, the interests of Germany and Italy were not easily to be reconciled in this quarter.

As to Russia, there was no evidence *so far* that Russia and Italy were going to make a bargain of it, and he thought it likely that Russia, backed by Germany, would renew pressure on Rumania and on Turkey before long. He expected pressure on Rumania before pressure on the Turks. He did not regard such pressure as being a *self-defensive* move by Stalin on the south; in his opinion it was expansionist and Imperialist and nothing else. There was a great lack of political activity on our part and had been ever since the beginning of the war. Right at the beginning we ought to have been active in the Balkans. We should have told Rumania to give southern Dobrudja back to Bulgaria. In the Balkan front Bulgaria was the weak spot. If Rumania had done this she would probably have squared Bulgaria, who would then have stood in with the rest of the Balkan Powers instead of, as now, endangering the whole structure. His advice had not been taken—and where were we now? People said it was too great a risk—that Rumania would have refused or Bulgaria, having got Dobrudja, would have demanded a port on the Ægean. He did not believe it, but the

---

1. Finland agreed to make peace on 12 March.
2. Hitler and Mussolini met on the Brenner on 18 March. Hitler told Mussolini of his preparations for an offensive in the west, and Mussolini promised to enter the war at a suitable moment.

point was that we would not take any risks and that in war risks must be taken. Well, he would have risked Rumania's refusing or Bulgaria's blackmailing afterwards. We would not take risks or 'take the initiative' with Rumania and the result we could see now! I said 'You mean Carol's bringing back the Iron Guard?' and he said 'Yes, of course; it's a first step of concession to Germany and probably more to follow.' I said 'Well, what can we do now?' He said 'Not so much because we have let slip various opportunities but we can put pressure on these peoples not to yield to Germany, but in that case we *must* back them up with armies and with munitions, e.g. aeroplanes.' Then he said that our production and our general effort were nothing like what they ought to be as yet if we were to have a vigorous diplomacy and make it effective.

So we got on to the question of the Government and I asked him frankly his views about the Premiership—Chamberlain, Halifax, Churchill, etc. I said that anyway there would be a change sometime, and that Halifax was much talked of. He said emphatically no, Halifax would not do. He would make a dignified PM, moderate, seeing both sides, judicious, conscientious and all that, but that was not enough. Rather than have Halifax he would much sooner keep the present PM, who—'*though I do not see him now*—is, I gather, highly resentful of the treatment he had from Hitler' (as well he might be!) and determined to go on in a spirit of 'determined indignation'. Then he went on to say that if N C should eventually go, the choice for PM lay between Churchill and Hoare. I said that the conventional argument against Churchill was his 'bad judgment', but that considering the judgment of Chamberlain and his lieutenants in recent years that did not seem to be decisive. 'No, indeed', he said, 'no misjudgment of Churchill could exceed the errors of the last ten years. I think that argument against him no longer holds. The truth is that Churchill needs people beside him who can say quite firmly "No", when he wants to do something wrong and insist that he must not do it.' [I interpolated that this is precisely what Lloyd George says about Churchill in 1915–16.] With that proviso there was much to be said for Churchill. But in his opinion Hoare had some qualifications. It should not be overlooked that Hoare, if he was convinced that something was the right thing to do, would take risks to himself in order to do it. We might condemn the Hoare-Laval scheme as much as we liked, but he (R V) and Hoare did that with open eyes because they believed that, with the Axis beginning, they thought it was the right and proper thing to do and they both of them 'laid their heads on the block' in order to do this. This was a not too common quality in a politician and it was to be carefully weighed. He did not think that Sir John Simon had this quality or that he was to be seriously considered as a possible PM. I said that J S was reported to hold a different view and he said that he thought what was decisive, anyway, was that J S had not a strong Parliamentary following behind him.

As to the future, he still thought that Hitler might attack through Holland if he felt that he must bring things to a head. He had been uneasy about the Sumner Welles mission because he thought that Mussolini, who was a cunning fellow, might put some plausible scheme over on a man who had little experience of Europe, but he was disposed to think now that the danger was less. He did not think the Germans were prepared to offer anything that would make a move by Roosevelt practicable.

Speaking of Mussolini, he thought that his idea might be not so much to go to war against us but at an appropriate moment to blackmail us and France into making important concessions to him.

Other points. He went back to the occasion a few days before Prague, when Chamberlain at No 10 had seen the press and, while forbidding them to indicate the origin, had given an entirely misleading estimate of the international situation. He had said that everything was fine and that a smooth period was beginning. He (V) was away at the time and was horrified when he read it. He wondered who had put it out and thought that it was shocking that such a thing should be circulated without a proper explanation of its source. The Press ought not to do it. I said that we had ourselves interpolated 'From an authoritative source' before printing it and that we understood that Chamberlain had disapproved. He said that Chamberlain had in this affair shown either a deliberate intention to deceive the public (which was hardly likely since he was liable to be exposed, as he was a few days later) or the grossest ignorance of the international situation.

4.00 P.M. SIR SAMUEL HOARE AT TREASURY CHAMBERS

There had been a meeting of the Supreme Council to-day; they thought that they ought to make Reynaud's acquaintance without loss of time.[1] It had gone off well and it was not just mere words; they had got down to practical business. The discussions had been useful; their motto was 'caution but enterprise' and he could assure me that they would seize every chance.

---

1. Reynaud had just become French premier.

It was easy to talk of seizing the initiative etc., but difficult at the present time to do. (a) There might be a German attack on Holland or Belgium, but they simply could not get Belgium to say what she wanted them to do or to make any arrangements in advance and, except in collaboration with the Belgians it was difficult for them to make the proper arrangements to assist her. Partly it was due to the young King, an 'invertebrate' person. Belgium would take no step in advance, always hoping that she at least would escape the deluge. It was very embarrassing. We had immensely strong positions in northern France, but if Belgium expected us to save her or if we were to save Holland *via* Belgium we must have our plans well worked out, in which case we could be at her back in six hours. But if she would say nothing and arrange nothing she would expect us to go in impromptu, and the result might well be that the German Air Force would have a good time bombing the Belgian roads (and the fleeing civilian population) while we would have to try to advance north to save her by improvised means. We could only go on trying to persuade Belgium to be more provident. I said that it had been thought that in January, when Holland was threatened for the second time, Belgium had told Germany in Berlin that she would go to Holland's aid, but he said it was untrue—she had said nothing of the kind either to us or to France or to Holland or to Germany.

(b) The Balkans. The difficulty was quite simple. The Turks were firm on our side and they were much better off in munitions and in money ('our munitions and our money') than in September last, *but they did not want to be at war with Russia*, and that governed everything. If Russia attacked them, well and good, but at present they did not want us to go through to the Black Sea, because this might mean war with Russia. He himself did not think that this was a certain consequence, because Russia could just ignore it if she did not want to be involved in a major war. But it was uncertain and the Turks at present would not run the risk. He did not think that the Brenner meeting had settled anything very important. Mussolini was certainly very hostile to us but there were other influences in our favour; certainly the popular feeling would be strongly against a war on the side of Germany.

He spoke of the Norwegian Territorial Waters question.[1] I said

---

1. Churchill had been advocating the mining of Norwegian territorial waters for some time, and it was in fact undertaken on 8 April—the day the Germans invaded Denmark and Norway.

that the PM had rather astonished us by saying that it was not proven that the Germans had sunk ships in Norwegian territorial waters, though Britain held that they had. He said he thought that the PM had not perhaps phrased the point very fortunately. However, there was an *immense* iron ore traffic coming down to Germany through the Norwegian territorial waters. It had been a bad winter and iron ore was piled high at Narvik, all waiting to be brought down to Germany. He said our scouts reported 'a long stream' of iron ore ships going southwards. What would be my reactions to the idea of going in and stopping them? I said that the basis of our action would presumably be either (1) Germany's attacks in Norwegian territorial waters referred to by the PM not very satisfactorily or (2) Germany's innumerable violations of international law against which we had already declared reprisals in certain forms. He hinted that number two would be more likely to apply and also that, instead of going in and cutting out these ships, we might adopt the course of mining Norwegian waters so as to drive the iron ore ships into the open seas. He said 'Well, I suggest that you might bear the possibility of this development in mind.' I asked was it likely in the next two or three days, if at all, and he said 'No.' I said I hoped that the Government, if it did this, would formally publish a reasoned justification on the ground of Germany's flagrant violations of International Law, and he said 'Yes, a solemn justification.'

I asked 'What about all this talk of reconstruction of the Government?' and he said 'If I know the way in which the PM's mind is working, it is this. A big reconstruction, such as the forming of a truly national Government, with Labour, etc. in, can only arise from actual developments in the war itself. There are, however, certain individual changes which should be made, but whether it would be worth while or advisable to make such comparatively small changes by themselves is doubtful. That, I think, is the present position but mind, in this matter I may be proved wrong during the next few days.'

About Air production, I asked whether the current reports were accurate. He said it was not as good as it might be because of (1) training machines, which had to be supplied in great quantity, and (2) training crashes but we should get over number one in a few months, not before, and then the increase would be great, very great indeed. Also, we were *beginning* to put out new types and at the beginning production was always and inevitably slow. There too in a short time the increase would be very great. As to the French the improvement was immense but, of course, 'they had started from nothing', so that it looked imposing besides ours, but they were getting on really fast now. At the same time, as in November last, they did not want to make an air offensive because they did not want to have one launched against themselves—they did not feel strong enough yet.

As to Scapa Flow[1] and the German raid on it, these lessons emerged—

(1) We were lucky.
(2) An unprecedented anti-aircraft concentration only brought down one German machine.
(3) Our aeroplanes could not go up because of the intensity of our anti-aircraft fire.
(4) The Germans were driven so high up that they could not bomb accurately. I asked if many bombs were 'near misses' and he said, 'No, few bombs fell in the Flow, most of them on the land.'
(5) It was a great mistake to speak of the Germans rushing in and precipitately fleeing to escape our attack. It was a vigorous raid and well managed and, like others, illustrated the methodical character of the German strategy.

He thought that we might see an air offensive directed before long against our North Sea Shipping and ports. That seemed to him more likely than any other sort of German offensive at present.

He mentioned Sylt[2] and said that all the evidence we had—the best was from Denmark—was that it had done very great damage indeed. Some people were puzzled that the Germans had not hit back. He thought it was probably because they had a methodical plan and that they were sticking to their one plan of operations whatever it might be—perhaps keeping everything in hand that they could for the big attack which, sometime or other, they would deliver.

5.00 P.M. COUNT REVENTLOW AT THE DANISH LEGATION

He said that Sweden could have done no other, in respect of the Finnish war, than she had done. It was his one reproach against the otherwise irreproachable Lord Halifax that in his message to Finland on her making peace, he had reproached Norway and Sweden. Sweden was absolutely bound to do what she did. A

---

1. Fifteen German bombers raided Scapa Flow on 16 March. The cruiser Norfolk was damaged.

2. In retaliation for the raid on Scapa Flow fifty heavy bombers attacked the German seaplane base on the island of Sylt on 19 March. No damage was done.

country in her position, between two powerful neighbours, could not and must not be on bad terms with them both. 'If she is, she is doomed.' Consider Poland, which had finally antagonised, for whatever reason, both Russia and Germany. That destroyed her. Now, if Sweden had 'gone in' officially against Russia, she would have made an enemy of her *on a long view*—which was not less important than the immediate present—and that would have been very serious for her. But if, in addition, she had given offence to Germany, she was lost.

As to help from Britain and France, he asserted positively that if they had either sent an expeditionary force or had sent troops of any kind, Germany would have attacked. She would not, and could not, have allowed the Allies to get a footing, or to seem to get a footing, in Scandinavia. And she would have had an army in Sweden long before the Allies could be there in force. [He referred to Denmark's past.] It was curious that there was little or no reference in the British press to Denmark and Denmark's dangerous position. That was in one way a good thing, since Denmark did not want too much attention drawn to her, but he felt also how dreadful it was from one point of view, since it showed that people in this country felt *and knew* how great was Denmark's danger from Germany and did not want to emphasise it. They all knew that if Germany attacked Norway and Sweden she would walk into Denmark and use it as a base. No, she had made no threats, Germany's attitude had been quite 'correct', but all knew what the position was.

He saw no easy end to the war, but he believed that the British were simply going on with it till they won. 'Of course,' he said, 'you can't trust Hitler. Whatever the peace, you could not trust him after what has happened. No one can trust him. Yes, I believe you are going through with it. I don't think your pacifists count for anything. I told him that not only would the people see it through but that they were much disposed, most of them, to want to have it out with Germany by more direct means than at present. I asked him if he knew that Napier, the historian of the Peninsular War, had said that the inhabitants of these islands were 'the least military but the most warlike' people in Europe. He was immensely pleased with the quotation; he repeated it and said 'Yes, that's a good saying—and it's very true too!'

He asked, as he always does, about Cabinet changes, and said that if Chamberlain went, the new PM ought to be Halifax and no one else. He was the right man for it, clear-minded, high-minded and so forth. I said, was there any reason to believe that he had as much efficiency and drive as Chamberlain himself? He mentioned Simon and said he gathered he was not liked. Also Churchill was, he supposed, possible but Halifax was his man from every point of view.

29 March 1940

10.00 A.M. LESLIE HORE-BELISHA AT OLD WARREN FARM

In Mrs Crozier's handwriting.

(Note: I had seen H B on Friday Feb. 16 and we had discussed his article on Scandinavia which was to appear in the News of the World on the following Sunday. This was the article which was to be 'the boldest of the war'. When it appeared it was found to have been considerably censored. At three separate points there was a note to say 'so many lines deleted by censor'. These cuts were made in the passages which argued that Norway and Sweden must grant the Allies right of passage through their countries under Article 16 of the Covenant and I have no doubt that they suggested that the Allies must demand compliance with their wishes.)

When I got to the Old Warren Farm I found Hore-Belisha sitting in a chair by the fire with his two dogs beside him. He was looking grey and ill and explained that on the Sunday before he had been seized with gastric influenza in the night. He had woken up suddenly gasping for breath and, when he got off to sleep, woke up again with the same disagreeable affection, which was several times repeated. I told him that he suffered from a tendency to a spasm of the glottis, that it was not serious, that it was caused by any sort of sudden irritation, and that a few hearty smacks on the back would cause the contracted muscle to expand again and then he would be all right. He said he had been told this last point and people had been applying it to him already. I told him that if no one was handy he must bang his back vigorously on the edge of a door or any sharp edge he could find, and he said very seriously that he would remember this. (It is quite an effective remedy tho' sometimes a little painful.)

His doctor had told him that he must go away for three or four weeks and that the rest must be complete. He would have to give up his Sunday article. No, he could not settle down to an article quickly, write it and put the matter out of his head till the next week. It worried him for days and if he was to have a rest he must certainly give up the idea of writing. Last week Sir Emsley Carr, the editor of News of the World, had come down to see him and had asked him not to write the next Sunday's article but he had insisted that he must and he did. But that would be the last for some time.

Then I said to him 'The last time I saw you was the Friday when you were talking about your article on Finland which was to be "the boldest article of the war", but I saw on the Sunday that they had censored it.'

'Ah', he said 'I must tell you all about that. It's almost unbelievable. It wasn't our people in the first place who objected to the article. It was the French censorship, and it was because of them that it came into the hands of our Foreign Office.

'On the evening of the day you saw me Lord Halifax's secretary rang me up here but I was out. He said he would ring up again later but he did not. Instead he rang up Sir Emsley Carr and said that Lord Halifax would like to see him on the Saturday morning at 9.00 a.m. Carr said that he would of course go to see Halifax. He was not told at all what the reason was for the interview and had no idea.

'When he went at 9 o'clock he found Lord Halifax sitting with a proof of my article (yes, he had got a proof of the actual article) before him. Halifax said that there were a few things in it that were undesirable and he hoped that Carr would be willing to have them modified. Carr replied that in his opinion this was a matter which he could not settle and that Halifax ought to speak to me personally about it. Halifax said he would.

'The next stage was that Halifax rang me up here at Warren Farm.

'He said that there were one or two things, quite small things, in the article that he thought were inadvisable and that "a young man here" (in the Foreign Office) had modified them and that he was quite sure that I would not object to the changes. He suggested that I should come to the Foreign Office and see what they were.

'I replied that I was sure that I would not object to the modifications if they were, as he described them, small, but in that case it seemed hardly worth while that I should go specially into town to see him. I suggested that he should send someone out to me with the amended script so that I could see what had been done. He agreed and a man came out. I was amazed when I saw what had been done. First of all a piece of the article had been deleted, but that did not matter much. But after that half the article—half the article, my dear Crozier—had been completely re-written by this man in the Foreign Office. It was entirely new matter, not my matter at all, and the scandal of it was that in his half of the article he argued the direct contrary of what I had argued—he argued the case for the Government whereas I had urged the policy which the Government was not pursuing and was not going to pursue. If I had allowed it to be printed it would have made it flatly impossible for me to make the speech criticising the Government in the Finnish debate of March 19. They would have tied my hands. And besides, the article made me say the opposite of what I believed. Of course, I flatly refused to accept the amendations.

'So the messenger went back to the Foreign Office with my refusal. Time went on and I could get no satisfaction and the whole thing remained unsettled. At 4.30 on Saturday afternoon, with the News of the World still unable to set their machines going with the article, things were becoming very serious. I got at the Press Bureau and the Ministry of Information, but they would only say that the whole matter was in the hands of the Foreign Office, that they knew nothing and that they could do nothing.

'At last it was decided that the passages most objected to should be omitted. I said that the omissions would have to be indicated when the article was printed in order to make it clear how much had been suppressed and at what points in the article, this was done.'

(As a matter of fact, what was done was without precedent in this country. The press is not supposed to indicate what is omitted by the censor but at three points in the article it was intimated; 'X lines omitted here by the Censor'.)

'I then took things up with Lord Halifax. I wrote him a hell of a letter. I told him that it was strange when we were supposed to be fighting for the liberty of opinion and all that sort of thing that he should try to suppress the views of his late colleague and prevent him from addressing the general public.

'I also protested to Chamberlain. He replied to me that he had no desire to stifle my opinions but that coming from one who had only just ceased to be in the War Cabinet what I said would be taken, especially abroad, to have a peculiar significance. And that in view of what I had actually said in the article might be a serious matter.

'And then, of course, John Simon intervened. He tried to blackmail me. You can always trust John on an occasion like this to emerge from the shadows in the most sinister way. He telephoned he would like to see me. Well, I was ready to see him if he wanted it. So I went. He said "If I were you, Leslie, I wouldn't do any more about this business"—he meant write about it in a newspaper—"You know, it wouldn't really be to your own interest. You know, people might say that you were doing it all *for the sake of money*!" I said to him "I'll be obliged if you will not continue to discuss what I am doing on that basis. If you went out of the Cabinet I imagine that you might very likely go back to the Bar to make your living. Well, I was writing (and making a good income out of it) before I became a Minister. It was my job in life and now I'm going back to it. I won't discuss the question of my writing at all on the basis that you're attempting to set."

'So *that* went no further.

'Then another strange thing happened. Reith came to lunch with me here, Minister of Information of course, and he suggested to me that really it might not be a bad thing if I let the Foreign Office do the writing of my articles for me. Of course, I was to have the money just the same. I would get the pay but they would supply the matter.'

I remarked that this was pretty shocking.

'Shocking', he said, 'and immoral!

'John Simon condemned me for taking money from a newspaper for writing my honest opinions but they wouldn't mind my taking the money so long as they could supply the opinions.'

I said I was astonished that Reith should make such a suggestion since he had such a reputation for rigid conscience and was bitterly opposed, as he had told me himself, to anything that could be called 'propaganda'.

'Well, of course', he replied, 'he didn't put the suggestion quite as crudely as I have said, but that was the meaning and the purpose of his suggestion.'

After breakfast he complained strongly of the docility of the Government supporters in the House. They were not critical and they did not like criticism of the Government. When he spoke on Finland (19 March) he could assure me that 'I did not have to try to avoid the applause of the Government benches. I had to try to avoid their boos. The moment I got up I felt the hostile atmosphere. Except for a handful there were no critics of the Government on the Tory side.'

I interrupted that there were some vigorous critics among the opposition and mentioned Clement Davies as a leader but he obviously was not thinking of Clement as an ally. 'Criticism on the Tory side' he said 'is stifled. No opponent of the Government will get anything in the way of reward from the Whips. The party truce has had effects. There is no expression of opinion from the country and because by-elections are not fought candidates are being accepted at Headquarters on the strength of subscriptions to the party funds.'

The Government, therefore, and Chamberlain had it all their own way and the conduct of the war lacked energy. In this connection he said that Churchill was a 'washout', he was lacking, nowadays in energy and, anyhow, was fully occupied with his own particular job.

'He's as good, of course, as ever he was *at words*. He can make fine speeches—speed the plough, dig the fields and all that, but in the Cabinet he's not the man he was or is supposed to be.'

He ended gloomily. 'We're not winning this war, you know, and if we go on as we are, we're even losing it.' He said he was going on the following Tuesday to Avignon and then to the south coast of France. If I saw anything of special interest in the English press would I send him a cutting. He referred to a Leader in the Manchester Guardian on the necessity for a liberal social policy during the war and said that it was excellent and that if there were any more on the same lines he must see them.

3.30 P.M. HERBERT MORRISON AT COUNTY HALL

Herbert Morrison was secretary of the London Labour party and leader of the Labour group on the LCC, as well as being a prominent Labour MP. There was no love lost between him and Attlee, the leader of the Labour party. This was Crozier's first meeting with a Labour politician other than Arthur Henderson at the time of the disarmament conference.

We needed more decision when we got a chance, but no more adventures. He thought that we ought to be a bit stiffer towards the neutrals. (He had told Churchill that he thought the Altmark affair[1] was the best thing done yet.) They were scared stiff of Germany and thought that while the Germans would always act as perfect blackguards the Allies would always behave like gentlemen. We ought to show them that we are capable of vigorous action if rights are flagrantly violated as they are systematically by Germany.

With regard to the iron ore traffic in Norwegian waters he was not supposed to know, but the Government had 'consulted' Attlee and Greenwood about the question of going in and seizing the ships. And, 'Well, you know Attlee!' He understood that Attlee had raised difficulties about the importance of rigidly observing

---

1. The German ship Altmark was boarded in Norwegian territorial waters, and British prisoners of war rescued.

neutral rights and not giving any opportunity to people abroad to reproach us. Well, as for himself, 'We've got to win the war' and if the Germans tore up every rule of war that there was to suit themselves he did not see why we should stand on the letter of the law and destroy ourselves, and if those iron ore ships were steaming down the coast to Germany, he would 'go in and pinch them'; he had said so to Churchill and he was saying so in an article which he had written for Saturday's Daily Mirror.

He said that things were not going too well in many ways and complained that there was much too great a tendency to say that we must not criticise the Government because of German propaganda; Lord Haw-Haw,[1] etc., would exploit it against us. When recently he brought up the question of contracts in the Ministry of Supply, some of his Labour people had said 'Oh, but we can't do that sort of thing. Lord Haw-Haw would make great capital out of it!' This was all wrong and was bad policy. It tended to stifle criticism, and it was silly. He would have taken this affair of the contracts and have boomed it on our wireless to Germany and elsewhere. 'Here in England, if there are scandals, in a few weeks they are brought to a Labour ex-Minister who exposes them in Parliament and the Minister is compelled to promise and to produce a new Order in Council to make such things impossible. But what have *you* got in Germany? What means have *you* to expose corruption and to stop it for the future? You have no means and you know it, and you know that therefore corruption must grow among you, and that our system is a great strength to us and yours a great weakness to you! That's how it should be handled, but too many people, including the Government, are all for hush-hush.' Even before the war, when he wrote two articles against Hitler in Forward, Lord Halifax sent a message that he would like to see him in order, as he learned, to protest against such articles and the harm that they would do abroad. He had sent word back that of course he would see Lord Halifax, but that if the intention was to get him to modify his methods in this matter it would be a waste of time. He was not asked to go!

There was no likelihood at present of a 'National' Government including Labour leaders. If they and the Liberals went in there would be no Opposition to assist by criticism. Besides, there would be trouble with the Labour people—they would either be 'yes-men' or they would be at loggerheads with their own leaders in the Government. With regard to the Premiership, he said that

---

1. Nickname of an English broadcaster, allegedly William Joyce, on German radio.

Chamberlain was a clear-headed, practical man, but he could not see things ahead and had no broad imaginative view, no 'vision' about anything. He did not like the idea of Halifax as Premier at all. He was a good man, dignified, religious-minded, etc. but he doubted whether he had the grasp and the drive required for a War Premier. Of Churchill he had a very high opinion; what he needed was a 'father' to put a firm hand on his arm and say, at certain times, 'No!—this cannot be done—no! you simply must *not* do this'—and stop him from doing it. Then he would be all right. (NB precisely the same view about Halifax and Churchill as Vansittart gave me.)

I asked him about his party and Russia and the question of Russia's being involved in the war. What would happen if Turkey let us into the Black Sea to cut off the oil traffic to Germany? He said that they did not want war with Russia, but if, under the circumstances named, Russia attacked us, 70% of Labour would stand with the Government, 20% would say that it was a misfortune but that it could not be helped and leave it at that, and 10% would protest. If we attacked Russia without cause, all would protest.

He said that the Government Tory party were a tame lot. Only a few (Macmillan, R Law, etc.) criticised and as they had constantly criticised the Government their opposition was now taken for granted and discounted. He thought that the Whips undoubtedly repressed criticism. They drew up the lists of speakers for the party and he believed that the Speaker usually accepted these lists.

He struck me as being clear headed and decided, a man who would know his own mind, stick to it and act. He asked me to come and talk again whenever I could.

5.00 P.M. WINSTON CHURCHILL AT THE ADMIRALTY

He seemed to be rather taken aback when I said that it did not look to me as though things were going too well at the present time, and I discovered that he had his eye mainly on the naval business. He said that anyway on the sea we were not doing any too badly. Only one ship—a tanker—had been lost in the last ten days. We were killing submarines quicker than they were—at present—being turned out, and both imports and exports were going through on the seas better than at any time since the war began. We could, of course, do with more ships of various kinds, especially destroyers. It is a pity that we had not had 50 or 60 more of them at the beginning of the war. They were indispensable for all kinds of purposes. Still, they were coming on. As to the new monster battleships now building he said that by the time Germany got two into commission we would have five against them.

He turned to the neutrals and said that the Germans were able to break every law in dealing with them and we were supposed to keep every little bit of it however much we suffered. We could not put up with it any longer, especially when, as in the iron ore business, they were supplying Germany with something that was absolutely vital to her in carrying on the war. We would have to stop it. It was true—in answer to my questions—that there now remained only about five weeks in which ore traffic would continue to go down Norwegian territorial waters as at present, but there was a great accumulation at Narvik and only about one-quarter of it had yet gone through. He would have interfered long ago 'but there are always so many people to persuade in these matters'.

I said I supposed the simple justification would be that if Germany was trying to destroy us by way of these indiscriminate illegal means there was no reason, in morals or in law, why we should allow ourselves to be destroyed through observing every jot and tittle of the law. He replied yes, and, of course, it would be most important if we in argument provided a 'cover' of this kind —'invaluable', he said, 'coming from a Liberal journal'—but he seemed to me to be himself contented with the point that this was a vital source of supply to Germany and that we were therefore going to stop it.

We spoke of the Balkans and he said that he himself had no desire for war with Russia. 'I don't want war with Russia. Germany is our enemy and I am not at all in favour of adding to the enemy that we have got. Of course, it is conceivable that she may herself come in but otherwise No!'

Speaking of the Home Front, I reminded him that he had said that a much greater effort was needed and that 'a million of women must come boldly forward' and asked him whether the effort was not being produced somewhat slowly. He said he was afraid it was, but that he thought things were at last moving.

Referring to the War Cabinet and the PM, he said that he got on very well with him. 'I have no desire at all myself to be PM, and any suspicions that he used to have that I might be dangerous to him have now disappeared. I determined—obviously I must— that I must work well with him and I do, and I believe that he now likes me.'

At the end he said 'You must come to see me again in about a fortnight—yes, in about a fortnight!' He had in mind, of course, our action against the iron ore traffic in Norwegian waters.[1]

5.00 P.M. BRENDAN BRACKEN AT THE ADMIRALTY

Things were rotten, and they were getting worse. We were not winning this war, we were on the way to lose it. The House of Commons was no good, the Tory party were tame yes-men of Chamberlain. 170 had their election expenses paid by the Tory Central Office and 100 hoped for jobs; what independence or criticism, then could be expected? The MG stuff about Margesson and the 'gag' was first-rate and it was all true. It was impossible to get rid of the notorious duds in the Ministry; Chamberlain and those round him could not be budged. The state of shipping was worse than was supposed. Air production was not good. I said, why? and he answered—personal differences between the professionals at the top and Kingsley Wood no good at putting his foot down and deciding. There were differences of opinion about new types and K W could not settle them. We had been promised that before long our single output should be equal to that of Germany and now we were told that the output of Britain and France and planes brought from USA were equal to that of Germany! If any Tory rank and file dared to raise their voice against the Government, they ran away the next day, and it was much worse now the war was on: e.g. on Palestine in June last the Government had a majority of 80 and now it rose to 200 or thereabouts. Margesson was largely to blame; he had declared, in respect of some man who had criticised the Government, that he would give nothing to any critic of the Government if he could help it. I asked him if he had read the Telegraph leader today saying that private members must not express opinions that would endanger the Government and he said 'I hope you'll give them hell!'

6.00 P.M. J W DULANTY

He had had a long talk with Eden and had heard about Italy. The French Ambassador to Rome (François Ponçet) had had an audience with the Pope, which was rather gloomy and gave the

---

1. The British action was taken on 8 April. A much more formidable German action coincided with it.

impression that he feared Mussolini would opt for Hitler. Maglioni, the Papal Secretary of State, had said that certain 'disagreeable possibilities' had to be reckoned with.

As to Sylt, the information from Denmark was that great damage had been done: in the destroyed hangars 15 aeroplanes and on the slips seven had been destroyed. The Government was puzzled why the Germans had not hit back.

· · · · ·

30 March 1940

12 NOON. BJÖRN PRYTZ AT THE SWEDISH LEGATION

Sweden had relief for the present but the future was dark and uncertain. Russia perhaps 'had enough' over Finland *for the present* but, the war situation being what it was, Sweden had just cause for anxiety. Russia she had always feared and she did not know whether Red Russia might not be worse than that of the Czars. Now also she had to fear Germany. The complete defeat of Germany by the Allies was her best hope, but how long was that going to take?

He thought it possible that if Sweden had gone to war with Russia as soon as Finland was attacked, she might have escaped invasion by Germany, but it would have been a frightful risk. Still, such risks had sometimes to be taken.

· · · · ·

If the Allies were going to stop the traffic along the Norwegian coasts it was going to be very serious for Sweden. Much Swedish traffic went *north* up the Norwegian coast to about Bergen and then struck *West*; that would suffer too. Ten times as much Swedish stuff went West as went to Germany—was it worth while to interfere? I said it was a question of quality as well as of quantity—and he said yes, the question was what the stuff was worth to Germany. In five weeks' time the Gulf of Bothnia would be open again and the iron ore would go that way to Germany. ('I wish', he added, 'that your people could get into the Baltic!'). Still, if it were all now stopped it would be a serious economic blow to Sweden, purely from the point of view of her trade. The iron ore was quite a large part of her export trade.

Speaking of peace, he said that the silent Mr Sumner Welles

had let one thing slip—that a British Government which included Liberals and Labour would go down better, and be more trusted, in neutral countries, including the USA. Was there any chance of a reconstruction? I said probably not unless there were 'developments' in the war. And these, he said, would be 'disagreeable' developments. I gathered that he would like to see Liberal and Labour in the Government, but he recognised the importance of an Opposition and its weakness (Labour) now.

.   .   .   .   .

What was to be done if the day came, he said, when Germany genuinely offered the reconstitution of Poland and Czechs? No peace, I said, could be acceptable that left Hitler, etc. there because we should have to go on arming just the same. He said, yes, it seemed that a good peace of any kind meant the downfall of Hitler; he could not accept any peace that would be tolerable. But he feared the after-peace conditions more than even the war. When Germany, which had been organising war for years, turned over to peace, what were the millions of men and women to do? The problem in Germany would be worse than in Britain and France, and that would be bad enough. I said that there would have to be international co-operation to save Germany as well as ourselves if we had the means, and he said that this was where the USA came in. She, and she alone, would be in a position to help save Germany (and others) by economic co-operation. He thought this was the only hope.

He spoke of the Balkans and said that power and money settled things there—especially money. A friend of his had said 'To be a Rumanian is not a matter of nationality; it is a profession.'

.   .   .   .   .

3 April 1940

3.30 P.M. SIR KINGSLEY WOOD AT THE AIR MINISTRY

Increase in production of aircraft. As Wood was on the point of leaving the air ministry, his remarks were of no significance.

4.00 P.M. SIR SAMUEL HOARE AT TREASURY CHAMBERS

Changes in the Cabinet were going to be announced that night.

They had been decided on since he saw me last Friday.[1] Yes, he thought that probably Gilmour's death had decided matters.[2]

Chamberlain had been thinking over the question of a genuine 'national' government, bringing in the Labour people and the Independent Liberals. Labour could not come in because it would split the party—that was the top and bottom of it. Attlee might be willing if he dare, but he dare not, and therefore Chamberlain would not propose it to the Labour leaders because he knew that it would be no use. But unfortunately there was scarcely any talent in the Tory party which they could promote and so Chamberlain was in a bit of a fix.

Kingsley Wood was changing places with him. Reasons (1) production had not been good; (2) he was a tired man and himself wanted to change; he had been for two years in the job and was tired out. No use keeping a man in that second most important job (after the Navy, that is) if he wanted to get out of it himself. He knew the difficulties. He had consulted his old friend Lord Trenchard about taking it and T had said 'Yes, you should take it, but it will be your funeral.' He knew it might be, but he would take the risk. He had spent seven years in the Air Ministry (up to 1929) and he and Trenchard had 'laid the foundations' of the whole thing. He would have the benefit of Trenchard's informal help and advice and Lord Riverdale (Arthur Balfour), the steel man, was going to have a job and organise production. Kingsley Wood would take on all the things that he had done as Lord Privy Seal— that is, the Home Front—including agriculture.

Chatfield was going.[3] No need for him with the three Services Ministers and they overshadowed by Churchill's 'tremendous personality'. Churchill had been offered Chatfield's job without Portfolio but refused; he wanted to stay at the Admiralty. So Chatfield was really only a co-ordinator and had no sufficient raison d'être in the War Cabinet. Hankey was stopping on in the War Cabinet but not, he thought, for very long. He was very useful indeed for purposes of reference. I gather that neither of these two were full of drive or 'personality'. Woolton would come in instead of Morrison—a very nice fellow but not very happy in

---

1. 28 March.

2. Sir John Gilmour, who had been minister of shipping since 13 October 1939, died on 30 March 1940.

3. Lord Chatfield had been minister for the coordination of defence since 29 January 1939. The post was now abolished. On 4 April 1940 Churchill was made chairman of the military coordination committee and on 1 May was given special responsibility 'for giving guidance and direction to the Chiefs of Staff Committee'.

these jobs—because what was wanted at the Food Ministry was not a politician but an administrator. He had always been in favour of bringing in a Rhondda for this job. He said that he did not know Woolton and asked me a lot of questions about him. I said that I hoped he would not continue to run Lewis's as Stamp was continuing to run the LMS, and he said no, he came as a 'whole timer'.[1]

Hudson was going to Shipping, and not Salter, because Salter had got across the shipowners.[2] I said that Hudson's reputation hardly suggested that he would be a tactful or long suffering person, and he said No, he supposed not, but we should have to see.

I asked whether we were going to get our 'small War Cabinet', and said 'Not this time', and I said I supposed not an Economic Minister either in the War Cabinet. To that he smiled broadly and said 'Well, you see, Simon and the Treasury won't have it.' I said 'Why not put the President of the Board of Trade in the War Cabinet with increased functions?' and he said that he thought that might come about in time. Duncan was an extremely able person.[3]

Other points:—

(1) Churchill had urged him to take the Air Ministry.

(2) Lord Swinton was a much abler man than Kingsley Wood, but failed at the Air Ministry because he could not deal skilfully with the people under him. I said I had heard that he could not choose the right man and he said he thought there was truth in that.

He was afraid Reynaud was in for a difficult time. The Radicals would not forgive him for unseating Daladier. In London they were afraid that the Right—Flandin, Laval, etc., the 'appeasers' —might be going to cause trouble, and, of course, Bonnet was capable of anything. Reynaud might fall and he doubted whether Daladier would be willing to form another Ministry. Possibly Herriot would—'a man of talk'. Reynaud had no party at all behind him—a great weakness. Daladier had not handled things

---

1. Lord Woolton, managing director of Lewis's the provincial stores, succeeded W S Morrison as minister of food. Morrison became postmaster-general. Lord Rhondda was a very successful minister of food in the first world war. Lord Stamp, president of the LMS railway, was adviser on economic coordination to the ministerial committee.

2. Sir Arthur Salter was parliamentary secretary to the ministry of shipping.

3. Sir Andrew Duncan was president of the board of trade from 5 January 1940 to 3 October 1940.

skilfully while Premier, partly in respect of the censorship but still more in the high-handed way in which he had treated Parliament. I rather gathered that in a personal sense he did not feel sure that he had a confident impression about Reynaud's ability.

30 April 1940

3.30 P.M. SIR ROBERT VANSITTART AT THE FOREIGN OFFICE

He was in a mood of complete and unqualified gloom.

'Now', he said, 'we are about to pay for the follies of our policy of the last five or six years.'

I said 'You mean Italy, and that she is going to come in against us?'

He said 'Yes, I think there is no doubt about it. You have seen all that the Italians have been writing and saying. It can mean nothing else. Even old Grandi—I never did think much of him when he was here—has declared himself as one of the war party. Yes, I think Italy is coming in. I don't blame the country for the line that it took about Italy in the sanctions period, because the country didn't know, but the Government knew the position and the Government did not arm and arm as it ought to have done. When did it really begin to arm in earnest? In 1939! Whereas the Germans had already been arming for three or four years! You can't give a great country like Germany three or four years' start in rearmament and not pay heavily for it. Well, there is a bad time coming now for this country. It is really a case now of "backs to the Wall" for us and the country will require a lot of guts to come through.'

What angered him was the *ignorance* of the men who had brought us to this pass. Chamberlain and Horace Wilson had entered foreign politics like two innocent curates knowing nothing of the world. They had even trusted Hitler after Munich although they ought to have known that the Munich settlement itself was the surest guarantee that Czecho-slovakia was finally doomed, not to mention, of course, the whole career of Hitler up to that point. 'In foreign politics you should never trust anyone unless you have *colossal* proof that he is trustworthy, and not often then.'

I asked what he thought about Mussolini's plans.

'Oh', he said, 'probably he will go for the Dalmatian coast in the first place, that being the easiest. If he goes to war he will carry the country with him. They will march. The King and Royal Family won't prevent him. Of course if he does badly there

may be popular reactions against him—perhaps in three months
—if he has serious reverses.'

'And then do we declare ourselves at war with Italy, or do we
wait and see?'

He shrugged his shoulders and said 'I don't know, I have no
idea what *they* will do (pointing his finger up to the ceiling to
indicate Lord Halifax, whose room is on the floor above). 'But
we may not necessarily go to war at once. We have enough to deal
with as it is. We really must cut our coat according to our cloth
and we have not enough cloth to spare to take on Italy if we can
avoid it. Moreover, the Germans can go to Italy's help—they have
cloth to spare.' I asked him if he had seen the Daily Telegraph
statement that we should be at war with Italy if she attacked
Yugoslavia, and he said No, but personally he did not know just
what the decision was or would be. 'The trouble is that these
people (German and Italians) have a plan for attacking each
country in turn. They open a certain drawer, take out a plan and
say "This is the country to attack to-day" and they attack it. The
Allies wait to see the plan, which is completely prepared to the
last detail, put into operation, and then they sit down and begin
to improvise some sort of reply. That is the case in Norway, where
we were not doing at all well.[1]

'The neutrals, of course, can only take one view of this sort of
thing. They have seen us suffer a long succession of defeats—
Austria (for that also was a defeat), Czecho., Poland, Albania,
Denmark—and probably Norway. The result is that they have
no faith in us or our *power* and they will soon sink, unless we can
do better, into poor terrified subjection to Germany. Why should
they support us? If you are at a gambling table and you go on
losing steadily—four times, five times, six times—you don't
expect the spectators standing behind to back you. No, and neither
will the neutrals support us.'

He did not see how the Yugos could hold up if Germany
threatened them in the north, and Germany could spare reserves
for this and lots of other campaigns. She had enormous manpower.
We had not.

I asked him about the prospects of an Allied war with Italy. He
said that we had no adequate resources to take on Italy as well as
Germany. I said that surely the British and French fleets in the
Mediterranean would be too good for the Italians. He replied
'Oh yes, we ought to be too good for their fleet but the point is

---

1. British forces withdrew from Norway, except outside Narvik, on 2 May.

that we have not the resources, naval, aerial, man-power and munitions to take on Italy as well as Germany. We may want the ships in the North Sea yet and the man-power in France, Belgium and Holland. Our "effort" has not been and is not anything like big enough—though we have had eight months to prepare. The Germans are turning out their armies well trained and always well-equipped. We are calling up men very slowly and cannot equip them properly.'

To everything I said about certain weaknesses in the Italian position—e.g. the situation of her army in Libya, between the French Tunis army and the Allied army of the East, he made the same unvarying reply that we had not the men nor the equipment nor the general force to take on a war with Italy. It made comparatively little difference whether Italy started with Dalmatia or not; once she started it meant that she was throwing in her lot with Germany and would fight it out side by side with Germany against the Allies. Whenever I had seen him, he said, he had always been gloomy, but so far I would admit that he had been right and today he was compelled to be gloomier than ever. If I came to see him in another two or three weeks the position would be blacker still. He thought that if we did badly in Norway, as seemed likely, and if Italy came in, which he thought to be certain, *then* Hitler would very likely strike at Holland and for Belgium. In that event the idea of holding the French Front economically with a few troops would be smashed, Germany would sweep round through Holland and Belgium from the north, and we should want all our available resources and more to hold the shock. Italy's coming in might make a most serious difference to the drain on us.

As to the Yugo-Slavs, he said that like all the small countries they had believed in 'collective security' and failed to arm themselves properly. Man for man, no doubt, they were a match for Italians, but that would not save them; nowadays munitions, equipment and aeroplanes counted enormously.

As to Turkey, no one could say what the Turks would do in certain contingencies 'but I don't think they are spoiling for a war, and they certainly don't want to be at war with Russia'.

What about Russia? 'Oh, well, Russia will very likely annex Bessarabia but she probably does not want to involve herself in a major war. She will probably be satisfied to see the rest of us destroying ourselves, and she will be treacherous, of course, if necessary.'

He said that he had pointed our repeatedly in 1935–36 that sanctions meant that Italy would throw in her lot with Germany, but no one would listen to him. When he saw what was coming he 'begged and prayed and shouted for rearmament', but no one paid any attention to him, and anyway it did not help us to recall that now. He said that in August [1939] a woman friend of his wife had consulted him about a motor tour in Central Europe. He had told her it was madness. A little later she had met one of our statesmen 'at the very top' who said he was surprised to see her as he thought she was motoring in Central Europe. 'Oh', she said, 'Van stopped that. He wouldn't let me go.' 'But why', said the statesman, 'do you listen to Van? He's always pessimistic.' This was about eight or nine days before war broke out. He was not too confident about the moral of the Home Front either here or in France, especially in France. If we had reverses Reynaud's enemies would be out against him in no time; it was only our naval successes against Germany that had saved him.

He was completely gloomy and offered me no encouragement anywhere. 'There's nothing to do, though', he ended, 'but stick it out to the bitter end. If we don't, we are lost.'

4.30 P.M. TOM JONES AT THE ATHENAEUM

Tom Jones was assistant, and then deputy, secretary to the cabinet from 1916 to 1930. In a feline way, he was Hankey's rival.

After we had talked of the question of a special correspondent in the United States he raised the question of the Government and the people in it, especially Lord Hankey.

He said that Hankey was a man with a remarkable memory, a great organiser and of great physical energy so that he could work day and night, which was an important gift. He was a magnificent secretary, but not gifted with constructive ideas or imagination. I said that I had heard that at a Cabinet meeting Hankey would look up and say on some subject 'on January 17, 1916, we did so and so,' or something of the kind. 'No', said Tom Jones, 'he would actually have said "we did so and so on *Wednesday*, January 17, 1916".' He did not think Hankey would be long in the Cabinet.

He spoke of Neville Chamberlain and said that C's character had been thus described to him. Give Chamberlain a file of documents on a certain subject and he would be excellent in deciding what should be done *within the limits of the file*, but he would see nothing at all beyond the file, nor be able to view the problem in the light of the surrounding conditions, direct and indirect. I told him how Sir John Simon had once explained to me the difference between Baldwin and Chamberlain—that every problem had a hard practical core and a surrounding penumbra made up of all sorts of elements bearing on it and that Chamberlain could see only the central core and Baldwin only the diffused surrounding penumbra. T J was much pleased with this. 'That's a very clever description,' he said, 'and a most true one.'

5.30 P.M. COUNT REVENTLOW

He was looking worn and sad. He said that recent days had been dreadful,[1] but he was much relieved to have got his wife back from Denmark. She had returned the night before. She had come through Germany. They had three children in Denmark, the youngest a boy of 16 at school.

I found, unexpectedly, that he was tremendously anxious to defend his countrymen against any suggestion that they were not deeply attached to their independence because they had not fought the Germans. He said he had read in some papers in this country that they had watched the German invasion with 'curiosity' and he assured me repeatedly that this was only because the whole thing had come to the people as a surprise—however remarkable this might seem—and all they could do for a time was to gape at the extraordinary spectacle. He was depressed by the different aspects of Norway and Denmark—Norway resisting and Denmark surrendering—but he wanted to say that the spirit of the people in Denmark was unchanged, only they were a small country and the 'tidal wave' had swept over them in a few hours. He did not think that the King and Government could very well have done anything else than they did, and he quoted Braatoy for the opinion that the King of Denmark, had he been in Norway, would have acted like Haakon, and Haakon, had he been in Denmark, would have acted like the Danish King. All the same— and this was unexpected to me too—he seemed to be worried lest Denmark's failure to fight might prejudice her claims in the eyes of the Allies at the end of the war, to her complete restoration. He obviously felt the difference between Denmark and Norway very keenly. I said that I had heard no one in my part of the country reproach Denmark for what had happened and I did not think that anyone did. Had he heard anyone in London reproach her? He said No, no one did, 'Everyone had been most kind to her.'

Here he added, for my private information, that he believed he was going to be allowed to stop on in London in an unofficial

---

1. Denmark was occupied by the Germans on 8 April.

way, and this pleased him greatly, because he not only liked London but he hoped to be of use there to his unfortunate country. At this point I referred to the Danish and Norwegian captains and seamen who were going to Allied ports and sailing under us, and he said that their action was really courageous as almost all the men had families in Denmark or Norway whom the Germans might conceivably persecute as a result. He discussed Denmark's international position and said that she was worse situated than any of the neutrals. A small neutral country must be able to lean on a Great Power or she would become the helpless victim of some other Great Power. She might, anyhow, but with a powerful friend she had some hope. Denmark had no such friend and no hope. He did not know what her future would be. Her economic position was now very grave. She had built up her main economy on the basis of exports to the British Isles and all that was now stopped. She could not get on without imported feeding-stuffs; she would not get them now and disaster would come upon her 'very soon'.

·   ·   ·   ·   ·

1 May 1940

11.00 A.M. HERBERT MORRISON AT COUNTY HALL

He thought that probably there ought to be a secret session about Norway. A secret session was useful to get and to give information. This might be better than an open debate; the House was 'nervy', too 'nervy' at present.[1]

As to the charge that our troops lacked guns and aeroplanes he suspended judgment for the time; we had to rush troops through the valleys to stay the Germans, otherwise they would have got to Trondheim in no time at all. But what he wanted to know was whether, when we decided to lay the mines in Norwegian waters, we had plans ready to put into operation if the Germans invaded Norway. 'There ought to be a plan for every country even if it is not carried out. These d——d Germans move too quickly; we are not quite quick enough for them.' Also it was important to know why the getting together of the Expeditionary Force for Finland had not been more useful to us, and what had happened to it when it was not sent to that country.

---

1. The debate on Norway on 7 and 8 May was fortunately not in secret session. Its outcome forced Chamberlain's resignation.

Italy. Would the Government go to war at once with Italy if she attacked Jugoslavia? He did not know but he was inclined to think that we ought to. We might not be bound to Jugoslavia by any obligations, but could we let them be invaded and defeated by Italy? I put to him R V's view that we could not spare the necessary resources. He said that the French ought to be able to hold up the Italians with a pretty small force and that we could do them a lot of damage on the sea. Of course the Germans might come down to the assistance of the Italians and organise them thoroughly. Italy, by the way, *was* supplying Germany with a lot of useful things. We had been behaving very nicely to Italy in order to keep her sweet, and he doubted whether it paid. He did not think the quality of the Italians was very good. The only person he knew who thought really well of them, having fought with them in 1914–18, was Dalton,[1] who both thought well of them as soldiers and had a soft spot for them in general. He had wanted Italy to have a mandate over Abyssinia. He (Morrison) thought that if Italy went to war with us there might be serious reaction before long against Musso.

5.00 P.M. WINSTON CHURCHILL AT THE ADMIRALTY

As a rule he spends a minute or two in chit-chat, but on this occasion he said at once 'I would like to give you the background of this [Norwegian] business', and he began to talk very earnestly. After a time he got up and for the rest of nearly an hour he walked up and down across the room, pulling at his cigar and every now and then striding up to and pointing at one of the two maps that he now had on the wall—one a general one of Europe, including the Mediterranean, and the other a great chart of the neighbourhood of Narvik. Throughout he was more grave and at the same time more animated than I had yet seen him.

The first principal point, to which he constantly returned, was that we could not afford to immobilise a large part of our fleet in the North Sea by setting it to escort and protect a big expeditionary force to the Trondheim area. The Trondheim enterprise, if pursued, meant 100,000 men or more. This meant a continual flow of supply ships across the North Sea—he gestured on the map —with the German Air Force on the flank, and we could not afford to have so much of our naval strength tied up there. We had disposed of nearly half of the German fleet—he was impres-

---

1. Hugh Dalton, a leading and very anti-German member of the Labour party.

sive about this—and we should see some results from it.[1] It would soon be announced—'probably to-morrow' (May 2)—as it was—that we had sent a battle-fleet to the Mediterranean—to Alexandria. I said I thought that there had been such a fleet there ever since the war began. 'Not at all', he said, 'but there will be one now and that will give the gentlemen there something to think about.'

Talking of the troops at Namsos and Andalsnes, he said that we were compelled to send them because the Government would have been strongly condemned if it had not sent them; the Norwegians were urgently demanding assistance. But there were not many of them. How many Allied troops did I think had gone? I said 'about 8,000'. 'Not so far wrong', he said. 'And how many Germans do you think there are in Norway?' '80,000', I said, and he replied 'Yes, or perhaps nearer 90,000.' Our position was bad. We had no aeroplanes there. We had sent a squadron which parked itself on a frozen lake and then the Germans came and smashed them up. And anyhow now the ice on the lake was melting.

What about the Finnish Expeditionary Force? I asked him. Well, he said, we really could not keep that together indefinitely and the French wanted their troops back. Besides, we did not know what was going to happen in Norway and so could not keep it together with Norway in view. Probably we should have to come out now. 'But', I said, 'we have just announced that we have made new landings.' 'Ah', he said, 'that is what we would like the Germans to believe. And you would do good service if you could help to get them to believe it. But if we come out we shall save our fleet from being immobilised in that quarter.' We did not know where the fleet might be wanted. There might be war in the Mediterranean, there might be war in Holland and Belgium, and we must have our naval resources mobile and well in hand. People should not forget that we had destroyed more than half Germany's fleet—'because we have, you know.'

How many Germans were there at Narvik? 'About 2,000', he said, 'or a few more. They hold the hilltop behind the town and we are there and there'—he indicated on the map. Important things should happen in the next two or three weeks, but everything was going slowly because of the snow—there was five feet of it—it was the great difficulty. The Germans could now only supply their Narvik people from the air, but they could get up to Bergen by coming along the coast. Talking of the British at Narvik, he

---

1. The Germans ended the Norwegian campaign with no major warship fit for sea.

said that they would be near the Swedish frontier in case they were needed, and I said that Germany would not like that and we might be in the position of pushing Sweden into war with Germany. To this he said 'Well, we must take care that that doesn't happen.'

He argued that the Germans' occupation of Norway, if we left them there, would have certain advantages for us. They would have to keep seven to nine divisions there and eventually we should get them out by forcing the Germans through war elsewhere to withdraw them. I said that the German air-bases, especially Stavanger, would be a nuisance to us, being so near, but he made light of it. 'It only means,' he said, 'that they will come more often to attack us but, if they do, we will put up a stronger fight against them.'

As to Italy, 'I don't want to declare war on anyone. I don't want any more enemies if we can avoid it. What will happen if Italy attacks Yugo-slavia? That depends. If it is a matter of a few bases on the Dalmatian coast, well, I daresay we shan't come in on that. If the Yugo-slavs resist valiantly and a long struggle follows, or of course, if the Balkans blow up all together, then we are likely to be in it. But I'm not for declaring war on anyone I can assure you. And remember this about Italy. If the Yugos fight her seriously she will come crawling to us not to intervene against her—she will then only want us to leave her alone.'

I again raised the question of the War Cabinet. I said 'You are now Chairman of the Military Co-ordination Committee. How in the world can you do all that plus the Admiralty, plus—?' 'Ah', he said, 'that chairmanship didn't mean so much until recently, but now I've got more powers—I've got more powers!' (He seemed very pleased about this and it turned out that since he had been made chairman some weeks ago Chamberlain had actually been presiding, but now Churchill was presiding himself.) Then I said 'Besides all this you've got to handle—' 'The general problems of the war', he interrupted, 'well, I don't feel the strain. I can do it. Look at my desk!' He drew me back to his desk at the other side of the room and said 'Look at it! It's quite clear, isn't it—except for this document.' There was one lying on the top of the top drawer and he picked it up and said 'Narvik!' and put it down again and went on 'I can do it all right. Even if I wasn't at the Admiralty or if I wasn't chairman I'd have to read all the principal documents as a member of the War Cabinet.' I said 'They say you never go to bed till 3 a.m.—is that true?' He replied 'Well, I'll tell you. I sleep for an hour every afternoon and after five I begin again as fresh as in the morning. Look here, do I look tired?' He came right up to me and pushed his face almost into mine. I was just going to tell him that the Parliamentary reporters had said how tired he had looked the day before when his secretary came in for the third time to say that Sir Percy Loraine, our Ambassador to Italy, was still waiting, so he said 'Good-bye and come again. I always read the MG, you know, there it is over there—on the table.'

4

The Battle of Britain, 1940

Crozier's interviews broke off just a week before the debate in the house of commons on the Norwegian campaign. He went next to London on 26 July. Churchill had become prime minister. There was a real National government with Labour and Liberal ministers as well as Conservatives. Under Churchill the war cabinet changed its character. It now represented the National coalition—two Conservatives and two Labour men with Churchill, not yet Conservative leader, as the national figure presiding over them. Churchill forgot his earlier insistence that the three service ministers should be in the war cabinet. They had merely departmental duties, and henceforth Churchill, as minister of defence, directed grand strategy almost unfettered. Only one member of the war cabinet—Halifax, the foreign secretary—had an administrative department of his own, despite Churchill's earlier advocacy that all members should have a department.

In the field of war, Belgium and Holland had been overrun. The BEF had been successfully evacuated from Dunkirk, though with the loss of all its heavy equipment. Italy had entered the war on the German side. France had been totally defeated and had signed an armistice with Germany. German forces occupied northern France and the entire French coastline. Hitler, after making an empty peace offer, was preparing to invade Great Britain or perhaps to reduce her by aerial attack.

Crozier made only two long visits to London in 1940 after the beginning of May—26–27 July and 23–24 August—and one short one on 6 August. Nevertheless the interviews of this time deserve a chapter to themselves. They cover much of the battle of Britain and recapture the feelings of that romantic time. The prelude to the battle began on 10 July and lasted for about a month, mostly in air fights over the channel. The first phase of the battle itself began on 13 August when the Luftwaffe attempted to penetrate inland. It led to a great victory by the RAF on 18 August and then tailed off. The second and most intense phase of the battle began on 24 August, and there followed a fortnight when the RAF was hard pressed. The final phase, which Crozier does not cover, came in mid-September, when the RAF re-established its mastery of the air and the danger of invasion passed away—as it proved for ever. Thanks to Fighter Command, Great Britain was going to survive the second world war.

Crozier's interviews present the days when the outcome was still uncertain. 'Will he come?' was the question in everyone's mind. It was expected that he would. John Scott arranged for control of the Manchester Guardian to be transferred to the United States in case of invasion, so that its tradition should be preserved for happier days.[1] Scott also expected that he and Crozier would

---

1. See David Ayerst, Guardian, 534.

have to go 'on the run' if the Germans came and equipped himself with an emerald necklace with which to raise funds. Crozier felt that history was indeed being made. His interviews were no longer designed as guidance for the paper, if they ever had been. They were now records for the future, and Crozier often kept them in his own handwriting in order to preserve their absolute secrecy.

26 July 1940

2.45 P.M. SIR ARCHIBALD SINCLAIR AT THE AIR MINISTRY

Sir Archibald Sinclair was secretary of state for air throughout the period of Churchill's National government. He regarded it as his duty to be the mouthpiece of the air staff.

I asked him if he was keeping well in spite of his strenuous job and he said 'very well'. In point of fact he looked ill, his face was white and I thought fallen as compared with the time I saw him last, and his clothes hung loosely on him.

I had intended to talk almost entirely about the Air, but that was not his idea. He was obviously troubled by the criticisms of recent government policy. 'Well now', he said, 'there are two things, aren't there—this aliens business and the Burma Road?' and he began to talk about them. He said:

'We decided to intern the aliens, you know, when France collapsed and we feared invasion, when there was, well I won't say a panic, but general apprehension that invasion might be coming any moment. Moreover—here he threw in a laugh—if invasion had come then I doubt whether anybody would have regretted our decision! However, there was no invasion and the thing was very badly managed, there's no doubt about that. The trouble was that no one looked after it adequately. I frankly admit that I did not attend to it; I have my own job to keep me very busy. It was partly Eden's job—and he is a liberal minded man too—but he was absolutely occupied with the business of getting the country's defences in order. Anderson had a host of things to see to also—he's a very humane man—and the result was that there was no one to look after it properly.[1]

'I know that many dreadful things have happened; I know of some of them myself. There's a family that my wife and I know personally. A boy belonging to it was taken from school and interned. His mother, distracted, did not know where he had gone

---

1. The government interned all enemy aliens, many of them Jews and anti-Nazis, after the fall of France. Anthony Eden was secretary for war, and Sir John Anderson home secretary.

and appealed to my wife. My wife rang up Osbert Peake, the Under-Secretary at the Home Office, who was very decent and promised to get the boy out. After a fortnight the mother rang up again and said they had heard nothing more about the boy. My wife got Peake again and he said 'I'm frightfully sorry, I can't tell you how sorry but, you know, we can't find the boy. *He's lost.*'

. . . . .

'Now about the Burma road.[1] I am bound to say that I think that there the Government was entirely right. Nothing else could have been done. Craigie, our Ambassador, reported that the Japs were determined to have the Burma Road question settled. Nothing else would satisfy them; that had to be conceded to them or Craigie told us the most serious consequences would follow, and that meant war. Then there was Australia. Australia had sent us her men and also her aeroplanes—those provided for her own defence, and her ships on condition that, if need arose, we sent the fleet—well, a fleet to Singapore to protect her. Well, now we had no fleet that we could send to Singapore—the defection of the French had settled that! So we had to give way to Japan.

'Remember, too, that we could not get the help of the USA. We tried all we could to get her help. We suggested that she guarantee the Dutch East Indies with us and that she should act jointly with us over the Burma road. She would not do either. She was completely non-committal. Perhaps, in three or four months, *after the Presidential Election*, she may be more forthcoming, but not now. And, perhaps, something will happen—in Europe, I mean—to make the outlook more favourable for us in negotiating with Japan. We must hope for that. As to Russia—well, Russia had certainly helped China and is still helping her, though not a great deal, but she is also negotiating with Japan and she is not doing anything to suggest that she would be willing to act with us.

'Is there anything in the talk of a "general peace settlement" in connection with the Burma road compromise? I think there may be. We have told Dr Quo that we shall not try to force anything on China or put any pressure on her, but we would like to see peace, and we shall tell Japan that we should be willing, if peace were made, to make things easy for her in the economic sphere.'

I asked some questions about the air. Was there not a chance

. . . . .

---

1. The British government had agreed to close the Burma road for three months.

that the Germans might suddenly turn up with improved machines that might deprive us of our present great superiority, and were we not only turning out our present superior machines but pushing on with still better types?

He said that our present types were greatly superior to anything that the Germans had but we lacked quantity. We must, as a first necessity, produce our present types in great numbers, and this we were doing.

I said that, nevertheless, the Germans might come out with something much better—they had known about our best machines for a long time now—and I was afraid lest we should not have better still with which to meet them.

He replied that already the Germans were appearing with better planes than they had in September last, e.g., the Heinkel 113 and the Junkers 88, but our Hurricanes and Spitfires, which 'ate up' the earlier German types, were 'eating up' these also. At the same time we were improving our own present ruling types e.g., in respect of firepower, the use of cannon, etc. Apart from this the answer to my question was that we were at work on more and more formidable types—two new fighters, of which we should eventually concentrate on one, and a great new bomber.

He then said '*if* we get Beaverbrook's 3,000 a month from USA' —and he laughed heartily—'we shall certainly make them produce a lot of their new machines for us'.[1]

Finally he said 'You need have no fear on this score. We are going on with the new types as well as turning out the present ones in numbers. We are not going to be left behind!'

BRENDAN BRACKEN

I ran into him in Whitehall when on my way to No. 10. He said:

'You're going along to see my boss, aren't you? You'll find him fairly cheerful, I think; things are looking a lot better than they were a few weeks ago. I wish to God the Huns would try to invade us. I am sure we should smash them up and such a defeat for them would be the best thing we could have.

'By the way, there's something I want you to do for me. Duff Cooper[2] must get some representative newspaper man, who really

---

1. Beaverbrook was minister of aircraft production, a new department established by Churchill. There was no love lost between MAP and the air ministry. No one would appreciate from Sinclair's remarks for instance that Beaverbrook had put cannon in fighter aircraft against violent protests from the air ministry.

2. Minister of information.

knows newspaper work from the inside, as his adviser. Would you see if you could think of someone who would be suitable? . . . I suppose you wouldn't consider the job yourself if you were offered it?'

I said 'No' and added that, if I had been Duff Cooper, I would have had a small private committee of important newspaper men to advise me from the start, and I wouldn't have adopted any public policy that the press would be discussing without knowing first what such a committee thought about it.

He said 'Perhaps your suggestion will give us what we want.'

5.00 P.M. WINSTON CHURCHILL AT 10 DOWNING STREET

In Mrs Crozier's handwriting.

He was in the Cabinet room in the Prime Minister's chair in the middle, with back to the fireplace. He said 'This is the first time I have had the pleasure of welcoming you in this room,' and I said I was glad to see him there. He asked would I have a whisky and soda and I said 'No' and he said 'Well, I will' and ordered one. It had ice in it and he put his hand in and pulled out a lot of the ice and threw it into the coal bucket.

Then he began by saying that he had read a Leader of ours on the 'dual position' of the Government, and he thought it was very sensible. 'You see', he said 'after all, Chamberlain and those other people represent the Conservative party which has a great majority in the House of Commons and they must have some consideration.'

I said 'I suppose that, as a matter of fact, it is a political necessity for you to have Chamberlain in the Government? He answers to you, so to speak, for the support of the Conservative party?'

'Well', he replied, 'I owe something to Chamberlain, you know. When he resigned he could have advised the King to send for Halifax and he didn't. And he consented to serve under me as Premier—not everyone in his position would have done that; Asquith, for instance, wouldn't serve under Lloyd George. But Chamberlain works very well with me and I can tell you this— *he's no intriguer.*'

I said 'The trouble is that when anything goes wrong a lot of people think—both here and in other countries—that it's Chamberlain and the Munich people working against you, and that makes a bad impression.'

He said 'They don't, and I can tell you that Chamberlain works hard and efficiently.'

'Then', I said, 'it isn't true that in matters of drive and effort in the war Chamberlain and Co are a brake on the wheel—I mean on your wheel?'

'No', he said, 'it isn't true at all.'

'Well', I said, 'I'm glad of that, but there's another point even more serious, and it's this. Do Chamberlain and those friends of his use their influence in any Government question of policy in the direction of "appeasement", pushing it on you and the Government?'

'I give you my word of honour', he said, 'it isn't true.' Then he went on 'Take this question of the Burma Road. Halifax is being blamed. As a matter of fact'—and he smiled broadly—'Halifax was opposed to the compromise. He said the Japanese were bluffing and that we ought to stand out against them. Our decision was *my* doing.

'Craigie, our Ambassador, a good man, warned us that if we refused the Japanese demand things would immediately become extremely dangerous.

'Well, I could not do it. I just could not take the risk of what might happen. I believe that I can pull the country out of this hole, and I will pull it out, if there are only Germany and Italy to fight, but if there's another great Power against us, I don't know whether it can be done. Therefore I couldn't do it. It's a three months' promise to Japan. I don't believe in this peace business at all. (That is, the suggestion that during the three months a way might be found of making peace), but I hope that things may somehow change during the three months to our advantage—that the Italians will give us a chance at their fleet in the Mediterranean or that we shall deal Hitler a big blow if he tries to invade us; and also, of course, after the next few months the United States, having got the Presidential election over, may be more disposed to be active in the Far East.'

He said that we had also Australia to think of. If there was war with Japan we should have to send a squadron to Singapore and how should we do that? Perhaps, if the Italians gave us a chance, we should so improve things in the next few months that to send something to Singapore would not be impossible.

It was clear that with him the major point was to stave off trouble for the time being in the hope and belief that our situation might become better in the near future.

About the improvement in our position he was cheerful and

confident. It was obvious that a great change for the better had come over the situation since the French collapse. He said so. 'We are much better off now than we were a month ago, and if we have another three months, if he does not invade us for another three months, I think that'—he looked at me and made a wry face—'he will have "missed the bus".' I said 'For goodness sake don't say that in public', and he said solemnly 'No, there's a time to say things and a time only to think them! But whether he (Hitler) attacks us and is beaten or doesn't attack us at all I think in a few months we shall be vastly better off than we are now.' 'Mind' he added, 'I don't mean that we haven't a great deal more to do, indeed, we have, a vast deal more, but things are much better than they were and will be better still.'

He then made it clear that in the air we were doing very well. He spoke with enthusiasm of Beaverbrook. 'He's done astonishing things these last few weeks. He's done miracles. He's giving himself to it wholly. He can't think or talk of anything else. He won't talk of politics—he's wholly taken up with aeroplanes. And when you've got the aircraft industry working like this with a never-ceasing dynamo like Beaverbrook behind it, things move at a great pace.'

He then sent for the graphs indicating the production in engines, machines, spares, etc. for many months past and showed them to me. The rise since Beaverbrook began the great spurt was very striking, and the comparison with the bad weeks in the spring (end of Kingsley Wood's term of office) was enormous. But *all* the weeks of the spurt showed a remarkable rise on the weeks immediately preceding.

Then he said 'I should say that our output now must be *a long way* ahead of that of Germany. We are turning out now about [number omitted] planes per week. The machines are all right' he said 'it's the question of pilots and the trained men of all kinds. It's going to be troublesome before long if we get these great quantities of machines—but we shall get them all right.'

He spoke of Russia and the Mediterranean. Germany was anxious to keep things quiet in the Balkans, but he believed that, if need be, she could tackle Russia at the same time as she was making the attack on us. After all, she had had two hundred divisions mobilised and she was so well off that she had already demobilised forty of them. She could carry on two campaigns if necessary though naturally she did not want to.

As to the Mediterranean, it must be remembered that the defection of France had made things very difficult for us. It was the loss of the French bases that was so serious. We had nothing now between Gibraltar and Alexandria (except Malta) to support an attack on Italy, and this hampered us very greatly. We had to hope that the Italians would give us a chance to get at them.

I referred to the Aliens internment policy and he said 'Yes, I'm sorry for that business, but you will see things will be better now,' and he said that he knew personally of some of the bad things that had been happening.

At the finish he said 'Come again and see me soon. I'm always glad to see you and I always read the MG.'

5.45 P.M. SIR ROBERT VANSITTART AT THE FOREIGN OFFICE

He was afraid lest people should begin to think that, after all, Hitler was not going to make a great attack on this country. He thought that because there was a 'lull' there was a tendency to think that Hitler might have dropped the idea of invasion. This was a great mistake. Personally he was sure that the attempt would be made. Hitler had committed himself too far, to his own people among others, to be able to refrain; the attempt was expected of him and he would make it.

There was no reason to suppose that Hitler would be unduly delayed by difficulties in the Balkans. He wanted to have things reasonably settled there when he was dealing with us, and he also wanted the economic resources of those countries.

As for Russia, there was no reason at all to think that Germany and Russia were near the stage of dangerous friction. He said they were doing what they had been doing ever since they made the non-aggression pact, namely, 'working together like this', and he interlocked the fingers of his two hands. He then made a rather curious qualification of what he had said by repeating there was no danger of any friction between the two 'at any rate before the winter', meaning, I think, that in his opinion there would be an attempted invasion of this country, and its fate would be settled before there could be any change in the relations between Germany and Russia.

He went on to say that any positive successes that we could gain would be of immense importance in changing the opinion that was held abroad about the end of the war. Any successes would diminish the number of the 'defeatists' in foreign countries about our prospects in the war. It would do this in the United States where, he said, there were people who were very much inclined to say that to help Britain was throwing good stuff away inasmuch as she was certain to be beaten, while there were others who went to the other extreme and said that now we were doing so well and building up our strength so fast there was no need for them to help us. Speaking of the need for positive successes, he referred to the Mediterranean and said that we had suffered a heavy blow from the French collapse since we could not use their bases on the French Mediterranean coast in order to attack Northern Italy.

On the subject of the Burma Road, he said that the compromise agreed to by the Government was 'of course absolutely necessary'; we could not stand out against the prospect that was held out to us if we refused to agree to the Japanese demand. He intimated that the United States had given us no encouragement to stand up to the Japanese.

6.30 P.M. J W DULANTY

In Mrs Crozier's handwriting.

He said that before we talked of more general things he wanted to ask me a question; he thought I might help him. Some weeks before, about the time when France collapsed there had appeared in English newspapers—notably the Daily Mail, Express and Mirror—articles suggesting that since Eire was likely to be invaded and since she could not (it was said) resist invasion, England should forthwith 'go in' to occupy the country so that Germany would not do so. Now, were these articles concerted and 'inspired' by the British Government? His Government would not believe that there was any other explanation. He did not himself believe it but could not persuade his Government, which insisted (and he meant De Valera) that such a stream of articles could not possibly have appeared without Government 'inspiration'.

I said that I had heard nothing directly or indirectly of any attempt to 'inspire' the press and I thought that I would have heard had there been any systematic attempt. He said it was also alleged that Duff Cooper had called the Lobby men together—and them only—and had 'called them off' from this inspired campaign.

Had I heard anything of it?

I said 'No' and that I would have heard as our own man (Boardman) would have attended the meeting and would have reported about it to me. I added that I would enquire and see whether I could discover any evidence of 'Inspiration' whatever by Duff Cooper or by anyone else in the Government.[1]

---

1. According to Longford and O'Neill, Eamon de Valera, 369–70, the campaign against Irish neutrality was a try-on by the ministry of information.

He said that it was, in his opinion, most important to disabuse his Government of their belief in this matter, as it affected their views of the good faith of the British Government in relation to Ireland, and if I remained of the opinion I had stated would I write him a private letter which he could show to the Eire Government. He was himself sure that there was no British 'inspiration', 'but they are convinced that there is something in it'.

(I afterwards enquired of Boardman and he told me that he was sure there had been no attempt to inspire the press; he said that on one occasion Duff Cooper had been asked about the state of feeling in Eire; he had replied that it was not too good and had added that it would not be a bad thing if the British press did not discuss the Eire business quite so much. That was all.)

D then said there were other awkward things. Tagart ex-Indian police official had been over in Ireland trying to stimulate De Valera's own supporters, *including his ministers*, against him. How was that to be explained? And certain British intelligence officers had been at work in Ireland. All this led to great suspicion in Eire.

He then spoke of what he said was 'terribly secret'. While it was absolutely true that De Valera could not abate Eire's neutrality in any way and could not agree that Britain should move a finger until Germany invaded Eire and Eire invited Britain to intervene, yet all the arrangements could be made in advance by co-operation between the two countries, so that Britain could intervene at once and efficiently so soon as the contingency arose. *And that had been done.*[1] Everything had been agreed between Eire and Britain, and everything had been worked out in detail between the staffs in the two countries. He was emphatic about the completeness and efficiency of the arrangements, but he repeated that all this was 'terribly secret' and, if it got out, it would 'blow De Valera up completely'.

He said also that their home defence forces in Eire were now pretty good and referred to a commanding officer who had said that if the Germans now came to Eire they would get a warm reception. All that they wanted was supplies of certain munitions from England. I asked him what impression he got of Caldecote as Secretary for the Dominions. He said he was pleasant to get on with and 'quite imperturbable'. He gave no great sign of capacity and had no 'drive', but capacity of a kind he must have or he could not have got where he had got at the Bar.

---

1. An unlikely story.

10.30 P.M. A V ALEXANDER AT THE ADMIRALTY

A V Alexander was first lord of the admiralty throughout Churchill's National government. He maintained doglike devotion to both Churchill and the sea lords.
In Crozier's handwriting.

I had been directed to go to the North Entrance to the Admiralty, where they would have instructions about me. My taxi was stopped about thirty yards from the Admiralty Arch by a sentry 'flashing a red light'. He told me to follow the barbed wire barricade along the footpath through the Arch until I came to an entrance on the left, when I should explain who I was. There were four sentries here and two officials who were waiting for me. One of them took me to the North Entrance, and inside the building, again, two sentries with fixed bayonets were marching up and down, meeting at the foot of the main staircase.

The First Lord was in the room in which I had always seen Churchill. He too had a big map on the wall. Under Churchill it had at first been Europe, then it became Norway. Now, under Alexander, it had become the British Isles and the coasts of Western Europe. Alexander had been at some naval base all day and had addressed 10,000 men connected with the Navy. He was in good spirits and was settling down to a pile of documents which were likely to take him, he said, till about 2 a.m. He is a direct and emphatic person, clear-headed, and seems to have energy and determination. He has the same habit as Churchill, Vansittart and Eden of jumping up from his chair and illustrating his points from the map on the wall.

I asked him first about the German motor torpedo-boats. I said that they appeared to be more numerous and more formidable in the Channel; how far were they to be regarded as a dangerous new weapon and what 'reply' to them had we? He said that, in the main, they were useful for raiding convoys but also they were used as 'bait'; the Germans, that is, sent out the mtbs, we spotted them and sent out destroyers against them; and then, in a twinkling, a lot of German bombers appeared from France and our destroyers were in danger.

I asked whether the destroyers were the 'answer' to the mtbs and he said that that was doubtful. The mtb was a small boat and the destroyer was a large one—all too large. The mtb carried two torpedo tubes, and possibly spare torpedoes; the destroyer had to be very careful lest she presented too good a target for attack. What, then, was the answer? I got the impression that as yet there was no definite answer. Every offensive weapon, he said, produced its antidote in time, but it might be some time before it did. I gathered that probably the answer would be some new form of craft—smaller than a torpedo boat but somewhat larger than an mtb. He told me about X types that were now under construction and spoke of the programme up to the end of the year.

I suggested that the mtb might be a formidable engine in a fleet action—against the battleship—but he did not seem to think there was much in this though he gave no particular reason. He said, of course, that the mtb was a fairweather boat and that the best time of the year for its operations was now coming to an end. When the autumn came and then the winter, with high winds and stormy seas—he shrugged his shoulders eloquently. He then returned to the subject of mtb raids on convoys. These ships that they had recently attacked, he said, were small vessels engaged in the coastwise trade. It might be extremely difficult to carry on such traffic in face of combined mtb and aeroplane attack, and his view was that it ought to be stopped and the goods sent by rail. 'I've begged', he said, 'that this should be done but so far without success.'[1]

Then the Mediterranean. He was cross with critics who had attacked him and the Admiralty about the delay in destroying the French battle-fleet. He seemed especially to resent the critics in the London clubs. They had all been clamouring to know why he was doing nothing—'a terrible twelve days!' He said that he had had to be very determined; he refused to act until he could assemble a certain force of capital ships to tackle the job at Oran.[2] He would not move without certain ships that he named; it would have been madness without an adequate force, and we had to be ready for anything also at Alexandria and in the North Sea. I raised the question of the rest of the French fleet and asked him where the ships were, and he said that they were pretty well scattered throughout the ports of the French Empire.

. . . . . .

1. Convoys were formed even for the coastal trade, and these continued to pass through the Channel. Motor gun-boats were developed in March 1941 and proved an effective answer to the German mtbs or E-boats.

2. After the fall of France, a strong French force, including two capital ships, was at Oran (Mers-el-Kebir). On 3 July Admiral Somerville presented an ultimatum to the French admiral Gensoul. He should either join Great Britain in the war, sail to internment in a British port, sail for demilitarisation to the French West Indies or to the United States, or scuttle his ships. When Gensoul gave no satisfactory answer, Somerville opened fire. One French capital ship and three destroyers were sunk or disabled. One capital ship and 12 other vessels escaped to Toulon. 1,300 Frenchmen were killed.

The loss of the French naval bases in the Mediterranean was an extremely serious thing for us. We had nothing now between Gibraltar and Alexandria except Malta and that was so persistently bombed from the air that it was really untenable as a naval base. However, he was not satisfied to leave things just like that. 'Something will have to be done about it!' he said.

He said that the Italian policy was, of course, to keep their ships at harbour. When the Colleoni, the light cruiser that we sank,[1] came into contact with our four destroyers, she had a sister cruiser with her, both faster than our destroyers, whom between them they might have destroyed before the Sydney came up, but they made no attempt. What was more, in the engagement when our battleship hit one of theirs, the Italian cruisers completely outnumbered our cruisers—they had six 8-inch gun cruisers and seven 6-inch gun cruisers, a force immensely greater than ours, and they made no attempt to engage (they had superior speed also). They relied on aircraft, but their attacks on our squadron on this occasion were very ineffective.[2] We needed the French bases in order to bomb Italy easily; now we would have to use aircraft-carriers or fly from a tremendously long distance; we had only been able lately to bomb their bases on the east coast of *Sicily*.

He rang for his secretary and asked where another secretary had put some exciting photographs from the Mediterranean showing how the bombs fell round, but not on, our ships in the fight off the coast of Italy. (They were taken from another ship.) The Secretary replied that Mr X, who had them, had gone to bed and was asleep. 'Oh, is he?' said A. 'I'm sorry. You might ask him for them.' They were brought and showed our ship with bombs bursting all round it but nevertheless missing the target. 'You might forget you've seen them' he said 'because I have not shown them yet to the people here.'

He referred to Churchill with admiration. I said that Churchill always showed an immense affection for the Navy. He said rather ruefully 'Affection? Oh yes! He thinks that he has only to ask that the Navy should do this, that or the other, and done it will be!' 'And so, of course', he added, 'it is!'

He thought the Germans might try to occupy the Faroes, Iceland or the Shetlands.[3] The Faroes would not matter so much;

1. The Bartolomeo Colleoni was sunk by HMAS Sydney on 19 July.

2. This engagement was off the coast of Calabria on 9 July.

3. The Germans made no such attempts. British forces occupied the Faroes on 23 May and Iceland early in July.

in Iceland we had a lot of troops; the occupation of the Shetlands would be 'very awkward'. With regard to preparations against invasion, he said that for three weeks past the Navy had been 'bringing in' a steady stream of munitions from USA, including X rifles in the last few days.

He talked to me for an hour and 10 minutes, and said as I left —'I've been more communicative to you than to anyone else since I took on this job.'

27 July 1940

11.00 A.M. ANTHONY EDEN AT THE WAR OFFICE

Anthony Eden was secretary of state for war from May 1940 until December when he succeeded Halifax as foreign secretary. The interview is in Crozier's handwriting.

He too had a big map on an easel against the wall. It showed these islands and the West European coastline.

I asked how he regarded things and he said they were much better than five or six weeks ago. On the day before he had been lunching with Halifax and H had reminded him that they had lunched together just a month earlier; after that occasion H had entered in his Diary—'I'm too lazy to keep one', said Eden[1]—that Eden 'had said that if I could have a month's respite at the War Office I should be satisfied'. Now, he said, he did not at all take that back but he would like another month or two more!

He had had to face a dreadful time when he took office. The BEF came back with all its equipment lost—a thousand guns were lost. Then he had to send off to France at once the only two fully trained and equipped divisions that we still possessed—the X Division and the Canadians, and then there was left in the country *only one Brigade* of trained and equipped men—only one brigade!

Yes, we certainly had a lot of men now but he could not share the satisfaction that others expressed so freely; we still needed so much equipment of certain kinds! For instance, we were still far behind our needs in such things as . . .—here he mentioned three important weapons—and he was in the disagreeable position that he had to think hard whether he dare move, say, an anti-tank gun from one district to another.

---

1. Lord Avon, formerly Anthony Eden, quotes extensively from his diaries in his published memoirs, though he states that they were kept sporadically.

He complained strongly of the way in which the pre-war Government had, he declared, multiplied numbers of men for the Army simply in order to make a show but without taking the proper steps to equip them. I said that probably the Government had never really believed that a great army would actually be needed as everyone had accepted the idea of the 'defensive' in France. He replied that at any rate the War Office had never believed in that theory; there were records which showed that they appreciated the possibilities of a heavily mechanised offensive, I said that in that case it must be the 'politicians' who were to blame and he said 'Well, in that case we'd better not go into it.'

He discussed the present military position in this country, described his plans for the coming autumn and winter—he was going to draw the present coastal troops farther inland and put the newer troops in the coast towns—and explained the general principles on which our defence against invasion was now based. He took the coastal areas and the country behind, explained the dispositions, and illustrated them from maps which he sent for and showed me (saying, like others, 'Forget that you have seen them'.) The essence of the system is its mobility. 'No Maginot Line for us', he said, 'or for me!'

He said he thought that the Germans, if they tried invasion, would bomb the areas in rear of the points where they meant to land. I asked about troop-carriers and the possibility of large numbers of them being used. He said, 'Well, how many do you think they've got?' I replied that I had no idea but that I had seen talk of as many as 3,000. He said 'Oh, no, they haven't anything like as many as that. Possibly a thousand. But anyway, if they come, you know, they would be fat sitting pheasants to our fighters.'

In talking of German plans for invasion, he said that it was at this moment the considered opinion of our General Staff that the attempt was coming. I asked whether there was evidence of actual preparation, and he said there was some. I enquired about Ireland and he said that we had made all our preparations in Northern Ireland to move south into Eire at once *when we were invited by the Eire Government*—he stressed that point—and he again illustrated his meaning from the map.

11.30 A.M. HERBERT MORRISON AT THE MINISTRY OF SUPPLY

Herbert Morrison was minister of supply from May 1940 to October when he became home secretary. He was now in a hurry to keep another appointment and had only time to say that the production of munitions was improving 'but I am far from satisfied'.

3.45 P.M. COUNT RACZYNSKI

.   .   .   .   .

He said that a day or two before he had been lunching with De Gaulle and Zaleski, Poland's Foreign Minister, whom he regards as a very great expert on European problems. He said that Zaleski had talked about the prospects of Hitler's invading England and had expressed the view that it was 50-50 whether Hitler attempted to invade us or whether he went south and joined Mussolini in a great attack on our position in the Mediterranean. Z thought that Hitler could not attempt both enterprises simultaneously. It would largely be a question of aircraft. They would, if they could, attack Gibraltar, but the main onslaught would be carried out by German aircraft from Italian bases, and the Germans would hope by keeping up a terrific attack in this way to smash our Mediterranean fleet. They had air force enough for this enterprise, and they had air force enough for a great attack on England, but they had not enough for both.

.   .   .   .   .

We then talked of Stalin's relations with Hitler, and he was very strong in the view that there was no likelihood of the two quarrelling yet. Hitler would swallow almost anything rather than quarrel, so much was that so that the Poles now feared that Hitler would hand over to Stalin the central section of Poland itself; this is the section which Germany has not annexed and which lies between the German and Russian portions. (The Poles fear, of course, that if Russia got this section from Germany she would never be got out of it however much Britain might defeat Germany.)

In talking of Hitler he said that what impressed him greatly was Hitler's immense efficiency as a practical man. He devoted all his attention to the practical side of things and ignored everything else. He cared very little about such things as prestige. For instance, he ordered the Graf Spee to scuttle herself[1] simply because he would not waste the lives of about a thousand men. He did not trouble about the loss of 'face' that the scuttling of the ship involved. Similarly, he did not fuss about the un-neutral acts of the United States, though he had plenty of ground for protest, because he knew that he could not prevent them. R thought that this was an important and remarkable trait in Hitler's character.

R thinks that Russia is playing a deep game and is completely untrustworthy. He illustrated this by telling me what Zaleski said about the long interview that Stalin had given to Cripps. 'Of course', said Zaleski, 'Stalin's idea is that Hitler would hear about this long and intimate interview and would begin to wonder what it signified and whether Stalin was perhaps tending to come a little closer to Britain, and this would influence Hitler to embrace Stalin still more firmly and to let him have a little bit more of what he wanted in the North or the South of Europe.' He thought it was on the cards that Russia would try to screw something more out of Finland, especially as Stalin must hate to see the Germans installed at Narvik.

Talking of the Vichy Government he said it was a curious fact that they were facilitating the departure of Polish soldiers (in civilian clothes) from France to England—he did not know why.

6 August 1940

L S AMERY AT THE INDIA OFFICE

Amery was secretary of state for India throughout Churchill's National government.

I had not met him for years; his face is now lined and wizened and he speaks as though he lacked teeth, though he does not. He was very pleasant and produced tea (China) served in a gilt set and very nice china (the whole thing much superior to the Foreign Office tea). He gave me a long summary of the Viceroy's declaration.[2]

·   ·   ·   ·   ·

---

1. After the battle of the river Plate, December 1939.
1. The declaration proposed to increase the executive council and to include two Congress members. Congress did not accept the offer.

He said that though the Declaration did not go as far as it might, he thought that it might reasonably be described as being a considerable advance—he repeated this several times—and also 'I think, you know, it goes as far as you could expect Churchill to go.' I said 'You mean, in view of his record on India?' and he said 'Yes, it goes a good long way for him'; and he gave the impression that Churchill had gone farther than he, A, had expected, and he added that he thought a good deal of credit was due to Churchill for having gone so far. . . .

．　　．　　．　　．　　．

23 August 1940

2.00 P.M. COUNT REVENTLOW

．　　．　　．　　．　　．

He defended Chamberlain (and Halifax) over Munich and when I said that at any rate a strong point against Chamberlain was that he had been hopelessly deceived at and after Munich, he said he sometimes wondered if Chamberlain really believed in Hitler's good faith after Munich, but he agreed (1) that Chamberlain slowed down the munitions effort in the months between Prague and September, and (2) that after his great blunder (misinterpretation of Hitler), it was apparent he ought to have resigned. He repeated that as a foreign diplomat observing the scene he considered that Chamberlain's failure to resign and so to procure a National Government illustrated the chief defect in his character as a statesman.

He said that his friends reported as something now certain that Chamberlain would resign, and probably Halifax too. He would be extremely sorry if Halifax resigned as he did not think we should get so good a man. Would it be Eden? It might be that the appointment of Eden would go down well in the USA, but he regarded that as a 'superficial' matter that should not be allowed weight in this connection. The story he heard was that if Eden became Foreign Secretary Morrison would succeed him at the War Office.[1] He had been greatly disappointed in Halifax's last

---

1. When Eden succeeded Halifax in December, Morrison was already home secretary, and Margesson, the Conservative chief whip, became secretary of state for war.

speech (the speech in which he appealed to the power of prayer). His former speeches had been good, but he was bound to say that something more was required of a Foreign Secretary of Britain than a pious appeal of the kind that Halifax had made.

.   .   .   .   .

4.30 P.M. SIR ARCHIBALD SINCLAIR

I asked him about Chamberlain, Halifax and 'reconstruction' of the Cabinet. Was it true that Chamberlain was going and that perhaps Halifax would go with him and that Churchill would reconstruct the Cabinet? He said that he thought that Chamberlain would not remain long in any case, but that he did not know the exact truth about his condition (after the operation); he rather thought that no one did. As to Halifax, he could only say that he thought it was quite likely that Halifax would go with Chamberlain. For himself he hoped that Halifax would not go, because he did not know who would fill his place. He thought highly of Halifax and that he did well in the job. I said that Halifax had not stood out with sufficient independence against Chamberlain and his policies and he replied that that might have been true up to the seizure of Prague but it was not true afterwards. He did not know what Churchill would do about the FO. 'Let's hope he does not appoint Beaverbrook—or Lloyd!'[1] His general view was that reconstruction of the Cabinet would come before very long, but not just yet.

Then as to the air. We had certainly done well in beating off the attacks of August 8–18. He thought that the next stage might be a series of mass night raids on industrial centres. The Germans were beginning to find their way about the country a bit better. They were not good at night-flying, though, they did not seem to like it. He repeated the point as of much importance that at night-flying they had not been very successful. Perhaps they had not had much practice. Certainly their Intelligence was not good—not nearly as good as ours. Our people were splendidly served with large scale maps and detailed photographs of their objectives and routes. The Germans often had 'stuck up in their machines' quite small maps—he gestured with his hands—of the English country through which they were flying. A good point in our favour had

---

1. Lord Lloyd, a die-hard Tory, had been appointed colonial secretary by Churchill. He died in February 1941.

been the excellence of our blackout; that had helped to baffle them. I asked about instruments. He said that he did not know whether our actual instruments were superior to theirs, but in everything classed as 'scientific equipment' we certainly had the better of them. I asked what was meant by 'scientific equipment' and he gave as an instance everything connected with wireless. I mentioned the story current in USA that our navigation instruments were much superior and that the Germans had not enough of them, or good enough ones, to go round, so that only the leader of a squadron was properly equipped and he had to lead the way for the others. Sinclair replied drily that in their daytime raids on this country they usually did not need the instruments and that by night they had not flown in formation but came on singly. He said that we did the same too in night flying; the machines flew in succession, one after another.

I asked about the Mediterranean and the possibility of reinforcing our people there. Was it true that we now had Hurricanes there. He said yes that was so. A month or so back we had been weak in many ways. The month's respite had made us much stronger but we had still a great deal to do. If we could have another four or five weeks before Musso (or Musso & Hitler) launched a big attack on Egypt we ought to be able to do a great deal more. (In this he was more cheerful than Churchill, who seemed to suggest that we should be able to do very little for some time.)

5.30 P.M. LESLIE HORE-BELISHA AT 10 DOWNING STREET

Hore-Belisha had not been included in the National government and never was. Churchill had not forgotten the rows between Hore-Belisha and the generals and in any case did not believe in buying over his critics. Hore-Belisha remained throughout the war in impotent opposition. Crozier's interviews with him have only a pathetic personal interest.

I was sitting in the waiting hall at No. 10 when the door of the Prime Minister's room opened and out came Hore-Belisha. He came over to speak to me and said 'What are *you* doing here?' I nodded at the door of the Prime Minister's room and said 'I'm seeing *him* for a few minutes.' 'Yes, I know', he said, 'but what are you seeing him *about*?' I said it was for a general talk about the war and he seemed a little disappointed (the reason appears later).

I asked him how he was and he said he was all right, but it was rather bitter to be doing nothing at a time when 'one feels that one really could help'. Then he said that he had found the Prime

Minister pretty cheerful and that the Cabinet was a 'one-man affair' completely. He himself thought that Hitler had suffered so severe a defeat in the air from August 8 to 18 that he would not attack in the same way again. What did he think Hitler would do? He replied, 'Probably go for us in Southern Europe most likely through Spain, won't he?'

I asked him if he was going to Wimbledon on Saturday morning, because if so I could not get out to see him as it would take too long. He said he was, but would I come round to his house in Stafford Place for a few minutes as soon as I had left the PM, and I said I would if I had time.

Then I went into the Prime Minister.

5.30 P.M. WINSTON CHURCHILL, PM AT 10 DOWNING STREET

First half in Crozier's handwriting.

As usual, he offered me a whisky and soda, and I said I did not take these things. Why? I said I did not care for them and I had had trouble with an ulcer. 'Whisky supposed to be bad for it?' he said. I said yes. 'It would probably be the very best thing for it', he said with a grin.

He referred to the 'air battle' from August 8 to August 18 and said we had done well. 'But I don't think it's over. Some people do. They say that he has had such a dose that he won't come again. But I'm not at all so sure about that. I rather think he'll make another attempt.' I said—'Invasion?' and he replied 'I certainly cannot believe that he will attempt to invade us without trying again to establish superiority in the air—*that* he must have.' Talking about the German losses of August 8–18 he said that on English soil alone—apart from the sea—we had recovered the bodies of 150 German airmen.[1]

He referred to the Mediterranean and I asked whether we should be reinforcing our forces in Africa before the Italians began their attack. He was not encouraging about that; he said we could not easily send troops and that we had to be careful to keep adequate air forces here against the German attack. 'No use to strengthen Egypt at the cost of running risks at the heart of the whole business.' He referred again, as on the last occasion when I

---

1. Typescript from here. The first phase of the battle of Britain ran from 13 to 18 August. On 18 August fighter command destroyed 71 German aircraft for the loss of 27. This was even better than the great day of 15 September (60 to 26) which ended the battle.

saw him, to the bad effect of the loss of the French Mediterranean bases. I enquired whether there was any sign that Italy was in any way being reinforced by Germany in the Mediterranean, e.g. in the air, and he said No, there was as yet no sign. If Greece were attacked by Italy we should gain a certain advantage by acquiring air bases nearer to Italy.

As to the USA he had no reluctance whatever to let them have bases on our West Indian islands. But he wanted 'the fifty destroyers' badly and he was very anxious that Roosevelt should be able to give them to us without having to go to Congress about it. That would be troublesome and might involve delays. He thought that it would be managed. 'You can never have too many destroyers', he said.

In a further reference to our Air Force, he said emphatically 'And it's larger now this evening, than it has ever been—larger than it has ever been since the war began.' I said 'after all our losses in the recent big battle?' and he replied 'After all our losses.'

He spoke of Duff Cooper and his present unpopularity and said that D C had done very well at the start.

In his last speech he had said that the invincibility of the British Empire inspired hope in many millions of the oppressed, and I told him of a passage in Milton's Samson Agonistes which expressed the same sentiment, used some of the same terms and spoke of God striking with 'winged expedition' at the oppressors. He read the passage with signs of great satisfaction and asked if he might keep the copy.[1]

ABOUT 6.15 P.M. LESLIE HORE-BELISHA

In Crozier's handwriting.

As I had a few minutes to spare after leaving the PM and before seeing Dulanty I went off to see Hore-Belisha at 16 Stafford Place. He was just about to leave for Old Warren Farm at Wimbledon but would not go till we had had a talk.

He was eager to know whether the PM had talked about the

---

1. Samson Agonistes, 11. 1283–86:

> With winged expedition
> Swift as the lightning glance He executes
> His errand on the wicked, who surprised
> Lose their defence distracted and amazed.

The quotation was probably too high-falutin' for Churchill, and he did not use it in any of his speeches.

'reconstruction' of the Cabinet and disappointed when I said that he had not. So he began to talk about it himself. He thought that there must be reconstruction soon as Chamberlain was going. The question was whether the PM would be able to reconstruct according to his own wishes and according to the merits of the available people. He was afraid that he would be prevented from doing so by the claims of the party machine, i.e. the Tory machine and by the dictatorship exercised by Captain Margesson. It would be 'monstrous' if the principle of a party balance in the Government had to be so rigidly maintained that Churchill could not choose the best men for the jobs, and this was now to be feared. (The Beaverbrook talk explains all this.[1]) He clearly implied that Churchill would *like* to make certain appointments but could not do so, or was likely to be prevented from doing so, by Captain Margesson and the 'machine'.

Then he gave some views of the existing Ministers, in order to show how defensive the present effort was. Herbert Morrison he described as a 'complete failure'; he had become suspicious of him when, only three weeks after he took office, as Minister of Supply, he had described the large improvements that had already taken place in his province. Morrison was all right, no doubt, as an Administrator in some such post as Minister of Health, but he was not 'creative'. Eden also was a failure; 'he hasn't given us an army; at the present time we haven't an army' (he did not particularise).

The PM, when he had seen him earlier, had been 'very friendly' to him. Then he mentioned that Beaverbrook, on the day that he entered the War Cabinet,[2] had called for him at the Farm, had taken him out to dine in the country, and had told him all about Chamberlain etc. Chamberlain had actually resigned at that time, but now he seems to be disposed to go back on his letter and to hang on.[3] He himself had had a letter from Chamberlain that day which ended 'I hope to return in about ten days', but what, he asked me, did that mean? Return to London, to work, to his job in the Cabinet? It was clearly a matter of great concern to him.

When I was leaving he spoke of his work in criticising the Government and said he had been the first in Parliament to point out that Duff Cooper was after a compulsory censorship. 'And now,' I said, 'he suggests there was no truth in the report'.

---

1. See 24 August.

2. Beaverbrook became a member of the war cabinet on 2 August.

3. Chamberlain, though in fact mortally ill, believed at this time that he could recover. He resigned on 2 October.

Inferences. Churchill and Beaverbrook would like to have Belisha back in the Government. The going of Chamberlain *might* open the way for it. Belisha hopes so, and that he might even get into the War Cabinet. The Tory party machine is insisting on the rigid maintenance of Tory representation in the War Cabinet, to Churchill's embarrassment. Churchill has been discussing prospects but *only vaguely* with H B, who does not know what exactly is coming or when.

6.45 P.M. J W DULANTY

In Mrs Crozier's handwriting.

He looked tired and when I asked him how he was, said 'Dead beat! I had been hoping to get away for a week in the country but I'm afraid its unlikely now owing to the trouble I'm having over the trade agreement with England. Its been hanging fire, you know, for some months now.'

'A question of the price to be paid, isn't it, for Irish produce into this country?'

'Yes, but more than that. I've been discussing it now for some weeks with Woolton the Food Minister. I used to know him years ago when he was at the Settlement in Liverpool. Now, when he talks to me about this question of price he always says "I'm just a business man; I look at this question from the business man's point of view; to me it's all a matter of the market price; I don't know anything about politics." He was dining with me the other night at the Athenaeum and he talked in this way until, at last, I lost patience and I said "I've been listening to you for three weeks talking about your being a business man and having nothing to do with politics and I'm tired of it."

'Nothing to do with politics!' said Dulanty 'and here are we in Eire who, in negotiating over this business with England, have agreed to joint action with her over freights and ships and purchases of various kinds, all in order to avoid competition and not to raise rates against her, and then to be told "I've no concern with politics!" ' But, he went on 'I'm afraid that the agreement won't go through after all because the British Government are now asking another (political) concession from us and I don't believe De Valera will accept it.'

.   .   .   .   .

Talking of English politics he referred to Beaverbrook. Beaverbrook had tracked him down one night at 10.30 to his club, the Athenaeum (which he said Beaverbrook called the Athenium). He found that Beaverbrook had been after him at his house and at his office before that. Beaverbrook wanted Dulanty to get some kind of 'concession' from the Eire Government which Dulanty said was 'small but quite impossible' and he had to tell Beaverbrook so. Beaverbrook replied that if he and De Valera could only get together all would be well but added 'De Valera doesn't know me.' 'I thought', said Dulanty, of saying to him 'and you don't know De Valera!'[1]

24 August 1940

12 NOON. LORD BEAVERBROOK AT IMPERIAL CHEMICALS HOUSE

IC House was the headquarters of the ministry of aircraft production. The interview gives a very good impression of Beaverbrook's method of working. It is tantalising that Crozier only gives initials to the other persons mentioned, and meaningless initials at that. Crozier may have met Beaverbrook previously over newspaper business.

His secretary had rung me up some days before about midnight to confirm the appointment and had mentioned that I might possibly have to wait a few minutes, as Beaverbrook had many interviews not all of which could be accurately estimated. I therefore got to the ICH at ten minutes to 12. After a few minutes in the waiting room I was told that Beaverbrook was almost ready and I went along to see him. He has a suite of four rooms opening into one another. A small room where a woman secretary is seated leads to one in which there were four men secretaries and another woman. This led to an inner room, where three or four people were sitting waiting for audience, and this again into a large room in which Beaverbrook works.

I had been in the secretary's room about a minute when Beaverbrook said he was ready and I went in to him. He was sitting at one side of an immense desk, with an Air Marshal covered with ribbons at the other side. Both of them had pads in front of them and were making notes. Beaverbrook got up, shook hands, said he was delighted to see me, pulled up a chair to the side of the desk for me to sit on, sat down himself again and resumed his discussion with the Air Marshal. I wondered whether he was

---

1. It is impossible to say what this small but quite impossible concession was.

proposing to talk with me while talking to the Air Marshal at the same time, but this was not his intention. He introduced me to the Air Marshal, Sir ABC, and then said to him 'I think I told you that I had an appointment with Mr Crozier at twelve o'clock, and so I've brought him in now because I don't want to keep him waiting.' The Air Marshal said nothing and went on with his points, but in a minute or two he said, 'That's all, I think', and departed.

Beaverbrook's conversation with the Air Marshal was most instructive about his methods. When I went in they were discussing some sort of gadget or other. It went like this:

B   'Well, it will be either the ABC or the XY.'

AM 'The XY! I know the ABC—I don't think I know the XY.'

B   'You don't know the XY! Oh, you ought to know the XY. Better find out about it at once. You had better go down to——and Z will tell you all about it. You can go down this afternoon? You will fly down, of course? Then you will hear all about it at once and settle the matter.' He pressed a button and a secretary with a notebook appeared behind me. Beaverbrook said 'Let Z know at once that the Air Marshal will be flying down this afternoon to see him and that he is to let him know all about XY.' 'Yes, sir,' said the secretary.

The full effect that Beaverbrook produces can only be understood if it is remembered that he talks the whole time in a strong American-Canadian accent, that his voice is harsh and his manner always incisive and sometimes abrupt. When he wants to emphasise something he raises his voice and almost barks out what he has to say. He makes an impression also by the fixed and penetrating eye which he turns on the person to whom he is talking.[1]

And then, said the Air Marshal, we want machinery for emptying aeroplane tanks quickly.

'Why?' said Beaverbrook.

'We already,' said the Air Marshal, 'have machinery for filling tanks quickly, and now we want it for emptying them. Because, an aeroplane can be mended if it is splintered, but not if it is burned out.'

Beaverbrook made a note, and the Air Marshal left.

'Come outside, Mr Crozier', said Beaverbrook and led the way to the balcony, where he leaned on the railing looking out on the

---

1. From here in Crozier's handwriting.

Embankment Gardens. 'It's the curse of my life', he said, 'having to talk to these Air Marshals for an hour or two hours every morning. I have to do it to keep the machine running smoothly but I can't bear having to sit down and listen to them talking, talking, talking.'—Then 'I'd like to get back to newspaper work', he said.

'Well, perhaps you will before long.'

'Why, do you think they're going to kick me out?'

'No, but people say so much about your performing miracles in producing aircraft that I thought you might have some more up your sleeve. But, seriously, what does your being in the War Cabinet mean? Does it mean that you are going to leave the Aircraft Production Ministry? I hope not, because it seems to me incredible that there isn't a vast amount still to be done there and, if you have been as successful as they say, I should have thought that was a reason why you should stay on.'

'I don't want to go at all. I want to stick at this job. It isn't at all true that things have now got so far advanced that everything will be all right. We are in a most dangerous position. I have no doubt that Germany will mobilise the industrial resources of Belgium and France to build aeroplanes against us and that will mean a great addition to their numbers. Another thing is the immense number of planes which we have to send to Canada for the training scheme.[1] Besides, there's a new job we've now got to tackle—the problem of *dispersal*. We've got to think of dispersing some of our works and sections of production so that they won't be so easily found and damaged. They [the Germans] are beginning to find our works now. They destroyed the —— works on the ——, and they've dropped 18 bombs on the —— factory. We've got to make up for that sort of thing, and we've got to hide our stuff away and "disperse" some of it as well.'

I said that the supply of training machines would repay itself in time. He said 'Yes, but the drain at the present time is very serious.'

Then he went on—'I don't want to go into the War Cabinet. But as soon as I started getting some success with this production business Churchill began to put one piece of work on me after another, until at last he wanted to bring me into the War Cabinet. And when I didn't want to go in he said that no one would ever do what he wanted, and so I had to give way.'

'Well', I said, 'is he going to reconstruct his Ministry? Chamber-

1. Beaverbrook was strongly opposed to this.

lain is going, so they say, and perhaps Halifax with him, and in that case there will have to be reconstruction, won't there?'

Beaverbrook 'I don't think there's going to be reconstruction —because I don't think there's anything to reconstruct. Chamberlain—well, he hasn't exactly resigned [see my talk with Belisha on the day before] but it doesn't matter, it makes no difference whether he has resigned or not, or whether he does resign or not', —here he raised his voice with a dramatic harshness—'he's done, he's finished, you need not reckon with him any more as a force in politics—he's got cancer of the bowels—he's finished—you can wipe him out in politics!'

'The same thing as Bonar Law then', I said (Bonar Law had cancer of the throat) 'and discovered, as with him, suddenly when he was Prime Minister.'

'And by the same man,' said Beaverbrook, 'both by Lord Horder.'

'And about Halifax?' I said, 'Will he go too?'

Beaverbrook 'I don't know that he would resign *because* of Chamberlain's going but I think it very likely that he would take the occasion to tell Churchill that if it would ease his task in constructing his Ministry he would be very pleased to resign his office.[1] For myself I hope that Halifax will *not* go. Who've you got' he said abruptly 'to put in his place?'

I said that Eden had been mentioned and, by some, Sinclair.

Beaverbrook 'Eden can't be spared: He oughtn't to be moved from the War Office. He's doing a fine job there. I can tell you that when I took office I regarded Eden with great suspicion; I didn't think anything of him. But now I think he's a good man. He knows his job, he sticks to it, and he knows his own mind and sticks to his opinion; he can, and does, defend it against others. Sinclair's a fine fellow, I like him; he's always cheerful and pleasant but there's one thing about him—he'll come along and state his view and set it out and defend it and then he'll go away and talk to one of his Air Marshals and then you'll find he isn't prepared to defend his view any longer—his Air Marshal has changed his opinion for him!'

Then he began to describe Churchill's difficulties—'He wanted to bring Herbert Morrison into the War Cabinet recently. [It was not clear but, adding in what Belisha had said, I surmise that Churchill, on getting Chamberlain's letter of resignation, on which Chamberlain afterwards went back, had then designed to bring

1. Halifax made no attempt to resign when Chamberlain went.

in Morrison.] But the Tory "machine" would not let him. The Tory managers, Kingsley Wood, Captain Margesson and others, held a meeting and decided that to have Morrison brought in would disturb the balance of parties in the War Cabinet and they would not have it. But'—he raised his voice again—'they decided that it would be all right for me to be brought in as a Tory, and when I heard that I was regarded as a representative of the Tory party I gave the biggest laugh that has ever been heard', and at this he laughed loudly again and again. 'Well, I'll tell you one thing, Mr Crozier, I'm not nearly such a Conservative as Herbert Morrison!'

He spoke of other Ministers. He has no opinion of Greenwood[1] but thinks very highly of Attlee[2]—a first-class man, he said, clear-headed and good in council. Chamberlain he greatly admires. 'I can tell you this, he's splendid at his job, strong and clear in judgment and in action.' He gave an appreciative laugh as he spoke of Chamberlain, as though he was remembering some good experiences.

Alexander, too, he thinks is first-rate. He has a 'fixation' about his job; he does it thoroughly, he doesn't bother much about things outside it; he stands up well for himself.

'But', he said, 'the man whom I regard as coming to the front in everything that relates to the war is the Chief of Fighter Command, Air Marshal Sir Hugh Dowding. He's a great fellow! There's no idea that he won't try. You tell him that there's some gun or gadget that is said to be useful and he'll have it on a plane the next morning and try it out at once. Do you know him? You ought to! I'll fix up an interview for you with him if you'll let me know the day. You'll see him? Right, let me know and I'll fix it up at once.'

A secretary came to the balcony 'New York on the telephone, Sir.' We went in, and I made as to go. 'No, no', he said, 'sit down, Mr Crozier, and stay a little longer.' He indicated a chair.

'That you, X?[1] Yeah, yeah. Well, when can they begin? I said, when—can—they—begin?—Yeah. How much? Well, we ought to get it settled. You go to Washington! Yeah, today. Can you go this morning? You'll fly of course. Yeah, fly this morning! Then you can settle it this afternoon and let me know this evening the result. Yeah, this evening!'

---

1. Arthur Greenwood, minister without portfolio and a member of the war cabinet.

2. Beaverbrook did not retain this high opinion of Attlee if he ever had it.

3. Presumably Morris Wilson, Beaverbrook's buying agent for MAP in the United States.

Enter secretary Sir D E F, sir, Air Marshal Sir G H I, and
           Mr J K L.

Beaverbrook   Bring them in. Sit down, Gentlemen, I'm on
                the phone now to New York. We're just
                settling it. Production begins by January.

Sir D E F   Delivery begins by January?

I got and made as to go. 'No, no', he said, 'sit down Mr Crozier.
It'll do you good to hear of our difficulties. Won't it?'—to the
three gents. 'Oh, let me introduce you, Mr Crozier, Sir D E F,
Air Marshal Sir G H I, and Mr J K L.' They all shake hands, the
Air Marshal somewhat coldly, as I thought.

Sir D E F   Delivery begins by January?

Beaverbrook   *Production* begins by January? USA Govern-
                ment manufacture priority for us. 400 to 500
                million dollars—say 80 million £.

Sir D E F   We'll have the result this weekend?

Beaverbrook   This weekend! We'll hear it this evening! X is
                flying to Washington this morning. It's 7.30
                in New York now. He'll get a plane by 9.30
                or 10; he'll be in Washington and settle it this
                afternoon, and he'll telephone the result to
                me this evening. (He gave them a decisive,
                final look which conveyed that that was that
                and all was settled.)

Sir D E F   (then said) Can you give us an assurance that
                we shall have fifty per cent delivered by ——?

Beaverbrook   I can give you no assurance of anything
                beyond what I have said. With these Ameri-
                cans—! [He looked volumes but said nothing
                more. (On the balcony he had said 'these
                Americans are a tough lot; they drive a mighty
                hard bargain with us.' He seemed to have no
                great love for them in these matters.)]

He pressed a button and a secretary appeared. Beaverbrook
said, 'Was that my call to New York or X's?'

The secretary   'X's, I think, sir.

Beaverbrook   'Find out, will you.

Secretary, a few moments later It was your call, sir.

Beaverbrook   Well, tell Mr. Q, if he makes another call to X in
                New York for me, not to get X up quite so early—
                it's only 7.30 there now, and that's a bit too early.

Then we all filed out along with him. In the next room were half a dozen others waiting to see him. It made a remarkable impression on me to see him standing there with all these people (two Air Marshals included!) watching him with tremendous respect and deference; he stood quite still for a few seconds, saying nothing and no one venturing, apparently, to address him. Then I said goodbye, and he woke up. He said 'When are you coming again?' and then suddenly he introduced me to the half dozen strangers. Then he said 'When?' and I said 'Perhaps in 2 or 3 weeks.' 'Oh no', he said, 'you shouldn't wait as long as that. You must come up specially to see Dowding. You must come specially. Let me know and I'll arrange it. You'll find it worth while.'[1] He looked at me fixedly for a second or two and repeated 'I think you'll find it well worth while.'

---

1. There is no evidence that Crozier ever met Dowding.

5

Holding on, 1941

Once more Crozier's interviews break off in suspense. When the last set ended, the battle of Britain was still being fought. The interviews resume in January 1941. The battle of Britain had been won. Great Britain was enduring the winter of the Blitz. There were the first great victories in North Africa which did much to restore British spirits. As the interviews proceed, things go wrong again. The failures in Greece and Crete raised an alarm for the entire Middle East. Instead Hitler attacked Soviet Russia. Crozier's interviews during the autumn breathed a different spirit. Great Britain was no longer alone. But it was by no means certain that Soviet Russia would hold out, let alone defeat the German armies. These interviews are a useful reminder how the Soviet-German war appeared at the time. The British could do little or nothing to aid Soviet Russia and they often feared that Hitler might emerge from the Russian war stronger than before.

31 January 1941

11.00 A.M. SIR ARCHIBALD SINCLAIR

He said that he wanted to mention that one day recently the PM had referred 'in Cabinet' to an MG Leader and said it was very fine. I said no doubt it expressed Churchill's own views on the subject and that perhaps he did not think so highly of some others.

. . . .   .

We were becoming stronger as against the Germans all the time—he meant not merely in quality, where we retained our superiority, but in numbers. We should go on getting stronger in numbers during the coming months, but it would be with the autumn that we should have an 'immense acceleration'. The difficulty would be to get enough 'advanced trainer' machines—the aircraft on which the pilot had to complete his vital training over a matter of eight or ten weeks. This was the great problem. Beaverbrook had concentrated on getting Hurricanes and Spitfires for the fighting line and had grudged effort on these advanced trainers. This was quite natural, but it was a very serious matter, for we must have these machines in quantity.

.   .   .   .   .

He spoke of the tremendous strain put on our Air Force by the summer and autumn battles of last year—in France, at Dunkirk and over this country. He gave certain particulars about the effects of the German attacks and the measures which we had had to take . . . I asked why the Germans had not persisted a bit longer and he said 'Oh, they got hell.' Our reports of losses were accurate except that occasionally the same German victims might be claimed by more than one of our pilots; though checking was very carefully done. 'And they could not stand the rate of loss, especially as they got no profit out of the business.'

.   .   .   .   .

He spoke of the aircraft which the Germans had sent to the help of Italy and said that there were not yet so many of them as to make any real difference to what they could use against us.

.   .   .   .   .

Thus he did not think that any German diversion to the East or South would make it impossible for them to attack us at home if Hitler chose. He thought that Hitler *would* come to invading us. By no other means could he hope to win the war in 1941. Enterprises in the Mediterranean and the East would not do it. He thought, therefore, that Hitler would press on with the U-Boat war and bombing our industries, etc. and would hope so to wear us down as to give him a good chance of invasion. In his opinion Hitler had no chance of doing this in 1941. He agreed that Hitler must also try conclusions once more against our Air Force before he could try invasion and thought that eventually he would do so.

I asked whether in the spring the Germans would not seek on a much greater scale to bomb our shipping from the air and to use torpedo-carrying aircraft, which seemed to me much more dangerous. He said 'Yes, but it is hard to hit with torpedoes; they have a nasty trick of getting a slight deflection and just running past the target.' I said 'Taranto!' and he replied 'Well, you know, I think we were a bit lucky at Taranto.'[1]

If Hitler decided that he could not win the war in 1941 and must face a long war, then he thought it possible he would go for *Russia*. In this war Hitler would get supplies of the kind that he would need for a war not ending this year.

.   .   .   .   .

Sinclair said that Beaverbrook told his secretary to ring up some aircraft works and to say that the Directors were to come at once to see him. The secretary came back and reported that the Directors were not at the works. He was told to find out where they were and to insist that the message must be given to them. The reply came back that, being worn out with all their efforts, they had gone off to play a round of golf at a nearby links. Beaverbrook said that they were to be told to stop their golf and to come at once. They replied that they must have their little relaxation and that they would come when they had finished their round. Thereupon Beaverbrook got on the 'phone to the nearest police station and told the police to send out a posse and bring the Directors to him.

.   .   .   .   .

12.15 P.M. J W DULANTY

He attributed a great deal to Churchill's influence. I asked how Cranborne, the new Dominions Minister, impressed him.[2] He said that Cranborne would appear to agree with what he said and would say that he would bring it before the War Cabinet, but he doubted whether when he did so he showed much sympathy for the Irish point of view. He rather hinted that a Tory and a Cecil was not likely to help them much.

.   .   .   .   .

1. On 11 November 1940 British torpedo-carrying aircraft sank three Italian battleships at their moorings in Taranto harbour.
2. Viscount Cranborne (later 5th Marquis of Salisbury) became Dominions secretary on 3 October 1940.

Referring to Churchill's reference to Eire, he said it would have been all right if Churchill had intended to follow it up at once by seizing the ports, but that if it was only an outburst of anger it was a mistake as it only made bad blood. One of Churchill's colleagues had said to him that it was unfortunate.[1]

3.30 P.M. ANTHONY EDEN

Eden was now foreign secretary and a member of the war cabinet.

He said 'Well, you've had some fine Leaders in the MG lately. Have you seen Sinclair? He was going to tell you how the PM praised the MG in Cabinet.' Then he enquired about Manchester's Blitz and its effects on the papers.

He asked 'What shall we talk about first?' and I said 'Vichy.' 'Oh Vichy', he said. 'That's a very difficult business, we go on hoping but no one can be sure what's going to happen. The Vichy people are asking much too much of us—in respect of our blockade. They want us to say that *none* of their ships must be stopped and of course the threat is that if we refuse they will collaborate with Germany. I don't see why they should be allowed to blackmail us. And, of course, they threaten Germany that if she puts the screw on them too much the French Colonial Empire will revolt. I've just heard this afternoon that Pétain has been talking to Herriot. That might be helpful to us; I hope it is. Herriot has been in the cold; may be Pétain is anxious to enlist his support.' 'Or', I said, 'perhaps he is explaining that he will have to give way to Hitler and that he wants Herriot to know why.' 'May be', he said, 'we'll hope it isn't that. Almost all we have to hope now is that Pétain will be an obstinate old man and refuse to yield anything not in the Armistice. It's no use hoping for much from any of the gang round him, whether Flandin or anybody else. I don't know that Flandin would be very much better than Laval, whom I had to deal with at Geneva and after the Hoare-Laval business. Laval is a first-rate scoundrel, and also he's ignorant; he reads nothing.'[2] I said Laval had been described to me as living from one shift to

---

1. On 5 November 1940 Churchill said in the house of commons that denial of refueling facilities in Eire was 'a most grievous and heavy burden, and one which should never have been placed on our shoulders, broad though they be'.

2. Laval had been vice-premier and virtual head of the Vichy government since the Franco-German armistice. Pétain dismissed him on 13 December 1940 and appointed Flandin who was expected to be less pro-German. The Germans however refused to accept Flandin and he resigned on 9 February, when his place was taken by Admiral Darlan.

another, and he said it was a good description. Germany wanted
Laval back in the French Cabinet but he thought Pétain might
continue to refuse. There was little doubt that Laval had tried to
put some crooked scheme over and to get Pétain to Paris for some
evil motive—hence his fall. But he repeated that even if Laval did
not return to the Government the whole Vichy gang were a bad
lot from our point of view. Among them, Darlan, who was anti-
British not merely because of Oran;[1] he was anti-British in himself.

Pétain, of course, had the childish idea of 'as one soldier to
another'! Goering was a Field Marshal and so was Pétain, therefore they could get on together and deal honourably with each
other! Still, Pétain's obstinacy might do us service. The other
possibility was Weygand and the North African Colonies.[2] The
FO, as I no doubt knew, had asked the Press not to talk about
Weygand. It was most undesirable that papers should suggest
that Weygand might hold up the African Colonies against
Germany. Germany might decide to demand Weygand's recall
from Pétain, and that was not at all what we desired. There was a
growing anti-Axis feeling in North Africa, especially in Tunis.
Opinion there was, and must be, powerfully affected by (1) our
victories in Libya (2) the part played by the Free French there.
The Free French force with Wavell was small but really good—
he had seen it. Both in France and in Africa its doings would be
heard of with pride—and this had to be taken into account by
Pétain and the Vichy gang. When we got full reports about the
campaign we should hear a good deal more about the Free French
contribution.

What did Germany want of Vichy now? It was *not* certain that
Germany had ever asked directly for the French Fleet or the
French bases, but he felt pretty sure that what she was after now,
though she might not have made the formal request, was facilities
in Tunis (Bizerta) so that she could get across to Tunis and help
Italy to hold out in Africa. He thought it was a serious matter.
I said it looked as though Germany had intervened too late to
save Western Libya (Benghazi),[3] and he said 'Yes, but she might
save Tripoli.' I said that it looked to me difficult for us to go after
Tripoli across 600 miles of desert and that, if we tried to take it,

---

1. Sinking of French battleships by a British fleet in the preceding July. (See p. 182).
2. Weygand was French commander-in-chief in North Africa. There were unfounded
hopes that he would turn against the Germans.
3. British forces entered Benghazi on 7 February.

we should perhaps attack it by expedition from the sea. He said he thought that was a shrewd suggestion. He had no knowledge that Hitler had yet sent his reply to Pétain *via* Brinon. It was to our advantage here that we were fighting German bombers in the Mediterranean. It was the first time in the war that we had forced the Germans to reply to *our* movements. They had had to get to the Mediterranean to try to thwart what we were doing and that so far was satisfactory.

.   .   .   .   .

The credit for the plan of the campaign was mainly Wilson's (of course Wavell deserved credit too but he had to plan for most of Africa—Sudan, Kenya, etc.). Wilson had planned the great attack.[1] The British army was very small—about half the Italian army at Sidi Barani—but the quality was great. Wavell and the others in November had expected the Italians to advance and attack. He had asked Wavell what he would do if they did not after all attack, and Wavell had said 'Well I think we shall have to go after them.' It would be most important if we could get the Italians out of North Africa.

'What worries me most', he went on, 'is what is going to happen in the Balkans. The loss of Metaxas[2] is serious. His successors will stand firm all right but I don't know who is going to fill his place. He was a remarkable personality in many ways, and we can only hope that the Greeks will throw up somebody good. I remember, by the way, the discussion which, four years ago, we used to have with you here about the methods of his dictatorship.'

'The Germans', he went on, 'are steadily increasing their numbers in Rumania and are "infiltrating" into Bulgaria. They will try to take Bulgaria from within. They will only go through Bulgaria when they think it is ripe for it and I doubt whether Bulgaria will resist if that comes. I have been working on all four of them—Greece, Bulgaria, Yugo-Slavia, and Turkey—to stand together, but I don't know whether it will succeed.'

.   .   .   .   .

---

1. Wavell was commander-in-chief, Middle East, and Maitland Wilson commander-in-chief, Egypt. The chief credit for the successful plan seems to lie lower down the scale.

2. Greek prime minister, died 29 January 1941.

Then there was Russia. We couldn't do anything with Russia. He wanted to get on good terms with her but he could make nothing of her. Neither could Cripps[1] who had done all he could. Stalin was inscrutable. (He laughed heartily at the report that he was a favourite of Stalin's.) The top and bottom of it was that Russia was afraid of Germany and would do anything to avoid offending her. The best that we could hope was that Russia would let Turkey alone if Turkey went into the war. He thought that she might, but one could not be sure. It was possible that, being afraid of Germany attacking the Ukraine, etc. (which Germany could easily do) Russia would agree to stab Turkey in the back if Germany attacked the Straits and made for the oil of the Middle East. Maisky spoke sensibly about German incursions into the Balkans and about Russia's position—but Maisky didn't know anything about what was going on and being thought in Moscow.

.   .   .   .   .

I asked what *decisive* aid towards winning the war Hitler could hope to get by campaigning in the Balkans and going south-east. He said that was the point; he had been debating this at length with the PM yesterday. He thought *no decisive gain*—that was the point against it—but he would gain bases in the Aegean and defy us to put him out; he would get oil from Irak; and he might try for the Ukraine also, Russia being no formidable opponent. [Sinclair thought Hitler *might* go for Russia.] He did not think that Germany could run *two* major campaigns—a big one in the East and an invasion one against us.

.   .   .   .   .

20 March 1941

11.30 A.M. SIR ARCHIBALD SINCLAIR

Increased strength of the RAF. Shortage of pilots now being overcome.

1.30 P.M. WINSTON CHURCHILL

I was waiting in the open lounge outside the PM's room when Sir Arthur Salter[2] came along. It seemed that he too was coming

---

1. Sir Stafford Cripps was British ambassador in Moscow.
2. Parliamentary secretary to the ministry of shipping.

to lunch. It had been announced that he was shortly going to the USA on shipping questions, so I said to him 'You are going soon, I suppose?'

He lowered his voice discreetly and said 'As a matter of fact, I'm going tomorrow.'

I said, for the sake of something to say 'By Clipper, I suppose?' and he laughed and said 'Well—er—I've been warned by the Admiralty that it would be better not to say how I am going.'

Presently the butler took us downstairs—two flights below ground, along a corridor, through two doors and into a very pleasant room which was on the same level as the garden at the side of the house (level of the Horse Guards' Parade). The walls and one or two pillars supporting the ceiling were in white paint and the sun was pouring in through the one window—the whole effect very pleasant. There was a fire at the left hand side of the room and a book case along another, with about a dozen or two books in it. I should say that perhaps the room had only lately been prepared for occupation. There were some daffodils in vases and Salter and I talked pleasantly and without indiscretion about bulbs in London and the north—he had actually seen some in bloom in the open etc.—and the prospective lateness of the spring. Churchill was kept at the House and arrived in about ten minutes. He advanced across the room with hand outstretched and a curious fixed, penetrating stare. He asked the butler 'Where is Mrs Churchill' and when the butler replied 'She is lunching out, sir' he said, 'Good, we'll be able to have a lot of politics.'

Then we sat down. The butler and a parlour maid both wore white gloves during the meal with the wrists unbuttoned, an old custom preserved either at No. 10 or by the Churchills.

He began to talk about what had been happening at the House that morning.

He said that he could see no reason why people who were opposed to the war and desired to obstruct our war effort should be allowed to hold posts at the BBC. I did not know what he was referring to, as this point had only turned up in the House that morning, so I said 'Well, anyway there is no reason, is there, why the BBC should refuse to allow musicians to perform their music simply because they happened to be pacifists!', and he said 'Oh, no, there is nothing at all to be said for that.' Then he added 'I dealt with both points this morning and you will see what I have said. I think you will approve of it.'

What Churchill actually said was (1) that avowed pacifists should not hold technical or similar jobs at the BBC, and (2) that the BBC should not ban musicians because they held pacifist views.

Later on, when some reference was made to the Dictators 'bumping off" people who were politically dangerous, he said 'It's not the dangerous people I would bump off, but the nuisances.'

.   .   .   .   .

He spoke hopefully about the United States. 'I don't agree', he said, 'with the ordinary view that it would be better for us if the United States didn't come into the war, on the ground that they can give us more help in war materials by remaining out. It is much more important that they should come in, and,' he added, 'I believe they will.' And then, slowly and with much emphasis, '*I'm sure* that they'll come in.'

He turned and said to Salter 'When are you going?' and Salter said 'Tomorrow morning.' Then, to my amusement, he said 'Ah, and how are you going? By Clipper?' and Salter replied 'Well, no; I've been told that I'd better go by ship. I'm going by so-and-so.' 'Ah', said Churchill. 'Cras ingens tentabimus aequor.' He said that you could not quote the classics in the House now. Salter added 'No, nor the Bible either!' I said 'why not?' and he answered, 'Because scarcely any of them know it. It's not read.' Salter added that he doubted whether any one could be a great speaker in English who did not know his Bible.

Then he spoke again of the United States. I had remarked that it was remarkable how Hitler had put up with every kind of breach of neutrality on the part of the United States and had scarcely even protested. Hitler had said scarcely a word until the other day when he had threatened that the U-boats would sink any ships that came across. 'No', Churchill said, 'he doesn't protest much because the last thing that he wants is that the United States should come into the war, and it is a good general rule that one should want and desire what the enemy clearly desires to avoid.'

Talking of opinion in America he said that he himself dated the decisive trend of it towards us from the moment when over there they heard of what we had done at Oran.[1] The Americans appreciated ruthlessness in war and they were up to that time

---

1. Sinking of the French battleships. This was also the first occasion when Conservative MPs gave Churchill unequivocal support.

doubtful whether we could be ruthless in order to save ourselves. They were converted when they heard that we had gone for the French battleships and when they knew that we would *do anything* rather than go down. He was at this moment looking straight towards the fire with me on his right hand a few feet away, and he turned suddenly towards me, looked straight[1] at me, and said with what was an almost savage glare—'and we will! We will do anything!'

Then he went back to the dreadful time when France surrendered. He himself had thought that we might perhaps rescue 100,000 men from Dunkirk and how the result had exceeded his expectation. He said that when he told the Cabinet that in spite of the defection of France we should fight on there had been a remarkable scene in the Cabinet. He had never seen such a display of profound emotion in a Government as he saw then. And what a change was there now! Then we had been in a desperate position, alone and expecting invasion. Now we were conducting war over half the world. Who would ever have believed that there could be such a change! It was the character of the British people that had done it. 'They are tough, immensely tough.' He thought they were the 'toughest people that existed anywhere'.

With regard to the Battle of the Atlantic he said 'We have a good lot of people at the Admiralty, a really good lot, and we shall pull through—I know we shall pull through.' He stopped and said 'But only just.' He spoke of Roosevelt, and the question whether he would convoy ships to this country. He thought he would, but, he said, he could not move until public opinion fully supported him. He had the *power* to convoy if he chose. Salter said he thought that this would be the way in which the United States would come into the war. They would convoy some merchantmen, the Germans would sink an American warship, then the United States would be at war. 'No', said Churchill, 'that does not necessarily follow according to present ideas. The Americans might sink a submarine and Hitler need not consider it an act of war unless he wanted to be at war. Equally, the Germans might sink an American warship, and the United States might not call it war unless it suited their plans to do so.'[2] The Americans had the crusading spirit; some day 'the fire would catch' and there was no doubt what they would do then.

---

1. From this point in Crozier's handwriting.

2. Churchill was correct. The sinking of an American warship, the Reuben James, on 31 October 1941 did not provoke an American declaration of war.

He was not in favour of a statement of peace aims. Something had actually been drawn up but he did not like it. The necessary thing was to win the war, and any statement of peace aims would either be a collection of platitudes or would be dangerous to the present unity. We did not want a statement that dealt with any of the hotly disputed things in domestic affairs, and it was going to be difficult at the end of the war not to have a breach on questions like property and Socialism. We could not expect the Conservatives to swallow the things that would be put forward by the Socialists. Some of the poor wretches were already taxed up to 18s. 6d. in the £. He could not have anything to do with Socialism. What he felt was that Socialism would impair or destroy the individual initiative of millions of small people in the country, which was an immense element in the national strength.

He spoke of the Italians in Africa and said fiercely 'We shall have them out completely', and then, going on to speak of the Italian people and the Germans in Italy he said, 'They hate, and must hate, the swaggering, beastly Germans.' He referred to the Voelkischer Beobachter, called it comething like 'Bobobachter' and said 'I can never pronounce their beastly language.'

.   .   .   .   .

He asked Salter to write to Beaverbrook or to go and see him and make it clear that he was not going to do anything in the United States that would encroach on Beaverbrook's field. 'I don't want to do anything that might upset him. He has had a bad time this winter. No, it's not duodenal ulcer; it's asthma, which won't let him sleep o' nights, and he has been working very hard at his Ministry. I don't want him upset. He's wanting to resign every week now.'[1]

Referring to the Burma Road he said that 'we were right to close it and we are right to open it'.

He referred to the sinking of three U-boats which had been attacking a convoy and said that five U-boats had been attacking together. We had lost five or six merchantmen but it was well worth while.

He showed me the letter that he had received from Roosevelt through Wilkie—the letter containing the Longfellow verse.[2] He

---

1. Beaverbrook did not send any letters of resignation between 6 January and 29 April when he actually resigned as minister of aircraft production.
2. 'Sail on, O ship of State!' etc.

had had it framed. On the other side was the address—'To . . . .',[1] the secret name by which his messages were always conveyed to Roosevelt. He also showed us a letter he had had from the Queen —also framed—in which she quoted a long piece from Wordsworth. He mentioned that at a suitable opportunity he was going to quote a passage from A H Clough, and he declaimed it to us (just as he declaimed some sentences that he was going to use in the next debate on war aims)—

> And not by Eastern windows only,
>   When daylight comes, comes in the light,
> In front, the sun climbs slow, how slowly,
>   But westward look, the land is bright.

He sat up with animation, using lively gestures as he recited. Then he said to me 'Mind you don't use that verse before I've quoted it!'[2]

Referring to racing, he said that it was absolutely essential to give the people recreation and among them must be racing; he hoped that we were not going to demand that all racing should be stopped. I mentioned the 'Dogs' and that they were almost entirely a matter of betting, but he denied any knowledge of that particular sport. He was in favour of Sunday theatres; he thought that the living theatre ought to be protected and he said that there was to be a free vote on the subject in the House. Salter commented that he did not think there would be any opposition to the opening of theatres on Sunday. (The proposal was lost when it came to the vote.) He thought that there was very little opposition in the country nowadays to Sunday entertainments and expressed surprise when I told him about the Puritan opposition in places like Manchester.

Churchill expressed great admiration for Smuts and then for Menzies and the Australians. He said that they were 'magnificent' people. He referred to their achievements at cricket, but he had no use himself for the game. 'You can have it', he said, 'so far as I am concerned. I've never liked it.'

He protested vigorously when I would have neither wine nor brandy and said he was sure they would do me good. Then he said pathetically 'Well, I work very hard and I think I am entitled to a little.' When he found that I did not smoke either he looked hard at me and said 'Good God, man, you have got nothing that you can give up.'

---

1. Former naval person.
2. Churchill used these lines in a broadcast on 27 April.

When the siren went he went to the window and looked out
and said, 'I wonder what it is all about, I wonder where they are.'
He rang and a secretary came in. He asked for information. The
secretary said, 'A single 'plane, Sir, approaching London from the
north-east.' He commented 'What a cheek! The sky over London
belongs to the RAF—at any rate in the day-time.'

Wanting to remember something, he very solemnly fished a
handkerchief out of his pocket and tied a knot in it, admitting that
he would probably not be able to remember what he had tied the
knot for.

3.30 P.M. A V ALEXANDER

Progress in the battle of the Atlantic.

4.00 P.M. SIR ROBERT VANSITTART

Interview not held or record lost.

21 May 1941

11.00 A.M. J G WINANT

Winant was American ambassador in London from 1941 to 1946. He advised
that the British press should emphasise the German threat to the security of the
United States.

LUNCH. LORD BEAVERBROOK

Beaverbrook was now minister of state with vaguely defined powers of supervision over war production.

I called for him at 1.20 at the offices of the War Cabinet as I was
to lunch with him at 1.30. We walked along what seemed to be
miles of stone corridor with endless rooms bearing the names of
Advisers and all that. He stopped at one door and said 'Lindemann! Let's ask him what the news is about Crete.'[1] He opened
the door and let out a loud shout, and then seeing that there were
other people inside he shut the door and said 'Let's wait, he'll
come out.' Presently Lindemann did come out and said he had
heard nothing so far and was going downstairs to find out. We

---

1. F A Lindemann, later Lord Cherwell, was Churchill's closest adviser. German
parachute landings on Crete began on 20 May. By the evening of 21 May the Germans
were already landing troop-carriers on the captured airfield of Maleme. British forces
finally withdrew from Crete on 27 May.

then went out and through the Foreign Office quadrangle into the top of Downing Street. As we emerged from the arch, Eden was coming out of No. 10 and B shouted at him loudly and then more loudly and Eden crossed over to speak to us. He was asked what the news was about Crete, and said 'Touch and go; it's going to be a very tough job.' He added that so far the Germans had not yet got any troops over by sea. He then added that he had been trying to get in touch with me as a Defence Committee had been called for 3 p.m., which was the time of my appointmen with him.

We then entered No. 12, where he took me into a large room on the ground floor. There was a long table and a few chairs and nothing else. He said that he had been bombed out of his home, and then out of the flat into which he had moved, so Churchill had placed this room at his disposal as an office. He seemed to be amused by the idea of its being his 'office'. I asked him about his health and he said that it was not too grand. He had had two operations recently, one of them to an eye which had been very painful and was not yet completely right again.

.   .   .   .   .

He mentioned that he had on the day before been having a long talk with American newspapermen in London. They were disgruntled because they didn't get enough news or enough of anything to send home and he was doing what he could to make things better for them. They had bombarded him with questions. 'They certainly gave me a tough time.' 'They must have material for their messages and it had somehow to be provided for them.' The real trouble lay with the Services, which were so horribly secretive. He was trying to do something now to make them more communicative. Ministers differed in their treatment of the press. Eden, for instance, in the way in which he dealt with the press was a Liberal, but Alexander—Alexander was a thorough Conservative.

He returned to Crete and he said that with regard to the prospects there he was himself a 'defeatist'.[1] If I asked the Government

---

1. Beaverbrook was the only member of the war cabinet who drew attention beforehand to the weakness of the air defences of Crete. He did so as early as 6 November 1940. He also criticised the lack of air support in Crete during the operations, much to the indignation of Portal, chief of the air staff. See A J P Taylor, Beaverbrook, 455 & 470.

they would not for one moment admit that there was any question of our possibly having to retreat, but it was no use saying that sort of thing to a 'hard-boiled journalist'. The Germans had so far landed about 14,000 men from the air. They hadn't yet actually tried to put men ashore from the sea but they would certainly try to do it. Now they had started they would keep on. I said that presumably our forces were better equipped, meaning things like guns. He said yes, but in his opinion the decisive thing was that our troops there were, and would be, subjected to bombing, and dive-bombing, which never stopped and which we could not prevent because we had, and could only have a small Air Force there. We had probably not more than 100 aircraft altogether in Crete. It was a terrible thing for our men who had to face this experience hour after hour, day after day, without being able to defend themselves properly, and he feared the result. Our general position in Crete was obviously a pretty poor one, because we had no good defensible air bases there. Our chance in his opinion lay in Libya, because there we had strong bases immediately behind us from which we could continually harry the Germans. That was very different from the position which we had to accept in Crete. (Note: This opinion was given at the beginning of the *second* day of the attack on Crete.)

.   .   .   .   .

With regard to the United States he was not satisfied at all; the trend in our favour had been slackening during recent weeks. 'The trouble is that Roosevelt is waiting on public opinion and public opinion is waiting on Roosevelt, and so there is a deadlock. Public opinion over there simply doesn't understand the danger to America; once they do understand it they will move forward indeed', and he gave a great sweep of his hands outwards and upwards to illustrate the force of the movement. 'How are we to help things on? Well, for one thing, the American press can help a lot and we must see what we can do to keep them thoroughly informed and supplied with information. The Germans do it better; we don't give the American papers information enough.'

He went on to say 'I'm thinking of flying over there myself for a few days just to see what the position actually is and what we ought to do about it. They try to tell me that I must not dream of flying over there, but that is absurd and I think that I shall go—perhaps after I have had a few days' rest in the country that I need.' Then he went on 'Flying the Atlantic is not the difficult thing it used to be. Did you hear of the Atlantic service which I started this last winter in the face of all authority and all advice—a direct service across the Atlantic which I started in mid-winter in spite of the dreadful weather, and 105 bombers have flown over by this route since and only one of them been lost! What is more, I operated that service both ways sometimes; Yes', and here he raised his voice, 'we have flown some aircraft over the Atlantic from East to West in spite of the weather.'

.   .   .   .   .

He would tell me why he had resigned from MAP. He had had two operations and he was tired out. He knew that some people, like Hore-Belisha, were saying that there must be some big man to look after the whole question of supply and that he was the only man who could do it. But he saw through them and their manoeuvres; all that they wanted to do was to use him to discredit Churchill and—here he chuckled loudly—'They've got hold of the wrong man for that!' He had eventually gone to Churchill and told him that he *must* give up MAP and Churchill had desired him to remain in the War Cabinet all the same. His first job was to look into questions of supply. There was a great *disproportion* that had to be remedied; We were getting vast quantities of some things and not enough of others. He had to see whether he could find a way through and introduce a *right proportion* into production and supply. He would spend a little time in examining the matter; and he would see if he could make recommendations. If not, he rather hinted that he would give up his job, but it was only a hint. He said that anyhow he *must* first have a few days' rest in the country. (His bad eye was 'watering' all the time; he grinned at me and said 'But I'm not crying!')

He spoke of aircraft and pilots. He said that he was 'terrified of invasion'. 'Hitler *must* attempt it; I am convinced that "it must come".' Then he said that we had plenty of aircraft but not enough trained pilots. It was 'a great crime' if we had not enough pilots to use the aeroplanes which were waiting for them. 'The cupboard is full of aircraft. But that's no credit to me! It ought not to be full of aircraft!' He raised his voice and almost shouted 'The cupboard ought to be empty. The aircraft ought to be in use. It's only full because there are no pilots for these aircraft!' He criticised the Empire Training scheme in Canada. He said that Canada should train Canadians and Britain should train Britons over here, but it was a bad system for Canadians to be training British who did not belong to their own country and for whom they could not have the same sort of responsibility.

Everything in war, he said, was a matter of 'urgency'. Urgency —urgency! and a sense of urgency was the most essential requisite in a war government and in every Minister in it. From that standpoint the present Government was *not* a good war government. Churchill had that sense—that was one of his greatest qualities as a Minister, but most of his colleagues had not. He laughed and said that he had no business to be criticising his colleagues in this way; it was dreadful, but he was being, and was going to be, entirely frank with me and knew that confidence would be respected etc.[1] Well, he had a good opinion of John Anderson, who was 'bold and bloody', a man of decision. (Beaverbrook referred to himself once as being 'bold and *wild-minded*'.) 'But the others, no! Look at Herbert Morrison, who tried never to make a mistake, who never offended either tories or labour, who carried on steadily with his "non-firefighting-racket" and never accomplished anything.' But what about Bevin? I said. Had he not the 'sense of urgency'? No, indeed, was the reply. Certainly he brought up proposals to the War Cabinet and certainly he pressed them, but put it to him that something was urgent and must be done and Bevin would say that he would think about it and come back with his views or with a scheme *in ten days' time*. Was that urgency? Sinclair: he was a nice man, indeed, but he was all for defending the Air Vice Marshals and for doing as they said. You had only to attack anything done by them as not being the best plan or as being inadequate or inefficient and Sinclair at once leapt in to defend the decision as representing the best that could be done. Was that the way to go about the job—to be contented with the doings of these Air Vice Marshals! Why, at one conference the question had to be settled of which high-up airman was to be appointed to a certain high command. Sinclair proposed X who, said B, had been 'Storekeeper' at Y and not a particularly good one either. 'I spoke up and said "Well, X has not made much of a success of being storekeeper at Y and I see no reason to believe that he'll be any more successful as chief of this command." Yes,

1. Of the ministers named, Sir John Anderson was lord president and a member of the war cabinet; Herbert Morrison was home secretary; Bevin was minister of labour and a member of the war cabinet; Sinclair was secretary for air; Margesson secretary for war; Cranborne secretary for the dominions; Greenwood was minister without portfolio and a member of the war cabinet.

that's what I said and X was present in the room at the time. Well, afterwards Sinclair went to the PM and said that such a thing was quite incredible conduct and so on and so forth. That's how he regards the job!' Margesson he thought was promising at the War Office, but he only spoke of him vaguely. The one Minister who had surprised him by pleasing him greatly was Cranborne (Dominions). 'I expected to think nothing of him when he started but he's good and I like him.' As to Greenwood 'Well, you know all about him.' 'No one has a true sense of urgency except Churchill himself.' He said it was a curious thing that the men who retained great energy and will power in oldish age were those who had been fighting hard and working hard all their lives, e.g. Churchill and Dill;[1] you would think they would be worn out but that was just what they were not.

We spoke of Syria and the German planes that went to Iraq. What were we going to do about Syria? 'Yes' he said 'What are we going to do? That is *the* question at this moment', and he made it clear that for his part he was in favour of standing no nonsense.

With regard to Dakar, he said that if Churchill made an occasional mistake he should be forgiven, seeing how essential he was and how good a leader; he thought not to be severely attacked. Besides, what happened about Dakar? When the Government was told that the French cruisers had passed Gibraltar the Dakar expedition was already at sea. The cruisers greatly changed the position and Churchill wanted to recall the expedition. He was persuaded not to do so by his military and naval advisers—by Wavell and Cunningham—and he allowed the expedition to proceed. Then he got all the blame.[2]

Production of aircraft had fallen in April, but March had been a record month. American production for us was good and coming on well. As to quality, it was inevitable that the Americans could not produce the same quality as we could because *they had not* actual war experience to guide them. We could, and did, send over our own knowledge but it was not the same thing as having the actual experiences of war always behind you and with you. He felt that he might have done more last year to help the Americans to turn out better machines, but the trouble was that his duty had been to produce quantities of machines here; that he *had* to

---

1. Sir John Dill, CIGS. He was in fact worn out by his conflicts with Churchill and left office at the end of the war, going to Washington as chief British representative on the combined chiefs of staff's committee.

2. British and Free French forces made an unsuccessful attack on Dakar from 23 t 25 September 1940. Neither Wavell nor Cunningham had anything to do with it.

do because he had been horrified at the situation when he took over MAP. Still, if he had to go through the same period again he would tell the Americans more about the situation and what was wanted of them. In the autumn we were going to have a great acceleration both of machines and of pilots—he mentioned October.

About Hess—he would give me his personal view.[1] It was to be understood that it was only his personal view based on such information as there was and his interpretation of it.

He firmly believed that Hess had come over here with the connivance and approval of Hitler. He did not believe it possible that Hess could have made the flight he did single handed and without a very great deal of help. A great deal of preparation had gone into this journey in the early stages. Hess had everything prepared for him most carefully and he found his way almost exactly to the spot at which he was aiming. How did he manage to fly all that long way, to cross the North Sea and to come down within a few miles of the place he was aiming for? He thought that not only had Hess been provided by others with all the possible aids to navigation but that very probably he flew to where he landed 'on a beam' from Germany.

Hess meant to land at a certain point in Scotland and in fact he got very near it. That was remarkable navigation, was it not! He reckoned that normally it would have taken *three* men to bring that machine accurately from so far off in Germany![2]

He thought that such was Hess's crazy idea that he thought he could come down in Scotland at this point, hide himself there, enter into communication with sundry pro-German dukes in this country—he mentioned names—inform them of his plans and then fly back to Germany.

I mentioned the difficulties and he said he knew them but Hess was a hopelessly ignorant man and he believed personally that this was Hess's plan.

I asked whether Hess has brought any proposals?

He said 'No proposals from Hitler or anything of that kind. But proposals of his own for peace, yes, and he thought quite seriously

---

1. Rudolf Hess, Hitler's deputy, landed in Scotland on 10 May. It is unlikely that Hitler knew of his intentions. Beaverbrook's account confirms that Hess did not at this time propose an Anglo-German alliance against Soviet Russia. He raised this idea only after the German invasion of Russia.

2. This paragraph has been pasted over another which begins 'Hess meant to land where he could see the Duke of Hamilton. . . .' The rest of the original paragraph cannot be deciphered.

that they would be entertained here and that his friends, whoever
they are, might put them across.'

What, then, are these proposals?

He said that they were—

(1) Hitler to have Europe.

(2) Britain to be left with her Empire except that the German
Colonies must be restored to Germany.

(3) No indemnities.

Then there were two conditions—

(1) Churchill and his gang must 'go' and a pro-Hitler Government be substituted.

(2) There must be no abolition, reduction or limitation of arms.

'And that means, of course' I said—

'Six months of safety' said B 'and then—!'

'And he believes' I said 'that this would be considered by us?'

'He does! He has the most extraordinary ideas. He thinks that
we are beaten and can't understand why we don't recognise it
and make terms while we can. And he thinks that the country may
easily overthrow Churchill and the Government since it doesn't
really support them.'

'And he really thought he could get back again to Germany?'

'He did.'

'I hope you have him well guarded because, if he escaped, I
think the Government *would* fall.'

He grinned as in a Low Cartoon and said, 'He's well guarded!'

I said 'How did he behave when he found that he was not going
to get back?'

'He was very angry' said Beaverbrook.

June 1941

WINSTON CHURCHILL

This is one of the few press conferences that Churchill gave during the war.
Beaverbrook had persuaded him to hold it. The reference to Syria shows that
it took place before 8 June. The earlier part of the interview is in Crozier's
handwriting.

The editors gathered in the open waiting room. It was to be 11
a.m. and he was a bit late. When he was observed coming from
the front door a manservant waved the little crowd aside on either
hand to make a lane for the PM, who advanced smiling to either
side and saying 'Good morning' right and left.

We sat round the Cabinet table. The PM in his usual seat, with

Duff Cooper on his right hand. The editors filled the table, with one or two in a second row. On the long Cabinet table there was one newspaper, lying at the PM's left hand,—the MG.

He began by taking a look back at the last six weeks—

IRAQ. By landing troops at Basra we had made the revolt (Taschid Ali's) go off at half-cock. So we had got in front of the Germans. They had sent about forty planes. They *must* have wanted to do more and they could not. 'Inference—they were not strong enough to do everything.' We had done pretty well in Iraq. When the trouble started and the Iraquis attacked Habbaniyah we feared that the place would be lost in a matter of days or even of hours—that was how bad it had been! Now we had taken Baghdad and the bad riots there had been put down not by us but by the new Iraq Government! 'Now we had a constitutional government there, or at any rate'—here a satirical smile—'a government that suits our book and follows constitutional forms.' We had taken Mosul—very important—by sending Gurkhas there by air and motorised troops by road.

LIBYA. First we had had a 'well organised' campaign against the Italians. Then, 'while we were not looking' the Germans came back and overran us. We lost heavily in tanks. If anyone complained that we had not done enough in Crete let him remember that we had lost heavily in Cyrenaica when the Germans came back in force and in sending tanks to be refitted after we took Benghazi. 'Our chances in Libya now are certainly no less good than they had ever been there.' The Germans had certainly been getting more stuff and men to Libya recently; also, they had suffered heavily. In the first advance 'they somewhat overran their strength'. Tobruk was, and would be, of great importance to us. We were becoming much stronger. We had now nearly destroyed Musso's Empire in Africa. Not long ago we had nearly 150,000 men entering Khartoum, including many Indians and 2 South African divisions. Now *all* of them were steadily moving northwards to the Mediterranean coast. The prospects were good.

CRETE. He spoke of the criticism of the Government and the demand for a debate. He did not think that there should be a debate 'with the Germans of course listening to every word to get benefit out of it for themselves'. He did not think 'that the Government should be arraigned or he himself put in the dock or the pillory or cross-examined every time there was a reverse'. He would not make a 'statement'. He had 'made a statement' only a few weeks ago. Others could criticise and ask questions if they chose and he would do his best to answer them, but that was all he would do. He thought it unnecessary that there should be a grand 'inquest' whenever there was a defeat. In the last war there had been a long series of defeats—at Ypres, Loos, Somme, Peronne, March 1918—and there did not always have to be a big debate on each occasion.[1] It was necessary to take risks. Unless one took risks one could not win. Ever since June of 1940 the Government had been taking risks. They could have too many debates. The best proof that could be given of the Government's ability as a war-body would be actual success. 'Of course, if Parliament is not satisfied with the present Government or with me, then naturally it will get someone better. I can only say that I shall be only too glad to hand over—if there is someone better.'

The Government had deliberately decided to defend Crete. 'We have to fight Germans.' We always knew that no strong air defence was possible there. Nevertheless we hoped that we would be able to hold on there and to win. We had fortified Suda very heavily. Our idea was that we would wipe out the first lot of parachutists, and then the second, until the Germans got tired of it and gave up. We had sent to the Middle East all the aircraft that we could possibly spare and we had been sending them 'by all the means that ingenuity and readiness to take hazards could devise'. (Nevertheless the Germans had an enormous advantage. They could bring their forces by short land hops in a limited number of days, whereas we had to go over many thousands of miles of sea.) As soon as it was established by events that the Germans were not sick of it, and were not likely to be, we knew that we were done—this was, he said, the third day.

We knew that our fleet, if brought in to prevent landings, would suffer heavy damage and that we could not maintain it off the island for long if the attack continued. But seaborne troops were *not* landed in Crete—the Navy prevented that. Harm had been done by silly statements made by officers. 'You and the BBC and my friend Duff Cooper here are partly to blame for that. I don't think that these "soldiers" ought to broadcast at all. I've stopped 2 or 3 of them already. Joubert de la Ferté, for instance, who said some very indiscreet things. Now there's this Air Commodore— what's his name?—I can't remember his name—Goddard, isn't

---

1. This was by no means Churchill's view when he was out of office during the first world war.

it?—well, this man Goddard said on the wireless that Crete *could not* be taken from the air alone! These people don't know half what the Government knows about the possibilities, but the Government doesn't say these foolish things, and on the other hand it can't vet all the foolish things that other people say. They ought not to be allowed to say such things at all.'

Casualties. We had about 25,000 men in Crete. We had brought away 17,000 and had lost 8,000 in all, mostly prisoners. The Germans had lost from 10,000 to 14,000, mostly dead. They had lost 250 of their fighting planes and about 400 transport planes. They had 1,000 planes in action.[1]

AA guns. It was alleged that we had few AA guns in Crete. This was true—because we did not possess enough of them altogether. Everybody wanted them for every purpose. The demand from merchantmen alone was enormous. The Germans had ten times as many AA guns as we—of their own stock, and besides they had all the guns that they had captured in the occupied territories. For nearly 20 years the Germans had been preparing to wage another war and we, until recently, had been doing nothing except trying to maintain peace and avoid armaments!

Why, it was being asked, did we not destroy the airfields? Because we hoped to use them again ourselves! If we could evacuate 17,000 troops, why could we not send in as many also? Answer—we could send the men, but supplies and equipment— no! It had been worth the cost. We had done more damage to them than they to us. It had been a deliberate decision, and worth while. Man to man we had shown ourselves superior to the Germans. The loss of Crete had certainly done great moral damage to our position, he did not pretend to deny that. But it was regrettable that people should look at one place only; they should look at the thing as a whole and on the whole he was confident. Crete was a salient thrust out into the enemy's front, and a most useful one. It enabled us to push our naval front into the Mediterranean further to the west. That was now lost. Nevertheless, it was only one place and its importance must not be overestimated. There were various signs that the Germans were not too rich in Air Forces in the Near East.

BATTLE OF THE ATLANTIC. May had been our best month for a long time in respect of (1) sinking of U-boats (2) imports to Great

---

1. According to later figures, British and Empire losses in Crete were 16,000. The Germans lost 6,000, of whom 4,000 were killed. They lost 200 combat aircraft and 170 transport planes.

Britain. The Focke-Wolf, ranging from Bordeaux to the coast of Norway, did more harm that the U-boats. He recalled Hitler's statement about the havoc he was going to do in the spring and summer. Hitler had been wrong but 'for Heaven's sake, don't say that. It would have a deadly effect in the United States!' He did not know what really was good propaganda in the United States. He had recently asked someone who had just come from the United States which was the better propaganda—our loss of the Hood or our sinking of the Bismarck[1] and his friend did not know![2]

He then said that he would be willing to answer questions, and things went as follows:

Q Have we still any hopes regarding the Turks?

A Yes, certainly. The poor Turks want to be faithful to their alliance with us, but they are in a most difficult position. They lack modern equipment. We have given them a lot, but they have not enough to meet an offensive by a great military Power. Of course, if we should lose the Suez Canal or the Battle of the Atlantic the Turks can do nothing, but they certainly want to help us, and if we only do well in a military sense I have hopes of them.

Q What will Japan do?

A I think perhaps nothing. Of course, if we do badly—or if we are invaded, the Japs will be down on us like a ton of bricks. But Japan is going cautiously at present. I always thought that the Tripartite Pact was a stupid business for Japan. What does she really say under that pact? 'I want to fight Britain, but I won't fight her until the United States comes in on her side.' What a policy! I believe that if Japan attacks us the United States will certainly come in. She may come in anyhow, and in that even my personal opinion—mind you it is only my personal opinion—is that Japan will find the means somehow to stay out.

Q Can you tell us anything about Syria? (This was at a time when everyone knew privately that we were about to invade Syria, and there was a general murmur of amusement.)

A (Smiling broadly) I would prefer to leave events to answer that, but I can assure you that the question of Syria has not been entirely overlooked.

Q What about Russia?

A That is a very difficult question. I can, however, say this, that Germany is now concentrating very large forces on the Russian borders—Poland, Rumania, all the way along. These

1. The battleship Bismarck sank the battlecruiser Hood on 23 May and was herself sunk on 27 May.
2. Typescript from here on.

forces are much more than is needed for merely defensive purposes. Hitler may conceivably be intending to strike for the Caspian, the Baku oilfields, and the Ukraine crops. I doubt whether Stalin will not yield even these things sooner than have a war, but the surrender would be extremely bad for Russia because the whole of Southern Russia's crops are run on Baku oil. Or it may be that Germany will demand the demobilisation of the Russian Air Force, and I doubt whether Stalin will not agree even to that sooner than fight.

.   .   .   .   .

Q Anything about Hess?

A I have been rather leaving the Hess question alone. There is nothing more to say at present. Better leave him to get thoroughly bored and he may talk more. He undoubtedly has ideas about a negotiated peace and hoped that we would accept them. He has the most extraordinary ideas about opinion here. He simply cannot understand how the British people can fail to see that they are already beaten and must be utterly crushed unless they give in. There is no evidence that he has been sent to put forward any particular plan.

Q Anything about Vichy?

A No, except that I have no hopes that any of them will treat us with anything but malice and hostility.

.   .   .   .   .

He described Russia as a formidable crocodile. He had no objection to Russia at all and would readily cooperate with her if she would consent. If a crocodile came up on one side of our boat and helped to balance it, so much the better. But you never knew with Russia. You give the crocodile a hearty kick and he may be agreeable to you. You give him a pat and he may snap off your leg. We had tried both methods and gained nothing.

18 July 1941

9.30 A.M. LESLIE HORE-BELISHA

Churchill, he said, was becoming a 'dictator'. He was 'drunk with power', 'tipsy with power' and this was 'leading to disaster'. In his opinion the physical strain on C was impossible to maintain for a long time; there were stories of his summoning meetings for two or three o'clock in the morning, and high up military men, who had been working all day, had to attend them. C was also impatient at criticism, and there was no one at all to stand up to him firmly. If anyone went to have lunch with him he was not expected to say anything except an occasional yes or no, and certainly not to express any opinion. He had recently lunched with C and had had this experience. It was the same in his treatment of the Members of the Government! He had been angry at the request for information about the new appointments in Egypt. He had been resentful also at the criticisms about Crete and about production. He had been annoyed even at the criticisms regarding our failure in Greece. Not being able to answer the criticisms that had been offered C had attacked him (H-B) for the alleged deficiencies of his term of Office. Unfortunately, however, for this attack, he had on an earlier occasion praised results of that term of Office in the highest terms.

.   .   .   .   .   .

He referred to the recent 'crisis' regarding the Ministry of Information—the struggle of the MOI to enlarge its powers. He said that Duff Cooper should resign by way of protest, but that, of course, he would not do because he had no supporters at all behind him, and if he lost his position he might lose it for good and all. (So also, he said, will Beaverbrook.) He had always liked D C very much because whatever else he was or was not he was a thoroughly 'loyal' man. He thought that the suggestion for a new Minister (Brendan Bracken) was a 'kite' to see how the public would respond. The only result, if that appointment (B B) were actually made, would be that whereas now the MOI mentioned the PM a thousand times it would mention him two thousand times in future. The whole explanation was that a 'yes man' was needed.[1]

The present Parliament was a weak and supine body. There was no parallel to the Parliament of 1900–16. In those days not only was there a Carson but Carson had an organised following. He did not himself intend to organise any following. There was no alternative Government possible, and there was no organised

---

1. Brendan Bracken became minister of information two days later.

Opposition. Churchill would like to pretend that there was a factious Opposition, and he would like to be able to make out that H-B was organising an Opposition of that kind. He did not intend to give Churchill the chance.

.   .   .   .   .

Reverting to Beaverbrook, he said that B was *not* ready to stand up to Churchill. He was entirely dependent on C. Since November 1916[1] no one in politics had trusted Beaverbrook. *That* was why he had been in exile for twenty-four years! Now he was back and in high office, but he had no following in Parliament and depended solely on C. He would not risk his whole political existence! Was B no good, then, at supply etc.? He was a 'production manager', that and nothing more!

12.15 P.M. ANTHONY EDEN

He said that he thought the Japanese were now going to get hold of Indo-China.[2] They would do this because it would be the cheapest acquisition within their reach; they thought that they could get it without having to fight. They intended to acquire Camranh Bay, not Saigon, and it was quite possible they would demand also some base from Siam. He then produced some maps, and we found that the Japanese, even with these new bases, would be something like one thousand miles from Singapore. We were much stronger at Singapore nowadays both in troops and in 'planes, but we were not in ships because we had not the ships to spare. I asked whether it was likely that the United States would send ships to Singapore, and he said, no, not unless she were actually in the war and then, of course, she would.

His opinion was that Japan certainly did not want to get into war at present with the United States, and probably did not want war with us either. It would be necessary to react sharply if Japan forced France to make concessions in Indo-China. We should at once issue orders which would deprive her of certain valuable materials, especially from the Malay States, without saying much about it, but she would understand.

.   .   .   .   .

1. When he had helped to organise the overthrow of Asquith and the elevation of Lloyd George. The remarks that follow come ill from one of Beaverbrook's former ghosts.
2. The Japanese secured bases in Indo-China on 23 July.

What would be the position in the Middle East if the Germans eventually came down by way of the Caucasus? It would be very serious indeed, and one of the things which we were now considering was how to build up against them in such an event. The position in Iran was not bad, but the Shah was a ruffian and we could not rely on him. Afghanistan was not too good, and neither was Iraq. We should certainly have to hold the air-fields in Iraq, and this was not at all popular with the inhabitants. I inquired, 'How are the Arabs in general behaving—about whom you say such pleasant things?' And he said, 'Not too well.'

.   .   .   .   .

The Russians and the Poles were 'awful'; they hated one another and persisted in quarrelling. Sikorski[1] was the best of them. They persisted in wanting the old frontier with Russia and would not accept the 'Curzon Line'.[2] The question of Teschen[3] had not yet been raised between the Poles and the Czechs.

The Russians were not doing too badly, and they still had a good air-force. If they kept an air-force going there was no need to lose hope; an immense amount depended on that point.

.   .   .   .   .

He made a short reference to Singapore, in the course of which he said that the Japanese air force was believed to be not at all good. It was described by people who should know as being 'as poor as Italy's'.

1.30 P.M. LORD BEAVERBROOK

Beaverbrook and Bevin were usually not on good terms. Here they are displayed in unexpected intimacy. To show interest in the other man's world was with Beaverbrook a favourite method of flattery, and no doubt he thought that he was flattering Bevin by recalling union leaders he could remember. This time the method did not work. Bevin detested all the men named, and with some reason. James Sexton had led the national union of dock labourers in Liverpool—the rival to Bevin's dockers' union. Tom Mann was first president, and Ben Tillett secretary, of the dockers' union. Mann had become a Commu-

---

1. Polish prime minister.
2. Approximately the ethnic frontier.
3. Acquired by Poland in September 1938.

nist. Tillett, an old friend of Beaverbrook's by the way, had been hounded from office by Bevin with peculiar brutality. A J Cook was secretary, and Robert Smillie president, of the miners' federation of Great Britain. Smillie threatened to involve Bevin's transport and general workers' union in a general strike. Cook did so. Altogether an unhappy choice by Beaverbrook. But then was there any union leader whom Bevin liked?

When I got to No. 12 I found Beaverbrook seated with Bevin and we continued to sit and talk for another 15 minutes. Beaverbrook was asking Bevin innumerable questions about Labour leaders whom he had known—Sexton, Tom Mann, Tillett, Cook, Smillie, Havelock Wilson, and so on, in each case being anxious to know what the Labour man's influence had sprung from, what sort of personality he was, and in particular whether he was an orator. The conversation throughout was on the lines of 'Was he an orator, Ernie?' and 'Oh, he was a great orator, Max.'

Presently the door opened and in came a gaunt lean man, with haggard sallow face and loosely hanging clothes. I thought that I recognised him from press photographs, and when they fell on him with loud cries of 'Harry' and he spoke with an American accent, I knew that it was Harry Hopkins,[1] who had been present at our Cabinet meeting the day before.

It appeared that the principal object of the luncheon was that Harry might find out from Bevin all about the way in which the Labour Ministry was running in respect of recruitment, labour conditions, shifts, canteens, women's work, and so on. Hopkins asked large numbers of questions and Bevin made a lot of interesting points about shorter hours and more rest spells increasing production, and explained in detail his methods of dealing with women.

Hopkins was also much concerned about one thing. He said that a lot of food supplies that America had been sending over under the Lend-Lease Act had been getting into the hands of middlemen in this country, and American opinion was disturbed about it. They thought that they were sending over stuff and it was being sold to people here at artificially increased prices. He wanted to devise some scheme under which the American food would go direct from the British harbours to the British munition workers; the American public would know this, the fact could be 'dramatised' and it would have a very fine moral effect in the United States. The two B's thought that it was a fine plan and said that the Government would certainly put the idea through.

1. President Roosevelt's closest adviser.

When they were talking about this country paying, or not paying, for supplies from the United States, Hopkins said 'I suggest that you should gather together all the things in this country that you don't like and sell them to us in return for our supplies. Send us all your statues, for instance.' Beaverbrook said 'No, you can't have our statues, but there is something you can have; take our bishops, take all of them. He can have our bishops, can't he, Mr Crozier?' I said 'No, our bishops are an ancient English institution and he can't have them; but he can have individual bishops provided one is allowed to choose the individuals.'

Hopkins struck me as an extremely shrewd and clear-headed man, knowing precisely what he was after and not at all afraid to say it.

3.00 P.M. SIR ARCHIBALD SINCLAIR

.   .   .   .   .

The question of a Minister of Production was mentioned and he said that he was against it. In actual practice it would mean that Beaverbrook would be the Minister. He had just left MAP and he had got Supply[1] and he would therefore be in a dominating position. He would be demanding tanks, which was what he was now after, and he, the speaker, would have to fight for aircraft.

He spoke of the Russian campaign and praised the unity of the Russians. He said that Cripps when he was in London had said that the Germans would go through the Russian army 'like a knife through butter', but then Cripps did not know any Russians when he was in Russia. He meant this literally—he was not allowed to meet or talk to Russians. He had had one meeting with Stalin, two with Molotov and perhaps half a dozen with Vishinsky and one or two other people. He had Russian guards always, but they were not allowed to have any talk with him or the embassy staff. The result was inevitably that he simply could not have any first-hand knowledge of things in Russia.

5.45 P.M. A V ALEXANDER

.   .   .   .   .

He referred to the sinking of the Bismarck and the tremendous fight that she had put up. He went over with me on the map the

---

1. Beaverbrook became minister of supply on 29 June.

movements that had been made by the various sections of our forces and expressed a great admiration for the work of Dudley Pound.[1] He then said that he would show me something that no one had seen outside the Admiralty, and he produced and read an 'appreciation' of the situation which he had written in the operations room during the night when contact had been lost with the Bismarck, that is the night before she was sunk. In this 'appreciation' he set down his views of the position as it then was and as he thought it might develop. It seemed to be sound, level-headed stuff, and he was pleased by some remarks that the Chief of Staff had made about it.

.   .   .   .   .

19 July 1941

12 NOON. BJÖRN PRYTZ

He spoke first of the general position in Finland. It was pretty bad. For two years they had been cut off from the outer world and Sweden depended, and wanted to depend for the future, on the outer world. Sweden refused to look to a closed Europe and to the German 'New Order'. She was international and belonged to the seas and would refuse to regard herself as part of a closed European Order. She was, however, in serious difficulties. She could get no oil to speak of. Two or three ships had come through from Mexico, but what was that in two years' time! She could get no oil, for instance, for her air-force or for her tanks, and how could anyone fight a war in these days unless they had oil for a mechanised army and an air force!

He had been in Sweden recently and he had seen Cripps on his way through from Moscow to London. Cripps knew little about Russia. He had told Cripps in Stockholm more about Russia than he had learned all the time he had been in Moscow. He found that there were two questions to be settled; and they were put to him thus—

    (1) Was Sweden to allow a single German division to cross over from Norway through Swedish territory into Finland.

    (2) Was Sweden prepared to give a general moral adhesion to Germany in her European policy.

His own view was quite clear. Never, never, ought she to agree

---

1. First sea lord.

to no. 2; never must she give a general approval under which the Germans could thereafter ask for anything they chose. London and the British people would never understand that. On the other hand, it seemed to him possible that Sweden should grant permission for a German force to cross Swedish territory in the north.

.   .   .   .   .

In the Russian-Finnish war of 1939–40 Sweden had refused to allow British or French troops to cross her territory in order to aid Finland. She refused in order to keep herself out of the war. Now she was permitting German troops to cross her territory to join Finland against Russia, and this was not inconsistent, because she thought it was the only way of keeping out of war with Germany. He reckoned that 90 per cent of the Swedish people were pro-British and pro-Ally, but Sweden had at all costs to stick together. The people did not like the action of the Government in letting the Germans through; but all felt that they had to approve it and that disunity in Sweden would be fatal to the Swedish people, since Hitler had always laid the foundation of his conquests by producing domestic disunity.

2 October 1941

3.00 P.M. LORD CECIL AT 16 SOUTH EATON PLACE

Viscount Cecil was of course not in office and, with the League of Nations moribund, politically inactive. His views on a resurrected League of Nations after the war are curious, and it is difficult to understand why Crozier, who liked practical talk, troubled to see him.

.   .   .   .   .

Principally he talked of the post-war settlement and the part to be played by Britain, the USA and Russia. He thought that we must not rely too much on the USA. Roosevelt was, of course, a much better politician than Wilson and would never make the same blunders. But there were tremendous ups and downs in American opinion. He thought that probably only 50 per cent of the Americans were disposed to go in whole-heartedly with us even now. When the war was over there would be a reaction; this was quite inevitable, and he thought there would be a strong disposition to withdraw again from Europe. Therefore we ought not to rely on them. Europe must rely on itself to maintain peace in the future. That meant that we and Russia must act together. He had great hopes of Russia, which was a great Power, really anxious for peace, and needing, after this war, very greatly to recuperate. We must therefore have a fairly rigid system of Powers who would be ready to intervene and fight for peace, and Russia and Britain must be at the head of this system. The small Powers also would come into it, and they would be good, e.g., the Scandinavian Powers, who had always been strong in this regard. One could not, however, expect them to go to war unless the great Powers were willing to bear the brunt. The system must therefore have Britain and Russia at the head, and then the smaller Powers equally pledged, and then again countries like the United States who were not rigidly bound like the European Powers but were nevertheless pledged to give all the aid that they could.

He went into past history. Japan was perhaps more difficult to control in 1931 than Italy would have been in 1935, but the failure of the League in 1931 made Italy think that she could get away with aggression against Abyssinia, and she was right. Our Prime Ministers and Foreign Secretaries had been a succession of disasters. Ramsay [MacDonald] perhaps had been the worst of them because he went back on all that he had ever said, and he disliked the League and the small Powers.

What was to be done with Germany at the end of the war? The problem was unsolvable unless a powerful international body was created that was ready to intervene with force against aggression. He was not in favour of dismembering Germany into a number of Small States, for that would only mean that they would never be contented until they came together again, and ultimately nothing would be able to stop them. They would have to be disarmed, and kept disarmed, for some time, and parts of the country would no doubt have to be occupied, but none of these things could produce a permanent remedy. If they tried to rearm it would be necessary to invade them at once. It would be fatal to let them do what they had done in the past—plunge into rearmament and get away with it. He was not very hopeful.

.   .   .   .   .

I had said something on the question of executing Hitler if we ever got him in our hands and suggested that that might only turn him into a martyr in the eyes of the German people. He said, 'I would risk it, but I doubt whether we shall get him. He will very likely escape to Switzerland, and I doubt whether the Swiss would give him up. I know all about the "hang the Kaiser" stuff at the end of the last war,[1] but I think that the guilty leaders in Germany ought to be punished. I think that Britain and the Allies ought to tell the Czechs, the Poles, etc., that the guilty will be punished if we can lay hands on them. Still perhaps it would be best if the Germans themselves would deal with these people—if they can capture them.'

4.15 P.M. ANTHONY EDEN AT THE FOREIGN OFFICE

I asked first whether there was any truth at all in the reports about a possible separate peace with Italy. He replied that there was absolutely nothing in it. Neither had Myron Taylor[2] said anything about such a peace on coming to London on his way back to the United States. He had talked a little about conditions in Italy. They were bad, but Italy was helpless. No one in Italy now believed in Germany or Hitler except Mussolini himself, but in any case Italy was an 'occupied country' and had no power to do anything of which Germany disapproved. I asked about the Duke of Aosta[3] and the rumours that he was sympathetic to us or might be of some use to us. He replied that there was nothing in this either. The Royal House was discredited and the Duke of Aosta was no better regarded than the rest, except that having made a fight of it in Abyssinia he had perhaps a little more popular respect. We thought nothing of him and he added that the King of Greece and the King of Yugoslavia seemed to agree only in one thing and that was their dislike of the Duke of Aosta. He thought that possibly there might be an outbreak of trouble in Sicily before the mainland was affected.

The position in general was better and was regarded by many people outside this country as being better. This was true of neutral countries. Our recent success in Iran was very important. I asked what route we should use to transport supplies to Russia, and he replied the Trans-Iranian Railway route up from the Persian Gulf to the Caspian Sea. It was simpler to do this than to use a railway broken by a stretch of road.

---

1. In 1919 Cecil had been strongly in favour of trying the kaiser as a war criminal.
2. US minister at the Vatican.
3. Former Italian commander-in-chief in Abyssinia and a cousin of Victor Emmanuel's.

He talked a good deal about the Poles now in Russia. When the Russians and the Poles made their recent agreement the Russians let the Poles out of prison and concentration camps in tens of thousands, 'literally tens of thousands'. Many of the Poles had had an extremely bad time; many of them had been tortured. They had been bastinadoed—a punishment which he thought was exclusive to Persia. He told a funny story about the Polish general who is to command the Polish divisions that are now being raised (four or six divisions). This Polish general had been thrown by the Russians into Lubianka Prison and there he had remained during all the war until just recently. The chief of the Russian Secret Service went to get him out of prison and to restore to him his liberty, etc. The Pole, who knew nothing whatever about what had been happening, did not understand this, and when he was taken to a good hotel and given champagne and a fine meal, thought that this was some new form of moral torture and that he was going to be thrown back again into prison. However, the Russians and Poles understood each other and expected mutual ill treatment and torture and there was no resentment between them.

．　　．　　．　　．　　．

He referred to Libya and said he was extremely keen on this front and hoped that we would be able to throw out the German-Italian army.[1] I inquired whether we could both give Russia all the assistance that we were proposing and at the same time run a Libyan campaign. That, he said, was a question which was at the moment being closely considered and he hoped that we should be able to do it.

I inquired about Japan. He said that the Japanese were behaving 'very queerly'. He mentioned the case of a British official's wife who had been kidnapped by the Japs, and on our demand they had restored her. I thought, he said, that she would have been beaten up, but actually she had not been harmed. The Japanese were undoubtedly suffering badly from the British and American economic sanctions and things were becoming very difficult for them. I said I had seen a report that the present Government (Konoye's)[2] might collapse altogether, and he said

1. The Eighth army opened an offensive on 18 November.
2. Konoye resigned on 16 October and was succeeded by General Tojo. This was a decision for war.

that he hoped that this was untrue, because if it did collapse it was very likely to be followed by a worse Government—made up of militarists and extremists. There was no doubt, he said, that at present the Japanese did not at all like the idea of being at war with America, Britain and probably some other Powers as well.

7.00 P.M. WINSTON CHURCHILL AT 10 DOWNING STREET

I had to wait a few minutes, as an important conference of 'Brass Hats' was taking place and the actual brass hats were piled up in magnificence on the table in the hall. The PM himself was looking a good deal better than when I saw him last. His face was fresher and his eyes less tired looking. He sat talking for about ten minutes and then for most of the time was marching up and down the room with his hands thrust down deep in his pockets, puffing at a cigar and occasionally stopping and demonstrating his points on a big war map.

'Things are looking better all round', he said, and proceeded to explain that he contrasted everything with the position in 1940. Above all he felt deeply that now we were 'not alone'. He ran over the sort of broad 'front' that we now presented to the Germans. It would be noticed, he said, that in his last speech he had deliberately brought in China, and with China what did our front look like? We had 400 millions in the British Empire, 150 million Russians, 130 millions Americans, 400 millions Chinese—'no, indeed, we are not alone'.

I asked him first about the Middle East, and he said that there was no need for us yet to anticipate the Germans coming down upon us via the Caucasus. The distances were too great; the distances in that part of the world were always enormous and they took a long time to cover. He would say that a war in those vast spaces of the Middle East must always be one of 'small armies'. But we had got a lot of men accumulated now in the Middle East, from Libya away up to the Persian frontier, and we were going to have more. We were going to get a lot of men from India and we were going to have a total of a million men there before long. About Libya and the prospect of early operations there he spoke with great reserve, no doubt because that was one of the subjects which they had recently been discussing. One thing he said was 'It is bad to attack across a desert.' He said that the Germans had greater difficulty in getting reinforcements and supplies to Libya than we have. 'We have the immense journey round the Cape, but the Germans have to face the difficulties and dangers of the Mediterranean crossing.' I said that perhaps in that case there was a rough maximum to the forces that the Germans could concentrate in Libya, but he said he could not accept anything so definite as that; still, it was the case that we could reinforce more easily than the Germans. He expressed great disappointment with the failure of our attack from Sollum in the summer. We had had lots of tanks and he had high hopes of it, but nothing had come of it.

He spoke of Russia and its strong resistance, but he said that we ought to realise that the Germans had scored very great successes there and the effect of these must not be underestimated. I asked him what precisely he had in mind when he said in his last speech in the House that our supplies to Russia were limited by difficulties of 'transportation'. Was he referring to our shipping or to the paucity of Russian roads and railways, and he replied that he meant both. Whether we sent material through Archangel or through the Persian Gulf it meant a tremendous sea journey before we reached the (inadequate) railways.

Then he got on to the matter of aid for Russia and discussed the problem of the 'second front'. I had not expressed any opinion at all about it when he said 'You are quite right to be critical of the idea of establishing a second front on the Continent of Europe.' He went on to say that such a project was one that Hitler would certainly welcome. Hitler would like the idea of our putting an army ashore on the Continent of Europe and he would certainly strain every nerve to collect all the force that he could and to throw against it an overwhelming strength. It ought to be realised that Hitler had in the field at the moment some 260 divisions and that he would have no difficulty at all in transferring a large number of troops from elsewhere and concentrating an enormous army against anything that we could land.

He then said he must, and would, keep a strong army in this country. We had to assume that during recent months—and we *must* assume it—Hitler had been building very large quantities of boats and barges which it was intended to run right up on to the English beaches and from which his tanks and armoured stuff would roll off on to the land.[1] Nothing must prevent us from being absolutely ready to defeat such an attack. The navy would do its part and so would the air force, but, he said, 'Don't ask me to give up a good strong army in this country, thoroughly well-equipped

---

1. This assumption was without foundation.

and above all well trained, which I can throw against any such invading force that may secure a footing on our shores.' He was emphatic that Hitler must have been spending time and energy in constructing an invasion fleet of this kind and he was emphatic again, as he always is, that the heart of the war remains in this country and that nothing must be done to jeopardise its threatened safety.

Returning to the United States, he said that if the United States came into the war we should gain enormously, and we should not lose American supplies as we might have done if she had come in much earlier. At that time she would certainly have had to keep a large proportion of certain supplies for herself, but now she had such an enormous programme and she was getting on with it so fast that if she came into the war she would be able both to arm herself and also to furnish great supplies both to Russia and to us. In alluding at another time to the United States he used the phrase 'When they come in' as though he regarded it as certain.

In Iran he said that Eden had done very well.[1] We did not want to have to run Iran ourselves, but to get it run by its own Government, and in that we had succeeded. He was glad that the 'old rogue', the Shah, had gone, as he had done nothing but rob his people. We were soon, he hoped, going to have a good treaty between Russia, ourselves and Iran.

The Turks, he said, were behaving well. You could not expect a small country like that to want to go to war with Germany. 'If a man comes out of his house one morning and finds five or six of his neighbours hanging in front of it, it makes him think a lot about what he himself should do.'

Japan, he said, was behaving well at present, but was just waiting to see what was going to happen. If the Russians showed signs of being badly defeated, or if Germany attempted to invade us, the Japanese would be down on us like a knife. But at present they were cautious and waiting to see.

·   ·   ·   ·   ·

As I left he invited me to ring him up if I needed information about some point that puzzled me. 'Don't ask me, though, about strategy or military policy on the telephone.' I said 'I shall try to

---

1. Soviet Russia and Great Britain concluded a treaty with Iran that in fact gave them joint control.

exercise a little commonsense,' and he grinned and said 'I'm sure you will.' He then told his secretary to inform me how I was to get him on the 'phone.

3 October 1941

11.30 A.M. BJÖRN PRYTZ AT 27 PORTLAND PLACE

I asked how Sweden was getting on and he said, 'Well, now, listen to this. What things people are capable of saying!' He then picked up a document and translated passages to me as he went along. 'Here is an account of a speech which Ribbentrop made the other day to my colleague the Swedish Minister in Berlin.' The Minister said that Ribbentrop spoke slowly, apparently weighing every word, so that he could write the whole thing down verbatim, which in fact was what he had done. Ribbentrop said that Germany was greatly grieved at the way in which Sweden was now behaving. He referred to the recent Trade Union Conference at Stockholm, to the presence of Gibson, the English trade unionist, and to the way in which the conference had referred to the dragooning of Norway. There were various other signs of Sweden's attitude. Sweden did not seem to realise the meaning of the 'New Order' which Germany was bringing into Europe, nor did she appear to sympathise with Germany's work; nor, again, did she appear to approve of the great crusade against Bolshevism by which Hitler was to save Sweden together with the rest of Europe. She had actually refused to allow volunteering in Sweden for the war against Russia. Actually it seemed that the Swedes sympathised not with their saviour, but with Britain, who was the friend of Bolshevism. He must mention that the Germans had just captured Poltava and he would remind the Minister that the great Swedish hero Gustavus Adolphus had attempted to defeat Russia and had himself been defeated at Poltava, but what a small country could not do a greater country led by Adolf Hitler was now doing. 'Sweden', said Ribbentrop, 'can't expect to escape from the great and historic events which are now taking place— nor from their consequences.' At one point he joined Switzerland with Sweden in his criticism and he also threw in the reproach that although Goering had always been a friend of Sweden (Goering's first wife was a Swede) the Swedes had treated him very badly. He went on to say that the 'New Order' which Germany was establishing would last 'for a thousand years'. 'Fancy', said Prytz to me, 'anybody talking about establishing anything for 1,000 years. What a man!' Finally, Ribbentrop complained of the attitude of the press in Sweden.

Ribbentrop had also attempted to sow discord between Sweden and Russia. He asserted that when Molotov came to Berlin in November 1940, he had made certain proposals affecting Sweden's vital interests. 'In the cellar of this very building', said Ribbentrop, 'Molotov had expressed Russia's strong interest in the Belt and the Sound, which interest could only be gratified at the expense of Sweden.' Ribbentrop had then gone on to contrast the attitude of the Swedes towards Germany very unfavourably with that of the Finns.

The Minister who was thus addressed had replied that for centuries the Swedish people and Government had based their conduct on the principle of law and of respect for law. If, therefore, the press had been acting within the bounds of the law that the Swedish people had adopted for themselves, the Swedish Government could not interfere.

He then gave me to read a report which had just been received from an observer in Germany about the state of things there. This observer said that there was a general feeling of depression and much fear of the future. Even the military were for the first time beginning to say that only a stalemate was now in prospect. Nothing of this kind had been heard from them before. Further, there were signs of discontent with the Nazi party. Gradually the leaders were dropping out, or being dropped. In particular, Goering was now taking no active part in the war or even in the work of his own Ministry. He was giving himself up to an idle and luxurious life. He took with him everywhere three detachments of Guards. One detachment he used to gather food and dainties of all kinds for him; the second he used to construct a tennis court or a swimming bath, or whatever suited him at the particular place at which he happened to be. This growing tendency to idleness and luxury was true also of some of the other Nazi bosses, including Ley. At the same time the military, the generals, were steadily growing stronger. The observer said that he would not be surprised if before long there was some sort of a 'purge' designed to get rid of some of the Nazi leaders;[1] and it might be a more drastic purge than that of 1934.

The observer went on to say that the food position in Germany was not bad. It was nothing like so bad as it had been in the winters of 1917–18, when the Germans lived mostly on swedes.

---

1. Quite the reverse happened.

The chief lack was of mineral oils and rubber. Buna, the artificial rubber, was being developed, but even for this a certain amount of natural rubber was needed and there was not enough of it.

.   .   .   .   .

[1]After he had told me about Ribbentrop's address to the Minister I said 'Mildly threatening?' and he said 'Oh, worse than mildly—very threatening.' The position was dangerous. Sweden had given us permission to do 'certain things' and, if we did them, the Swedes 'would be for it'. He thought it would be better all round if we did not do these things and Sweden remained as now 'and not be conquered'. Germany could quite easily run a campaign against Sweden in addition to what she was doing now.

3.00 P.M. PRESIDENT BENEŠ

Beneš resigned as president of Czechoslovakia after the Munich conference. He established a Czechoslovak national committee in exile when Hitler occupied Prague, and the British government recognised this committee as the Provisional government of Czechoslovakia after the fall of France. Beneš, being once more in theory a head of state, had to spend most of his time in security in the country and talked the more volubly on the rare occasions that he came to London. His assertations were based more on Czech optimism than on hard information.

He is a little man and very quiet, highly repressed but burning with fires within. He talked rapidly for over an hour, at times with intense feeling. His face all the time is that of a man who has gone through bitter experiences.

He asked what I would first like to hear about, and I said the Czech opposition movement. He said, 'The war did not begin for me in September 1939; it began with Munich and has gone on steadily ever since Munich. I myself prepared the broad lines of the national opposition before I resigned and left Czechoslovakia. I arranged things with the chief people and arranged the means of communication that were to be maintained between Czechoslovakia and myself. When I came to London I perfected these arrangements.[2] Now there is a highly efficient and rapid system of communication between my people and me. Everything that

---

1. Handwritten addition.
2. Most of this is imaginary.

happens over there is communicated to me in London, very often within a few hours, nearly always within twenty-four hours. Everything is done from top to bottom on my instructions, and the whole people obey me. That is the strength of the movement. It is national and universal. Everyone is engaged somehow or other in opposing the Germans. If a German officer or official asks a Czech girl in the street the way to some destination she gives him the wrong directions, and that same spirit is carried out in every possible way.' Because the movement was national it could not be put down or defeated, and for the same reason everything that the Germans did was known to him. The Germans had been compelled to maintain large numbers of Czech officials in the Administration because they could not do without them. These officials knew everything that the Germans did and everything that was being planned; within a few hours they had communicated their knowledge to him, including the most secret orders given by the Germans, and very often, of course, also the orders that were sent to Prague by the German Government and staff in Berlin.

For a long time Neurath[1] had tried a policy of clemency with the Czechs. He had tried to get them to work with him, and he had failed completely. Then came the war against Russia, and the communications through Czechoslovakia to the Eastern Front were of extreme importance to the Germans. There followed incessant obstruction and sabotage and the German communications were seriously embarrassed. The German General Staff had declared that this must somehow be stopped, and the German Government thereupon deposed Neurath and sent Heydrich. Heydrich would butcher a great many Czechs and then the German Government would say 'You see that it is useless to rebel. You only injure yourselves; now we will give you another chance to behave well,' and they would send someone less brutal than Heydrich. Perhaps they will even send Neurath back again. It would all be no good, the Czechs would pay no attention and the same national opposition would go on unabated. But there must be no open revolt. He had told the Czechs that whatever was done to them there must be no open revolt until he gave the word, and he would not give the word until German fortunes had so far declined that a Czech revolt could not be suppressed and would help to produce a decisive victory.

.   .   .   .   .

1. Neurath was appointed Protector of Bohemia after the dissolution of Czecho-Slovakia.

He believed that the Russian national unity would last however great Russia's trials. He believed that the Germans would fail to win over the Ukraine or any part of it. No pro-German ruler, like Skoropadsky would last for an hour at Kiev unless he were supported by German bayonets. He had had early information, he said, in the spring of 1939 that Russia would compound with Germany. Ever since then he had known, and Russia also had known, that Hitler would attack her. But Russia had desired to stave off the attack as long as possible in order that Germany might be weaker and she might be stronger. In May of this year he had declared openly to Churchill that Hitler was about to attack Russia and he had been asked (by Churchill, and by everyone here) whether Russia would resist. He had replied that she would and must resist, but at the same time if Stalin could have compromised with Hitler up to a week before the attack he would have done so because he still desired to put the attack off as long as he could, although he well knew that it was bound eventually to come.

Russia would go on resisting throughout the winter. The Germans would win more successes, and very likely they would win successes still in the early part of next year, but he thought that then the tide of the successes would begin to slacken. He believed that politically and economically the position in Germany was worse than our own people in London would accept. He thought that there would be a growing disintegration in Germany in the middle and latter half of next year, and that the people would not face a fourth winter of war. He insisted that a process of disintegration was already beginning in the Nazi Party. He believed that 'the Generals' or 'the army' were beginning slowly to push the Nazi Party out of its position as ruler of Germany and that it was their intention to continue this process until Germany was ruled not by the Nazi Party but by themselves.[1]

One sign, he said, was that beyond all doubt Goering had been 'put byside', a phrase which he repeated frequently. He said that only a few weeks ago a high Gestapo official had gone to the police headquarters at Prague and had ordered the pictures of Goering on the walls to be taken down. The same official had then, on the next day, visited the Prague Town Hall and ordered the Vice-Mayor to take down Goering's portraits. The same thing was happening to Dr Ley, and he predicted it would happen before long to Goebbels. The important point was that all this was the doing of the military; they were deliberately putting the Nazi

---

1. This is entirely inaccurate.

bosses 'byside'. Soon only Hitler would be left, and then it was possible that they would keep Hitler for their own purposes, but it was also possible that they would get rid of him, too, and establish a military dictatorship. In that case they would put forward to Britain and her allies proposals for a nice reasonable peace on the basis that they had got rid of the evil Nazis and their leaders, and if they succeeded in obtaining such a peace they would settle down quietly to prepare for the third great war. That, he was convinced, was what was coming and what they were even now beginning by this process of excluding the worst of the Nazi leaders. A German Government in the hands of these military men, he said, would be as bad from the international point of view as the present—and as any that could be conceived.

When talking of Hitler's war on Russia, he asserted it to be true that the German General Staff expected to win the war in six weeks. He said that just when the war began, a high Gestapo official had been sent to Prague and that almost immediately after getting there he received instructions from Berlin, which were immediately known to the Czechs, that he was to proceed to Moscow and take over police control in six weeks' time.

He said a good deal about the end of the war in regard to a settlement with Germany. An ideal settlement was not possible, never had been possible and never would be. 'We must be courageous enough,' he said, 'to defend conditions of peace which are necessary, although not ideally right.' He was obviously referring to the mountain belt inhabited by the Sudeten Germans. He suddenly took out his pocketbook and produced from it a map of Czechoslovakia on which the regions with a German population were shaded. He ran his finger round the Sudeten belt and said that without it Czechoslovakia could not live. Ten million Czechs[1] had to be considered, and it was not right that they should be sacrificed for three million Germans. He believed that every possible piece of Sudeten territory inhabited by Germans that was not essential to Czech existence should be left outside the Czech frontiers, but otherwise the Czechs must have the Sudeten belt, and the solution, in his view, was that as many Germans as possible, say, one-and-a-half millions, should be transferred on to German soil.

I asked him about 1938, and he said that he was absolutely certain that Russia would have fought alongside of the British and French if they had made war for Czechoslovakia instead of con-

---

1. This figure is correct only if the Slovaks are counted as Czechs.

cluding Munich. He said he knew Russia well, and 'I know Russian', and he was positive about it. In referring to Elias, the Czech Premier whom the Germans had just arrested, he described him as 'their own man'.

As I was leaving him he made some remarks about the Chamberlain-Munich period, and I said that he must have had a very bad time. He replied simply, 'I went through hell.'

9 P.M. A V ALEXANDER AT THE ADMIRALTY

.   .   .   .   .

In the Mediterranean we had a very tough job. We had to supply Tobruk entirely by sea from Alexandria and that meant that our ships had a longer course to make than the German aeroplanes which came to attack them from Crete and the Dodecanese; these air-bases were extremely tiresome to us. If we looked at the map of the Mediterranean—and during this talk he was continually jumping up and going to point to these maps—we should see that the Germans had every place on our northern flank, except the Syrian coast and Cyprus, and this gave them a great advantage. The reason why we were attacking Sicily so persistently was because of the air-bases there. As to Libya, he would like very much to have a campaign there if it were possible and to sweep the Germans clean out of Africa. He would like to go right up to the border of Tunis, and if we did he thought it would have an immense effect for good both on the Vichy French and on the French Colonial Empire.

The three big German ships were still bottled up in Brest; we had now immobilised them for seven months, which had been of tremendous assistance to us.

Speaking of the chance of invasion, he said that there were no preparations by the Germans visible at present compared with those that were to be seen at this time last year.

.   .   .   .   .

4 October 1941

11.00 A.M. IVAN MAISKY AT HARINGTON HOUSE

This was the first time that Crozier met Maisky since the outbreak of war. Maisky gave a survey of the fighting on the eastern front that was clearly based

only on what he read in the English newspapers. He also said that, failing a
second front, the British should send an army to Russia and 'occupy the
attention of from thirty to forty German divisions'.

24 October 1941

3.30 P.M. SIR ARCHIBALD SINCLAIR AT THE AIR MINISTRY

Sinclair described the bombing offensive in glowing terms. It is now known
that during 1941 the RAF lost a bomber for every ten tons of bombs dropped
and that its strategic offensive killed more members of the RAF than German
civilians. In November 1941 the bomber offensive was broken off. According
to the official history (Strategic Air Offensive, i. 299): 'This was no less than
a formal expression of the belief that the results which Bomber Command
was achieving were not worth the casualties it was suffering.'

.   .   .   .   .

He said he was troubled about one opinion which he thought he
had detected in the MG—'a paper to which I pay more attention
than to all the other papers put together'. The point related to
the effects of our settled bombing policy. I asked whether he
referred to our having said that it was difficult to estimate the
effects of our bombing policy on Germany because so little information ever emerged, and he said 'No, not at all; I thought
that I had detected a suggestion that our bombing policy was so
ineffective that we could hope little from it in the way of reducing
Germany's strength and that we must look to a land campaign
first and foremost to defeat her.' I said that I did not know how
that impression had been given because it was certainly not the
interpretation of the bombing campaign that we had intended to
give. Our view was that we had to rely on bombing to reduce
Germany to the point at which our land campaign could be
regarded as having a chance of success.

.   .   .   .   .

5.00 P.M. J G WINANT AT THE AMERICAN EMBASSY

.   .   .   .   .

He thought that public opinion in the United States was pretty
good from our point of view and improving. The Roman Catho-

lics were not giving very much trouble and would not give much trouble in the future with regard to freedom of religion in Russia. The Isolationists, of course, would make the most of what trouble there was. He added that a very great relief to Roosevelt was that the Irish were no longer the thorn in the flesh that they were to Wilson in 1916–17. Except for a few in places like Chicago and Boston they would not give trouble to the Administration. Roosevelt was managing the situation in Congress very skilfully. The arming of merchantmen had already been agreed to.

.　　.　　.　　.　　.

6.00 P.M. SIR SAMUEL HOARE AT THE DORCHESTER

Hoare was on a short visit to England. Most of the interview is devoted to an account of conditions in Spain.

I asked him how he was and he replied 'As well as anyone could be after sixteen months in a lunatic asylum.' He was thoroughly wearied of what he called the 'iniquities' of Spain.

.　　.　　.　　.　　.

He talked a bit about the way in which British opinion in this country thought of Spain. The most important thing in his opinion was that we should make it clear that the Spanish were to settle their troubles under all circumstances for themselves. He said, for instance, that if Suñer[1] were killed by the generals the British could declare that all Spanish generals were as bad as one another, but they ought to treat the killing as a purely domestic Spanish business. It was a great error to exult over anything in Spain as being an anti-German victory. When Suñer recently nearly fell from power and some British newspapers immediately exulted over it, Suñer used this vigorously to declare that British opinion was interfering in Spanish politics to his detriment. Britain, he said, was 'dictating' to Spain. The Germans also worked very hard in Spain all the time to suggest that Britain and the British are putting pressure on Spain and interfering with her affairs.

The same in his opinion was true of France. It was highly desir-

---

1. Suñer was Spanish foreign minister.

able to let the French settle their troubles for themselves and not so
to treat Vichy or de Gaulle as to appear to be suggesting, let alone
dictating, to the French what they should do. It was a very lucky
thing for us that in both Spain and France the pro-German leaders
were the best hated men in both countries—Laval and Darlan,
Franco and Suñer. It was a great mistake to be continually holding
up de Gaulle as a great political statesman. He was in fact a most
difficult man to deal with and he was much disliked by Frenchmen both in and out of France. In his opinion we had made two
very bad mistakes: (1) it was an act of folly to withdraw our
representative from Vichy. Not only had we need to know at first
hand what was happening in Vichy, but also Pétain would have
been glad to have a British representative with him, and indeed
such a representation would have been most helpful; (2) de Gaulle
ought to have been treated exclusively as Commander of the Free
French Army and not as a political leader, and then all the
French would have welcomed him. Now, unhappily, it was
different.

.   .   .   .   .

25 October 1941

10.45 A.M. LORD BEAVERBROOK

Beaverbrook, who had been expecting to go out of town on
Saturday did not go and his secretary was looking for me on
Friday. It proved to be impossible to make an appointment and
Beaverbrook then rang me up at 10.45 on Saturday morning and,
after saying that he wanted to see me the next time I was in London, he talked for a minute or two on production and manpower.
He said that much greater effort was needed than was now being
made in various directions. There were so many claims on us that
we had got to do much better than we were at present doing. This
applied specially to MAP where we must get more women to
work. At present women's labour amounted to 30 per cent in
MAP and at the very least 50 per cent was required. He knew
that we had already had a great deal on this subject, but they
required all the assistance they could get and he hoped that we
would keep on pressing this point about women's labour.

12 NOON. COUNT RACZYNSKI

Difficulties in Polish relations with Russia.

20 November 1941

2.30 P.M. ANTHONY EDEN AT THE FOREIGN OFFICE

I first asked about the Russian request that this country should declare war on Finland and Hungary and Rumania. To leave out Finland for the moment, was there any objection to our declaring war against Hungary and Rumania? For instance, did any of our Allies object? It had been said that Poland did not want us to declare war on Hungary. He replied that really it was only a case of deciding what to do about Finland. It was not practicable to declare war on the other two if we would not declare war on Finland. If that difficulty were not in the way the objections of any of the Allies would not stop us. We should simply declare war on the pair of them. [Beneš afterwards told me that he took the view that war most certainly ought to be declared on Hungary and Rumania—see notes of talk with him.][1]

With regard to Finland there were a good many difficulties. The United States objected. There was in that country a very strong sentimental feeling for Finland. There was a strong feeling also against Russia. Finland, the Americans thought, was fundamentally fighting for her liberty and therefore they did not want us to be on the other side against her. Were they influenced by the remembrance that Finland alone had paid her war debts? He thought there was something in that. It helped to make up American sentiment but there was not very much in it. The next point was that the Cabinet was not at all united on the point. Labour was against declaring war; it had always had a close connection with Finland and maintained its friendship. He was a little puzzled by the insistence of the Russians in this matter. His own personal view, and it was only that, was that the Russians were really trying to get from us a certificate of virtue; they were asking us to whitewash them for their past sins in respect of Finland.

'The trouble between the Russians and the Poles,' he said, 'is going better now. The position had been pretty bad; the Russians refusing to let Polish soldiers out of prison and labour camps, and so on. Now things are much better and that is due to Stalin himself. We and the Poles have managed to get personal access to him and he is behaving very well indeed. The general diplomatic position is extremely difficult. The Ambassadors, including Cripps,

---

1. Great Britain declared war on Finland, Hungary and Romania on 5 December 1941.

are all at Kyubishev and have no direct touch with people at Moscow. They are not allowed, any of them, to go back to Moscow although they are very anxious to do so. Stalin, however, himself remains at Moscow and with him all the time is Molotov. There is reason to think that Molotov is the real trouble. He is anti-British, indeed anti-everybody. He won't let the Ambassadors or Cripps go back to Moscow and so there is no personal or direct touch with him. In spite of all that we have done and do the Russians still remain highly suspicious. Until quite recently they have refused to let Sikorski go to Russia. Now they have withdrawn their objections and he is on his way. My idea is that I should go to Moscow myself, not at present when things are so difficult in every way, but at an appropriate moment when things are looking better—then I will go. I have been there before, which will help, and I think, and at any rate I hope, that it will do good if I can establish direct contact with Stalin.'[1]

. . . . .

4.30 P.M. BRENDAN BRACKEN AT THE MINISTRY OF INFORMATION

Bracken became minister of information on 20 July 1941.

He said that the position was rather serious at the moment. There were very ugly reports about the Vichy Government having surrendered to German terms and he added 'It looks as if they had gone over completely.'

He talked of newspapers and complained that Lord Kemsley has just printed in the Daily Sketch an article by the highly anti-British Col McCormick. He then went on to discuss Lord Kemsley and his policy at some length.

He spoke of the MG, inquired about the supply of paper, asked how we were fixed in respect of having men called up, and said that he would be willing to help us, supposing there were a good case, if he could.

He mentioned the PM, said that he was very fond of the MG, read it closely, and wherever he went, even if it was to Scapa Flow, always had it sent after him.

He had a good deal to say about Kemsley's social ambitions; about his standing at No. 10 under Neville Chamberlain and now under Churchill. What Churchill liked about journalists and what

---

1. Eden visited Moscow and had talks with Stalin from 16 to 18 December.

he did not, and why he had 'no use for K'. He said that Churchill
had not yet met the new editor of the Times, (Barrington-Ward),
but must soon do so.

7.00 P.M. WINSTON CHURCHILL AT 10 DOWNING STREET

While I was waiting the door of the room opened and several
people came out. I looked up just in time to see the last of them,
who was Arthur Greenwood.

Then I went in and found Churchill sitting in his usual place
at the centre of the table with back to the fire. He said to me, after
the usual invitation to a whisky and soda—or rather in this case
water—'I have just been helping to reconstruct the world—I
don't know, but I think we have got to do a lot to win the war
first.'

.   .   .   .   .

He began to talk immediately about Libya.[1] 'Let's look at the
map', he said, and took me to a tremendously detailed map of
Northern Africa which was covered over with a sheet of trans-
parent paper on which the position of the principal units of both
sides was marked. He showed me the big stretch of desert roughly
south of Bardia where the two German armoured divisions had
their station, and south-west of them was marked the one Italian
armoured division. He put his elbow on the coast just east of
Sollum and swept his fore-arm round from due south up to the
coast west of Tobruk, indicating that the whole of our movement
was a sweeping, encircling one pivoted on the North-South line
from Sollum to Sidi Omar. 'It appears to be going well', he said,
'but one can't say whether we are going to win. We ought to, and
I am hopeful that we shall, but in such things one simply can't
tell. This offensive has been postponed; that was sad but it had to
be. The army out there had to be reinforced and I have sent out
force after force to join them. It is very strong now, very strong—
a really big army.' I asked about numbers and he said that it was
reckoned that within the great curve which we had made about
the enemy, there were 150,000 of them. I asked whether the
enemy had really suffered a surprise, since they must have been
expecting something like this day by day, and he said that nevertheless in a tactical sense he thought that they had been surprised

1. A British offensive in Libya began on 18 November 1941.

and that was a great gain to us. One strong point was that our Air Force had been much too good for them while we were concentrating our forces in their new positions for the immediate attack. This was the reason more than any other why the enemy had not spotted what we were after. It had been a tremendous operation to get the army up to the battle positions. 'Nothing walks, nothing! Even the tank is a baby that has to be carried. It is carried on a lorry right up to the position from which it begins to attack. Everything is carried—everything.' He mentioned the relative work of Auchinleck and Cunningham; the great responsibility that fell on Cunningham and the success that he had so far achieved. 'This is', he said, 'Cunningham's battle.'[1]

It had just been announced that Dill had been removed from the position of Chief of the Imperial Staff, and that he had been succeeded by Alan Brooke; also that Nye, a man forty-six years old who had risen from the ranks, had been appointed Deputy CIGS. The official War Office announcement had merely said that Dill had retired on reaching the age limit of sixty and that he had been appointed Governor of Bombay. Some of the newspapers had said that this age limit reason was obviously ridiculous. So I asked about it. The conversation went like this:

WPC   I wish you would tell me whether the age limit was the real and the only reason for Dill's departure. It seems rather rummy if a man who was held as a great military genius when he was appointed, should be allowed to go just because he reached sixty.

Ch   I didn't say that about him mind.

WPC   Perhaps it was the newspapers that said it!

Ch   Well, of course, they have to, don't they.

WPC   It is curious just to let him retire and not to give him another military job?

Ch   Well, at any rate he was not as good as his successor, Brooke, and as he was reaching the age limit I saw no reason to stop the normal process.

WPC   Still, couldn't he be given another military job?

Ch   Ah, but you can't do that. When a man's been CIGS, the greatest post in the army, you can't just go and give him some other military job—it can't be done.[2]

---

1. Auchinleck was commander-in-chief, Middle East, Cunningham commanded the Eighth army. He was relieved of his command on 26 November.

2. After Pearl Harbor, Dill became chief British representative on the combined chiefs of staff's committee in Washington.

WPC Still, isn't it a bit curious that when a man has held this highest of all military post he should be made just Governor of Bombay?

He was very amusing at this time. He stood with his back against the table facing me and he was only about two feet off. He had the whole time a quizzical and half-mocking look on his face.

Ch Well, (he said) I like to reward merit and he is a very able man.

WPC Yes, but Governor of Bombay!

Ch Well, it's an important place and I like to raise the status of Colonial Governorships! At any rate his successor, Brooke, is a very good man, and so is Nye, I can tell you, very good indeed; he has risen from the ranks.

WPC Sir William Robertson[1] rose from the ranks, didn't he, and he was not at all good, and he had to be got rid of, if I remember rightly?

Ch Oh, Nye is not that sort of man at all; he is not in the least like Robertson. He has a very good mind and is a really cultivated man. Besides he's young, and that's good. Don't forget that Napoleon had won some of his greatest victories by the time he was twenty-seven and had finished at forty-six.

Then, starting on a journey round the table, he said abruptly 'And I am not going to change Ministers either. I know what people are saying. They are saying "Why don't you get rid of Greenwood?", but in point of fact he is doing very good work, and besides Attlee wants him, and remember that Attlee is leader of the Labour party in the House.' He then went on to give, very vigorously, a little exposition of the party system. 'I am a Parliament man; I am a leader according to our Parliamentary system; I am devoted to Parliament myself and I am dependent on it. Well, the Conservatives in the House have a majority of about a hundred over all the other parties, and I have to think of that, I have to take account of that in what I do. And at any rate I have left no genius out of the Government that I know of. There's only the "awkward squad" of opponents, including Shinwell—and when I offered him a job in the Government he would not take it.'

WPC I know all that, but nevertheless I am sure that people

---

1. CIGS, 1915–18.

don't like the idea of too much attention being paid by you to the party system.

Ch   Well, if it comes to that, the Conservatives have not had more than their due share of places in the Government; as a matter of fact, they have not had their due share. The Labour people have had more than they should, and so have the Liberals. Why, only the other day I gave Sinclair another Under-Secretary because he asked it of me: I gave him little Seely.[1]

I said that I should have thought that the Conservatives had had, to say the least, their share of offices, and mentioned various names.

Ch   Oh, there are a whole lot of non-party men in the Government—Leathers, Anderson, ——

WPC   But Anderson sits as a Conservative for a Conservative constituency.

Ch   Yes, I know, but he is not a party man at all.

I said he would be if there were a party question. 'And what about Beaverbrook, doesn't he rank as a Conservative?'

He said 'No', with great emphasis, and I said, 'Well, maybe not. I know it amuses him to be called one, but all the same the party machine reckons him as one when it tots up representation in the Government.'

Then I asked about the demand for a Minister of Production which he had recently refused. He said 'The truth is that such a Minister is not needed. The thing works without him, and that is what matters. Whether it is a perfect system in theory or not it works in practice.' Had Beaverbrook chosen to take it he could have had the job at the end of his time at MAP; he could, that is to say, have combined both jobs into one office, but he didn't want it. One of the principal reasons was his health.[2] 'When he is all right he can take on anything, but when he has his asthma he is miserable, and he wants to get out of things. And, mind you, I need him; I need him. He is stimulating and, believe me, he is a big man.' Then he went on to say that the reason the present system worked was that supplies for the Army, the Admiralty, and

---

1. Lord Sherwood, formerly Sir Hugh Seely, became additional under-secretary for air on 20 July 1941.

2. Beaverbrook repeatedly refused the job of minister of production because he did not believe he would be given effective power, and Churchill claimed that the existing system, or absence of system, was satisfactory because he did not want a minister of production with effective power.

MAP all had their definite allocations and one could not encroach
on the supplies of the other. I said, might it not be true that B
would go and 'pinch' some of the material that belonged to the
other Ministries, and I reminded him of the old story that B had
sent lorries to collect the material that he wanted regardless of the
just claims of other people.

'Oh, yes', he added, 'I know that story, but it belongs anyway
to the beginning of things when he first started at MAP; he could
not do it now if he wanted to; he simply could not get the stuff.
It could not be done under the system. MAP has to have so much
of this and so much of that and it can't be deprived by anyone
else of those quantities. Any such charges of buccaneering are
simply not true.' Then,

> Ch   Tell me this, whom am I to make Minister of Produc-
>   tion, anyway? Who is it to be? Anderson, Reith?[1] Well,
>   neither, of them knows anything about the subject,
>   and in any case Reith is difficult enough.

I asked him about Japan and did he think that she was going
to war. He said 'Until a few weeks ago I did not think so; now I
am not so sure.'

LIBYA Ch 'If we get possession of Libya we shall have within
our reach all the Eastern Mediterranean and everything northwards up to Central Italy', and here he swept his hand up over
the lower part of Italy. I inquired about Bizerta, and he said that
he thought that undoubtedly the Germans would like to send
supplies and reinforcements over to Bizerta and they might be
able to make Vichy agree. If they did, 'our submarines would be
active'.

He referred to Malta and said 'That place has made a great
show. It never could have been expected.'

He then said that he agreed with almost everything that had
appeared in the MG, but on one subject he disagreed, and that
was India. He would be prepared for the British getting out of
India if he were sure that all India was agreed about it, but he
would not agree that we should get out and leave our Army, Navy
and Air Force to defend India while the Hindus oppressed a great
minority which, if left to itself, would be capable of dominating
the Hindus and ruling India. 'If that is what they want,' he said,
dropping his voice to a subdued and obstinate note, 'well, they

---

1. Sir John Reith was minister of works and buildings. Churchill said of him: 'There,
but for the grace of God, goes God.'

won't get it.' I said my point was that however difficult the situation the Government must keep making fresh efforts and not abdicate. The Viceroy had declared that nothing at all more could be granted, and then had granted much more. He intervened vigorously and said, 'No, in point of fact they didn't get much more.'

As I was leaving he spoke of the gravity of the whole situation and said, 'But, I'll pull you through yet—if you let me.' And at the finish, when shaking hands, he said, 'I think it is going to be a good show in Libya, but I am not predicting, and I have not predicted, a great victory—have I?—but you wait and I'll give you a much better show than this before long—you wait—a much better show.'

21 November 1941

9.30 A.M. LESLIE HORE-BELISHA

I asked him about his health, as I knew he was on a duodenal diet. He said he had given up smoking and he was sticking to the diet. He did not, however, believe that it was 'scientific'. He found that he was suffering from a certain amount of skin trouble and it was due to the lack of vitamin C in his blood. The diet did not contain any vitamin C. He had had blood tests and the specialist had told him he had no vitamin C in him. 'You also,' he said to me, 'probably have no vitamin C in you.' He was now having vitamin C injected into him.

He was much concerned about the Gort Despatches on the BEF in France. He said that the two reports, one relating to events before the German offensive and the other relating to the course of the offensive, were not consistent and were not accurate. 'It is rotten.' In his first dispatch, he said—before the German offensive —Gort had praised all the preparations made for and by the BEF, and then when it came to the story of defeat and retreat he suddenly announced, 'I had misgivings' about the preparations and the supplies. As a matter of fact it was obvious that he only had the misgivings when we were driven back. The simple truth was that the BEF had been well equipped for its intended task, but it had never been intended to fight a very large part of the German army so concentrated against the British and in no scheme that had ever been envisaged by the Government, War Office Staff, or by anybody else, had this been expected or provided for. He considered that the advance into Belgium when the Germans attacked had been a great blunder. The French had insisted on it, but why had not the Government resisted? Neither the Government nor Gort need have been a mere cypher. He considered that the policy for which he had pressed when War Minister in the winter 1939–40 was the right one. He had urged the building of a strong line across the North of France to join up with the Maginot Line, and then they should have stood on the defensive while the Germans battered themselves against the wall. The Germans had only destroyed the Maginot Line by out-manoeuvring it; that is to say by breaking through the unfortified French front, so that there was no proper defensive line at all.

Discussing the collapse of France, he said that in his opinion there were too many symptoms in this country of the same sort of decadence. 'At the top there were', he considered, 'all the signs of a nation in decay.' Everywhere there was the Public School tie spirit. It was bad form to make one-self disagreeable to anyone. The War Office would not put up any fight against the Air Force. Everyone was for working amicably with other old-school-tie friends, rather than demanding and fighting for what they needed and what they ought to have. Instead of the War Office demanding aircraft from the Air Force people for their own legitimate purposes, what they said to the Air Force Command was, 'Now let us have a few more planes, there's a good chap.' Nobody must be offended or affronted and, of course, nobody must be dismissed. The question was whether we could undermine this caste system from below. For himself he very much doubted it. The governing classes nearly always succeeded in absorbing those from other classes who pushed themselves into the governing world. He thought they were beginning to absorb even Bevin. Look at his own experience. As soon as he began to stand up to any of them they said he was rude and proceeded to get rid of him. To come back to France, it was true that one great cause of her collapse was corruption. He did not think that we had that in this country, but in other respects there were similar symptoms and he thought that as things were going now there really was a danger of our losing the war unless we dealt with these defects.

11.30 A.M. BJÖRN PRYTZ AT 27 PORTLAND PLACE

I asked him about the question whether we were going to declare war on Finland, and he said he had been trying hard to persuade us not to do it; it was all wrong if we did do it. That is to say, he meant that it was morally wrong. The Finns were only fighting to regain what had been recently taken from them by Russia and we had no right to declare them to be our enemies. Moreover, it was the fact that border States like the Turks and the Poles all disapproved of our declaring war on Finland, and especially the Turks did. He could point out that the next thing that would happen would be that Japan would attack Russia and then we should be called on by Russia to declare war on Japan, with the United States not in the war at all.

The Finns, he said, could not trust the present Government of Russia at all, and for obvious reasons, 'No one does.' I mentioned the obvious arguments why Finland would have to be regarded by us as an enemy, and he said that in his considered opinion the disadvantages of declaring war on Finland would more than counterbalance the advantages and, once more, it was morally wrong. Actually, he said, the Russians had promised very little in the way of concessions to Finland if she should be willing to make peace and there was very little doubt that she was not willing to make peace. I reminded him that he had often spoken to me about the danger that Finland was running if she made a permanent enemy of a great power like Russia. He said that he knew of this, but above all he did not want Great Britain to be a formal enemy of Finland.

He said that if Sweden was in danger of being thrown into the war it was because there might come about a great battle in the North, e.g. the Russians pressing into Finland and being met there by a German army, with the battle spreading over the Swedish frontier. Or possibly the time might come when we would invade Norway and the danger would come from the other frontier. Moreover, it had to be remembered that Sweden was not badly off for food and that as conditions grew worse in Germany the Germans might regard her as a 'very tempting morsel' which they could, and at any moment might seize.

1.30 P.M. LORD BEAVERBROOK AT SHELL MEX HOUSE

I found Beaverbrook with Citrine of the TUC.[1] He presented me to him as 'The Editor of the Communist paper—the MG.' Then he told Citrine about the Labour meeting in Manchester the Saturday before, when a member of the audience had asked him why the Daily Worker could not be re-established, and he had

1. Sir Walter Citrine, general secretary of the TUC.

replied, 'Why, what is wrong with the Manchester Guardian?' This, he said, had got him out of an awkward corner.[1]

Then he took us to a big map and showed us the Libyan front. He pointed to El Rezegh and said that actually the British were 30 miles or so to the west of this place and were about 140 away from Benghazi. I asked what had happened to the German tank forces, and he said that we had gone looking for them and that we had found them 'dispersed' and would have to find a way of dealing with them.

When we went to lunch I asked him how he had got on with Stalin,[2] and he said he thought that they had liked each other very well. 'I could not understand him, but I liked him all the same.' After that he turned to an article which Citrine had written in the Daily Herald on the 'Second Front', the last of a series of articles that Citrine had written after coming back from Russia. He said, 'I don't like what you say in this article, Walter, about the "Second Front".' (He called him Walter throughout the conversation.) 'However,' he said, 'I'll come back to that presently. Only I'll tell you what I want you to do. Stop all building!' (waving his arms violently). 'What,' said Citrine, 'do you mean stop all Government building?' 'Yes,' he said, 'there are a million men involved in it.' 'No,' said Citrine. 'There are not a million men.' Then followed a brisk argument as to what ought or ought not to be regarded as coming under Government building— hostels, huts, factories, and all that sort of thing. Beaverbrook insisted on his figure and finally summoned a secretary and demanded documents. As a result of the documents he declared triumphantly that a million men was right. Then he began again, 'Look at the factories that have been started; the new factories these last few weeks; three or four factories have been started this very month. The MAP says that it wants factories and must have them. The War Office says that it wants buildings of this kind and the other kind which is not much better. There is no one to stop any of them and we at the Ministry of Supply have to obey. Well, that is what I want you to do, Walter. Stop it all and save the labour.'

I intervened and asked who settled a thing like that and who stops the building.

Citrine   The Cabinet, it is the Cabinet that stops it.
Beaverbrook Ah, but then, of course, there is the labour

---

1. The Daily Worker had been banned on 21 January 1941.
2. Beaverbrook went to Moscow in October 1941.

representative, the Minister of Labour, who has to be considered—a strong, independent man, full of ideas and most outspoken [roars of laughter].

Citrine   Well, I have sometimes differed very strongly from Bevin.

Beaverbrook What, differ from Bevin! Why, it's a crime for anyone to differ from Bevin.

Then they came again to the question of the article in the Daily Herald, which Beaverbrook had been looking through. When Beaverbrook said, 'You know it contained so and so', Citrine replied, 'How do you know that? You have not read the article!'

'Oh, yes I have,' said Beaverbrook, 'I have read it.'

'When?' said Citrine. 'Just now', replied Beaverbrook.

'You can't have read it in three or four minutes,' said Citrine.

'Yes, but I did', said Beaverbrook. 'Shall I give you a summary?' He then proceeded to give a very lucid and connected summary of the whole article from start to finish, and Citrine had to admit that he had done it very well.[1] Citrine then proceeded to speak at great length on his own views of British policy regarding Russia and about Labour in this country. It was all addressed to Beaverbrook, who presently got up and walked about the room, going round and round the table. Sometimes his back was presented to Citrine, who then addressed his argument to me. After a time Beaverbrook wandered towards the door, which was right behind Citrine, and Citrine kept looking over his shoulder to make sure that Beaverbrook was still there. After a time Beaverbrook, who was within my sight all the time, quietly slipped out of the room and disappeared. Citrine went on addressing me for about a minute until at last, noticing the complete silence behind him, he looked round and found that there was no one there. At this, with immense seriousness, he leaned over towards me and said in a penetrating whisper, 'He's a ——, isn't he? He *is* a ——!'[2]

Beaverbrook having returned to the room, gone out again with a secretary and come back in the conversation went on to Russia and the Russian army, and the question of a token force. B said that to take advantage of Russia's man-power and to arm it

---

1. Citrine also tells this story in Two Careers, 43–44. He places it in Beaverbrook's early days at MAP and says the article was from The Manchester Guardian. As Crozier's record is contemporary and Citrine's is not, no doubt Crozier is right.

2. Experience of the trade-union world suggests that the missing word was bugger, not bastard.

efficiently was much the best thing that we could possibly do. The Russians wanted us to open up a 'second front' in Norway or France but that was not advisable.[1] Citrine said Yes that was so and he had been told that they also talked of our opening a front in the Caucasus, but he did not believe that. He added that when he was in Russia he found that there was still great distrust of this country. The Russians were suspicious and secretive and he thought that they would remain so during the war 'and at the peace'.

Beaverbrook spoke of the great difficulties in regard to shipping. What was the use of talking about a second front when all the available shipping was needed in any event to carry materials to Russia?

3.45 P.M. PRESIDENT BENEŠ AT 9 GROSVENOR PLACE

This interview is Beneš at his most fanciful.

.   .   .   .   .

He said that in his opinion a peace offensive was coming pretty soon. 'The Generals know that they are beaten and are preparing the way for a peace overture. The German army is becoming steadily weaker and they know it. They will, of course, shout all the more loudly about their strength and their terrible intentions. They will threaten to "destroy everything". That is what Von Papen has just been saying in an interview given in Ankara. He says that Germany's enemies had better make peace with her when they can because if they do not the German armies would exact a terrible penalty.'

Things were moving very rapidly in Germany. He knew that Bishop Von Galen, who had recently been denouncing the Nazi Party and praising the Army, had been put up to it by the Generals and it was because of their protection that no harm had come to him. Not only, however, were they protecting him, they had actually instigated him.

He said there was no doubt about the sort of terms that the Generals had in view and would like to get:

(1) They wanted to have a string of small vassal States set up to the East and South of Germany—Croatia, Slovakia, Bohemia, Poland, etc.

---

1. For once Beaverbrook was loyally toeing the official line. On 19 October he had submitted a memorandum to the war cabinet, advocating some military action in the west, and had been overruled.

(2) They would offer to evacuate at once all the countries in Western Europe that they had occupied.

(3) They would undertake to get rid of the Nazis and they would be ready to do it. Whether they would get rid of Hitler himself would depend entirely on circumstances. They had used him and would continue to use him if they could, but if need be they would get rid of him along with, or after, the Nazi party and the other Nazi bosses.[1]

Any such peace overtures would, of course, be extremely dangerous if there were any idea of considering them. To him the Generals were just as bad as Hitler. I asked what would happen if the peace offensive failed. He was not prepared to say; the Generals would act according to the circumstances at the moment, but we must be ready for violent action by them in the Spring.

He thought that if the Russians held firmly and the United States came in we might get to the end of the war within twelve months. We ought to win the Libyan campaign outright and then smash Italy. In his view Italy would then crumble, she would have to be occupied by the Germans, just like Rumania, and even this would be good for us; nothing, he thought, would prevent Italy from crumbling into bits.

I asked whether he was in favour of our declaring war on Hungary and Rumania. He replied that he certainly was. He said that it was a moral duty to show that fraud and violence such as they had been guilty of could not be rewarded, but must be punished. Both of them would have to be punished, but this need not prevent Hungary from coming later on into some sort of federation of the South-Eastern States. It was wrong that Britain, the leader of the Allies, should continue to be in a state of peace with countries which had behaved so wickedly.

He insisted that things were a good deal worse with the Germans and with the German Army than people in this country thought. He gave an illustration of what might happen in such a matter. In August, 1918, he was informed that the Austrian Government was about to allow a secret delegation of Czechs to go to Geneva in order to meet him and find out about possible peace terms. So, first of all he went to have a talk with Foch in order to find out what Foch thought about the military prospects. Foch told him that he ought to base his plans on the assumption that it would be six months or more before the condition of Germany and her Allies

---

1. This may have been the programme of some members of the so-called German Resistance. It was not seriously supported by any of the generals on active service.

would make peace possible. After a short interval he went and met the Czechs in Geneva and he spoke to them on the basis of this advice from Foch. On the very day, he said, when he was telling them about the 'six months', news came that Vienna was in revolt, and this was in effect an announcement that war was over for Austria-Hungary. He had never forgotten this lesson and he mentioned it now because he believed that Germany and the German armies were in a worse condition that we in this country thought.

6

Defeats and Discontents, 1942

On 7 December 1941 the Japanese attack on Pearl Harbor brought the United States into the war. A fortnight later Churchill and Roosevelt, with their military advisers, met in Washington for the first of their war conferences. On the eastern front, the Soviet armies halted the Germans at the gates of Moscow and soon afterwards began an offensive of their own. Great Britain now had two great allies. Total victory, previously so remote, now seemed sure or at any rate likely.

There were still dark days to come. The first six months of 1942 saw an almost unbroken record of defeats. Crozier's interviews, which run only from January to May, cover most of this gloomy time. In the Far East, the battleship Prince of Wales and the battlecruiser Repulse were sunk on 10 December 1941. Hong Kong fell to the Japanese on Christmas day. Singapore fell on 15 February 1942—the gravest capitulation in British history. The Japanese overran Burma and broke into the Indian ocean. There were fears for Ceylon and for India itself. In Libya Rommel launched an offensive on 21 January and drove the British forces back to the Gazala line. The Soviet offensive petered out. Most challenging of all to British pride, the two German cruisers Scharnhorst and Gneisenau passed through the English channel from Brest to Germany on 12 February 1942 virtually unscathed.

These setbacks provoked considerable discontent in England. There were complaints that some ministers were incompetent and that Churchill was taking too much on himself. His critics demanded an independent minister of defence, a proposal which, if carried out, would have dislodged him from supreme direction of the war. Churchill rejected this proposal firmly but he yielded to some extent. The reconstruction of the government on 19 February, fortunately coinciding with one of Crozier's visits to London, was the nearest thing to a political upheaval in British politics during the second world war. The reconstruction had a number of causes. One was the attempt to establish an overlord of production—a position that Beaverbrook attained on 4 February, only to abandon it in disgruntlement a fortnight later. A second was the return of Sir Stafford Cripps from his post as ambassador at Moscow. He enjoyed an undeserved popularity as the saviour of the country. He was brought into the war cabinet and made leader of the house of commons, partly to render him harmless, partly to cloak Attlee's ineffectiveness. At the same time seven ministers of cabinet rank were dismissed or moved to other posts.

The discontent was not allayed. The rank and file of the Labour party were restless. In March Churchill wished to ban the Daily Mirror. Herbert Morrison had difficulty in persuading him to be content with a stern warning.

By-elections ran steadily against the National government—between March and June four Independent rebels were returned. On 20 June Tobruk fell. At the beginning of July a vote of no confidence in Churchill was moved in the house of commons. It was heavily defeated, but the surge of discontent ended only with the victories of the autumn. Crozier's interviews do not cover the end of this period. They give only a dramatic picture of the months when men railed against failures that were to prove the prelude to victory.

15 January 1942

3.30 P.M. ANTHONY EDEN AT THE FOREIGN OFFICE

With Churchill absent at Washington, Eden, though not officially deputy prime minister, was the only minister qualified to give general information of the course of the war.

.   .   .   .   .

I asked first about Finland and he said that he had no knowledge whatever of any peace feelers being put out by the Finns. Russia would want the 1940 frontiers—all of them and would accept nothing less. He thought that in point of fact this was not so bad for Finland. I then asked about possible imperialist designs on the part of Russia and against Finland. He said that Stalin had told him 'quite definitely' that he had no such designs against Finland or anywhere else.

Eden went on to say that we had to make up our minds about Russia. Either she was International Communist in her intentions or she was a Peter-the-Great Russia. Personally he was convinced that Stalin's policy was that of a Peter-the-Great Russia and that we could, and therefore must, live with her in Europe. I said that this was all very well, but one would like to know how far the ambitions of a Peter-the-Great Russia might extend; and he replied that Stalin had convinced him that Russia was, and would be, reasonable in her aims. She would, however, certainly want the Baltic States, and Stalin had said so.

Then he turned to Singapore and the criticisms of inadequate preparations. He said there were two points: (1) so far as the Singapore authorities had asked for men to be sent out the British Government had sent them all that they had asked for and even more; (2) it had not been able to send out as much equipment as it would have liked, and this was because it had to meet the drain of the Libyan campaign and still more of the Russian campaign. The simple truth was that we had given to Russia what we ourselves needed here now and that in consequence we had not really got enough for ourselves. It was very unfortunate. In 1940 we had to repair the enormous gaps made by the loss of the BEF equipment. We had done that, sent masses of stuff out to Libya, and then just when the war material was coming out in great quantity for our own use we had to send away a large part of it to the Russians.

I then told him of the suggestion which I had heard that the defences of Singapore had been considered only from the side of the sea and not from that of a land attack. He ridiculed the idea and said it was completely untrue.[1] What was true was that things had turned out very differently from what anyone, Generals included, had expected. 'I am not a soldier', he said, 'but the soldiers also had been wrong about events. Hong Kong, for instance, had held out for two weeks only, whereas all the plans had been made on the assumption that the place would hold out for four months.' He was in Russia with General Nye when the news came that Hong Kong had fallen and he had said to Nye, 'However has it happened?' And Nye replied to him, 'I don't know, I just don't understand it.' Then he said 'It may be the same with Singapore. However, we are not only sending reinforcements, but reinforcements have already got there, including fighters. It is a risky business and I tell you that I was very glad to hear that they had got there.'

Then he went on, 'There was another thing that we never reckoned on. We never expected that the Japanese would have sea supremacy. We never thought that such a thing as the disaster at Pearl Harbour would come about and, of course, we never expected to lose our big ships.' I asked about aircraft not being available because (as the official report had said) their airfields were under attack. He replied that as a matter of fact there *were* aircraft available, but the big ships, according to the usual practice, did not use their wireless lest they should disclose their position to the enemy. Finally, he said, one of them did use its wireless, but by this time a Japanese plane had spotted them and in another four hours the attack came. I inquired why no fighter protection had been sent with the two ships when they were on their way to Singapore. He said [as afterwards stated by Churchill] that there was no aircraft carrier on which to send them. He agreed that we must somehow save Singapore, and he sincerely hoped that we should, but . . . ? I said that the Japanese were now spreading

---

1. It was true.

themselves over the seas just as though there were no American fleet 'in being'. To that he said 'And I am afraid that is just about true!' The question, to his mind, was whether we ought not to have retreated more quickly in Malaya than we had done. In a further reference to the battleships, I questioned whether under the circumstances they could have greatly delayed the Japanese landings, as there must have been Japanese battleships waiting for them in the background. He said 'No, so far as we were aware, there was no Japanese squadron anywhere which could have interfered with our big ships. The Japanese battleships were then strung out south and south-east of the Philippines waiting for the American fleet.'

He turned to Libya, and said that the new demands from the Far East were unfortunate. Last year we had to choose between Libya and Greece, and now Auchinleck had to choose between Libya and the Far East. He very much hoped that we would be able to go right on to Tripoli, but he was non-committal. He wanted us to go on because it was so important for reasons of prestige and political objects. We could rely on it that the Germans would do everything in their power to get reinforcements over to Tripoli, and they were already attempting to neutralise Malta. Our position along the whole north coast of Africa was difficult, especially for our fleet, because of the German possession of Crete, from which they were sending their aircraft to scour up and down all the time. He mentioned that we had lost a battleship in those waters (the Barham).[1]

He mentioned the French Islands and their seizure by De Gaulle's people.[2] All that had happened while he was in Russia and he had had a 'terrible time' since he came back, between the Free French, the Americans, and Churchill in Washington. De Gaulle had promised not to seize the islands, and then he had gone and done it. When we asked him about it he said, 'Well, I knew that the Canadians were going there, so I went there myself.' The Americans had been disappointing; they had made so much trouble about it. Once the Free French had gone into the islands it was quite impossible to get them out. France had had sovereignty and it still belonged to her and De Gaulle felt that he could not risk losing it to anyone. Personally, he believed that the American annoyance was all a part of Pan-Americanism. The

---

1. Sunk by U-boat on 25 November 1941.
2. On 24 December 1941 Free French forces occupied the islands of St. Pierre and Miquelon in impudent defiance of the American government.

United States did not like any foreign Power at all in those islands and was therefore annoyed when there was any change of status, even if it involved no change of sovereignty.

Churchill had been very funny over this business. 'He got me out of bed at 3.30 in the morning to talk to him about it, and the trouble was that Churchill, being at Washington, had absorbed the American point of view.' 'You must get them out', he had said, and later, 'I don't think you have done at all well over this!' He did not mind what the PM said to him. 'The PM can be very nice to those whom he likes, but if he doesn't like you he can be very disagreeable.'

Criticism was blowing up strongly and he thought that Churchill when he returned ought to strengthen his Ministry. 'I know he did not want to recently, and he may refuse to do it now, but I think he ought to agree.' I remarked, 'The best thing would be to avert the storm by not losing Singapore', and he said, 'Oh, yes, but there's a lot of trouble coming.'

.   .   .   .   .

16 January 1942

12 NOON. BJÖRN PRYTZ AT 27 PORTLAND PLACE

I said I had noticed that Goebbels was making himself unpleasant to Sweden, and he said, 'Yes, and not Goebbels only.' Sweden, however, was keeping a firm course. She was determined, if possible, to keep out of the war and her defences were now pretty good. Her chief trouble was that they had no supplies of oil for the air force (he had complained of this before), and they had no means of obtaining it. They were running tanks on wood spirit, but wood spirit was no use for aeroplanes.

Regarding Finland, he said he had no knowledge at all that the Finns were putting out, or were intending to put out, any overtures for peace. Sweden had done what she could and had had no success. All he could say now was that they hoped that some moment would come when the Russians would still be willing to make a reasonable peace with Finland and Finland would be in a position to defy Germany, but that moment at any rate had not come yet. In Sweden they were still afraid that they might become involved in the war through Russia driving the Finns and Germans back across Finland until the German army finally retreated into Sweden. Then the Russians would, of course, expect

Sweden to intern the Germans and the Germans would threaten them with attack if they did any such thing.

Incidentally, he said that he considered that Sweden had conferred an enormous benefit on Britain when she had refused point-bank to allow a British expeditionary army to go across Sweden to the help of Finland. If she had given permission there was no doubt at all that Britain would have been at war with Russia long ago, and that would have complicated matters very considerably. Sweden ought to be thanked because she had made it possible for Russia and Britain now to be full allies against Germany.

With regard to Hitler, he considered that the Generals had manoeuvred him into taking the job of Commander-in-Chief and that it had been a very clever move on their part.[1]

He was not enormously impressed by the victories of the Japanese. Certainly it would take a great deal of time now to win the war in the Pacific, but he declined to regard either that war or Singapore as being decisive. Hitler and Germany were the things that mattered, and he went on to say that in his opinion the greatest achievement of all that Churchill had brought off in America had been to persuade the United States Government to regard Germany as being the enemy no less than Japan.[2] He thought that it was a tremendous piece of work and it showed that Churchill is 'a great man'. He put it alongside of Churchill's action in declaring immediately that Britain stood with Russia when she was attacked by Hitler.

He was rather amusing about the loss of the Prince of Wales and the Repulse. He said he regarded it as 'almost providential' that they should have gone down. He had heard such scathing criticisms in London about the inefficiency of the Americans at Pearl Harbour, that if the British had not had something to confess about their own inefficiency 'the American alliance might have been in danger'.

He had had a talk with Maisky, who had only one complaint to make about the British. It was that the British did not really want to win victory in 1942. I said that such an idea was ridiculous. 'Well', he said, 'you may be right, but I know a man in the FO, not very high up, who said to me "I hope to God that the Germans won't suddenly collapse now, precisely at the moment when the Russians would be top dog at the peace conference, having done

1. This was not so. Hitler took over the job because he decided that Brauchitsch, the commander-in-chief, was no good.

2. The American decision had been taken long before and owed nothing to British encouragement.

more to beat the Germans than the British and much more than the Americans!" '

He mentioned that the Swedish Government had had to put on a stronger censorship of the Press in Stockholm because, he said, the newspapers were printing such astonishing stories, and Stockholm seemed likely to become 'the mother of all lies'.

He made an interesting observation on the effect in this country of the loss of the two battleships. He said he had been greatly struck by the calm and restraint with which public opinion had received that disaster. He said that he thought it implied a steadiness of mind and reserve of strength which were a great advantage to the people of this country. They were grieved and hurt, but they were not badly shaken and it made no difference at all to their determination to go straight on to the end.

3.30 P.M. PRESIDENT BENEŠ, AT 9 GROSVENOR PLACE

He reminded me that on the last occasion he had talked about the signs of disagreement between the Generals and the Nazi party. Now, with the assumption by Hitler of the command of the army, the quarrel had become graver, whatever might be done to patch it up. Three conferences of great importance had taken place in Germany or on the German front towards the end of last year.

The first was at the end of November and took place at Berlin. It consisted partly of Generals, including Brauchitsch, and partly of civilians, including Himmler. Brauchitsch had made the principal speech and had insisted that things were not going at all well with the offensive on the Russian front. He also declared that he had always advised against the move along the Black Sea and the Sea of Azov towards the Caucasus (a German army had, of course, been thrown out of Rostov-on-Don). He mentioned all the serious difficulties which he had foreseen as affecting this advance. Thereupon Himmler interrupted and said, 'Why, then, did you not tell all this to the Führer', to which Brauchitsch replied 'Why should I alone tell him the truth when all the others tell him lies?'

On 1 December a conference to discuss the situation was held at military headquarters. All the principal Generals were there and so was Himmler. Brauchitsch again addressed the meeting. He announced that in his opinion the offensive against Moscow could no longer succeed and that the German army must fall back on a line running from Leningrad on the north, through Smolensk and Kursk to Taganrog on the Black Sea. Hitler refused to accept the decision. Brauchitsch was supported by five of the senior Generals, namely Bock, Leeb, Kleist, Guderian and one other. Hitler was supported by Himmler, Keitel, Jodl, Reichenau and one or two of the younger Generals. The meeting broke up without a decision and was resumed the following day. Overnight the six Generals all decided to hand in their resignations, and in fact when the conference began again on the next day they had done so. Their resignations were not accepted, but Brauchitsch was shortly afterwards dismissed, and he said that four out of the other five had been got rid of [Von Bock was afterwards reinstated by Hitler].[1]

Beneš said that not only was he sure that the Russians would go on attacking the Germans right up to the spring, but that he thought that the German armies would have to retreat to a line running through Riga, on the north, to Odessa, on the south. He thought that the Germans would undoubtedly open a new offensive against Russia in the spring, but that this would be stopped and broken sooner than that of 1941. Then the Russians would open a great counter-offensive, and the Allies also would have to do something equivalent to support them. He foresaw the possibility that Germany might collapse in the late summer or the autumn of this year. He would not predict it, but he thought that we must reckon with its possibility, and that in itself imposed a great obligation on us. There was undoubtedly great gloom and depression in Germany and he did not doubt at all that the Generals has come to the conclusion that they could not now win the war. On the whole he was disposed to think not only that the Generals had pushed Hitler into the supreme command of the army, but that they were now at heart against him as well as against the Nazi party. You could always trust German Generals to escape the internal consequences of their own defeat. Ludendorff and Hindenburg had done so in 1918–19, and the present Generals would manage somehow to evade responsibility and to push it on to Hitler.

He said he wanted to mention one great danger. He knew what was going to happen when the Russian armies approached Germany. The German people would revolt. They would sack Hitler and the Nazis and they would appeal to the nice kind British to send troops to occupy all Germany in order to keep the dreadful Bolsheviks out. At the same time they would, of course, seek peace, but the whole thing would be a plot to play on the feelings of the lenient, forgiving, sentimental English in order to avert a Russian

---

1. All this is quite imaginary.

invasion. It would not do. Of course, the British must invade and occupy Germany, but they must do so along with the Russians, the Poles, the Czechs and all the other Allies.

He ended up by saying that although he did not believe that an early collapse of Germany was coming, it was absolutely essential to assume that such a thing was possible and to prepare for it. Britain, Russia and the Allies must on no account allow themselves to be taken by surprise—by an early peace. They must have all their plans for the settlement worked out and agreed on before-hand lest a sudden collapse of Germany, however little we might expect it, should find us *un*agreed. 'I am always pressing the necessity for this on your Foreign Office, because you know, Mr Crozier, British policy is not always marked by an excess of clarity.'

17 January 1942

11.30 A.M. IVAN MAISKY AT 13 KENSINGTON PALACE GARDENS

I began by mentioning to him that I knew that he was being asked to accept an honorary degree at Manchester University, and I inquired whether he was likely to come. He said he was much pleased by the invitation, but otherwise he was rather non-committal, saying that he was still waiting to hear certain further particulars. [Actually he wrote a few days later saying that he could not for various reasons accept the degree; his special reason was that he knew nothing about the Law!]

With regard to the Russian front, he thought that things were going well and would continue to go well. 'I feel very confident. We are going to keep on fighting all the winter and we do not intend to let the Germans get away from us.' The German Generals had disagreed with Hitler about the last offensive against Moscow and he had insisted on it. As to Hitler's having taken over the supreme command of the army, he thought that partly he had pushed himself into the job and partly the Generals had helped to push him in in order that he might be forced to bear the responsibility for anything that might happen. 'Hitler has now been in supreme command of the army for nearly a month and'—[here he was much amused]—'nothing very favourable has been happening to him so far.' It was now clear, he went on, that the Russian people possessed a unity which had hitherto always been denied in this country. They had none of the inward rottenness that afflicted Tsarist Russia in 1916–17—'and which has afflicted France in this war'. I asked him whether he had expected the collapse of France, and he said, 'I certainly never expected it to be so complete, but I began to fear something of the kind in 1938 to 1939.'

He described the Russian strategy. They had begun their counter-offensive just at the right moment, when the Germans were at last held up. There had been two extremely dangerous moments when Russia had looked like losing Moscow altogether—once in November and once in December, when the diplomatists had been hurried off to Kuibyshev. It was Russia's 'New Armies' that had brought about the German retreat. Ever since the war began in June one set of armies had stood up to the German attack and had carried out the retreat. Meanwhile new armies were being organised in the rear. These came into action in mid-December and they would carry on the fighting till spring. Then they would be withdrawn and another set of armies (the third) would be ready for the next stage. The morale of the Russian soldiers was much better than that of the Germans. They had captured many letters on German dead or prisoners, and these were letters freely written which had not yet gone through the hands of the German military censors. They showed a growing gloom and nervousness, reluctance to go on fighting, and a dread that they would not get back to Germany. The German Army in Russia today was by no means as formidable as the army which attacked in June.

He had really only one anxiety. The Russians were preparing for victory in the course of this year (1942); they believed that they could decisively defeat the Germans in the autumn or winter of this year. The British, however (and the Americans) were preparing for victory in 1943. There was thus discrepancy in the time-programme and therefore in military preparations, and therefore in politics also. 'I don't like this position.' He thought that we ought to do something big to join with the Russians in forcing a decision in 1942. This something, this new enterprise, might conceivably be in Western Europe, but it need not be. It might be in the Balkans, or it might consist of a tremendous attack on Italy. He did, however, contend that there ought to be some big new enterprise of this kind in our programme for the latter part of this year.

What was Hitler going to do? 'I am convinced that he must do something. I fell sure of this. I think he may easily do something desperate. For instance, he may use poison gas, not certainly on the whole of the Russian front, because it is much too long for that, but on a restricted part of the front, say before Moscow, in the hope that by its use he might make a big breach in the Russian front and pour through it.' Certainly Hitler might start another offensive against Russia in the spring, and if he did he might take a certain amount of territory and might inflict some reverses, but on the whole a new offensive would have a poor prospect of success. I referred to Hitler's sense of a Divine mission and that this might drive him to attack again. He professed to be much amused and said, 'His Divine mission won't save him from finding out that he has made a great mistake.' No German offensive was likely to be so strong or so well equipped as that of 1941. His own view was that Hitler's wisest tactics, although probably he would not do it, would be to stand strictly on the defensive in Russia and go for another front altogether. There were two or three alternatives from which Hitler could choose:

(1) Malta, but an attack on Malta was in itself too small to satisfy Hitler. The Germans might be able to neutralise Malta, but this by itself would give Hitler neither enough military advantage nor enough prestige.

(2) Hitler might go through Spain to Africa. His idea would be to gain a large number of bases in Spain, Portugal, and Northern Africa from which he could operate both U-boats and aircraft against us in another great Atlantic war. Such a march would be comparatively easy from one point of view. Hitler would only need, say, ten divisions, of which two or three might be armoured. He would get the bases, and he would also get a large prestige from the new conquests. To such an enterprise he could add the neutralising of Malta.

(3) Hitler might decide to go through Turkey. He had definitely now lost the chance of going round the Black Sea into the Caucasus to get its oil. He could hardly strike across the Black Sea because of the Russian Fleet, but he might try to make his way through Turkey to the Middle East. This, however, would be a formidable business. He would need not ten, but forty, divisions to do it, and when he landed at the other side, if he did, he would find the Russians and the British waiting for him there again. I said, what about Bulgaria? He replied that he did not believe that the Bulgarians would be at all willing to fight Turkey for the sake of the Germans. It had to be remembered that Bulgaria was not at present at war with Russia. It was an odd thing, but it was true, that Russia still had her Ambassador in Sofia and Bulgaria hers in Moscow.

He thought that if Hitler were to break out somewhere new it would be through Spain. Yet, on the other hand, the most important question of oil supplies was involved. There was no doubt that the Russian campaign must have made a tremendous drain on Hitler's oil reserves and before long he might be running short. His only principal source was now Rumania, and if he came near to running short he would have to get fresh supplies and, if need be, take more risks to get it. That point was, of course, all against the Spanish campaign, which would cost him heavily in oil and not produce any for him. The oil argument favoured the idea of a Turkish campaign. Well, anyway, Hitler needed action now and might perhaps trust in his famous 'intuitions'. He had always been right, had he not—[then, with a big chuckle]— except in regard to two things, Russia and Britain. These were big enough mistakes for any man. Napoleon had made exactly the same two mistakes—he had achieved everything else but had under-estimated both Russia and Britain.

Returning to Libya, he said he did not like the look of things. His fear was that Rommel would retreat right past Tripoli into Tunis and seize Bizerta, while Hitler was neutralising Malta. Wouldn't that be extremely disagreeable for us? We should be completely cut off in the Eastern Mediterranean. Southern Italy, Sicily, Bizerta and neutralised Malta would be very bad for us. It would be worse still if Spain 'went' and Hitler got the North African ports as well; then we should be doubly blockaded. In his view it was imperative that somehow we should find the means of preventing the Germans from acquiring Tunis and Bizerta. 'I see it reported that Rommel, after making a stand at Jedabya, is now making another stand at El-agheila. I only hope that he will make a lot of "stands" of this kind, because if he does he won't be able to hurry off into Tunis and seize Bizerta.'

He returned to the possibility of deciding the war in 1942, and said that he was, of course, speaking in terms of Europe. To settle the war in the Far East would obviously take longer. I replied that his demands for some new big enterprise meant a tremendous drain on us for material, and that it was largely because of lack of material that we looked like losing Singapore. It was difficult to see how we were going to get all the material that was needed for these campaigns, including Russia, and start a new one as well. He replied that the material had to be got from Britain and the United States between us and that he was sure that this additional effort had to be made.

What was to happen after the war? He said, 'We are determined to march to Berlin.'

I said that I had always had the idea that when the Russian Army came within invasion range of Germany the Germans would offer to make peace.

'That', he replied, 'will not in the least prevent us from marching to Berlin. Others must march with us too.' Speaking of the demand for 'vengeance' about which so much had been heard, he said that the Russian Government would resist any campaign for indiscriminate vengeance, but that it would be very difficult to restrain those who had suffered so badly. The worst thing about the outrages in Russia was that they had not been committed merely by leaders and high-ups, but by the individual German soldiers and especially by the young soldiers.

Then came the question of what should be done with Germany in a political sense. It was quite true that Russia was in favour of a series of strong independent Border States—Poland, Czech and so on, but that was a quite secondary matter. The real question was what was to be done with the German people itself. That was the crucial European problem. 'We know a great deal about the mentality of the German people. We have captured any number of German prisoners in Russia and our intelligence service has been systematically finding out how they feel and what they think. Well, we divide them up into two classes. We find that the young men up to about twenty-seven or twenty-eight are entirely hopeless; they are completely inoculated with Hitlerism, have no other ideas and can't be trusted to have any other ideas. Above thirty they are different; they are not hopelessly Hitlerised, but they are hopeless in another sense, because they are completely docile and spineless and ready tools for any future Hitler. So what conclusion do we come to? We say that no doubt there will be a revolution in Germany, and to that extent a new Germany. That is all right, but whether the new regime be democratic or socialist or communist, we have come to the conclusion that there will be no internal guarantee whatever that the new Germany will not go precisely the same way as the old—that is to say will not fall a victim to new aggressive leaders and will not make yet another war for domination. Well, then, if there can be no internal guarantee we must provide external guarantees and that is definitely what we intend to do.

'(1) There will be a new regime.
'(2) There will be an effective military occupation of Germany which will for a time prevent this peaceful regime from being overthrown (Germany, of course, will be disarmed).
'(3) Since Germany cannot be occupied permanently there will

be an international army pledged to intervene at any moment in order to stop rearmament and the manoeuvres of any Government likely to be aggressive. That is the only thing that can keep Germany from waging another war.'

I asked him whether Russia had any idea of breaking up Germany. He said that she had not, in the sense of breaking up Germany into a large number of small units, but certainly she might insist on dividing Germany into certain large units, e.g. South Germany might be detached in order to form an homogeneous State along with Austria.

I said that I thought opinion in this country was much sterner this time with regard to making Germany harmless than it was in 1919, and he said that he was very glad to hear it, as Russian opinion on the subject was drastic.

He then spoke of some other countries and said that he did not believe that either Rumania or Finland could get out of the war even if they wanted to. The German grip was too strong, but in any case the 'Mannerheim Group' meant to stick with Germany. As for Rumania, he thought that there would be considerable uneasiness in that country as the Russian armies gradually approached its borders. He was amused by the idea that Odessa had been promised by Germany to the Rumanians. 'Yes,' he said, 'but Odessa is Russian—it is a Russian town.' And he laughed again, as though he found the idea of the Rumanians thinking that they were going to get it, highly amusing. He reverted again to the attack on Moscow and Leningrad. I mentioned a curious idea which some people were airing, that Russia had enticed the German armies up to the gates of Leningrad and Moscow and then turned on them. 'Yes', he said, 'that is an absurd idea. Indeed, the Russians did not attempt to lay a "trap" for the Germans around the two cities. On the contrary, they tried to prevent them from advancing every yard. What happened was exactly what Tolstoy in War and Peace attributes to General Kutusov, who said he did not try to draw Napoleon on or anything of the kind, but that he had always been compelled to do what he did by a "combination of circumstances".' That was what had happened now. It was quite true that Russia had determined from the start on three deliberate points of policy:

(a) That her retreat should be a fighting retreat.
(b) That she would wage against the Germans a guerrilla war.
(c) That she would practise against them a 'scorched earth' policy.

Having made these three decisions the Russians had decided

to hold on desperately to Moscow and Leningrad and to organise fresh armies in the rear. As it happened, the last German offensive of all against Moscow petered out just at the time when the Siberian regiments in the rear of Moscow were ready to advance. It was a vital, critical moment and the Russians seized it and counter-attacked. They had acted all the time 'according to the combination of circumstances'.

He made one rather nice reference to Turkey. I asked him about the relations between Russia and the Turks and he said, 'Oh, they are quite satisfactory.'

'All the same,' I replied, 'they seem to remain very suspicious of you.'

'And of you!' he said, with a wide grin.

19 February 1942

4.30 P.M. ANTHONY EDEN AT THE FOREIGN OFFICE

.   .   .   .   .

I said to Eden, 'Well, are you reconstructing the Cabinet?'

Eden 'You *would* ask indiscreet questions, wouldn't you?'

I said, 'Not indiscreet! The last thing you said to me when I was here a few weeks ago was that you were going to urge Churchill to reconstruct, so naturally I ask about the result.'

Eden 'I think he'll have to reconstruct. I don't think it can be avoided. . . . I was with him until two this morning—that was what we were discussing.'

I said there was so much dissatisfaction—and some of it touching Churchill himself, that he ought to make changes in order that the Government should not only be but also *look* formidable.

Eden 'Well, I think you'll find a change *is* coming and that it will be "pretty good".'

Then he talked of Churchill: 'I'm sorry he was so rough with the House last week. It was a pity. But you know he's had to put up with a lot. It isn't only the people and the House that feel these defeats—Singapore[1] and so on—he feels them himself enormously and he is always blaming himself, sometimes quite unjustly. He blames himself now—wrongly—for things that took place long before Singapore. And then, when he's worried to death himself

---

1. Singapore fell on 15 February.

and the critics in the House go for him, he gets irritable and turns on them. He's really a very sensitive man. He's a warm-hearted man, you know, and most kindly, and all this affects him deeply. Also, he's overburdened.'

I said the job of attending so often in the House was too much and that ought it somehow to be lightened.

Eden 'It's really intolerable. It doesn't leave him time to conduct the war. Since he came back from America he's spent a tremendous lot of time in the House. Sometimes he goes there three days a week to answer questions. How can he devote himself to the war in such circumstances? It was never intended when he became PM that he should do this any more than Ll G did. But he has become so much the one personality that now the House won't have anyone else to explain and to answer, and he won't easily escape from the burden.'

I said he would have to escape somehow.

Eden 'Yes, some one rather better than Attlee will have to take on the job of speaking in the House.'[1]

Then the war. In Burma it was a race in time between us and the Japs. We were sending all we could as quickly as we could— mainly from Calcutta across the Bay to Rangoon. People talked about all the Indian troops available in India and asked why they were not sent. The reason was that they were only half-trained and that it was no use sending untrained, unhardened troops (we had found that out in Malaya).

I said that I supposed that before long we should not be able to use the Bay of Bengal at all owing to the Japs coming round from Singapore.

Eden 'Well, that won't happen immediately. So long as we can hold Trincomalee in Ceylon we shall embarrass their efforts to come north-west and west. Trincomalee is a naval base and a good one in its capacity to take ships, etc., but not good in respect of actual strength because we have so little there. But it will help us as long as we can keep it.'

Java was a difficult business. We ought to save Java, but the trouble was to get the reinforcements there, or there in time. All the chief ports to which Allied forces would go were on the wrong side of the island, the north coast, and were subject to attack from the bases on the islands round about which the Japs had seized.

From this we went on to Singapore and the Libyan campaign.

---

1. Cripps attempted it unsuccessfully. In November Eden took over the leadership of the house and did it very well.

I asked him what he thought of my view, that a large part of our misfortunes was due to the inferiority of our direction, staff work and the general level of our more or less leading officers. I asked him to tell me whether in the years preceding this war our staff of professional advisers generally had ever worked out plans based on the assumption that the Japs *might* one day attack Singapore from the land-side, from Malaya.

He said that there had been *one* plan and one only in respect of land attack on Singapore. That was a scheme for having an army at, or sending an army to, the Kra Peninsula in order to hold off an army advancing from the north, but nothing had ever been done about that.

He said that in general with regard to inferiority of direction he feared that I was very right. The army since the last war had been an institution in which many officers remained 'in order to have something to do'; it has not in the least attracted the brains of the country. He thought that our generals at the very top were good, e.g. Wavell, Dill and Brooke, but there were too many of inferior quality and the process by which youthful talent could force its way to the top was very slow. He had asked Lloyd George what he thought about our generals, and L G had replied that at any rate they were better than those *he* had in the last war.

We were certainly doing 'something' now to get better and younger men into the important positions, e.g. they had put a very good man into command in Burma. But it was a terrible problem—they had to find the new talent and promote it and do it *quickly*.

I asked whether the process worked at all and whether we should not need a ten years' war to get the right people into the right posts.

He said that it was working now, but only slowly. He named one very able young officer who had by merit now got to be Lieut-General. This difficulty had worried him greatly when he was Secretary of State at the War Office.

I said that when our three generals were captured in Libya an intelligent officer had said to me that the capture of one of them was one of the greatest pieces of good fortune we had had.

Eden 'Ah, I think I know whom you mean! Unfortunately one of the other two was one of our very best men—O'Conor.'

I said, 'How can we explain Libya except by this same reason—the general quality of our leading generals?'

Eden 'That *is* the reason. We have been out-generalled. People talk of the superior German tank gun! One of our chief staff officers said to me the other day, "Yes, but the Germans had this greatly superior gun", and I said, "They had it when we were driving them back from Sollum and Benghazi!" Besides, we have the 25-pounder that everyone praises so highly. We have had air ascendancy. We have had almost everything in our favour. But there are some things difficult to understand. At any given time the proportion of tanks and aeroplanes that we have actually available for use in the "front line" is always low, and always has been low—compared with the total we possess in Libya—and we cannot understand why. We had made all sorts of enquiries into it and done all sorts of things to remedy it, and still the proportion remains unaccountably low.'

I asked what was going to happen in the spring. He thought the Germans would go mainly for the Caucasus and the Middle East, perhaps by-passing Turkey, taking Sevastopol and seeking to destroy the Russian fleet, then cutting across to Batum, or perhaps even attacking Turkey. He thought that the Turks would resist; they themselves admitted nowadays that they had *some* equipment, but they wanted more and we were short of shipping. Shipping, shipping, that was what we wanted! Part of their plan would be that Rommel should simultaneously attack Egypt.

I asked about Vichy and Rommel. He said that Vichy had not sent a great deal to Rommel, mostly foodstuffs, and anything sent took a long time to go via Bizerta and Eastern Tunis. The USA ought to handle it. They had been much too kind to Vichy. The USA had all the arguments to use against Vichy—its gold, shipping, West Indian islands. Therefore they should teach Vichy what to do, and it looked as though they were going to get a bit stiffer.

His final word was that what between the Japs and Hitler's push to the East (backed by Rommel from the West) 'we're going to have an awful time this year—an awful time.'

9.00 P.M. LORD BEAVERBROOK

In Crozier's handwriting. Beaverbrook had resigned the previous evening. He was dissatisfied that, as minister of war production—the post created for him on 4 February—he had no powers over shipbuilding or labour and few powers over anything else. He was also opposed to the appointments of Attlee as deputy prime minister and Cripps as leader of the house of commons, believing rightly that they were lukewarm in their desire to aid Soviet Russia. Beaverbrook remained out of office until September 1943.

As I arrived at No. 12 at 5 minutes to 9 a big car drew up just behind me and someone walked rapidly into the house. It was B himself and when I asked him how he was he said he had asthma, and I thought it would do him no good to be out in such a night —with a bitter east wind and slightly freezing and generally raw and disagreeable. I noticed that in his 'office', as he calls the big room where he has his desk and where we dined, there was a steam kettle (bronchitis kettle) pointing towards his desk, with a thick jet of steam coming out of it.

'I've just come back from Maisky', he said. 'I've spent an hour or two with him. He said that he couldn't come to see me as he has a bad cold, so I've been to see him.'

Here he stopped and said, 'What do you think of the new Government?'

I said that I had only seen a few lines in the Evening Standard and did not know whether the changes mentioned there were correct or not.

'Oh', he said, 'But the changes are *out*. I'll tell you the new Government!' He then proceeded to walk up and down, giving the names in full and explaining what the changes were. Presently he said—'Me—out of the Cabinet and out of the Government.'

'Out of *the Government*, did you say?'

'Out of the Government altogether! Why? Well, I'll tell you. I'm not too well, my asthma is troublesome, and I'm very tired and I've had about enough. I've told Churchill so. I haven't agreed about everything these last few weeks, you know. I didn't like the Ministry of Production White Paper. After I'd accepted it very reluctantly two new paragraphs which I hadn't seen were added to it and I was then asked to accept the whole thing—asked to accept it one morning and told that it was to be published later the same day. I asked for it to be postponed and was told it couldn't be. Churchill sent a man over to show it to me in the final form—with these added paragraphs—and to ask that I should accept it. If I would not, he was to present me with a personal letter from Churchill which he had brought with him. I refused to accept it. Then he gave me Churchill's letter. It was an angry letter—a very angry letter, the sort of letter that he writes when he is angry. I read it and said again that I would not accept the White Paper. Then Churchill got me on the phone (his envoy still being there) and appealed to me to help him and so forth. So I pushed the letter back to his envoy and told him to take it away and I accepted the White Paper, but I didn't like it. And I haven't liked his making Cripps Leader of the House, either. He says I don't understand the House of Commons, that I've been too long away from it and all that sort of thing. I thought that Eden should have been leader of the House. I think he would have been better. Look what's happened in the case of Cripps. What's got him into the War Cabinet?'

'The Russian victories!'

'Yes, that's so. But he never much liked Russia, and the Russians never liked him. When I went to Moscow it was necessary for me to see Stalin alone—without Cripps—I had to. And you know what he thought about the Russian armies when he came back to London. He thought they would be done in a few days. And, besides, when Churchill made the great decision to stake everything by the side of Russia, what did Cripps do? I was summoned to No. 10[1] and I found Cripps there with Churchill. Churchill announced that he was going to recognise Russia as an out-and-out ally and do everything to support her. And I said "you're right. Go to the limit in support of Russia, and I'm with you and will help all the time." But Cripps—oh no, Cripps didn't approve —he was all for *negotiations* first!

'And that's why I've just been to Maisky. The Russians know that I'm leaving the Government and that Cripps is going into the War Cabinet, and they think that I'm being *dismissed* because of my insistence that we shall send supplies to Russia and that Cripps, whom they don't trust, is taking my place. I've been to tell them that it isn't true, and we are sending a telegram to Moscow to reassure them but they are intensely suspicious. And they have reason to be. Do you know that our Services have each of them put in memoranda urging that our supplies to Russia should be cut down? Do you know that when I went to USA the supplies to Russia stopped, or greatly slowed down, and that as soon as I came back the full flow started again? The Russians know it and suspect that my retirement from the Government means trouble for them.'

'But Cripps must be all for Russia now?'

'Oh, he's playing them up no end now—now that they're winning but he was not before. Mind, he's able enough in himself —he's a very able man—but it isn't an exchange, as between him and me, that the Russians like.'

For himself, he was weary of present methods and present people. 'This country is going to be defeated unless we are careful, because it is over-organising itself. Too much organisation, talk and committees everywhere. These committees! I had one yesterday which I intended to be of 12 people. Bevin made it into

---

1. The summons was to Chequers.

one of fifty. What did it do? It talked for two hours and then adjourned without deciding anything. That's what's always happening. That's how we are making war. I tell you that a lot of these people are only happy when they have a new committee at work. Something important has to be decided—something ought to be done, and done quickly. How do they do it? appoint a committee! and then they accumulate documents and minutes and plans and memoranda a foot thick—[he made rapid gestures with his hands]—and when at last they've got affixed to the pile the red label saying "passed to such and such a Ministry for action", then they think they've accomplished the object, the end in view and that they're winning the war. But they're losing it. They think that this interminable committee business is all that's needed whereas what is required—[he raised his voice furiously and beat with his hands]—is to act, to burst through, to bomb and blast until we've done what we had to do. Ministers are like that, nearly all of them. I told Churchill the other day that I was going to change to the other side of the Cabinet table because I couldn't bear any longer to look at the same faces. They weary me, they *exasperate* me.'

I said, 'Of course, your idea of a committee is one man isn't it', and he said, 'May be, but it doesn't alter the truth of what I've been saying.'

He began to talk about some of the Ministers. He said he was free now and he would tell me.

ATTLEE 'His chief idea nowadays is to stick out obstinately for positions in the Government for Labour people. That's what he thinks of.' He mentioned here that the Tory Under-Secretaries had met and decided to send a letter to Churchill putting their posts collectively at his disposal in the reconstruction.

MARGESSON[1] 'He doesn't count. He isn't any good—and he's "going".'

BEVIN 'He's able, he's a very able man. But he has this passion for committees. Whatever has to be decided, Bevin is always for a new committee.'

ANDERSON 'A capable Civil Servant. He'll always put anyone else's plan through very efficiently, but that's all.'

ALEXANDER 'A very faithful lieutenant of Churchill—that and no more.'

CRANBORNE 'Very good. When he's made up his mind what is the right thing to do, no one can make him budge.'

---

1. Secretary of state for war. Succeeded on 22 February by P J Grigg.

He returned to himself and said that Churchill had made great efforts to keep him in the Government. He had had a very disagreeable interview that afternoon with a friend[1] whom Churchill had sent to persuade him to withdraw his resignation. He had refused. One office that Churchill had offered him was that of Lord Privy Seal. He laughed aloud. 'I suppose it was thought that the title would be appropriate for a nobleman like me', and he laughed uproariously again.

I asked him why Belisha did not get back into the Government and he said, 'I think he ought! I want him to and I have pressed it on Churchill. But he is disliked by so many people.'

Then he said suddenly—'By the way I must speak to Herbert Morrison. Some time ago I gave him a pledge on behalf of the Prime Minister that no other Labour man should go into the War Cabinet before him—Morrison—and now Cripps has gone in.' He called a secretary and said, 'Get me Mr Morrison.' In a few minutes he was through and talked to Morrison.

'Oh, is that you, Herbert? Well, I want to say I did my best for you, my very best. . . . What's that? You don't know what I mean? . . . You've seen the new Government, haven't you? . . . What, you don't know about it? It's out, it's out! Weren't you at the Cabinet this afternoon? . . . What! you were and nothing was said about it? . . . Well, I'll tell you who they are. Cripps is in the War Cabinet . . . Yaas . . . [slowly and emphatically] Yaas—in the War Cabinet. That's what I meant, I did all I could just as I said I would . . . Me? Oh, I'm out, out of the Cabinet, and out of the Government . . . out of the Government I said—yaas, yaas, well, I'm tired and . . . oh, I'm not finished, you know, but once again I'm in the wilderness—I'm the "cat that walks alone"— . . . What am I going to do? I'm going to propagand . . . yaas, yaas, propagand—why, in my two papers, of course, the day after tomorrow I'll begin . . . you'll see, you look—the day after tomorrow . . . yaas . . . goodbye.'

I said, 'Do you mean it—the day after tomorrow?' He laughed, 'Well, soon', he said. 'I'm going to attack this system, these methods. But not Churchill. I'm going to strengthen him all I can —and he needs it. My God, if ever there was a man at this time who needs to be supported, encouraged and comforted, its Churchill. You do all you can to help him because it's a terrible time we're going through and going to go through. Look at the Far East. The Japanese can go where they like and take what they like.'

---

1. Presumably Brendan Bracken.

I said something conventional about retrieving our fortunes there.

He said, 'Oh yes, of course, sometime; sometime, but when?' in a completely sceptical tone. Then he suddenly sat back in his chair, dropped all excitement and speaking in a very calm, composed voice said: 'When we were flying back over the Atlantic in the night, in the darkness we saw snow beginning to fall thickly. We saw it drifting past the windows and falling on the wings and the engines. And Churchill, who was sitting by me said—"It's all right. There's no need to worry. We can turn off to Lisbon or to the Azores, or we can turn back and return to America, so everything will be all right." And I knew that it was not true. We could not turn off to Lisbon or to the Azores, and we could not return to America. We could do nothing except go straight on, hoping that the engines would go on working and that we would come through. And that is where this country is now. We can't turn aside to the right or to the left and we can't turn back. We just have to go on straight ahead, and hope that the engines will go on working and that we shall come through.'

I said to him that I felt sure that he would be back in the Government before long and that I thought that if the moment came he would certainly respond. He said, yes he might—if the occasion was compelling enough but not otherwise. He was tired of it. He must, he said, have threatened to resign at least twenty times (this seemed to amuse him), and certainly five times over one single issue. He jumped up, went to his desk and brought back a typed slip. 'This', he said, 'is the official announcement about my resignation. Churchill sent it over for me to approve and I sent it back without a word of alteration!' He seemed to think this a rich joke.

It said that he had resigned on the ground of health and that he would be going shortly to USA to complete arrangements with regard to supplies. I said, 'Anything in that under present circumstances?' and he laughed and said, 'Nothing at present.'[1]

He said one other thing about Russia—that Russia wanted our approval of her getting the Baltic States and that he had been working on the Government 'for weeks' to secure this for Russia. He was dissatisfied about the delay. I asked him how far they had got. As far, he said rather sourly, as sending to the United States to ask what they thought about it!

---

1. Beaverbrook went to the United States a month later, but to agitate for a Second Front, not to discuss supplies.

Harold Macmillan rang up and B had him told to come 'right along'.[1] 'He's coming', said B, 'to tell me that he's sorry I'm going.' Apparently they had got on very well together. Macmillan arrived and I got up to go. 'No, no', said B. 'You stop and talk to Macmillan and me.' But I thought Macmillan would sympathise more freely if I went.

B said that he was sincerely grateful for the kindness he had had from the MG and that he had made good use of our support!

20 February 1942

9.30 A.M. LESLIE HORE-BELISHA AT 16 STAFFORD PLACE

A sad episode in the life of a disappointed man.

He was very anxious to see what all the papers were saying about the reconstructed War Cabinet and told me with great animation what the leaders in the papers that he had read were saying. But as soon as we started breakfast, he said that he wanted to tell me as a journalist about something rather astonishing that had just happened to him. He said that a week or two ago he had received a letter from the editor of one of the popular illustrated weeklies asking whether he would give an interview for publication on the political topics of the day. He had replied that he had always made it a rule not to give interviews and that he must still observe it. On the other hand, as he was something of a journalist himself and had no desire to rebuff a friendly journalist, he said that if the editor would like to come to tea with him he would be very glad to have a little private talk. Accordingly the editor had come and had a talk, in the course of which he had chatted and given his opinions quite freely about such topics as the promotion and personality of Cripps, trusting entirely in the obviously confidential character of the conversation. To his amazement he had that morning received from the editor a proof of what was neither more nor less than an 'interview' with him; the whole thing done in a way which was extremely inaccurate, highly offensive and calculated politically, if published, to be injurious to him. He produced the proof and proceeded to read it to me. It was a remarkable production. It spoke of the 'full-lipped, prominent-nosed Israel Hore-Belisha'. It mentioned 'plaster busts' on his

---

1. Harold Macmillan was parliamentary secretary to the ministry of supply, while Beaverbrook was the minister, and had strongly urged that Beaverbrook should become overlord of production.

shelves, and described the whole place as lined with oak. His name was not 'Israel', the busts were Sèvres porcelain or marble, there was no oak on the walls, and he mentioned that his nose was not prominent. A second offence was that he had spoken to his secretary about some private engagements of his, and the editor had put the conversation, mentioning the secretary by name, into the article. Worst of all was the fact that the editor had picked out all the critical and disagreeable things about Cripps and had omitted all the appreciative things that he had said about Cripps's abilities and merits. He had said various things about Cripps's earlier career—the violence of his attacks on our institutions, the way in which the Tory party regarded him, the fact that he had been expelled by the Labour people, and that after all these things had happened here was this man suddenly translated by the Russian successes to the very highest office. This sort of treatment was grossly inaccurate and unfair and, at a time when the reconstruction of the Government was contemplated, might have very serious results. So he said he was going to write to the editor and say to him that this must not be published.

WPC You must not wait to write. You must telephone to him
        at once and say that this must not be published in
        whole or in part, in any shape or form; then write and
        confirm the prohibition. If you don't telephone to him
        at once and be extremely firm you will be told that the
        article has already gone to press and that nothing can
        be done about it.
H-B All right I will get my secretary to telephone at once.
WPC Your secretary won't do; they won't take any notice of
        her. You ought to telephone yourself immediately, insist-
        ing that nothing can be published, and if they don't agree
        tell them that you regard it as injurious to you and that
        you will have to do what you can to protect yourself.

So the secretary got through on the telephone, found the editor, and H-B proceeded to address him. A spirited interchange then followed for about twenty minutes. H-B speaking something like this:

'I just wanted to speak to you about this so-called interview. It is good of you to have sent me a proof, but you know this can't possibly be printed. . . . Well, in the first place, the whole thing is inaccurate. . . . Yes, the whole thing. . . . Really there is hardly an accurate statement in it. . . . What's inaccurate. Why, everything is inaccurate. You call me Israel, which has never been my name and isn't, you talk of plaster casts when they are not plaster, and of oak when it isn't oak, and you actually say that when you entered the room I was reading Rosebery's Napoleon, the last Phase, and closed the book and rose up to greet you. As a matter of fact, as you know, I was not in the room at all, but came in from outside. However, these things do not so much matter. The point is that you have written this as an "interview". . . . Oh, but of course it is an interview. You describe me as actually saying so and so and you put words into my mouth. . . . But if not an interview, what is it? And you know that it is a dirty trick. You were told explicitly that I never give an interview and I received you privately as a guest into my house and then you choose out some of the things that I said and give them as an interview. . . . Well, obviously the things that I have said about Cripps I never would have said if I had supposed that they were going to be quoted. . . . No, you have no right to do it at all. I have the very highest opinion of Cripps in many ways and, what is more, I said so, and you have gone and took out some particular things that I said about his earlier career and given a wholly inaccurate impression. If published it would be most injurious to me. . . . Well, but you can't publish it; it is incredible. I asked you here in a friendly private way and I must appeal to you now to respect my confidence. . . . Of course it can't be published. I will appeal to you, if you like, as one journalist to another, but you must see, my dear man, that you are not entitled to quote anything and that this doesn't anyway represent my views, and that the whole thing was entirely private. . . . What! What! you don't see why you should not print it? . . .'

I put in front of him a slip of paper saying, 'Tell him again that you consider it damaging and injurious.'

H-B   'Well, I must insist you don't print it, or any of it. . . . I consider the whole thing damaging and injurious to my reputation. . . . What do you say? What sentences in it I complain of? No particular sentence or phrase, but the whole thing. . . . Well, in that case. . . . What do I intend to do? I don't know, but I shall have to take whatever steps I can to protect myself. . . .'

They went on this way for sometime and then H-B said he would not have minded if this man had speculated on how he, who had so many changes of fortune, must be feeling when he saw the great changes of fortune that had befallen Cripps. H-B didn't mind an objective account of his house and his views so long as nothing was attributed to him personally. The editor then began to say that he would be willing to re-write the article on some such lines. So I put in front of H-B another piece of paper saying, 'Insist on having another proof or, if not that, a draft,' which he then did and the editor said he would re-write the stuff and telephone the new version to H-B. H-B then said that he wondered whether he ought not to get through to Lord Southwood,[1] the proprietor, and asked me whether he ought to do so at once. The editor had told him that the article was already made up in page four of his magazine and that it was very difficult now to get it out. I said that I thought he had better give the man an hour and if nothing happened get Lord Southwood to intervene and squash the article. However, in twenty minutes time the editor rang up and read a new version, which H-B said was innocuous and acceptable. But he added, 'This has taught me a severe lesson; I shall take great care not to receive any such person again without knowing him or without knowing all about him. This man is a bully and adopted a very bullying tone in the early part of the conversation. One phrase he used was, "I can tell you I am getting heated and I am going to do what I like about this." '[2]

The point about the private secretary and his engagements was that he had been invited to some 'do' at the Kemsleys' and also by a friend, to dine with him and Dorothy Hyson, the actress. He, H-B, had said something while the editor was there about these two engagements and the editor, in the 'interview', had said that at a certain point H-B 'shouted out, "Miss Sloane, Miss Sloane, is it to be the Kemsleys' tonight or dinner with Dorothy Hyson?" ' (whom he had never met).

It was clear that he hoped to regain office during the 'Reconstruction' that was going on at this time. He said that Eden had asked him to go and see him, and had said that they would like to get him back into the Government. He had said that he would like it but was afraid he had too many enemies. 'Not in the Government', said Eden, 'so far as I know.' So he thought something might come of it. He had an idea that he could do useful work by undertaking one of those special Missions that leading politicians are carrying out, and he had mentioned this to Eden. A little time afterwards—all this was quite recently—Beaverbrook also had wanted to see him and when they met he said—

'Leslie, I understand that you would like one of those Commissions. What do you want exactly? Is it the Scottish Commission

---

1. Chairman of Odhams, who published The People, The Daily Herald and many weeklies.
2. From here in Crozier's handwriting.

or the Ecclesiastical Commission, or what? You can have any Commission you like.'

'I told him', H-B went on, 'that I didn't want anything of any kind, and he said, "I'm very glad to hear it".' B also wanted to get him back into the Government. He (H-B) thought that the Reconstruction would involve all three Service Ministers and not just the War Office.[1]

I said that I imagined there was no certainty about his getting back until the results were actually announced, (Beaverbrook's reference the day before had suggested that the appointment was not coming), and he laughed very cheerfully. 'Oh no, I'm not confident. I've been as close as this to getting back 2 or 3 times before now, and it's always come to nothing!' Speaking of the Reconstruction he said that Churchill was behaving just like Neville Chamberlain had done over the Ministry of Supply— refusing everything until he was *compelled* to give way and so losing the credit that he might have had.

LUNCH. 1.30 P.M. WINSTON CHURCHILL AT NO. 10

In Crozier's handwriting throughout.

I got there at 1.25 and was taken downstairs to the same two rooms, one opening into the other, as before. They are away below Downing St level, very pleasant rooms, white panelled, with low ceilings and looking out on the garden. Mrs Churchill was there. She said that the first of the two rooms, in which we were, had been Violet Asquith's[2] sitting room in the Asquith Premier days. She told me that Sir Stafford and Lady Cripps were coming to lunch—his appointment as Leader of the House had been announced among the War Cabinet changes that morning.

Mrs Churchill said that other changes were now under discussion and she expressed great disappointment that the Labour people were making a lot of difficulty about jobs. 'They seem to think of nothing else than of getting what they think to be their proper share of the appointments. If it came to a real division (of opinion) I am sure that the public won't think at all well of them if it knows what has been the cause of it.' I said No, but they would never allow a quarrel to come about on any such ground; if it came, it would always be represented as being on some high

1. Hore-Belisha was wrong. Alexander and Sinclair survived in office until the end of the National government.

2. Asquith's daughter, later Lady Violet Bonham Carter, and later still Lady Asquith of Yarnbury.

ground of public policy. She made it clear that the trouble was at all events quite a serious matter (cf Beaverbrook, 19 February, on Attlee and Labour claims).

Then the Crippses came, he very cheerful and spirited. Talk of their journey in the East some time ago, Lady Cripps saying that what dismayed her most in Japan was the enormous numbers of babies and young children which made her fear the worst for the future, unless the Japs changed. Sir Stafford was hopeful about the Far East, saying that the Chinese had far greater composure and endurance than the Japanese and, whatever might be happening at the moment, would eat them up in time. For that reason on a long view he felt sorry for the Japanese.

Then there was some talk about a blue egg or eggs which they had sent to the PM. They apparently had some hens which laid genuine, natural blue eggs. They were Peruvian hens, of which there were one or two lots in this country. Then Churchill arrived. He announced that he had had his blue egg and enjoyed it greatly. As we went in to lunch he and Cripps stopped to glance at a morning newspaper and Churchill said, 'We'd a pretty good press this morning?' and Cripps agreed with great heartiness. They described the Herald's leader as 'rather grudging'.

The Crippses had lunched the day before with the Crown and Churchill said to Sir Stafford, 'Well, did you make your peace with Buckingham Palace?' and he replied that it had been very pleasant. Mrs Churchill asked if the Queen had been there and Lady Cripps said she had, and had been very charming. They all agreed that she was always very charming. A further reference was made to newspapers and Churchill spoke of himself as reading them late the night before or rather early in the morning in order to get himself off to sleep. The others recommended thrillers, especially Lady Cripps, who said she read them very lightly and remembered nothing much about them afterwards.

Then we began to talk about the war, and to put questions to Churchill. The difficulty was to get a subject finished, as, with five present, there was a lot of cross-talk and sometimes two conversations were going on, so that it was sometimes difficult to get things clear or to get answers, or the final answers which the talk was leading up to.

The escape of the German ships through the Straits soon came up.[1] Churchill has an amusing trick both of saying violent things

---

1. The German battle cruisers Scharnhorst and Gneisenau passed through the Channel from Brest to Germany on 12 February without suffering serious damage.

about his critics in a good-tempered way that takes all the sting out of them and also of attributing to them extreme statements which in fact they have never made and would not think of making. So, in this matter, he spoke with a derisive contempt, but with a grin, of the people who thought that the admiralty were entirely incompetent duds and good for nothing because the German ships had got away. (He threw in parenthetically the remark that if the House and Country wanted another Premier he would be very glad to go back to the Admiralty, 'where I have always been extremely happy'.) About the actual escape he said:

'People talk as though these were the first German ships that ever got through the Straits in the war. Lots of them have got through—*hundreds* of them—they got through every week, and big ships too—7,000 and 10,000 tons.'

WPC	Merchantmen?
PM	Well, they get through! That's the point.
Cripps	What's puzzling is that these ships should have been in such good form when we thought we had done them such a lot of damage.
PM	We did do them a lot of damage!
WPC	Not in the engine-rooms if they could steam 20–30 knots on their own through the Straits?
Cripps	Seeing the damage was so small I've wondered whether the Germans didn't build a new deck over the old one, allowing just the funnels and the top of the superstructure to show through.
PM	shook his head dubiously. 'It's a dreadfully hard business to hit a small target in a dock like that. You can't torpedo it because there's no water and no run-up. There's a tremendous AA defence and you have to come very low to have any chance at all.'
WPC	Everybody's wondering about the point of there being only six Swordfish torpedo-carrying aircraft. It's very small. We understand that torpedo-carrying aircraft are needed elsewhere and with the fleet and all that, and still are puzzled that there were so few to tackle these ships. If one may ask, have we developed this weapon busily since we ourselves showed what it could do at Taranto? Everyone's said that the Germans must be developing it against us and we wonder whether we have been, or are now, developing it ourselves.

PM   Yes, but it's like everything else—there are so many demands everywhere for the weapon. If we haven't enough here it's because we've sent such forces of it to the Middle East, and remember that we have to be prepared for attacks which could bring the main fleet into action, and we have to fulfill its needs.

WPC   Well, are we multiplying this weapon?

PM   What we are after especially is to develop and increase *carriers* for aircraft. That's the need, that's what we're after—carriers—carriers!

WPC   Well, another point. The Admiralty says that we are the better off because the German ships are in German ports. Suppose that one of them, or one after another, of the whole lot sally out into the North Atlantic or round by Ireland, to attack our convoys and hurry back again, how much better off are we if we don't catch them, and how about torpedo-carrying aircraft for catching them?

PM   Well, we have our dispositions. It will be like the pursuit of the Bismarck, and we sank her. Aircraft spotted her, shadowed her hour after hour, and then torpedoed her, reducing her speed until our own ships came up.

Cripps   I wondered whether something couldn't be done in the way of a naval expedition against Brest.

I could not catch the answer, if any, that the PM gave to this, so I said—

WPC   And I wondered, when we got to Benghazi last year, whether we could not have run a naval expedition against Tripoli at once, there being none but Italian ships there at that time, and taken the whole show with perhaps 5,000 or at most 10,000 men—finishing off the Axis in Africa.

PM   (giving a sarcastic grin) Well, at that time there was a country called Greece which called for some attention from us! and besides, you know, the Germans were already in Tripoli—they had begun to arrive.

He referred to the coming debate, and I raised the question of those who said that he could not both be Premier and Minister of Defence. I said, how much of the job of Minister of Defence did he in fact do. He was very emphatic. 'Not much', he said. 'Of course the big decisions have to come before me, as before any

Premier, but I *assure you I don't run the war*.[1] The chiefs of staff run the war. I don't often preside over their meetings. When I was in the USA for five weeks they ran the war without me, I assure you.[2] If I wasn't Minister of Defence at all, I wouldn't do anything different from what I do at present. And if there were another Minister of Defence, I wouldn't do anything very different, either.'

WPC   People talk as though you ran the whole defence show, whereas it appears that the title really makes no difference.

Ch   No difference.

Mrs Ch Then you should tell them so, Winston.

Ch.   I'm going to tell them next Tuesday—when I make my Swan-song (a very large grin). The title of Minister of Defence does *not* matter to me—but mind, you *I'm not giving anything up!*

In talking about the Cabinet changes announced that morning he said he was determined that the Germans should not learn of them as early as they seemed to have learned of some other things and he had accordingly ordered that no cables were to be cleared from this country on the night before until 12 midnight. Cripps asked if there was any reason to suppose that things got out through Ireland.

The talk turned to bombs and bombing.

WPC   People are feeling troubled about our bombing policy in Germany. We have lost a lot of planes and men and, though the results to German production *may* be good, we can't see them and begin to wonder whether all is right.

Ch   Well, we began this policy in 1940, after France collapsed and we have no way of fighting Germany except by bombing. It was our only weapon. Now it's rather different, with Russia and USA both in.

WPC   The point is that people like me at any rate don't know what the effects of this bombing policy are on German production, but we do know that we haven't enough Air Force in Libya or anywhere else.

Ch   Don't forget the 'near misses', which are almost as im-

---

1. This is not confirmed by other accounts.
2. Two out of the three chiefs of staff were in Washington with Churchill for much of the time.

portant in some ways as the hits. After all, the destruction of the morale of the German people is a military
objective. (Cripps amused[1])

WPC   If bombing hasn't hurt British morale nor, in the
[Spanish] Civil war, Barcelona morale, nor Russian
morale since June 1941, why should we think it has
hurt German morale, and have we any evidence that it
has? (There seemed to be some approval for this,
especially from Mrs. Ch.)

I got no answer to this owing to the general talk, but he said that
it was quite true that at night there was no such thing as 'precision
bombing' which was so much talked of. I then asked, why not have
sent a lot of our aircraft to places where they might have helped to
decide events.

Ch   It takes a long time, you know, to transfer aircraft to
distant fields—with all the men and the spares and the
repair shops and the rest. And have you any idea what
our total AIR FORCE is now in all the Middle East
countries together? Well, guess!
WPC   I have no idea at all.
Ch   Well, but you must guess.
WPC   A thousand pilots?
Ch   Pilots! Pilots! Any number of pilots! We have a total
Air Force of all kinds in the Middle East today of
—,000[2] men!

The talk about bombing touched on this country and he said that
he thought of all the places he had seen Plymouth had suffered
most. It was not only the bombing of the town, however, but the
loss of men on the warships. There were whole streets in Plymouth
that were plunged in mourning when a ship like the Barham[3]
went down. No other place did, or could, suffer like Plymouth
when there was a heavy naval loss.

He spoke of Randolph's maiden speech[4] and it was clear that

---

1. Word difficult to decipher.
2. Blank in the original.
3. Sunk in the Mediterranean by a U-boat, 25 November 1941.
4. A mistake presumably by Crozier. Randolph Churchill, returned unopposed for
Preston, made his maiden speech on 26 November 1940. A violent attack on the critics
of the government, made on 26 January 1942, was his next contribution to parliamentary proceedings.

it had not been a wholly happy occasion for the father. (There had been a good deal of personal interruption of a pretty 'personal' speech.)

Then the Crippses went and Mrs Churchill, and we had some further talk about the Reconstruction and his 'burden' in the House. He spoke intimately:—

'I've had a bad time this week with the Reconstruction of the Cabinet. I don't like this business of getting rid of people that I like and telling them they've got to go. It's very disagreeable to me—I don't like it a bit.'

I mentioned the stock saying of Asquith that a PM had to be a 'butcher'. 'Oh I know,' he said,—'he said that to me, but I don't like it all the same.'

WPC	And there are more people still to be changed about, aren't there?
PM	Oh yes there are, but I don't mind about them. They've got to do what I tell them.
WPC	I'm sorry Beaverbrook has gone.
PM	So I am, indeed. But he needn't have gone. He could have had any one of three or four offices if he had liked to stop. He could have gone back to MAP if he had chosen. I didn't want him to go. He was good for me! Any number of times, if things were going badly, he would encourage me saying 'Look at all the things on your side. Look what you've accomplished. Be of good courage!' and he put courage and pep into me. But he wouldn't stop.
WPC	I daresay he'll come back sometimes.
PM	I daresay he will, but in the meantime, when his health gets better and he's had a good rest in California or on the coast of Florida he'll come back again *and he'll be very fierce.*
WPC	I'm glad you're going to get some relief from all that speaking in the House.
PM	I must. I've got to get some relief. In the weeks since I came back from America I've been constantly at the House of Commons. Mind you, I do my work all right—I do my work, but it is a strain and I feel it. It isn't actually making statements in the House that matters. That's nothing. It's preparing them that counts, for I dictate or write every word of them myself. I've got to start dictating next Tuesday's statement this

evening in the car as I drive down to Chequers.[1] And
that isn't all. The point is that when I have to make one
of these statements the whole thing *hangs over me for three
days* before it actually comes off. I do my work but this
hangs over me all the time. (He was tremendously
earnest about this. No one could doubt that it is a
really serious matter for him.)

Then Sir Archibald Sinclair was announced, and greeted me.

PM   Ah of course—(very solemnly) let me introduce to you
the Editor of our leading Liberal paper, no the *only*
Liberal paper, for who could apply that great name to
a paper which, like the News Chronicle, is moved only
by nervous hysteria? (To Sinclair) you Liberals!

AS   Well, you didn't think so poorly of Liberal support
when you wrote and upbraided me the other day for
carrying *only four* Liberals into the Lobby in support of
your Vote of Confidence![2]

I made as to go but PM said no need and if I had some other
points to raise he would like to hear them.

WPC   Yes, there's one about Libya and the reason why we had
done so badly there.

PM   I think we've done pretty well there all the same, you
know.

WPC   Not as well as we hoped to any way, and there's one
thing I would like to hear about. It has been said for a
long time that the only answer to the tank is a tank, and
obviously that isn't true. Nor does it seem to be a
bomber because the tanks are small and widely
scattered and your bomber doesn't and can't hit them.

PM   They hit a good few.

WPC   And they don't hit a good few. Well, isn't the answer
then, an aircraft firing armour-piercing shells that can
chase the individual tanks, fly from one to another, and
pepper them with these shells?

PM   A very sensible military idea, I think!

---

1. The statement of 24 February 1942 on Changes in the Government is given in
The Ends of the Beginning, 64–74. Churchill's peroration was taken from the speech
which he made when he left Asquith's government in November 1915.

2. 29 January 1942. Churchill was not hard pressed for votes. The vote of no
confidence was defeated by 464 to 1.

AS   We haven't got dive-bombers of course.[1]

WPC   You don't necessarily need them for this, do you—You already have fighters with cannon firing $1\frac{1}{2}''$ shell or something of that kind. Well, why can't you fire $3''$ shell or whatever is needed—I don't know the technical side at all—from low-flying fighters? Then you chase the tanks all over the place.

AS   Well, as a matter of fact—and of course nothing must be said of this at all, but between these four walls (favourite expression of A S) we are after that sort of thing now. We're doing something of that already.

PM   But for goodness sake don't say so.

WPC   We could say that's the way to deal with tanks?

PM   Oh, if you're saying what in your opinion is the right way to deal with them, yes! (To A S) What about that plane (he gave some description) that you are going to get to Libya? There are none of them there.

AS   Oh yes, there are! There are difficulties but—

PM   No, they're not there. You should have come to me and I'd have seen to that.

AS   But they *are* there! I got them there without coming to you!

PM   And how many? *One*, I should say! And that one probably never been in action yet! And what about that plane that was going to 'PUFFBALL' the German tanks?

AS   Oh, we've got some of them all right!

PM   And have you puffballed 'em yet? No, I thought you hadn't!

SOME OTHER POINTS —

SPAIN. PM   The position regarding Franco is rather better. The Generals don't like the Germans much. The experiences of the Spanish 'Blue Division' fighting in Russia—Cripps:—'Blue with cold!'—hasn't helped the Axis with Spanish opinion. They have had an awful time. You know that when Hoare first went to Madrid he kept his plane waiting for a week

---

1. The lack of dive bombers was the fault of the air ministry which first tried to prevent the ministry of aircraft production making them and then stirred the war office not to ask for any.

because he thought he would have to leave at any moment.

GIBRALTAR. PM The Spaniards could have made Gibraltar useless to us at any time, not by capturing it but by shelling it, which would have soon ruined it as a base.

RUSSIA. PM I'm afraid the Germans are preparing a tremendous attack on Russia for the spring. They are getting *200* divisions together against Russia out of a total of 280.

5 P.M. COUNT REVENTLOW AT 29 PONT STREET, LONDON

.   .   .   .   .

He said that life was proceeding fairly well in Denmark and that all attempts to Nazify the people were a failure. The Nuremberg laws against the Jews, or part of them, had been proclaimed, but little or nothing had been done to put them in operation because the people would not have them. The Danish Government continued to administer the country and the German representative, who was the former Minister in Copenhagen, was not a strong or a harsh personality. He said that he wanted to make one point on behalf of the Danish people. They were sometimes compared with Vichy France. It was quite true that they were helpless and offered no resistance nowadays, just as the people of France offered no resistance, but there was this difference on which he desired to insist, that the Danish people maintained their democratic institutions, their democratic way of life, whereas France was being converted into a Fascist State in every possible way and was collaborating as such with the Germans. The Danes had not done this and under no circumstances would do it. He referred to Sweden and hoped strongly that Sweden would succeed in keeping herself out of the war. He said there was no Scandinavian who was not anxious that there would remain a centre of neutrality for the rest of Scandinavia to look to.

He was very much interested in the reconstruction of the British Government and asked many questions about it. He had listened to Churchill's last broadcast and had not much liked it, thinking it too rhetorical in the grave situation in which we were. He had also listened to Beaverbrook and he did not like the personality which he thought came through in the broadcast. He said that the broad-

caster was lacking—how should he put it?—'Kultur'. And I said
that I thought the broadcaster would probably assent to that
judgment very cheerfully himself. He had also heard Cripps
broadcasting and had been much impressed by him. He had not
met the man, but thought that his broadcast showed a clear and
vigorous mind.

21 February 1942

12 NOON. IVAN MAISKY

He was keenly interested in the changes in the Government and
was anxious to know what the country thought about it. Then I
asked him. He said he thought that Cripps would be a great
improvement, as he didn't think much of Attlee; Cripps had more
force 'he is a very able man'. But he was greatly disturbed about
the retirement of Beaverbrook. This raised the whole question of
supplies for Russia. Beaverbrook was the force that drove on the
flow of supplies, that got it going, and now that he had left the
Government he feared very much that supplies would diminish.
Why, when B went to USA recently the result was immediately
that the flow slackened. And it was essential that the flow should
be kept up. Russia needed it absolutely for the spring campaign.
He reverted to this time after time and was obviously deeply
concerned. I said that B would be able to do a lot to put pressure
on from the outside and would do it, but he said it was not at all
the same thing as being able to watch the problem and act from
the inside of the Government. He repeated that B had got on very
well during his visit to Russia. He said also that B had done a
great work for Russian supply at Washington.

About the actual war, he said he hoped that the Russians would
still be able to free Leningrad. I asked about the thaw and he said
(1) in the south (Ukraine, etc.) there was still a month of
winter. About mid-March the thaw would begin, but it
would make fighting difficult till mid-April. When people
said that the armies could fight during the thaw because
the ground in the south was sandy they were badly wrong.
It was black soil and would be 'sticky mud'—very nasty for
campaigning.
(2) Moscow and Leningrad. Leningrad was not quite so cold
because of the Baltic, but in general it would be end of
March or a bit later before the thaw and active campaigning would not be till the end of April or middle of May.

The Russian advance had exhibited a different method as compared with that of the Germans. The German light mechanical forces had advanced, when they broke through, far in advance of their infantry and had then frequently been cut off by the Russians. The Russians had gone slowly, closely followed by their infantry. They had not advanced so rapidly, but they had not lost so many troops and they had consolidated their ground carefully.

He was disturbed about the Scharnhorst and Gneisenau episode. It was a serious business for Russia. These ships might go out into the Atlantic and raid commerce, but they were also a very grave threat to the northern supply route to Russia. This was extremely dangerous. He did not worry much about the Baltic and he doubted whether the Russians would in fact use the ships there much, but the supply line from Britain was vital to Russia. In his opinion, the break-through of the German ships had been extremely disappointing.

He was also greatly disappointed about Libya. I reminded him that when I saw him last he had been glad that Rommel was 'making a stand' at Agheila, because he feared that R would go right into Tunis and seize Bizerta. Now R was near Tobruk! 'Yes', he said ruefully, 'I wish he was back at Agheila again!' Then he went on—

'Do you know what has caused this setback? I will tell you. When your army drove Rommel back to Benghazi and El Agheila your generals thought that Rommel was done, finished. He was far from done, but your Intelligence did not know it. So your generals sent back your tanks to Egypt to refit—exactly as they did before when they had chased the Italians to Benghazi. They made exactly the same mistake as before. Of course Rommel also got some reinforcements, though not perhaps a very great deal, and he got his machines more quickly repaired, but the real point is that he *out-generalled* your people completely.'

Then he said that he had been talking to a certain British person who had been in Egypt last year and who said that the British were then going to double the railway track from Egypt to Mersa Matruh and to make a great road from MM eastwards, and to take repair units right up to the front line, and this person now told him that nothing of the kind had yet been done. 'Well, if that is so, what can you expect?'

From this he got on to the general question of the *quality* of our direction and staff work in the war. He had a very poor opinion of it. 'Perhaps I ought not to say these things to you about your people, but we are friends and allies, so I can do it.' He said the great problem was to get brains into the direction of our army. It had to be done urgently, quickly, and it was not being done. He had heard of one man, Alexander, who was being sent to Burma and who was a good man.[1] When the Russian Military Mission was over here they saw the work of our generals and they said that Alexander was the best they saw, and that the work under him and the troops under him were good, and they thought nothing of most of the others. 'At manoeuvres they did not know what they were about. . . .'

He himself since he came to England (October 1932) had met and knew our highest officers. When he came he had asked the CIGS and others to dinner. The CIGS was ——.[2] 'Well, I was dumbfounded when I saw him. He was seventy-four; he could not hear properly and he could not see properly and he did not seem to me to understand modern weapons. They do not think in terms of modern war, those people. Then there came a new CIGS ——.[3]

WPC Could he see and hear?
X   Physically yes, but mentally no. He also was much too old-fashioned. After him came ——.[4]
WPC He did well in the retreat of the BEF in France?
X   Yes, he might be a good commander in the field, but he was not a general of the staff. And, after him ——.[5] He laughed at this name as though greatly amused and said nothing more. ——[6] he said was better, and he thought well of ——[7], the present Deputy CIGS, whom he had met on the visit to Russia.

I said that perhaps our best hope was to find and promote the "new men' whom the war brings up. He said 'Yes, but they have to be trained and trained. You can't get them easily, for war is

---

1. General Sir Harold Alexander, later Field-Marshal Earl Alexander of Tunis

2. The CIGS in 1932 was Sir George Milne. He was sixty-six, not seventy-four, and not unreceptive to new ideas, at any rate in his younger days. He was succeeded in 1933 by Sir Archibald Montgomery-Massingberd, aged sixty-two at the time of appointment. Maisky's description fits him except in regard to age.

3. Sir Claude Deverell, CIGS 1936–37, also adequately described by Maisky.

4. Viscount Gort, CIGS 1937–39 and C-in-C of the BEF 1939–40.

5. Lord Ironside of Archangel, CIGS 1939–40. He had commanded the British force in Archangel after the first world war, and his title sufficiently explains Maisky's amusement.

6. Sir John Dill, CIGS 1940–41 and thereafter chief British representative on the combined chiefs of staff's committee until his death.

7. Sir Archibald Nye, Vice CIGS 1941–46. He accompanied Eden to Moscow in December 1941.

now a most tremendously complicated business far more than it ever was before. So you cannot expect to get these young new men so easily.' He seemed to want good professional soldiers, but did not know how we were going to get them in the British army. He was contemptuous about Percival who had been in command in Singapore and said that he could see no sign that he was or ever had been adequate to the job he had to do. Then he went on to talk of the British in a military sense. 'The British in general', he said ,'are not in the least what they make themselves out to be. They like to say "Oh yes, we know we are stupid, slow people, no good at anything".' He laughed at this as at a great joke. 'No, they're not that sort of people at all—they're very much cleverer than that! But they don't shine in military affairs. There were only four military nations—Germany, Russia, Japan and France. France has gone and now there are only three—Germany, and Japan, that is two, against one, Russia.' He spoke very gloomily. I reminded him of Napier's saying that 'the British are the least military and the most warlike of all peoples'. Oh, he said, 'I know the British are tough but that is not enough.' I explained to him that they were not only tough but pugnacious, warlike and determined, and would so win the war. He asked when would all these things become apparent and that it was not a question of many years but of this year and next. I added that the Americans were of the same kind and would organise and fight until the war was won. He was highly sceptical and said 'I never have thought much of the Americans'. He thought they had all our faults, and more. He did not think very highly of the Dutch either. They had become 'soft'. They had lost their old tough aggressiveness during the last two hundred years. He did not expect much of them now. Roughly speaking, the only Powers that seemed to him to be formidable in the war, the only Powers that were effectively 'military', were Germany, Japan and Russia.

.   .   .   .   .

16 March 1942

TELEPHONE CONVERSATION WITH LORD BEAVERBROOK

I had wanted to meet him in London on Thursday or Friday and he had replied that he would telephone to me direct. He came on almost immediately afterwards and asked me if I would go down and dine with him tomorrow (Tuesday) afternoon. He said that he would be at the Savoy until Wednesday, but would not be available at all on Thursday or Friday. I said I would have to look forward to seeing him on my next visit to London a few weeks hence, and he replied 'I shall not be here'.[1]

He then talked for a few minutes about the war. He said that they were getting a move on in America with the war effort. It was slow, but they were moving and they would in time do great things. We had to expect a good deal of misfortune yet, especially in the Pacific and all we could hope for therefore was that the Americans would carry on guerilla warfare against Japanese communications.

He was hopeful about Cripps,[2] but said that the position was as indicated in Low's cartoon—Cripps going in at one door and Japan at the other, and Japan was extremely close and threatening. Cripps had been doing well, but he would describe him as having 'the genius of the untried'. The hearing on the wire was bad and I asked him to repeat and to explain, and he said that Cripps was a man of great ability, but in these matters of high policy he was as yet untried and had to prove his skill. 'He is a very able man indeed but, you know, he has his defects; he is in some ways difficult.'

He spoke of Russia and said 'In my opinion the result of the coming Russo-German conflict this spring and summer will be decisive. At any rate in this sense—if the Russians hold up the German attack, for which the most tremendous preparations are now being made, Germany will have lost the war; the war in Europe will have been decided.' 'Therefore,' of course, he added, 'all possible supplies must be got to Russia.' I asked how they were going on and he said 'Well, quite well'. Nevertheless he would like to see still more going. I said that I imagined that he was doing all that he could in that direction and he said that he was indeed putting his back into it. He added that he thought that on the whole he was perhaps at present of more use outside the Government than in it, and when I tried to draw him on the subject of a possible return to the Government he repeated that he thought he could perhaps do the things he was trying to do better from without than from within. He used phrases which suggested that he was very energetic in pushing the idea of 'urgency' and getting certain things done which he didn't particularise. He also made a few references to the PM.

1. On 20 March Beaverbrook went to the United States, where he campaigned for the Second Front.

2. Cripps was in India, settling a constitutional settlement. He was unsuccessful.

19 March 1942

3.30 P.M. A V ALEXANDER AT THE ADMIRALTY

Empty talk about torpedo bombers and excuses for not damaging the Scharnhorst and Gneisenau.

5.15 P.M. BRENDAN BRACKEN AT THE MINISTRY OF INFORMATION

The Daily Mirror published a cartoon of a distressed seaman on a raft with the words: 'The price of petrol has been raised by a penny.' Churchill wished to suppress the paper. Morrison, the home secretary, contented himself with a warning.

. . . . .

He began at once about the Daily Mirror, about which a statement had been made in the House that day. He said that the Mirror campaign about officers was really serious and that the Government was genuinely afraid that the moral of the rank and file might be affected. He quoted the Mirror passage to me. He said it had to be remembered that our long series of defeats could not have had a good effect; the present inactivity of large forces in this country was not a good thing for morale; there were certain things relating to our defeats in the Far East which were puzzling and made us more anxious about morale here. The Government was very much in earnest about the Daily Mirror question and had every intention of treating it very seriously.

. . . . .

At this point a secretary came in and handed him a slip of paper which proved to be a Reuter telegrame. It was the first intimation that Curtin, the Australian premier, had been annoyed by the appointment of Casey[1] to Cairo. Curtin announced that he had most specifically told Casey that Australia wanted to keep him at Washington, etc.—a slap in the face for Churchill and the British Government. B read the message and said 'Crikey!' jumped up and told his secretary to get No. 10 Downing Street. He asked the personal secretary to tell the PM all about it and to

---

1. R. Casey, an Australian MP, had just been appointed minister of state in the Middle East and a member of the war cabinet.

say that presumably they would have to issue an official statement on the subject later on that evening. Then he said to me 'I don't understand this at all.' The PM had told him himself that morning that he had made the appointment with Curtin's concurrence and, of course, he would not have made it unless Curtin had concurred. Everyone in the House thought that it would please Australia. 'What do you make of it? Is Curtin being attacked by some of his own people or is he unfriendly to Casey because of party political feeling or what?' The longer statement by Curtin had not come in when I left.

20 March 1942

9.30 A.M. LESLIE HORE-BELISHA, AT 16 STAFFORD PLACE

He was animated and pretty positive regarding the Government's position. Cripps had just gone off to India and he said that it was truly remarkable that immediately after a so-called reconstruction of the Government in which Cripps's appointment was the only thing that mattered, Cripps should have been sent away to India. 'Thus,' he said, 'the "vitalising" influence that was to do so much for the Government, and therefore of which the public expected so much, has been sent out of the country, although certainly through his own volition. Incidentally, the man who would have been the strongest critical force has been taken into the War Cabinet.'

I inquired about the position of Cripps relatively to the Government when he came back to this country. 'Oh,' he said, 'he was offered the Ministry of Supply and he would not take it but wanted a seat in the War Cabinet, and now that he has got it I believe that he has become a Moderate.' He said this in a semi-jesting manner with much amusement. I said 'What did you want him to do?' He replied 'I wanted him to stop out of the Government and to take the lead of all those people who are discontented with the way in which things are going and are anxious to get the war won with more energy and efficiency. Because if things are not changed we are going the right way as fast as we can to lose the war. Look, for instance, at the rapidity with which commanders are changed from one day to another; you hardly know what Wavell's command is at the moment.'

I referred to the fact that he had not been called on to take office in the recent reconstruction, and he said the only reason why he had thought that something might be happening was the positiveness with which one or two people (Beaverbrook and Eden) had approached him and broached the matter to him. He mentioned one of them (Beaverbrook) and said that the trouble was that he only told you half the truth and that there was always something behind which he concealed. However, he was on the whole relieved to think that he had not been brought into the Government because unless he had an office in which he would be able to have a good deal of authority and achieve something, he would have to share in the responsibility for failures and for a great many things of which he didn't approve. He felt that he could do better work outside.

He then went on to talk about the effect of recent reverses on Churchill's prestige and on the effect which success or failure in India might be expected to have on Cripps's political fortunes when he came back. He also speculated as to who might be a successor to Churchill as Premier, and he said he wished very much there had been some way of calling in Lloyd George. He was a statesman, a great statesman, and it was deplorable that it hadn't been found possible to make use of his immense talents in spite of his age and of difficulties; he sincerely wished that it might still be possible.

LUNCH WITH WINSTON CHURCHILL

There were there Mrs Churchill, a Miss or Mrs Muriel Ward, a Lady Colefax or Colfax[1] or something like that, Commander Stephen King-Hall,[2] and Churchill himself who came in a few minutes late. The ladies were old friends of the Churchill family and apparently 'up to the eyes' in the politics of the day. e.g., the Miss or Mrs Ward said to Churchill 'Well, I see you've sent young Alex to Burma', meaning General Alexander, the new C in C in Burma, and Lady C spoke intimately of the De Gaulles and all the Free French lot. She said 'So they're trying now to arrest one another!' The conversation was largely between the ladies and the PM. King-Hall was almost entirely silent. I got in a few questions. Towards the end Bracken arrived and sat down at the table and joined in the talk.

Once or twice when the talk at the other end of the table was busiest, Mrs Churchill turned to me and told me amusing stories about the Free French.

She said that General de Gaulle was extremely touchy and

1. Two well-known society ladies.
2. Journalist and independent politician.

when he took offence struck the most dignified attitudes. She had been much puzzled on one occasion when, on thinking that he was slighted about something, he folded his arms with great dignity (she gave a comic imitation) and said 'Je me retirerai dans mon FIEF'. She could not for some time understand what he meant until he said something else which showed that he was referring to Brazzaville, the capital of French Equatorial Africa.

She had had an awful fiasco with a luncheon party she had given in his honour. Things politically had been a bit strained, so she thought it would be a good thing to give him and Madame de Gaulle a luncheon. Only she and Winston—they both spoke French—were going to be present. The De Gaulles do not speak English, or not well. A day or two after it had been fixed Lord Crewe rang up, said he had not seen them for some time and would like to come and see them. She thought this was a great idea, as he had been Ambassador in Paris,[1] and asked him to the lunch. Then, by an odd coincidence, Lord Derby, another ex-Ambassador at Paris,[2] rang up in the same way, and she thought this was a great chance, so she invited him also to the lunch. 'Would you believe it, those two old men came and from start to finish of the lunch, they would neither of them speak a single word of French. It was all very flat, and a terrible failure.'

Churchill referred to India and said bitterly 'Yes, it's a fine thing, isn't it, that we should be sending all these troops and equipment to India only to be kicked out at the finish when we have saved the country!'

Among other things that he said during the lunch were these:

'I was always afraid for a long time that Japan would come into the war and the United States would be out of it. I would have liked to have the United States in and Japan out. Now both of them are in—well, would anyone prefer to go back and to have Japan out of the war at the price of having the United States out also?'

He thought nothing of the people who criticised the escape of the Scharnhorst and the Gneisenau. The loss of Singapore—that indeed was something to lament, but as for the German cruisers, why four or five hundred ships of all kinds had gone through the Straits with impunity and nothing had ever been said about them.

1. 1922–28.
2. 1918–20.

I asked why the Gneisenau and Scharnhorst had not been discovered sooner. He said they were discovered by a reconnoitring aircraft, but he was attacked and had to fight, and his wireless apparatus went wrong, so he had to fly back home in order to report. That lost precious time. I asked why we had not more destroyers available to attack the G & S. He laughed rather wryly and said 'Because so many are busy hunting U-boats and convoying British merchantmen. That's why there aren't enough of them at Harwich!'

He did not like the speculations about future strategy which constantly appeared in the press. He would like to stop them all, because he thought that they were really dangerous. I said that people would hardly be stopped from general speculations about the coming course of the war and he said 'No, but they speculate about the likelihood of a coming blow here or there or in some third place, and the enemy, studying all this, may think that a certain suggestion has something behind it and they may take action accordingly; and, in fact, by a pure fluke the suggestion may be right and then they will anticipate us and great harm may be done. It is really dangerous.'

Bracken came in at this point and said that he had been lunching with Barrington Ward of the Times, and as he was leaving he ran into Cowley of the Daily Mirror. He had begun to talk to him about the attacks that the Mirror had made on the whole of our officers and he had pointed out to him that Nye, for instance, now Deputy CIGS, had actually risen from the ranks. Churchill thereupon burst out in violent explosion—'Why did you tell him anything about Nye? Why do you argue with him about these subjects at all? You should have told him simply that we will go for them and that,' here he hammered the table with his fist, 'we will flatten them out.'

I said I thought that this was a mistake—that he should tell them that he quite admitted that more merit was wanted in the army and then he should go on to tell them how much there was already, using Nye as an illustration, and how much he intended there should be in the future.

He said 'Oh, well, anyway it's not the provincial newspapers that I complain of, but some of the London papers like the Mirror, the News Chronicle the Daily Mail and its Sunday paramour, the Sunday Dispatch.

At 3.15 I said I must go, as I had an appointment at the F.O. He said 'Oh, but you can't go. I want to talk to you upstairs.' Bracken said 'Who's it with?', and when I said 'Eden', he said

'That's all right. I'll fix it. I'll tell him'.[1] So I went upstairs with the PM to the Cabinet room.

He began to speak of the Casey episode and said that he was astonished at the reported protest of Curtin. He had certainly obtained, as he understood the full concurrence of Curtin before he had actually approached Casey. He sent for copies of the cables which had been exchanged and went over them one by one. He pointed to the almost apologetic phrases which he had used, especially in mentioning Menzies, and said that at any rate there could be nothing there to hurt Curtin's feelings. He read over the cable in which Curtin asked that Casey should remain in the United States long enough to meet and consult with Evatt and in which Curtin withdrew his opposition if that condition were satisfied. He then said "I took care to satisfy that condition and, in fact, as the news shows, it has been satisfied, and, that accomplished, I went ahead. If Curtin had in this cable, which was the second cable, renewed his opposition to Casey's appointment I should have done nothing and the whole thing would have fallen to the ground and been finished with.' He went on to say that at present he could not understand what had happened. I suggested that possibly Curtin had acted without consulting some of his colleagues, that they disapproved of what he had done, and that he had therefore to find fault with the proceedings. He thought that might be so, but that it was at any rate very puzzling and it looked as though he would have to publish the whole correspondence in self-defence

He turned to the Daily Mirror question and was very hot and strong about it. He said it was dangerous to have a constant stream of stuff which was calculated to undermine the moral of the soldier; very serious issues were involved.

He then spoke of Singapore and of what had happened there. I said that the surrender was a great mystery and worried people very much. He said 'it filled me with anguish and self-reproach. Whether I am responsible or not I feel it intensely. And some of them accuse me of complacency!' I said I would like to explain what was worrying me. It was that the quick surrender suggested that there was no real fighting spirit in the defence, a lack of quality, and that if it was so in Singapore it might be— 'I know what you mean', he said. 'That there was a lack of nerve and that it might conceivably be the same here. Some things that happened are as yet inexplicable.' He drew patterns with his finger and

---

1. The meeting with Eden was cancelled.

explained that when the Japs landed on the island one would have expected the troops posted at certain points would have counter-attacked and driven them back to the beaches, or be wiped out. 'It gnaws my heart' he said.

He was searching everywhere for military talent and intended to encourage and promote it all the time. That was his great desire. He resented the 'Carping, niggling criticisms' that he and the Government received day by day from certain quarters and certain newspapers—from the Daily Herald, 'which represents the second largest party in the Government', and from the News Chronicle—'the most stupid of all the papers'.

He was vehement about this, and I said 'You don't mind if I speak quite frankly about that?', and he replied 'No, that's what I want you to do'. I said 'Well, it puzzles me that you should bother, or worry, about these papers so much. No doubt they irritate you but do they matter all that much. You have your great majority in the House and you know that you have the country behind you firmly. Why should you let one or two papers who nag day by day disturb you so much?' He said he didn't think he got reasonable treatment from such people, they were injuring the prestige of the Government which was very important etc. But what he obviously felt most was that the disaster in Malaya etc. hurt him bitterly—'anguish and self-reproach'—and that he did not get a fair deal from the daily critics. (Both A E[den] and B B[racken] told me how much he was hurt by these constant newspaper attacks.) He insisted that, though times were bad, he could and he would pull the country through to victory, but 'Give us a chance!' he said.

A small point. He referred, a little ruefully, to the generals who 'are always wanting more and more (before acting), but of course they've got to be given by us all they want.'

Another casual reference 'We are sending all possible quantities of aid to Russia, and we are going to go on. There are great difficulties but it is going, and it is getting there.'

5 P.M. SIR ARCHIBALD SINCLAIR AT THE AIR MINISTRY

I began by asking him what he thought about the Daily Mirror business. He said that speaking for himself he never saw the Daily Mirror and therefore could only judge in the light of the passages which had been collected and put before him as a Minister; he was bound to say that they were pretty serious. He would put it this way—that if the objectionable passages had been collected together by anyone in a leaflet and circulated to the troops in a camp, the printer and the author or authors would have been liable to be prosecuted for sedition, and he understood that there would have been every reason to expect a conviction. It was not in his view a matter of freedom of criticism at all; it was a constant drip, drip, of an attack on the officer class in the army and it was likely to do serious harm. He then got on to the question of his recent speech in the Commons in which he had said that RAF officers resented criticisms and were angry at the idea that they were not doing all that they ought to do to help the army or the navy. He said that there was a tremendous esprit de corps in the RAF as an independent air-force. However it had begun and however it had grown up its members now regarded themselves as members of an individual service and he was bound to say that any idea of the 'dismemberment' of the service, which was how they regarded it, was much resented by them. I said that I thought this was all wrong in two ways. It was not the individual man or officer in the RAF who was ever criticised. So far as there was criticism it was directed either against the system or against those in authority who defended the system, namely the air staff and the parliamentary chief, meaning himself, to which, of course, he would not object, and that I thought it was very unfortunate if individual officers were either encouraged or allowed to regard themselves as being the target of criticism which was never directed against them. He replied—as these people always do—that there was, of course, no objectionable references in the MG or any similar paper, but that there had been definite articles and that there had been definite speeches which appeared to attribute failure or insufficient effort to the RAF as a service, and he had evidence that the men and the officers strongly resented this. I said that shortly a time might come when it might be necessary, and might be generally agreed that it was necessary, to take away certain functions from the RAF and give them to one of the other two services. He replied that in his opinion any such thing would not have a good effect, and he added that the formation of the naval air arm had not in its time had a good effect either.

.   .   .   .   .

20 April 1942

3.30 P.M. ANTHONY EDEN AT THE FOREIGN OFFICE

The Russians were insisting that recognition of their annexation of the Baltic states should be included in the proposed Anglo-Soviet treaty of alliance. At the last moment they dropped the demand, and the treaty was signed without any reference to the future territorial settlement.

.　　.　　.　　.　　.

He talked about Russia and her desires in the matter of frontiers. He described what was proposed with regard to the Baltic States and admitted that it was a disagreeable business. He hoped to secure the insertion of a clause in the treaty saying that anyone who desired to leave those States after the end of the war settlement should be allowed to do so and to take his property with him. He hoped that Russia would both agree to this and would carry it out. He said that some of his friends had suggested to him that we should simply allow Russia to do what she chose in the matter and should ourselves stand aside; neither agreeing nor opposing. He did not think that this was a courageous policy and he did not think that we ought to do it. We ought to take up a definite position in the matter one way or the other. In his view the issue was this—did we or did we not desire to co-operate with Russia with regard to the future of Europe? He believed that Russia was willing to co-operate and that we could work together and he held that this would be of immense importance. If we now refused what Russia desired and maintained what she was entitled to on the grounds of her bare security we should run the risk of alienating her and preventing what ought to be a most fruitful co-operation in the future. Further, we could not, of course, prevent Russia from absorbing these States if she desired to, so that if we refused our consent we might be proclaiming a good principle, but it would have no practical effect on the fate of these countries, while on the other hand Russia might decide that we really did not desire to work with her and might pursue an isolated independent policy of her own.

.　　.　　.　　.　　.

5 P.M. WINSTON CHURCHILL

I mentioned the visit of the American representatives—General Marshall and Harry Hopkins—and said that it was comforting to think that things had gone off well. He said 'Yes, there was one thing in particular that was comforting and that was that, contrary to expectations, the Americans took the view very strongly that the first thing to do was to defeat Germany; once that was done Japan was in fact finished even if, of course, it took a considerable time to defeat her altogether.'[1]

He then spoke of the Far Eastern war and I asked about the likelihood of Japan attacking India, moving westward, etc. He said 'We have had a very anxious time these last few weeks; we never knew whether the Japanese would appear in the Bay of Bengal with a large fleet or whether they would bring a great expeditionary force and throw themselves on Ceylon or invade India. An invasion of India is, of course, quite possible. No, they are not likely to attack India overland from Burma; the country would be terribly difficult. If they attack it is more likely to be from the sea. Yes, one would expect them to make an attempt on Ceylon first, but Ceylon is a bit stronger now than she was. We managed to get a good many aircraft there in time and they gave a good account of themselves when the Japs attacked Colombo and Trincomalee.' He gave some slight account of how the reinforcing aircraft had got there.[2]

I said I supposed that instead of invading India, which might bring them nothing in the long run, they might attack Ceylon and then, using it as a base, penetrate farther westward on the sea towards the rear of our Middle East and Suez positions. He said 'Yes, but they won't find that quite so easy as they did a little time ago; we are putting some additional weight there now.' In this connection he mentioned the Atlantic and American assistance there, enabling us to move further East.

Then we got on to Europe and the Mediterranean and I asked about Libya. He said 'I think very likely the whole of the fronts—both Libya and the Russian fronts—will be ablaze in May. It is quite likely that Rommel will attack then in conjunction with Hitler's onslaught on the Russians. It is there—pointing to the Russian front on a big map—it is there, especially in the south round Rostov and all that region, that the big things are going to

---

1. General Marshall, the American chief of staff, and Harry Hopkins, Roosevelt's personal representative, were in London for conferences with the British chiefs of staff from 8 to 14 April. Though they certainly agreed to put the defeat of Germany first, they were also set on an early landing in Northern France. The British chiefs of staff, while ostensibly agreeing, really wished to continue the campaign in North Africa and in July got their way.

2. The Japanese were concerned only to establish a defensive front in Burma and at Singapore and made no serious attempt to dominate the Indian Ocean.

happen. That is what is going to decide a great deal and we have got to help them all we can.'

I said 'Supplies, you mean, and are they still going out of the country regularly and a lot of them?'

'Yes, tanks, aeroplanes, guns and all that—our own life-blood that we are sending to them. And they are getting there, but it is a tough job—ships taking them in all weathers, through storms and snow, and they have to be well protected because the Germans are looking for them all the time with submarines and great bombing aircraft that they send out from Norway, and then there is always that great Tirpitz, not to mention others that we have to be ready to meet. A ship—of what size?—well perhaps 50,000 tons.'

I said 'How much? If it is that it is near the limit, isn't it, of what is supposed to be the size limit for battleships?'

He asked what I meant and I said I had always understood that designers and engineers regarded 55,000 tons as a practicable maximum. He said 'Oh, I thought you meant some sort of a legal limit in the past. I don't know whether it is 50,000 tons, but anyway it is far beyond the limit of 35,000 tons which we and the Americans observed for so many years, and while we were observing it the Germans were building these great monsters. Lord! How they must have laughed at us!' He gave an exclamation of great disgust.

I asked about Malta, and he said 'It is a remarkable business. The Germans have got at least 400 bombers engaged in attacking Malta and there are a lot of Italians engaged in the attack, perhaps 700 in all, and it is still going strong.' I asked whether they would not be wanting these bombers soon on the Russian front, and he said 'It is only intelligible on the supposition that they have said to the Air Commander there "You have until such and such a date to complete the job and on that date, whether or not you have completed it, off you go to the Russian front".' He thought, however, that the bombing attack on Malta still had a week or two before it would have to be stopped in the interests of the Eastern Campaign. I remembered how on an earlier occasion he had insisted that it was a tiresome and long business to transfer all the equipment and personnel that went with air units to a new theatre of war.

In a sort of summing up way he said 'Burma—no good! Libya, well—' and without saying anything he moved his hands up and down in a see-saw manner. 'Russia—that is the great issue.'

Then he suddenly broke off and said 'I hope you do not think anything of all this bunk about a Combined Staff that is being put out by these ex-Ministers! It is aimed at me, of course.' I said that I thought that Chatfield's letter in that day's Times arguing against a single Chief of Combined General Staff was a pretty good argument. And he said 'Oh, yes, he wants a committee instead of a single man. Well, we have got a committee already—that is the Defence Committee of the Cabinet. I may tell you that I am thinking of issuing a White Paper on the subject in the next few days. It sets out exactly what the position is about the Chiefs of Staff's Committee and its relationship to the Defence Minister and the Cabinet. It will be a good thing to tell people exactly what the position is, don't you think! I am sure a lot of them don't know.' He then sent for a copy of the white paper, which was already printed, and went over it paragraph by paragraph. He pointed out that General Ismay represented him as Minister of Defence on the Committee and reported everything to him; also that Ismay managed the secretariat of the Committee and also that of the Cabinet Defence Committee, so that there was, so to speak, a complete interchange of knowledge and close 'co-ordination'. He also drew attention to the point that the Chief of Staff's Committee had now included a Joint War Production section, so that the whole business of production was brought into the most intimate connection with the war plans of the staff. He exhibited the strongest distaste for the proposal that there should be a single Chief over the three present Chiefs, and said that under no circumstances would he accept it.

28 May 1942

4.30 P.M. PRESIDENT BENEŠ

I congratulated him on his birthday (he was 58 this day) and he said 'I hope to spend the next one in Prague.' He referred to the attack on Heydrich and said: 'There will be a terrible persecution. Heydrich is dying.' I said I only knew that he was wounded, but he said 'He is dying, I have news from Prague. I have heard it already today from Prague—he is dying.'[1]

.   .   .   .   .

Then he talked for an hour about Germany and the war.

---

1. Heydrich, the German Protector of Bohemia, was assassinated by two Czechs sent from England on 27 May.

'The winter has been terrible for Germany—worse than is yet known. There has been a catastrophe in respect of food-stuffs, especially potatoes; of coal, the production of which has fallen off enormously; of electrical energy; and of transport.

'There is another crisis between Hitler and the Generals. Last year as you know, they disagreed with him about the attack on Moscow. He insisted on the offensive but they were right. Now they are right again. Hitler insists on a renewed offensive against Russia, and he must; he cannot avoid it because of all the things that he has told his people. But the Generals are against it. They want a general *defensive* on all fronts. They want simply to stand fast, both against Russia and against Britain and USA, and then to say to the Allies "Now see. We are on the defensive and we can maintain a defensive for five or six years. And we will—we will defend ourselves for five or six years unless you agree to make with us a negotiated peace." [1]

'It may easily come to that position yet. All depends on the Russians! If they do well, if they hold off the German offensive. then the Generals may yet present the Allies with these alternatives. Moreover, if the Allies refuse, as of course they must, then the next stage may easily be that the Generals will get rid of Hitler and the Nazi system, and again ask the Allies to make a negotiated peace with them and the German people but without Hitler.'

I reminded him that he had said in December that the Generals knew they could not win the war. He said:

'Not only do the Generals know it now but I believe that Hitler and his Nazis know it also. I believe that they too know they cannot win but that they too hope to get a negotiated peace before they collapse.' The winter campaign had cost the German army enormous losses—1,000,000 dead from all causes; 250,000 dead of *cold alone*; 2,000,000 wounded and disabled, of whom *1,600,000* would never return to the battle-line. Hitler's views of his own position was shown by this—he was reorganising his SS and his SR throughout Germany, distributing them in new formations as a safeguard against the coming counter-revolution, which is now being prepared. But he is doing it wrongly. Generals are always wrong about a war. They prepare not for the next war but for the last war. The French Generals prepared not for the war of 1939 but for the war of 1918—with their Maginot Line and all that. Hitler is preparing now not for the next revolution but for the last

1. All this is quite imaginary.

one in 1918–19, and he is wrong. It will come but it will come in a different way. That crisis is coming, but there will be two crises— one in the Home Front, another in the army.

'To me the whole Hitler process has the inevitability of a Greek tragedy. The onslaught and the over-running of much of Europe— inevitable! The fall of France—inevitable! The attack on Russia— inevitable! The resistance of Russia, the throwing back of Hitler, the collapse of Germany—the inevitable climax! I don't think now that the war will end this autumn or winter. I have been told that I prophesied an early end of the war so I prophesy no more, but, speaking to you privately. I will tell you what I think. I think that —provided Russia holds out, and I believe she will, but all depends on that!—Germany will face and struggle through most of next winter but that in about February and March of next year the strain will be too much for her and she will crack. I am fairly well satisfied with what has happened so far on the Russian front. For two or three days things looked pretty black, but I think that the Russians have got the position in hand at present. As for the Crimea, the Germans have exaggerated their victory and captures by three or four times. There is in the military reports both of the Russians and of the Germans a certain element of propaganda, but the German reports of the Crimea fighting are fantastic—over 160,000 Russian prisoners when the Russians had perhaps two or three divisions in all in the field!'

He thought that we should establish a Second Front as soon as possible. It was true he had suggested to me in the autumn that an offensive against Italy would serve but he felt now that what was needed was a Second Front *in the Low Countries*. That would destroy the Germans—provided again that the Russians kept their end up. He knew, of course, that it was a question of practical resources. In the meantime he wanted our bombing campaign against Germany to be maintained at the highest pitch.

He was well pleased with us militarily and he very much wanted that the Germans should have to surrender to us and the United States as well as to the Russians. He thought that was very important. 'Politically, if I may say so, I am not quite so satisfied. It is essential that this country and the USA should make up their minds *before the Peace Conference* about certain fundamental questions. What *is* Czecho-Slovakia today in the mind of your Government? I am President of Czecho-Slovakia and shall go back to it as President, but of what geographical country with what boundaries am I the President? I want to know, I am entitled to know and so is my country. But your people can't tell me, nor can the USA. What about the Munich Settlement? Oh, they say, that does not exist—we take no account of it.[1] Very well, I say, but is it, then, Czecho-Slovakia of the status quo ante, with the boundaries that we know, with the Sudeten regions included? But they won't say—they say everything will be settled at the Peace Conference. After the last war it was 1921 before the boundaries were all settled—two years. Am I to be in Czecho-Slovakia for two years, trying to help the country to recovery, before I know what Czecho-Slovakia is to be, how it is to be constituted? How am I under such circumstances to settle my policy, the Czecho-Slovak policy, towards Germany? It is incredible. I agree, I am willing to agree with your people, that all things must come up and be discussed at the Peace Conference. The Americans don't want anything at all discussed before the Peace Conference. But that won't do. I want the principle accepted, some principle accepted, about the post-war position and after that certainly everything can come to the table for discussion. What about Yugo-Slavia—is that to be as before or not? What about Hungary—is she to profit by her crimes and retain the new territory she has got? And so on. Unless something is settled, nothing will be settled and there will be hopeless confusion, especially if the peace comes suddenly—and peace may at some moment come much more suddenly than your people now think. They must prepare plans for such a contingency. There must be something settled, even though subject to the discussions of the Peace Conference about such questions as I have mentioned, especially of course—to me—Czecho-Slovakia. But I am troubled, for I know the Anglo-Saxon mind. Your people say that we have the Atlantic Charter as an expression of Anglo-American aims—but it is much too vague and general.'

He returned to the state of things in Czecho-Slovakia. He said the Czechs were the most formidable of all Germany's opponents in occupied Europe. In their opposition they are quiet, persistent, industrious and entirely unforgiving. All of them—private persons, officials and the rest—were determined to do something damaging to the Germans every single day, and they did. The nation was as one man in this and the Germans could not, and never would be able to stop it or grapple with it.

---

1. In August 1942 the British government informed the Czechoslovak government that it did not recognise any territorial changes made in regard to Czechoslovakia 'in and since 1938'.

Of Himmler he said that he was the most powerful man in Germany now after Hitler—more powerful than Goering.

Of Libya, he said that a great British success would be a powerful moral blow to Hitler's prestige *in Germany*.

5.45 P.M. HERBERT MORRISON AT THE HOME OFFICE

Morrison had run into difficulties at the annual Labour party conference. Three by-elections had been lost to Independents. The Labour party executive put forward a resolution, committing the party to active support of any government candidate, regardless of what party he belonged to. The resolution was carried only by 1,275,000 votes to 1,209,000.

Further a resolution in favour of lifting the ban imposed on The Daily Worker in January 1941 was carried by a narrow majority. As the Communists were since the German invasion of Soviet Russia the most wholehearted of all parties in support of the war, the ban was rather absurd. It was lifted in September 1942.

On both issues Morrison was the executive spokesman.

I referred to his 'telling off' the Labour Party Conference on the day before. 'Yes', he said, 'I've had a hard week. I had a pretty stiff time yesterday. The Executive made a mistake in circulating that resolution about the electoral truce beforehand. We ought to have kept it quiet, disclosed it at the Conference and put it through, but we wanted to be so nice and reasonable. There was a lot of opposition—MPs; and a string of candidates. Quite naturally I have to do the dirty work on those occasions. Really it's Attlee's job, not mine, but they put it on to me. Not that Attlee hasn't done a good job at the Conference because he has, but when there's a really nasty job like this I have to do it—I don't mind, either.'

He referred to the Labour Party vote on the Daily Worker, told me what it was and said he would have preferred that it had been a narrow vote the *other way*. If he restored the DW it would be said he had surrendered to the Bolshies. He wouldn't be able to restore it for a bit now. I got the impression that he might restore it before long.

'Most of the Labour people are for the war effort and Coalition all right, but the trouble is that they won't face the consequences of their acts. They are for the party truce until they find that they don't like its consequences, and then they want to run away from them—in short, to have things both ways. They're suffering from too much soft leadership in the past.

'About coal—yes there's undoubtedly going to be trouble over it, but I don't think that at the finish it'll lead to a Government crisis.[1] First we have trouble over Rationing, then we add on Organisation, and now on top of that we've got wages. Something will have to be done about wages—there are real injustices. The miners are always difficult people—I've a great admiration for them, mind you—and very tough to deal with. I'm told that there might even be danger of a national coal strike over this wages question. The recent rationing business was mismanaged, of course. The PM, by the way, doesn't like rationing—he doesn't much like rationing anything in a severe way. He's full of sympathy, you know, for the ordinary British man and woman, and doesn't like inflicting hardship on them—[he was much amused when he was talking about this] He's the old benevolent Tory squire who does all he can for the people—provided always that they are good obedient people and loyally recognise his position, and theirs. Well, it was agreed on in principle by the Cabinet but no details, no scheme, and down comes Dalton to the Commons and says we're going to have rationing on coal but he can't give particulars and he can't answer any questions (and there are lots of questions), and so he goes away and all the critics get busy and there's no end of opposition worked up in no time at all. But that's no way of doing things. The principle ought to have been decided and the scheme worked out and then the Government ought to have made a short formal statement of its intentions to the House and after that it ought to have stuck to the scheme whatever happened.

'The coal business hasn't been well handled in various ways. The Mines Department has been too soft with the owners for long enough. Well, now we have to tackle organisation. There's the Labour scheme, which is open to a good deal of objection, and there's an alternative. The Government might set up a National Corporation to do the job and on it they should *appoint* representatives of the mineowners and the miners. These, however, should be chosen and appointed *by the Government*. They should *not* be delegates chosen by the owners and the men. That would be dangerous because the owners might choose some of the most crusted reactionaries and the men might choose some of the most

---

1. Early in 1942 there was a coal shortage, owing to a decline in the labour force and in productivity. Dalton, president of the board of trade, commissioned Sir William Beveridge to prepare a scheme for rationing domestic consumers. The scheme leaked out before it was in operation. Conservatives protested, and the scheme was dropped —the only successful Conservative revolt against Churchill's government. There followed a cut in supplies to domestic consumers, increased control of the industry by the board of trade, and increased wages for the miners.

difficult of their leaders.' He didn't see why the alternative scheme shouldn't work.

I asked him about the general position of the Ministry and of the PM. He said that he thought that recently the PM's stock went down a good deal but that it was now recovering. His last broadcast also had helped.[1] He was bound to say that, so far as he was concerned, he considered that 'the old man's' gifts—and he alluded to him also as 'the old rogue' and 'the old rascal'—were so pre-eminent as a war leader that he could not think there was any alternative to him. He had, no doubt, some tiresome habits—like that of working till 2 a.m. 'I myself work till 2 a.m.—I knock off a bit about 7 p.m. and then go on till 2.' I said I thought it was a small matter anyway for these bigwigs to be asked to work till 2 a.m. and he said 'Oh yes, but they find it awkward. The old man sleeps in the afternoon and then starts again for the night's work as fresh as a daisy. And they have a routine and it involves getting early to work at their desks in a morning, so they don't like it.' Here he mentioned that Shinwell was 'out to bust the Government' and bring it down altogether, but he would not succeed. The PM, of course, had his faults and about some things was too headstrong. Not, however, about all. In many ways he was not only cautious but remarkably cautious. When Churchill became PM he had expected [like me—I had mentioned this expectation] that he would be too impetuous and would 'jump' to doubtful actions, and that this would be a danger, but he had found that he was wrong and that Churchill was in many directions extremely cautious in the direction of the war. It was, however, necessary to stand up to him sometimes. Some people were too ready to agree with him or, after beginning to oppose, to surrender to him quickly, especially when he glared at them, saying nothing. He said that it was quite amusing that sometimes, when he was crossed, Churchill would glare at the offenders or 'all round the table', saying nothing at all 'for nearly two minutes' but looking extremely baleful. Well, you must stand up to him and he might be at the time extremely angry but nothing evil came of that. 'On three occasions I have whacked him.' I asked for particulars and he gave them.

(I) THE DAILY MIRROR. 'I opposed him on that. He—and some others besides, whom you might not have expected—wanted to suppress the Mirror at once without a word of warning. I wouldn't do that. Bevin was hot and strong about it—highly emotional. Well, you can't conduct your policy on the basis of emotion. You

1. Prime Minister for Two Years, 10 May 1942. The End of the Beginning, 100–7.

must base it on reason and then stick to your decision whatever happens. Bevin was emotional about the Mirror cartoon. How, he said, was he to "press" people almost into the merchant navy if they were then to see the suggestion (in the cartoon) that they were being "pressed" in order to put the price of petrol up for the owners. I at once said that we could not suppress the DM out of hand. It must go to a Committee first. So it went to the Committee (with Anderson as Chairman). Then there was a funny thing. The Law Officers held—and it is the first time, so far as I know, that such an opinion has been given—that even if it is admitted that a paper is trying to aid the war effort, nevertheless its criticism of the existing system may be such—by showing that the whole of the defence or the army or something like that is rotten and useless— that it comes under the regulations and can justly be suppressed. Well, I said, that may be so, but we have never had that stated before, and I doubt very much whether opinion is going easily to accept an interpretation which was certainly never dreamt of when the Regulation went through. So when it came before the Cabinet again I opposed the suppression bluntly. I said I couldn't agree but that I would cheerfully see the DM people and tell them what the position was and warn them, and if they did not amend I would certainly suppress them. And that was how it was settled, but Churchill didn't at all like it at the time.'

(II) NORTHERN IRELAND. 'I opposed conscription in Northern Ireland. Again, Bevin was the moving spirit in this case; it was really he who put it up to Churchill, who was quite pleased with the idea. I knew there would have been great trouble and that it was I who would have to deal with the trouble when it came. They got me down to Chequers to discuss it and when I was leaving Churchill walked with me and put his arm through mine and said "Now you'll do this for me, won't you?" and I said "I can't give you any promise. I don't know. It's a big thing and I must think more about it." Then I got two of the Ulster people over and I said to them "You've got to tell me the truth about this because a lot of the trouble is going to fall on me if there is trouble. Is this going to mean shooting or not if it goes through?" and, well, in effect they admitted that in all likelihood that is what it meant. So, when the discussion came again, I would not agree. Others supported me. Then Churchill glared "all round the table" for about two minutes, saying nothing, then some gave way but others didn't, and the project was dropped.'

(III) THE BLACK OUT. 'Churchill and Beaverbrook were for abandoning the black out—depressing, gloomy and all that—a

Beaverbrook stunt! They didn't understand the practical details and difficulties. They said, "Put all the lights on, and then, when the Germans come, turn them all off again." I said, "Well, if you do this, you needn't worry about turning the lights *off*—the public will do that quick enough for you, I assure you." Anyway the practical aspects were all against them and they soon dropped it— it was a quite small matter anyhow.'

Of the Home Office he said that it was most important that its functions in social matters, health, etc., should never be taken away and given to another Ministry. If that was ever done the Home Office would tend inevitably to become a Police Department with a Police mind, which would be a disaster. Its functions in social policy were a liberalising influence on the whole department, and in his opinion a most essential part of its work. He could himself feel the constant danger of the Police side growing and colouring the work of the whole Department.

Of Attlee he said that he had had a lot to do with the more liberal policy of the cabinet towards India—it ought not to be undervalued.

He was fairly satisfied about the ARP now. The NFS was vastly better though there could still be improvements. They had learnt a lot from the Blitzes. There had been unjust criticism about ARP at Bath and Exeter.[1] Those places were out of the usual track for Blitzes and you could hardly expect that ARP would be as good in Category C places as in the most threatened. He did not think it had been bad. In casualties Bath had suffered worse, in proportion to its population, than London on the worst of all its days of Blitzes.

· · · · ·

29 May 1942

11.30 A.M. BJÖRN PRYTZ

I reminded him that he had been in Sweden since I last saw him and I asked him how Sweden is getting on. 'Not so badly', he said, 'considering that she is cut off from so much of the world.'

WPC The Germans still don't seem to be too pleased with you.
P   And, neither, I'm afraid are your people sometimes.

---

1. The 'Baedeker' raids, undertaken by the Germans in retaliation for a bomb dropped on Heidelberg.

Nor Russia either. Nobody is particularly pleased with us.

WPC Perhaps that shows you are being successful as a neutral?

P   Maybe; at all events there is no doubt about our attitude towards Norway. We are always showing our sympathy for our unfortunate neighbour. There is the strongest public opinion in Sweden about the German treatment of Norway. With regard to defence we go on working hard. Do you know that taxation in Sweden is relatively as great as in this country—mostly for defence purposes?

He began to speak of the discussions that were going on in London with Russia. He was glad to say that he understood things looked much better—in the sense that the idea of making detailed territorial arrangements about Eastern Europe now had been abandoned. What was the sense of starting to determine now how the frontiers of Poland of any other of those countries be delineated? All that should be kept until later.

He spoke very strongly of the way in which Germany was treating the occupied countries. He said that at the beginning of the war Sweden represented the interests of Poland, but that was no longer so. The Germans would not have it; they would not have the wretched Poles, whom they maltreated so much, represented by anybody, so that no one would have the right to intervene or to try to find out what was being done to the Poles. He said that in Germany, when labour from the occupied countries was handed over to the farmers, the farmers would pay (to the 'Labour Management' Office) say, 50 Marks for a Frenchman, 30 for a Dutchman, and so on down to 5 for a Pole. There was a tariff which exhibited the value put on the Poles by the Germans—they were regarded not as human beings, but as animals.

He thought that the Russians were doing fairly well at present, but one thing troubled him. There were good authorities in Sweden who did not believe that Russia could last out beyond this year. Up to the autumn, yes—but after this year—these people said—doubtful. That was why this question of a second front was so important. He did not believe that the Russians were demanding a second front *in order to win the war this year*. That was not the point. The point was that Russia wanted the second front in order that she should not herself collapse; it was to hold her up over the winter; and in his opinion the question ought to be carefully regarded from that point of view. On the other hand—or rather therefore—he hoped that Britain and the USA would not depend so completely on Russia as they appeared to do. That was wrong and he was alarmed about it. He was afraid that they might depend too much on Russia only to find that Russia was no longer there.

In Germany itself 'no one any longer smiles'. Hitler's and Goering's speeches were very significant of the gradual crumbling of morale. Railway transport was very bad. Germany had been due to send coal to Sweden but did not send it. She said she would send it if Sweden would herself provide the waggons. Sweden refused, knowing that if she sent the waggons she would never get them back.

He asked me what I thought about the position of the Government and Churchill and then said 'What is Beaverbrook up to? What is he after?[1] I don't suppose it's true that Churchill and the other members of the Government got him out [Curious how that idea persists], but what will B do now? I will tell you what some people here say to me. They look at his promises to Russia when he was in Moscow and his speeches and the articles in his papers about a Second Front in aid of Russia. They say that if Russia wins all will be well, but that if Russia loses B will accuse the Tories of having failed to fulfil the promises which he made to Russia on behalf of the Government and that he will again try to be a "kingmaker". No doubt the country would not have him himself as Premier, but they think that he might try to make a Premier of his own choosing,—Churchill being no good for the purpose—and having got a Government to his liking he would declare for a negotiated peace with Germany on the basis that Britain should stick to the British Empire and the USA and clear out of Europe. This was his policy before the war and it might be his policy, if Russia collapsed, again. That is what these people think and suggest to me.'[2]

I said that B was a great individualist, 'The lone wolf', but that I did not believe this account of him and, anyway, there was a good deal to reckon with in public opinion, etc. etc. before any such thing could be conceivable; also I believed B to be attached to Churchill just as Ch liked him and regretted him going. I told

1. Beaverbrook was conducting a campaign in favour of an immediate Second Front in Northern France.

2. These and other suspicions about Beaverbrook were common at the time. They were without foundation. Beaverbrook preached the Second Front because he believed that it was the most effective way of winning the war.

him that I thought the idea that Ch or the Government had 'got rid' of B was entirely false.

Prytz himself is always very 'nervy' about the idea of Britain withdrawing from Europe and retiring into the Empire and USA. He does not understand the British character or public opinion very well. He assured me in the summer of 1939 that Britain would never go to war 'for Poland';[1] his view was based on the talk of the society, political and financial people he mixed with.

3 P.M. WINSTON CHURCHILL

'Well', he said, 'I think this battle in Libya is going fairly well.[2] I'm quite satisfied about it and I'm following it hour by hour. We'd better have a look at the map.' He rang for his secretary and said 'Bring that Libya map'. The secretary brought in a sheet-map about 3 ft wide by 2 ft deep, showing the Libya region in great detail, and the positions of the forces and lines and arrows indicating the movements of the Germans up to that morning. Running from the west to Bir Hacheim was the German line of advance, which then curved up north and north-east: the words indicated that the 21st and 15th Panzer Divisions were in this, with some part of the Italian Ariete Division—up to that time 250 tanks in all. The rest, he said, were being held back somewhere. The advance to the north-east had been repelled and this column, swinging westwards, had joined up with the left-hand column moving more or less due north. The fight against this united column was now going on. Meanwhile, he said, our aircraft were attacking Rommel's supply lines from the west to and beyond Bir Hacheim; these were open to attack from the northern flank and this should give us good chances. The enemy had lost 148 tanks. So far we had lost 150, but 'we have more than they', so we had the better of it. He said that in everything—tanks, guns etc—we had more than they. There had been no surprise at all by the enemy. Ritchie[3] had anticipated the lines of attack and had prepared for them—he had prepared for just such an advance on Bir Hacheim.

Then he went on—'I'm glad they have attacked—very glad. It suits us better than if we had had to begin. If they hadn't attacked now, we should soon have had to go for them, but I prefer it this

---

1. This was presumably at the interview of 17 June 1939, the account of which has not been preserved.
2. Rommel took the offensive on 26 May.
3. Commander of the Eighth army.

way—it's much better. Now we shall have to hold up their attack and then, if we drive them into retreat, of course, we shall go after them. You know, this tank warfare is quite different from anything hitherto. Before it came, we thought that if the enemy got behind your positions, it was dreadful, you were "cut off" and all that sort of thing. But it's quite different with tanks. If they get behind you, you take no notice of them; your other troops fight them, of course, but in your prepared positions you just take no notice of them until they withdraw or are disposed of. That's what's happening now with those German tank columns going right away up north there'—indicating on the map—'right in the rear of our prepared position from Gazala to Bir Hacheim.'

He then began to speak of the recent two-days' war debate in the House.[1] He said that he was not at all pleased there should be these long debates on the war in which about thirty members—and always the same thirty—got up and attacked the Government often in the most extreme manner and gave the world a quite wrong impression of the position of the Government and of himself. 'I am not going to have two-day war debates on the adjournment in future. There is no vote of confidence in the Government on them so that these thirty critics hold the field and what they say goes all over the world without the only adequate reply, which would be a vote in favour of the Government showing that the house was almost solidly behind it.

'I think very strongly that if these people attack the Government as they do they ought to have the courage to go into the Lobby and record their votes against it. Then it would be seen for how little they really count. In future if they want to make a full-dress attack on the Government they can do it on the motion for the Consolidated Fund Bill, on which anything can be discussed, for they can put down my salary, or they can put down the salary of some other minister, and then we shall have it out with them. I will tell you the sort of damage that these debates do. I made my broadcast the other day and I am told that the effect was good. Then, the day after the war debate in the House there comes a message from Hoare in Spain saying that every newspaper in Madrid had carried streamer headlines across the whole of its front page, splashing Hore-Belisha's declaration that the Government was losing the war for the country and all that sort of thing. If that kind of impression is going to be sent abroad then it is necessary that the House should take a vote so that the news of

---

1. 19–20 May 1942. Churchill did not speak in the debate.

the Government's majority would also go abroad at the same time and neutralise the effect of the attacks.'

I said that once or twice some months ago he had insisted on a vote of confidence and it had been very salutary for the reasons which he now put forward. The only question seemed to be whether it was necessary to have a vote every time there was a debate and a succession of critical speeches; clearly that seemed to depend on the effect which such speeches were held to have abroad. He repeated that it was wrong to have a succession of such attacks without forcing the attackers to go into the division lobbies to prove how few they were in comparison with the support behind the Government—and that was what he was going to do.

From this we went on to the critics who were demanding that he should accept a Chief of Combined General Staff and himself cease to act as Defence Minister. He said:

'I will tell you more about that. As I have told you before, it is not true that I run the war or try to. I don't in general interfere at all with the Chiefs of Staff. I have nothing to do with the operational conduct of the war. But it is quite true that I am active as Minister of Defence. I conceive it to be my duty to stimulate the Chiefs of Staff, to offer suggestions for discussion by them, and to bring before them all subjects that ought to be considered. I am prepared to say to you that I am better fitted in some ways for this job than anyone who would be likely to be made Chief of Combined General Staff.

'I know a lot about war. I have studied war all my life—studied it and written about it—I was for some years in the army and two or three times I have been First Lord of the Admiralty. Well, they talk about Trenchard as a possibility for this suggested post. I say that if he had it, and I say it most seriously, I would know more, much more, about the army and the navy, than he would. And if a new chief came from the navy, I would know more about the army than he would. And if he came from the army, I would know more about the navy. What I am saying is simple fact—it is true. I daresay that if someone else were Premier, he would, and ought to, have a man holding the position of CCGS. But I don't require such a man and he ought not to be imposed on me. If they are not satisfied with me, then they can get someone else. They can take away all my powers altogether if they like, but I am not going to have them taken away from me bit by bit.'

From this he turned to Singapore and to the suggestion of an Enquiry. He said 'You are in favour of an Enquiry into all that led up to the Singapore disaster, I know, but I am not. We cannot possibly be spending our energies at this moment on enquiring into all that led up to it, and anyway I have got enough to do without it.' I said that we hadn't in fact suggested that the commission should start at once and should call on him and other ministers to spend their time in appearing before it, but there was surely a great deal to be done in finding out what had been thought and advised and provided for, if anything, in the years before the war, before his Government, and before Japan entered Indo-China. 'Maybe,' he said, 'but who is to gain by this Enquiry? What good is it going to do? What good is the country going to get out of it?'

I said I saw no reason why in this case, as in others, the exposure of weaknesses and inefficiency should not help us to do better afterwards. 'I can tell you,' he said, 'some of the things that it would do and I doubt very much whether they would help us. For one thing, it would divert energy, and it would divert my energy and that of other Ministers from the war, and I can tell you that I, and we, have a great deal to do already and not much time to spare.' (He spoke with an air of humorous understatement.) I said that I supposed that even in the last war Ministers were pretty busy and nevertheless they managed to hold the great Dardanelles Commission and to publish an important report while the war was still going on.

'I'll tell you about that too' he said. 'Who or what gained by that Commission? I did, and I alone. Before it reported I could not get a place in the Government at all, but *after* it had reported and exonerated me, I went back into the Government.[1] *I* gained but no one else!'

At the finish I asked a few questions. I said that for some time there had been no bombing raids over Germany and people were puzzled. 'It is because of the weather', he said 'and entirely because of the weather. The weather interferes with our campaign much more than people imagine. They don't think how ground mist or fog, to take only one point, can make it extremely danger-ous for aircraft to land and cause heavy losses. I can assure you,' he said, 'that the recent lull in our bombing has nothing to do with any losses that we have suffered. It is simply and solely the weather and we shall soon start again, though,' he said, 'I feel sorry for the Germans when I think of what is coming to them this summer.'

I mentioned Cripps's statement in the Commons that we had ordered dive-bombers in 1940 and that they hadn't 'come forward' for reasons into which he was not able to enter. 'What happened,'

---

1. Churchill became minister of munitions in July 1917.

he said, 'was that we had ordered quantities of dive-bombers in America, and America "fell down on it". We were getting them now. Another reason was that some people, the Air Force chiefs, didn't believe in the dive-bomber as the best weapon. They believed that we should do better with the aeroplanes that flew low over the enemy and bombarded him with machine gun bullets or cannon shells.'

He sent for a collection of papers and read me the text of (1) a dispatch from Wavell at Singapore about the lack of defensive preparations (2) a list of twenty or more suggestions for defensive measure which he himself drew up and sent to the Chiefs of Staff for their consideration. (3) the despatch actually sent out by the Chiefs of Staff's committee. This actually embodied many of his suggestions. He said 'I sent them these notes to consider, accept or reject. That is how I am useful'. His note to the Chiefs of Staff began 'I am appalled to hear—of the lack of preparations reported by Wavell,' and he *was* appalled. He told me all the things that had *not* been done at Singapore and all the things that ought to have been done. There was a long list of defensive measures to put into operation in the island of Singapore behind the 'moat' that is the Straits of Johore, and none of these things had been done. He described the island of Singapore as technically the 'gorge' of the fortress, the straits being the 'moat' and said it was incredible that with a great 'fortress' the 'gorge' should have been left so completely undefended. It was *elementary* in the establishment of fortresses that the 'gorge' must be equipped and defended by certain well understood means and methods—but nothing had been done! He said about these notes of his—'they are suggestions which I rough out—I dictate them in bed.'

'Of all our home production of munitions of all kinds we keep only 30 per cent here—all the rest we send somewhere abroad.'

COAL 'I don't think there's going to be any Parliamentary crisis—you'll see. We should not have given way to the 1922 Commission? Well, but why should not the poor, wretched Tory be able to criticise if he wants to? People like Shinwell and so on can criticise and oppose all they want to but the poor, downtrodden Tory is not allowed to open his mouth to the Government without loud cries of protest being raised!'

SHIPBUILDING I asked was he going to increase our shipbuilding programme in this country?

'No, it wouldn't be worth while to take away the labour from other things that would be needed. Better to leave it to the USA. USA can produce *seven millions* of tonnage in one year when she gets going. The small amount that we could produce would not be worth the diversion of labour from other things.'

'Beaverbrook is going to demand an increase of our programme —in the Lords?'

PM (Grinning and saying it twice over) 'In secret session, then. Only in secret session!'

NEW MINISTERS

PM   Can you suggest any really able man that I *could* put into the Government?

WPC I've often wondered why Hore-Belisha does not get back. He's able isn't he? And he had courage when he sacked the army chiefs?

PM   Yes, he's able, very able, and he has courage. But, you know, he didn't get on well with people at the War Office. Antagonised officers, when he went to the front. (He went into details of this, and also referred to   ).

LLOYD GEORGE

'He may have more imagination and more depth as PM than I have, but I have more experience, and know more, of war.'

HOME DEFENCE

'Yes, the defence of the inside of England is thoroughly and systematically worked out, I can assure you.' (I had said this troubled some people) We are stronger now. But in June, 1940! If Hitler, when France fell, had only said to his generals "Now, get over there!" we would have been in great danger. We had only 200 guns! We had scarcely any Air Force and, mind you, the French had been demanding that we should send them our last squadron—after they had already decided to surrender!' He spoke with great bitterness.

THE GENERALS 'They are apt to be very cautious. One must take *some* risks in war. Do you know that in any particular case the negative forces *against* action are as 20 to 1? Some of them were against our going to occupy Madagascar—oh yes they were— because they were all for caution. They quoted Dakar! Well, this was no Dakar'.

MADAGASCAR[1] 'We decided on that 3 months before the actual stroke. I wanted USA to join in it, but they wouldn't. But they supported us to the full and went and told Vichy so at the very

---

1. British forces occupied Diego Suarez in May and the whole island in September.

moment when we struck. And they stopped warships southwards so that we could send our ships to the right place.' (The USA stood out from the action so as to avoid a breach with Vichy.)

When he spoke of Russia coming in through being attacked by Hitler and then of USA coming in through being attacked by Japan and contrasted the situation as it was when we stood alone, he said with some emotion 'It's impossible not to see the finger of Providence in all that'.

4.30 P.M. A V ALEXANDER AT THE ADMIRALTY

General talk of no great interest on the naval situation.

30 May 1942

11 A.M. COUNT RACZYNSKI

He had been for two months in the USA and had come back at the beginning of April. He was pretty well satisfied with things there, though he admitted others were not. Production, he thought, was speeding up all right. At the Federal Reserve Bank they had told him that this year 60 per cent of the US income was being spent on the war and next year it would be 80 per cent. What made others uneasy, though not him, was the feeling among certain sections about the war. There were many anti-British influences— Irish, masses of Germans, and a good many isolationists. They made a lot of all British reverses, depreciated and sneered at the British effort. He was appalled at this when he first landed there. He had no idea there were so many bitterly anti-British people. It was a good thing there had been Pearl Harbour to counterbalance Malaya and Singapore! The British habit of self-depreciation and understatement was not understood by the US people. He had been at a great meeting. Litvinov had praised Russia to the skies, every other speaker had backed up his own country and been violently cheered. Then Sir John Dill—a very nice man!— had spoken for England. He had devoted nearly all his speech to eulogies of Russia and all the other Allies and, at the finish, about Britain, he had said that the British Empire 'was doing, and would do, its best'. On sitting down Dill had said to him that he was afraid his speech had fallen a bit flat. In America they did not understand that sort of reticence.

He referred to the London discussions (without mentioning any names). He said that in USA he and Sikorski had discussed the political questions privately—about Russia's boundaries, that is. The USA did not want them discussed publicly, nor in any way settled before the Peace Conference. Russia had pressed for this very vigorously—at any rate in London. He got out documents and read to me what Sumner Welles had officially said to him. (He said that S W was 'pompous but precise'.) It was that USA did not approve of these territorial issues being settled before the Peace, though there was nothing to prevent Russia and Poland privately from discussing the questions between their two countries. That was the whole position of the USA. He was glad to think that, as a result of the talks in London, these questions had been set aside now and that the only agreement likely to be made between Russia and Britain would be of a wider, vaguer kind about working together in the future. He said that Russian diplomacy was very interesting. In USA Litvinov was 'an angel with great white wings'—he made spreading gestures—who never mentioned the necessity of discussing these awkward questions, while in London was Maisky—'you know, the little black devil'— who was putting on pressure all the time to get Russia what she wanted in these territorial matters. 'Roosevelt said to me that if it was a question of Russia's *security*, he would be perfectly willing to consider the principle of security for Russia as one of extreme importance at the Peace Conference—he would certainly take that view—but it was not a matter to be settled now.'

On the subject of Stalin's policy, he said once more that Stalin represented a Peter the Great policy, and that the more the policy became 'Peter the Great' the better the Russian people were pleased. It would be found, if all went well for Russia, that she was 'Peter the Great' in Finland. As for the south-east of Europe, it was true that Stalin accepted the collaboration of Poland and Czecho-slovakia, but that was as far as he went. When Yugo-Slavia and Greece got together he was cold and hostile, and he did not like signs of independent action in the Balkans. No! the Balkans were, in his view, a sphere of Russian 'penetration', there was no doubt of it.

. . . . .

Stalin was 'a great gambler' and 'a great bluffer'. Even last year, when the British offered to organise the Poles on the Russian left-flank and perhaps go there themselves, he would have none of it— he would have Russians or nothing. He was a man of great courage

—of strong nerve. He was determined to hold Moscow at all costs. He had told Sikorski that he would never surrender it; he would fight for it to the end. In spite of the unpleasant speech of Stalin some months ago when he spoke of driving the Germans out of Russia and nothing more, he did not believe that Stalin would make a separate peace, or that Hitler could either. Hitler had gone too deep into Russia and had involved himself too far. He did not think that either *could* make peace with the other now. 'No, they will have to fight it out.'

I said the German figures of their successes in the Donetz counterstroke were suspicious—they said they had annihilated 'three armies' and taken over 160,000 men.[1] If this was true they must have advanced through the breach a long way before the Russians could stop them. He was not sure about this. Last year it would have been so, but he was told that *this year* the Russians had 108 to 110 divisions in the field and the same—another hundred or more—immediately in reserve. So they might have filled the breach quickly. In general he thought both the Germans and the Russians were weaker this year than last. Say the Germans were 25 per cent weaker; if the Russians were less than that much weaker, they would win. He remarked that the Russians always 'boosted' their own production to the utmost, saying how much they produced in the Urals and all that. They never gave us credit for helping them, but a friend of his who had been in Russia told him that the greater part of their equipment seemed now to be British plus some American. And we played up to this. [He was vastly amused.] When the Russian Air Force did anything great it was, according to the British papers, always Stormoviks and never British Hurricanes, which often it really was.

The state of Poland, he said, was dreadful and he feared that at last some of the Poles out there were becoming really discouraged. When they saw the German massacre of hostages, etc. they demanded some sort of reprisal in kind, but that was not a thing that Britain or the USA could do. He thought, though, that more formal notice ought to be taken of the German outrages—Churchill or Roosevelt ought to make more frequent references to the dreadful things the Germans were doing and to threaten them with retribution.

---

1. Two Soviet armies were destroyed, and 241,000 Soviet prisoners taken.

9 November 1942

4 P.M. MRS ROOSEVELT, AT THE MANCHESTER TOWN HALL

Mrs R, after going to Avros, etc., came to have tea at the Town Hall with the new Lord Mayor (Ald. J. Septimus Hill). J R S[cott] and I were introduced to her and she said that she had been told by Winant, the Ambassador, that when she came to Manchester whatever else she did she must see the MG people.

We sat down, there being at the table the Lord Mayor and Lady Mayoress, Wright Robinson, ex-Lord Mayor who had just gone out of office, and Lady Reading, the head of the WVS, who was going round the country with Mrs R. Mrs R talked quite simply and interestingly about what she had seen and seemed to be a very sensible and clear-headed woman. She said that her husband had told her that she could come to this country 'provided that she made a good job of it', and that she had been very busy carrying out the timetable prepared for her. Wright Robinson raised the question of the development of institutions, social principles, religion and all that and in regard to religion Mrs R said that she thought that young people had more or less ceased to be interested in any 'theoretical religion', but were still prepared to be interested in it if it was related to their ordinary lives. During the talk on progress, I asked her whether there were in the United States Republican diehards who didn't appear to want to change anything at all, and she said yes there were, but there were even worse diehards in the Democratic party.

Finally she left to stay the night with the Stopfords.[1]

---

1. Sir John Stopford, vice-chancellor of Manchester university.

7

Victories and Policies, 1943

In the field of war, 1943 saw the first long run of successes. North Africa was cleared of Axis forces in May. Italy surrendered unconditionally in September, and the Allies re-entered Europe at the supposed 'soft underbelly'. On the eastern front the Russians won the greatest tank battles of all time at Kursk in July. Crozier records some of these events. Many of his interviews have a different interest. They suggest, however tentatively, the political issues of the future. The Beveridge Plan of national insurance was published in December 1942. Three months later Churchill tried to stave off the popular enthusiasm for it by talking vaguely of a Four Year Plan of his own. Men began to debate whether the wartime coalition should be continued after the war was over. Curiously, Herbert Morrison, who when the time came did most to swing the Labour party to independence, seemed in 1943 to be the leading advocate of coalition. Not surprisingly, Sinclair took the same line. In foreign affairs relations with Soviet Russia, rather than the chances of her survival, became the leading topic. Rupture between Soviet Russia and Poland was already in the air.

25 March 1943

3.30 P.M. SIR ARCHIBALD SINCLAIR

He began by saying that privately he agreed with every word in that day's MG leader about the Four-year Plan and the necessity of doing more in a positive way before the election. He hoped I was going to see the PM and would talk to him about this. I would find, he said, that the PM held very strong views about the importance of the Government's not committing itself too far to positive legislation. Partly, of course, it would be settled by events. If the war in Europe went on to the latter part of 1945 then he was quite sure that the Government would have to do a good deal in the way of legislative measures, etc. It was right to remember that a great deal of administrative preparation was going on already in various directions and would go on continuously, e.g. preparation for the great building programme. I said that the main point was what was going to happen to the Beveridge plan.

I felt that, whether Churchill liked it or not, he would have to go a good long way in putting that through before the election. He replied that his own feeling was that the country meant to have it and that no Government would dare to refuse it. But he repeated that a lot depended on when the next election came. The farther off it was the greater the pressure to get things done.

Then he came to the question of the election and the parties. One thing he felt was that we did not want Churchill to go to the country simply as head of the Conservative Party. If he did he would be the man who had won the war, the man who was the equal of Roosevelt and Stalin, the man who was going to make the peace treaties, the man who had a great social programme, and the man who would put through the Beveridge plan, which in fact he would do if it hadn't been put through before. The consequence would be that he would sweep the country and he would undoubtedly have in his Government a number of detached political leaders who would carry weight in the country; he mentioned particularly Woolton.[1]

He did not believe for a moment that Churchill had any idea of wrecking, or any desire to wreck, the Labour Party by forcing a crisis on it or by splitting it up—those who were for coalition and those who were not. Such an idea was entirely foreign to Churchill's character. No one had ever lived who was less of a political intriguer. Churchill's ideas of political intrigue were 'boyish and puerile'. In the days before the war, when they were both of them in opposition, Churchill's idea of conducting a plot against the Government was to call out loudly to Sinclair 'Come on out and let's have a talk,' and then he would conduct Sinclair out of the House before the eyes of the assembled members. He was the most candid, ingenuous and impulsive person in the world.

Churchill was not thinking of a centre party; also, he had let it be known the day before that he did not intend a coupon election. The truth was that he hadn't thought it out at all; he had probably given very little thought in any way to it, and in fact no one else had got far in thinking it out. We did not want a coupon election and most certainly we did not want the present Tory block returned to the House. I said that if the Coalition Government went to the country it would publish a manifesto signed by himself, Churchill and Attlee; they would have to support the pro-Government candidates and the Tory block would substantially

---

1. Lord Woolton, minister of food, and in November 1943 minister for reconstruction.

be returned. He suggested that there might be a conceivable way out. He had not thought a great deal about it and he was not sure that it was practicable, but his idea was that more than one candidate could accept the Coalition platform and promise to support the Coalition Government if returned, but each candidate would support the Coalition on the basis of his own general party views—the Tory with Tory principles in mind, the Labour man with a special slant of his own and so forth. There had been, he thought, a few by-elections fought on that basis and he just wondered whether a general election could not be fought in a similar way. The party leaders, would, of course, have to stand down in contests between pro-Coalition candidates; these candidates would have their dog-fight. I suggested that the Tory machine would be very averse to an arrangement under which Labour and Liberals were free to attack Tory seats under the general cover of a coalition umbrella. He said, yes he was himself aware of that difficulty.

.   .   .   .   .

He then came to the question of the air weapon and Air Force. He said it was unfortunate, but really the only thing on which he disagreed with the MG was his own province, the air. He wished we would send someone to see him a little oftener.

.   .   .   .   .

There was now an absolute priority for everything needed for the U-boat war; second priority was for everything needed for the bombing of Germany. It should be remembered that the bombing of Germany was our only active offensive against her except what was proceeding in Africa, and that only occupied from six to eight German divisions. Our bomber offensive was in fact giving a great deal of help to Russia, and Stalin was most keen about it. We were doing great damage to the Germans' production of munitions and we were damaging their manufacture of aircraft. The Germans were being forced to build fighters rather than bombers in order to deal with our bombing offensive, both the present and that which they knew was to come. More than half the whole of the German fighter force was stationed in the west against us and only one-fourth of the whole on the Eastern front from the Baltic to the Black Sea.

.   .   .   .   .

We had a considerable discussion of the airmindedness of the Admiralty which, so far as the present was concerned, he defended. He insisted that the Air Ministry had a full and adequate influence on decisions relating to the U-boat war and anything else that concerned it. Also he paid tribute to the PM who, he said, was a very good impartial judge and saw that justice was done to the air weapon. He said that the gravest part of the U-boat campaign was undoubtedly that it could delay military operations.

.   .   .   .   .

26 March 1943

9.30 A.M. LESLIE HORE-BELISHA

I had not seen him for six months or more and he began by explaining what had happened to him in respect of his digestive troubles. He had been put on a diet for duodenal ulcer and then he found that he was having skin trouble. He asked the doctor about it and the doctor said that the skin trouble was due to the diet (prescribed by himself) containing no vitamin C. Thereupon he left the doctor and went to a specialist, who confirmed the first opinion and gave him a course of injections of vitamin C. This had put his skin right and he thereupon decided to pay no attention to medical opinion about his duodenum, but to eat and drink moderately what he thought suited him. This he had done and the result was quite satisfactory.

He began at once on Churchill's references to the post-armistice election and the relationship of the parties. He had seen Arthur Greenwood, who was very gloomy and thought that the Labour Party was likely one way or another to come a cropper. He himself thought that Bevin would certainly stay with Churchill, that Morrison probably would, but that Attlee would probably come out and remain with those who were throwing over the Coalition. His belief was that Churchill, in spite of his denials, was thinking of founding a Centre Party. He might lose the extreme men on one side or the other, but he would like to lead a Centre Party which would include 'the best men of any party or of none'. He was not at all sure that Churchill would not prefer to lead a party and a government of the 'best men' rather than to lead a Coalition Government which included some very uneasy followers in the Labour Party. He said that Churchill had during the last war openly contemplated the formation of a Centre Party and that there was an account of this in Beaverbrook's volumes (I could not remember this). Next he called attention to young Randolph's speech at Preston in which he had openly advocated a Centre Party, and he said that he thought that Randolph was only reviving the plan which his father had cherished during the last war. He then went on to say that there was no room for more than two parties in the country, which meant Conservatives and the Labour Party; the Liberal fragments were too divided to coalesce and the inference was that they would disappear.

He then went on to speak of his own position. He had not made any considerable speech of any kind in the House since June of last year; he had ceased to make highly critical speeches such as he had made on the capture of Crete and the catastrophe in the Far East and he didn't intend to make any attacking speech for the time being unless there was some event which could be compared with those two so that he was morally compelled to take up a position and criticise the Government.

With regard to the Beveridge Plan, for instance, he would like to offer any constructive criticisms that he could, but he didn't want to take up a position which would appear to be definitely hostile to the Government, nor was he attacking the Government, with questions that might be interpreted as definitely hostile. I remarked that anyone who adopted what might be called a nagging policy was liable to be bracketed with Shinwell, Bevan and Clem Davies, and very reasonably. Some of their criticism might well be regarded as pursuing a personal campaign against Churchill. He said he well knew it and that anyone who has sided with them in asking even fairly harmless questions was tarred with the suspicion of their animosity. He was, he confessed, much troubled at the present moment as to what he should do. He did not want to remain idle and apparently useless. He felt that he could do really useful work at the present time.

I suggested that he might follow for the present at any rate a policy of examination, but beneficent examination, of the Government's policy in respect, for instance, of the Four Year Plan and Churchill's desire to postpone almost everything until the war was ended. He said that he was disposed to think that this was good advice and he thought that he would do something of the kind in his coming speech at Devonport. He would examine and analyse and ask questions, but not in a spirit of hostility to the Government and its present policy. He really didn't know what influences were keeping him out of the Government. The PM was very friendly to him in a personal way; Beaverbrook had declared himself on his side, and Eden had gone as far as to say to him plainly 'Why don't you join us?' There must be some influences behind the scenes which were strongly against him. Winterton[1] had taken him aside one day recently in a very friendly manner, walked him off to the Smoke Room, and talked to him about future policy. Winterton had said that he didn't want a General Election (that is to say before the post-armistice election), but that if things became very difficult, that is to say, for instance, if Labour broke up the Coalition and went into opposition an election, however disagreeable and tiresome, might nevertheless be inevitable. I reminded him that, according to Beaverbrook, when in 1916 Bonar Law had threatened an election in order to get rid of the Tory critics in the House, Winterton[2] had said that he could not imagine anything more immoral than to hold a General Election in the middle of a great war.

11 A.M. BJÖRN PRYTZ

.   .   .   .   .

He spoke about the future policy of Russia after the war. He hoped very much that she would not be aggressive, that she would be thoroughly cooperative with the rest of Europe.

I said that there seemed to be signs of it, e.g., the Anglo-Russian Treaty and that it was difficult to think that Russia, having made alliance with us and the United States, would want to retire into seclusion again.

'No one knows,' he said. 'She might say that after the last war she had had to go into seclusion for twenty years in order to recover, and now after this war she felt that she would have to return into seclusion for another twenty years.' He hoped that it would not be so, but no one knew.

I suggested that whatever else happened Russia would always have Japan on the one side of her and Germany on the other.

'Yes,' he said, 'but you know there are some people who think that if Russia does not get all she wants, or if the situation suits her, she might ally herself with a Sovietised Germany. I hope not, but

---

1. Lord Winterton MP, one of Churchill's most persistent critics.
2. This should be 'Winston' [Churchill]. Beaverbrook, Politicians and the War, ii, 106.

that is what some people think possible. As for the border States, Russia, of course, wants to have Governments in them that are favourable to her. If you ask the Russians themselves they will say "Nonsense, there is no danger whatever of an imperialistic Russia. All that Russia wants is to have friendly countries on her borders." But what is meant by friendly countries? Do they mean "friendly" in the sense that the Baltic States have to be friendly, and do they mean that Finland must be friendly in the sense that it must have a Kuusinen[1] Government? It is all rather like Hitler, who said that everything would be all right if Germany only had a friendly Poland on her borders.

Russia had proved to be much stronger than had been expected, but the food shortage was worse this winter than last. There would be food all right for the army and officials, but a lot of the common people would die.

.   .   .   .   .

12.45 P.M. WINSTON CHURCHILL

He was looking rather washed out, but said that he felt fit again.[2] He said it was the new drug M and B that had pulled him through; they had told him that but for M and B 'it would have been 50-50'. He was the usual mixture of grimness and good-humour. It was, he said, 'with great resentment' that he found himself being constantly told that he must talk about the post-war plans when we had nothing like won the war. People were always getting ahead of events. He was dismayed when he opened his paper on the morning after the break-through on the Mareth coastal stretch. From the headlines 'you would have thought that we were in Tunis already, so, when I got the bad news of the setback, I went straight down to the House and gave everyone a stiff warning'.

Then he reverted to his broadcast.[3] I said that traces of his 'resentment' came out at the beginning and at the end, and he said 'Well, anyhow, I *did* it—and I took three weeks to think over what I was going to say.'

Then he got on to the domestic politics of the broadcast. 'I don't know at all what Labour are going to do. I don't want them to come out of the Government and, on the whole, I don't think

1. Finnish Communist leader, an exile in Russia.
2. Churchill had had pneumonia while in North Africa.
3. A Four-Year Plan, 21 March 1943. Onwards to Victory, 32–45.

they will. I think they'll finally decide to go on—perhaps for another twelve months anyway. I don't want a General Election either—not if it can be avoided.'

I said a General Election would mean a big upset in the middle of the war.

PM 'Oh yes it would. They have them in America, of course, and in New Zealand, but then they're farther off—they don't feel the war so much. I wouldn't like the idea of the fight and noise of an election when we ought to be concentrated on the war. Besides, you might have German bombers casting a vote—they would know all about what was going on. I wouldn't like it.'

I said that I remembered that he had expressed very strong views about the idea of an election in war time—during the last war, when Bonar Law talked of it as a means of getting rid of Tory opposition.

He made a grimace and passed on without comment. 'But, however much I disliked it, I might have to do it—if they [opponents whoever they might be] created such a state of things that we could not get on efficiently with the war.'

I enquired what his view was about the method of a post-armistice election and its effect on the parties, whether one used the word 'Coupon' or not, did it not mean that the Coalition leaders would put forward a programme together and therefore would support the candidates accepting that programme?

He said 'Yes, and they could not support anyone else.'

I said it would be very awkward for the Labour Party—would it not stereotype the numbers of the parties and confirm in possession the great Tory block now in Parliament?

He said, 'Well, he couldn't tell any Tory constituency not to defend a Tory seat, could he? The trouble was that Labour would naturally want to increase its strength and to diminish that of the Tories and under a Coalition Government election, that could not be done. That was the crux.'

I then broached the suggestion that S[1] had thrown out—that more than one candidate could support the Coalition Government but fight for the seat among themselves, each with his own party slant. He looked very dubious and said meditatively 'They would soon be slanging each other and extending their differences —it would be an awkward business. At present we must leave things to events.'

We then got on to the four-year plan and the question of how

---

1 Sinclair. See interview of 25 March.

much should be put through Parliament before the election. I said I thought it would be a great mistake, and the country would be much disappointed, if it was understood that the election was to be followed not by the carrying into action of plans already passed but by long sessions of legislative debates. He said 'Well, but I included in my speech *legislative* preparation. There will be all kinds of preparation—some administrative and some legislative. There's a lot of preparation going on now—as e.g. with regard to building. There's going to be legislation about education. There will be other things. But, regarding this insurance question, I don't think that the time and energies of Parliament ought to be distracted, because they *would* be distracted to the details of a great programme like that, instead of devoting its mind mainly to the job of the actual war. I feel that most strongly. And a great deal depends, of course, on the length of the war and how much time we have.'

From this he turned to the war and began with the U-boats 'You don't need to worry about the U-boats. I think it is going to come out all right.' December, January and February were much better and so was March 'except that they got into two convoys'. We had much more strength coming along in the next few months. We preferred the summer months because we were going to have a lot of aircraft at work and they could look down into the water for the U-boats. I asked did he mean that we were going to put aircraft into the middle zones of the sea away from the coastal regions, and he said yes he did indeed. I said that that meant more, and many more, auxiliary aircraft carriers and were we going to get a lot of them, and he replied 'Oh Lord yes.' They were the only things that could give proper air escort to a convoy in the middle seas and we were going to have them.

On the subject of publicity for figures of losses, he was unyielding; he wasn't going to tell the Germans anything. I enquired whether it could tell the Germans anything if we gave the figures for the first half of 1942, and he said yes he thought it might (he did not say what). The Germans were always exaggerating shockingly and trying to find out what happened in particular places and at particular times or with some particular tactics. They claimed to have sunk twelve million tons last year! He had had an estimate at the beginning of 1942 that they would sink seven millions and they had not done that. Besides, we really must not forget that on the last seven months or so we had a net gain of two million tons, and the shipbuilding programme of the USA was enormous, incredible.

I said that the thought had always worried me that the Admiralty was not, in fact, sufficiently air-minded—did not appreciate either the danger of attack by plane or its power in defence against the U-boat. He said that this was not true. The Admiralty was intensely anxious to get hold of anything and everything in the aircraft way that would help. He could tell me that if he didn't check them they would nowadays seize all the aeroplanes they could get their hands on and starve the bombing offensive. He had to decide, he had to strike the balance and we must have planes to bomb Germany. (He made a comic gesture of despair.) 'Apart from Tunisia, bombing is the only offensive thing we can at the moment do to beat Germany. We *must* keep on at them—we can't let *all* the planes go elsewhere. And we were hitting Germany hard! The Essen attack was the greatest of the war. These great bombs—and they are enormous—tearing and rending'—he made a gesture with his hands as of tearing a thing violently asunder.

I suggested that the public ought to know some of the figures so that they could *feel* the seriousness of the position.

'Well', he said, 'I know and I feel them. I feel them most acutely—I feel them in my bones, and I can assure you that no one can do more than I do all the time to press on my colleagues and on the Admiralty the immense urgency of the whole question. I know the Germans will do all they can to impede us. The serious thing is that while we must keep up the minimum of food, etc. to our people the U-boats *can* slow down our operations. Of course they will do all they can to obstruct the Second Front wherever it is. Will their surface ships come out also? Maybe. They are now at Narvik. They have moved them farther north— to Narvik. 'But,' he made an eloquent gesture, 'we've got strength enough to take care of them all right. And we made our plans for all contingencies at Casablanca.'[1] Reverting to bombing the Germans, he said they would have caught it hot this last week but for the bad weather, and, as soon as the weather improved, they were going to catch it hot again.

Regarding the Second Front, he spoke of the immense supplies that were needed. He wished the Americans would send their troops over quicker. 'They send such enormous quantities of supplies with them—much more even than our own men want—all sorts of things!' (He gave the impression that this was holding things up a bit.) This was why we must finish in Tunis quickly. We must get the extra shipping. I asked whether we would have

1. Roosevelt and Churchill met at Casablanca, 14–24 January 1943.

to get Sardinia and Sicily as well as the African coast before we could 'Go through the Mediterranean.' He said 'Oh no, not at all.' Once we had the Africa coast we should send merchantmen— 'not perhaps, big troop transports'—along the coast under continuous air cover and the gain in shipping would be 'enormous.' We ought to be all right in Tunisia. He still hoped we should clear everything up by the end of April.[1] We had immense superiority in numbers and material. If the Axis had a quarter of a million men we had'—he threw his head up and meditated—'well, half a million, and a good many more.' And our supremacy in material was overwhelming.

He referred to the idea that the Axis might achieve a 'Dunkirk' from Tunis. He said that we got away from Dunkirk because we had air superiority but at the Tunisian ports the Axis would not have air superiority—we were taking steps to make very sure of that.

If the Second Front were to be in France, our task was terrible. To land in Europe without a single port! Every expedition had always had at least one port of disembarkation. We had to capture ours before we had anything at all, a terrible task!

He went back to his aims in his speech. 'You know, I put something good in about the League. These people—they tell me that the League was no good, that the League failed. Well, it never need have failed if they had done the right thing. It never need have failed as late as 1937 when it was clear that Russia wanted to cooperate and make a strong thing of it. It wasn't the League that failed. Yes, and I said a good thing about Free Trade, didn't I?' He was pleased with this. 'Why, if the Protectionists had had their way and we'd had a Corn Law in England we should have gone under long ago.'

As I got up to go he said 'Well, I like the MG. I always read it. I've been reading it today'. He pointed to the paper lying spread out on the table. 'The Yorkshire Post has a good line too—a good paper. But most of the papers infuriate me. They exasperate me.' He marched up and down a few feet of carpet, with his hands in his pockets, glaring savagely—very comic. I said, to draw him, 'The News Chronicle?'

He said 'Oh, the News Chronicle! All over the place! Geese! Geese!' Then he said 'But the paper that I can't stand, the worst of all, is—the Daily Mirror.'

I said with some astonishment 'The Mirror?'

---

1. Axis resistance in North Africa ceased on 12 May.

He said 'Yes, the Daily Mirror.' Then with enormous energy 'It makes me spit.'

When I mentioned the question of Hitler's air force and what he could or could not do with it, he said 'I think he's in a tight place now.'

Of China he said, with a sort of rueful laugh, 'I can't bring myself to speak of China as on the same level in this war as the three really powerful countries—America, Britain and Russia.' I said 'She will have a bigger part to play someday?' and he replied 'Oh yes, certainly, when we have to go there to get at Japan.'

5.30 P.M. BRENDAN BRACKEN

He inquired first of all about Evelyn Montague[1] and said he thought that he was the best of the war correspondents. The Express had a good man also in Alan Moorehead, but, as a writer, Montague was the best of all. He mentioned that Montague had that day started on his flight back to Africa, and that Barrington Ward of the Times had pressed for early facilities to be granted to him.

.   .   .   .   .

Things would go all right in Tunisia, though he did not himself expect the end of the campaign there before the end of May. The Americans had not been doing too well in the Centre. The trouble was that at the beginning they will not be taught. ('We cannot teach the Americans anything.') It was much the same when they had to face the U-boat war. We had been running convoys successfully ever since the beginning of the war. They would not adopt convoys; they had very heavy losses off their coasts; and then they did at last adopt them, and very successfully too. One reason why he was very confident about Tunisia was that we had a definite superiority in all arms (3–1 in aeroplanes and guns, 4–1 in tanks); the trouble was that we were unable as yet to deploy our great superiority in tanks. Once we got them over the famous Wadi we should be able to operate them freely and get the benefit of our superior strength. Before the beginning of the battle a letter had come from North Africa (from Montgomery to Churchill) telling us that the Tunisian contest was bound to take a certain amount of time, but there was no ground for discouragement as

---

1. MG correspondent in North Africa.

we should certainly put the business through successfully in the end.

Cardinal Spellman,[1] who was now in London, had given an account of his visit to Italy. (He had dined with him the day before.) Spellman said there was complete and general depression there. The people wanted quite simply to get out of the war. The Pope had said that Germany was 'as bad as Russia', and of course the Pope could not say anything more damning than that. He had also said that the only thing which could save the situation was the complete and early victory of the United Nations. While the Cardinal was in Italy two interesting things happened. The Italian General Staff had sent him an invitation to go where he liked and to see what he liked. More remarkable still, the Crown Prince had sent him a letter asking him to go and have a talk. Spellman had declined, saying that he was in Italy solely on ecclesiastical business. The Crown Prince had then written again, sending a longer letter, and urging, still more strongly, that they should have a talk. The inference was clear that he wanted to sound Spellman about the prospects of peace.

He then had something to say about second fronts. With regard to an invasion of Italy the question was whether the Germans would come down in great force into Italy. If not, we should only be killing Italians and not Germans, and it was at any rate quite certain that the Russians attached little importance to the killing of anything except Germans. It was inadvisable to disperse your strength between two fronts, and the Italian front was open to the objection he had named. The inference, therefore, was that there should only be one front and that in a different part of Europe. Also it should only be opened when Tunisia was completely in our hands, the Mediterranean had been opened, and a large quantity of shipping had been released.

He did not think that an invasion of France was as terrible an enterprise as some people did. There were twenty-four divisions of Germans in France, of whom perhaps 100,000 were really good men. Germany's 'total mobilisation' measures might produce forty-five new divisions, or 700,000 men in all. He thought the total force available from these sources was not very discouraging to us. There was, of course, the question of the transfer of German troops from the East, and he admitted that he himself thought that the Germans might fall back on the defensive and find a considerable force for the West.

---

1. Leading American cardinal.

On the U-boat war he thought that the Germans were probably building more than one new boat a day. It was not so much, however, the total number of U-boats that was formidable, it was the number of 'aces' that they possessed at any given time. Submarine 'aces' in any navy were the men who possessed a sort of special gift or genius for this job, and it might easily be found that nine or ten 'aces' were responsible for almost the whole of the destruction done by a big submarine fleet.

Our resources in the air against the U-boat were soon going to be increased and the Allies were building a large number of auxiliary carriers.

He criticised the foreign policy of the Times, said that they were 'all over the place', and described their principal writer (E H Carr)[1] as 'loopy'.

27 March 1943

11.15 A.M. COUNT RACZYNSKI

.   .   .   .   .

He had received from the Polish Ambassador to Russia, Romer, an account of the interviews which he had had three times with Molotov and once with Stalin. The way in which they had treated Romer was extraordinary, quite incredible, just as bad as Hitler.

I said, 'You mean bullying and hectoring?'

He said, 'No, not at all. I meant this. When Romer remonstrated about Russian policy, Molotov replied "The decision has been taken and Russian policy on this point is immutable."

' "Well, but", says Romer, "I want to suggest that your policy is inconsistent with such and such treaties, and so on, and I beg you to consider this."

' "Russian policy", replies Molotov, "has been finally settled on this point. It cannot be changed and nothing can be done about it."

' "Well", says Romer, "but look at the way in which it is being carried out. I have evidence which I want to show you and I only ask you to consider it and, if you find that I am right, give instructions to your officials."

' "Russian policy", replies Molotov, "has been communicated

---

1. E H Carr, historical and political writer. At this time very pro-Soviet.

to the appropriate officials in precise terms, and they are carrying out their instructions faithfully." '

And this, he said, was the method on every occasion. They were up against a blank wall. They could get no hearing, no redress, no change. 'The Russians have introduced into the world a new diplomacy which consists in saying continually they have settled something for good and all and nothing whatever can be done about it.'

What Russian policy amounted to was this. They meant to annex the Polish Ukraine and Eastern Poland and to get it recognised that this was an accomplished fact, over and done with and not open to discussion. Apart from these annexations, they wanted the rest of Poland to be under a Soviet form of government. Sikorski had done his very best to secure friendly relations. He had been to Moscow, he had taken great risks with his fellow Poles in pursuing a policy friendly to Russia, and now Russia treated him as though he were a sort of Quisling—not indeed a Quisling for Germany but a Quisling for Britain, and they put him on the same sort of level as Darlan.

He did not think that the way in which British policy was treating Russia was altogether wise. For two years now Britain had been appeasing Russia in every possible way, taking the view that she could not oppose Russia in anything and must not put pressure on her to do anything that she herself did not want to do. In his opinion this was a great mistake. Britain and the USA ought to use their influence with Russia now. It was no use saying, as some did, that when we took a more active part in the war, opened a second front, and so on, we should have more influence with Russia when we tried to get her to do what we thought ought to be done. That view assumed that Russia would be grateful for the increased aid that we were going to give her, but Russia had no gratitude for anything. She was much more likely to listen to us when she was hoping and expecting that we would do something for her than when we had actually done it, and it was therefore now, not later, that we ought to try and persuade her to behave differently about the questions that we had been discussing.

He added that he did not like the way in which people in this country were talking as though everything was going to be settled in the future by four great Powers—Britain, USA, Russia, China—and the smaller Powers would all have to sit round and do as they are told. He expressed great resentment against the Times leader of March 10, which said that Russia was entitled to have friendly Governments in all the countries on her frontiers. He

knew that the leader was by Professor E H Carr, and he knew
what Carr's idea of Eastern Europe was, but it was not the idea
of the Poles, and they knew very well what Russia would mean by
friendly Governments.

.   .   .   .   .

27 May 1943

3 P.M. ANTHONY EDEN

I asked him how things were going at Washington.[1] 'Pretty well,
I think,' he said, 'pretty satisfactory. But there have been difficulties, you know. It hasn't been at all easy going all the time.'

WPC The 'Pacific First' people, I suppose you mean?

E   Yes, not the President, he's quite sound on the point; it's
     the Service people that are the trouble, and especially
     the US Navy—they've very strong about it.

WPC I suppose they think that the Pacific is their ocean, so to
     speak, after the war, rather than the Atlantic?

E   Yes, though they don't in the least deny our right to be
     interested in the Pacific, mind you. None of them do.

WPC They think about the future of Japan and the necessity
     of keeping her harmless as we do of Germany?

E   Yes, but it's only partly Japan. They think an immense
     lot about China too. No one who has not been in the US
     can imagine how much they think about China, and its
     position. It's always been so, of course, even before the
     war, but it's much more so now. That explains, of
     course, why they're so enormously interested in Madame
     Chiang Kai-Shek—a remarkable woman.

WPC Not too pro-British, it is said?

E   No, and that's why I wanted to get her to come to
     England. I hoped it would do good.

WPC She's not coming?

E   No, her health's bad—she might have a complete
     breakdown. But T V Soong is coming in June—and
     he's the ablest of the lot, I think. There was a frightful
     fuss, by the way, when Churchill in his last broadcast
     here forgot to mention China. In the USA they thought
     it was a terrible omission. I was there at the time.

---

1. Churchill was in conference at Washington with Roosevelt.

WPC I saw him just afterwards and he referred to his omission. He seemed to be rather rueful. I wonder if you sent him a message?

E   I did indeed. I sent him a strong message. Well, he will have been able to put all that right now. Madame Chiang is a bit difficult, though. She was in New York and the President invited her to come to the White House while C was there. She thought, however, that as she is the wife of the head of a State anyone else ought to go to New York to see her. That's rummy, for after all R is the head of a State and has the right if he chooses, hasn't he, to invite another head of State to visit him? I've a good story about Mme Chiang, by the way. Someone asked her what she thought about Roosevelt. She thought a few seconds and said 'Sophisticated!' And what, she was asked, about Wendell Willkie? She thought again and said 'Adolescent!' C, by the way, (went on E) doesn't like Willkie.

WPC No? Too young and boisterous?

E   Well, that sort of politician who really knows nothing and is just picking up what he can as he goes, doesn't appeal to C, with his great experience, his tremendous sense of history and all that.

He went on to speak of the Republican candidacy in 1944 and said he doubted himself whether Willkie would get the nomination (in spite of his book). He was slightly apprehensive about what might be coming at the election.

RUSSIA He was on the whole satisfied with the prospect and with Stalin's doings. The Russo-Polish business was very difficult but even that was slightly improving and he was not unhopeful. Of course the crux of the whole business was simply that Russia wanted all Poland roughly east of the Curzon line.

WPC And Moscow wants to present the Allies and the Peace Conference with a fait accompli about that?

E   Yes, that is it exactly. All else flows from that. However difficult they are in many ways I have a good deal of sympathy with the Poles over the way in which they have been treated in this matter. I'm hopeful, though, that something can be done. If, for instance, the Russians can be got to let out of Russia the wives and families of the Polish soldiers now with the Allies, that would produce a better feeling and something might be built on it. That's what we're now trying to do. Sikorski is good and is genuinely anxious to work with Russia, as he has been all the time.

WPC   How would you solve the territorial puzzle?

E   Russia wants something like the Curzon Line and that is, roughly, just. I think that the Poles will have to have East Prussia. Danzig and the Corridor—I don't think that sort of thing is any good. The Germans in East Prussia will be given a free choice to go to Germany or to become Polish citizens. I certainly don't want any more of minorities and minority treaties. I don't want provision for minorities in the peace treaties. Such provisions never have succeeded and never will. They are a constant and immediate source of grievances and friction and they will always be used by some other Power to ferment trouble. That's what happened after 1919 and it would happen again. Therefore transference —voluntary transference—is the remedy. Those who don't want to go can remain and become citizens of Poland.

WPC   And the Sudeten Germans?

E   Most of the Sudetenland should go back to Czechoslovakia—not necessarily the whole of it, and the German population in the part that reverts to Czechoslovakia should be given the option of going elsewhere or of becoming Czechs for the future. That is the solution. But no minorities under treaties which they, and their 'protecting' Power, will always deny are being carried out!

The TURKS Again, general relations quite good. 'They are now very friendly indeed to us. I have been a bit surprised that things have gone so well. I was, I may tell you, rather against C's going to Turkey from Africa. I was afraid it wouldn't come off, but it did—it was a great success.'

WPC   In view of C's visit, and those of the Air and Army Chiefs, since then, the Germans must suspect that Turkey is turning against them?

E   Yes, no doubt they do, but so long as Turkey does nothing, concedes nothing to the Allies, they need not worry much. And she has conceded nothing so far.

WPC   She is receiving munitions from Germany and from us?

E   Oh yes, rather. She takes munitions from both of us in order to protect herself against Russia.

WPC She fears Russia as much as ever?

E   She always fears Russia. Our Tunisian campaign succeeded too soon for her liking. She would have preferred that Germany had launched a new offensive against Russia before we struck in Tunisia so that Russia would have been fully involved.

WPC I can't see why Turkey should do anything particularly for us. What would she get out of it?

E   A good seat at the Peace Conference.

WPC She has no territorial claims?

E   Very little in that line. Some slight adjustments of the Bulgarian frontier, some similar points in Syria—no great difficulty about those but nothing much in them anyway. It would be more awkward if the Turks wanted the Dodecanese!

I then asked some questions about the ways in which Turkey could help us if she chose. He said the Turk Ambassador was in Turkey. He had talked frankly to him before he left.

ITALY There was no reason at all to suppose that the Italians would not fight against an invasion. They would not yield, he thought, until we had scored more definite military victories. He was not yet sure that the Germans were going to come down in great force to defend Italy and the Balkans.

.   .   .   .   .

28 May 1943

11.30 A.M. BJÖRN PRYTZ

.   .   .   .   .

He was keenly interested in Churchill's speech to Congress.[1] 'I'd like to know what you think about one point. Some of my friends (he meant himself) were puzzled by the little that he had to say about the imminence of a Second Front. They wonder whether his silence really indicated some sort of postponement of it—for the time at any rate. I hope it didn't.' I told him that I thought the comparative lack of emphasis was caused by (a) Churchill's usual great caution about anything imminent and (b) the 'Pacific First'

---

1. 19 May 1943. Onwards to Victory, 91–102.

atmosphere in USA; if he was emphasising our own very definite intentions about the Far East it was almost inevitable that he should go a bit easy about Western fronts. P's anxiety that there should be a Second Front or Fronts as soon as possible was significant. He said 'I'm very glad you don't think it means postponement.'

Thence to Russia. He said that the belief of himself and his friends was that neither Germany nor Russia would make a big offensive this summer.[1] Germany would not because she could not afford to tie up large resources in the east when we and USA might be going to set about her, and Russia, he implied, was now likely to wait for us to start the long demanded offensive. This led him to mention the Turks and I asked what Turkey had to gain by coming into the war on our side. 'A seat at the Peace Conference', he said very seriously in a way that made it clear that politically this was of considerable importance. He added that he wished Russia would do more to remove the anxieties of the Turks, e.g., give their solemn guarantees about the Dardanelles and the security of their frontiers on the Persian side.

Then to the Comintern, where Stalin's latest move seemed to give him great enjoyment.[2] He thought it was a logical development of Stalin's policy. He was obviously looking forward to the Labour Party conferences with much interest as a student of British politics. He told me a story of how he had entertained to lunch the members of the British Council and had asked them how they managed to adapt their work in various countries to the widely differing political systems. After they had told him a great deal about them he had said to them: 'All this is most interesting; it seems to me you conduct your organisation rather as the Comintern does its work in various countries.' They were astonished and indignant! 'I shan't be able to say that now,' he said.

.   .   .   .   .

3.30 P.M. HERBERT MORRISON

I said 'And how is the architect of the new Centre Party?'

M   Ah, they've not got it quite right there. I'll tell you presently. But this Communist Party business is inter-

---

1. The Germans began an offensive on 5 July. The Russians answered with a counter-offensive on 12 July.
2. Stalin had just abolished the Comintern.

esting. We've been at it today and we've issued a statement for tomorrow's papers. You've had some good leaders in the MG—articles that no other paper except the MG could have had. I suppose Wadsworth wrote them? (I told him, Oh yes.) Well, we've confirmed our decision today about the CP—we were almost unanimous.

WPC You told me last time that you were always put up to do the nasty jobs. Are you going to take it on this time—are you going to wind up?

M Yes, that's the idea. Ridley is going to open and I'm going to come in at the end. I did think at one time it might be better for me to open but no, on the whole I think it's best that I should wind up. I'll tell you the line I'm going to take—I told them today. I'm going to say that this isn't a small matter for petty disputation or wrangling—such as we've so often had. Let's try and raise the issue to a higher level—to the level of a matter of great national moment. Here's Stalin has made this great move[1]—well, I don't like him for many things in his history, there's this and that against him and there's a good deal of blood about his hands—but here he is now making a remarkable gesture, striking this blow against discord between the Allied nations and opening the prospect of a co-operation that should be immensely fruitful. I shall appeal to the Communists to act in the same sort of spirit and looking to working class unity, to dissolve the Communist Party.

WPC How do you think things will go at the Conference on this issue?

M I think we shall win all right, but of course you can't be quite sure.

WPC Is any other subject likely to be lively—will the question of the continuance of the Coalition and the post-war election come up?

M Not directly, but it may arise out of discussion of the electoral truce.

I asked him his views about Coalition, election, etc., and he said: 'I hope there won't be an election immediately at the end of the war. I don't want an election until twelve months at least after the end of the war—then we shall see how things are shaping and

1. Abolition of the Comintern, 22 May 1943.

may be we shall have had time to get the war ended with Japan also. As for the election itself, I don't like the idea of *Coupons* at all, and it wouldn't do for us. It's bad enough as it is for our young and enterprising candidates not to be able to attack Tory seats and that is what would happen, of course, in a Coupon election.'

WPC If the Coalition Government goes to the country it will be led by Churchill with a more or less Tory progressive programme and the three leaders will sign the manifesto?

M There needn't necessarily be such a manifesto, I think.

WPC But there would be a Coalition platform which everyone would be expected to accept?

M Churchill's programme in his four-year plan broadcast was a 'social welfare' programme, wasn't it, and that was all? I have the idea—it is tentative only and I know that there are difficulties but I have the idea that candidates in the constituencies might be allowed, while giving a general support to the coalition, to present the case from their own political angle, on their own political basis—Tory or Labour as it might be. I think that *might* be possible, but you know, with the war as it still is, we really haven't got anywhere near considering details of that kind. But—he was very cheerful here—if the war suddenly collapsed we should be considering it very quickly!

WPC But isn't the point, or a very material point, that, if there were this free-for-all, the Tories would think that their representatives were being attacked whereas they want to keep that representation undiminished.

M (seriously) Yes that is the trouble—that is what Kingsley Wood would say.

WPC Isn't it true, then, that the election must take one of three forms—it will look towards either a Coalition, or a purely Tory Government, or a 'Government of the best men', in each case under Churchill?

M I think nothing of the last idea. So far as I am concerned I have no use for membership of any Government if I am disjoined from a party behind me, cut off from popular support. That is impossible. It's possible only to non-party men like Woolton or Duncan.[1]

WPC But the point is that in any of the three cases supposed it is Churchill, the man who has 'won the war' and will

---

1. Sir Andrew Duncan, minister of supply.

'win the peace' who is going to the country and that the Tory party will try to capitalise that so as to keep its enormous majority and that it is difficult to see how it can fail, broadly, to succeed?

M   Undoubtedly that is what Kingsley Wood and his people will aim at and expect.

He then spoke of the character of the Labour Party and the 'revolts' in Parliament, especially the recent split over pensions, which he said was stupid and annoyed him. He said that the party needed to be 'educated for governing'. It was much better in opposition than as a governing party. To some extent it was a question of leadership. There was now, as there had been before, a 'crisis of leadership'. There was one under Ramsay Mac, who had no idea of handling, and educating, the party. When he wanted to do something, and meant to do it, which would certainly arouse opposition in the party, he ought to have met them frankly and said: 'Now, my lads, this is what I propose to do and I'll tell you why, and you can tell me why you disapprove and we'll have it out here, and then, unless you've given me sufficient cause, I'm going to do it.' And there would have been a lot of trouble three, four or five times or more but they would have learned in time, and some such process had to be gone through. There was a lack of leadership now also and the position was very serious.

Then he mentioned his personal position. He was standing for the Treasurership with Arthur Greenwood opposed to him and therefore he was going off the Executive. He *thought* that he would come through all right, but if he didn't, then it would be bad for him and he thought it would be bad for the party also. Then he said: 'I don't know whether you would think it right to help in such a matter—it's of course for you to say—but I think it would help if you thought fit to argue about this question of the election to the Treasurership—in view of my disappearance from the Executive—and the effects which the choice may have on the fortunes of the party.'

WPC   You don't think that it might prejudice you?

M   No, not if it's the MG. Any other paper yes, but the MG is the only paper that they will all listen to because of the general respect in which it is held.

He told me that he had written most of the Introduction to the Labour Party report. It had foolishly been sent out along with the whole of the sixty-page (actually ninety-page) booklet and so had got next to no prominence. 'Those idiots at Transport House!' He said something at another time also about the necessity for reorganisation at Transport House.

1 July 1943

3 P.M. ANTHONY EDEN

I asked him how he was and he said it was an awful life that he was leading—having the two jobs, the FO and the Leadership of the House.[1] They had had trouble in the House that morning over the pensions business; he had been sent for suddenly from a Cabinet meeting; poor Womersley was in an awful fix, and he had to come and deal with a subject about which he really didn't know a great deal.

I was sympathetic and said that of course the Leader of the House had to know about everything?

Yes indeed, he said, and he had the FO as well. He would like to give up one of them and, of the two, he would prefer to stick to the FO and let the other go. He had told Smith[2] so and Smith had said 'Well, it's for you to say, but of course, if you give up the Leadership I shall have to take it on again myself.' And no one wants him to have to do that, said E.

He went on to say that the trouble was that there were so few members of the War Cabinet who were 'good Parliamentarians'. The average Minister could not become a 'good Parliamentarian' unless and until he had had a pretty long experience of the House. There was the Lord President of the Council, for instance (Anderson[3]), a very able man indeed but not at his best with the House; and there was Oliver Lyttelton,[4] too, about whom the same could be said, and in each case the trouble was the man had not been long in the House. There were only two or three who were really good at this part of the job. Bevin was good 'considering', and so was Morrison, though Morrison's tendency to be a bit dictatorial (he laughed here) came out at times.

---

1. Eden became leader of the House in November 1942 when Cripps resigned from the war cabinet and became minister of aircraft production.
2. i.e. Churchill.
3. Sir John Anderson, a former civil servant, and virtual controller of the domestic economy.
4. Minister of production, a former businessman.

Then he spoke of Algiers, USA, etc.[1] The position was certainly difficult though he was not disposed to be gloomy about it. His view was that we must press the claims and the position of the National Committee and not let it become a matter of personalities. De Gaulle was indeed difficult and also foolish. He was responsible for a large part of his own troubles. He had, for instance, said many most offensive things about the Americans and these had been reported from London to the USA.

I said, 'He's said a lot of offensive things about us too, hasn't he?'

'Oh Lord, yes, and of course he doesn't love us—and no more does Giraud either. Nor is he, de G, much of a democrat either! But the thing is that, whatever his faults and whatever the blunders, De Gaulle has come to be a symbol to France and of France. He represents the resistance movement more than any Frenchman living. I'm trying to get the Americans to see that and to recognise its importance.'

I said 'Who is it that's against De Gaulle so much in USA—some say Hull, some say "influences" in the State Department, some say Roosevelt himself—who, for instance, inspired that AP message?'

'I think it was influences in the State Department, perhaps obscure influences. But undoubtedly Hull detests De Gaulle. His dislike for him is extraordinary. It has become almost a vendetta. I found that out when I was over there, and it's grown since. You know, the Americans are *all* difficult about France. The Lafayette business! They are convinced that because of that they understand France and the French much better than we do. They really think that France is *their* problem and they alone know how to handle it. They thought that all the time they were dealing with Vichy and they think so now. What we have to do is to support the National Committee, to get power into its hands rather than those of individuals, to support the reconciling influences like Massigli and Monnet, and to try and bring the Americans along with us.'

I said—'There is a growing suspicion here, and also among the smaller peoples, that the United States is on the side of semi-

---

1. De Gaulle and General Giraud were in dispute over the control of French North Africa. On 3 June a committee of national liberation was set up with both de Gaulle and Giraud as members. The British government recognised the committee on 27 August. Giraud left the committee in November, and de Gaulle reigned supreme. Both Hull and Roosevelt were implacably against de Gaulle for different reasons. Eden was firmly for de Gaulle. Churchill oscillated between admiration for de Gaulle and violent irritation with him.

Fascist persons and Government, that this is being exemplified in its policy at Algiers, and that it is likely to follow this course in European countries when it gets there and at the peace.'

He said 'I don't believe that. At all events Hull denied to me positively when I was over there that there was, or could be, the slightest truth in such a suggestion. Hull said that nothing exasperated him so much as any suggestion that he, a Democrat all his life, would dream of lending his assistance to setting up or anywhere supporting a non-democratic regime. I think it was attacks in American papers, not British, that had angered him. It is remarkable that a man brought up like Hull in American politics should be so sensitive to criticism. But I don't myself believe that American policy will turn out to be bad in this way. France is a special case. They had to handle that problem when they took charge in Africa and they've looked at it largely from the purely military point of view *plus* their dislike of De Gaulle as an individual. I don't think we have cause to fear them elsewhere. They are not particularly interested in Spain, and, if it comes to that, we've been rather kinder to the Franco regime (though disliking it) than the Americans. Nor are they interested specially in the future of Italy and I don't think we need to be anxious about them there.

I asked about the likelihood of a semi-Fascist Government under the King, Badoglio, Grandi, etc.

He was cautious. He said we just didn't know what was going to happen there. There was undoubtedly a queer state of mind brewing and he had thought it advisable in the House yesterday to be 'pretty rough' about Italy. But what it would lead to no one could say nor with whom, if we succeeded rapidly in Italy, we could negotiate. No one knew whether there would be anyone to negotiate with at all. The prospects were cheerful. Moral in our Mediterranean forces was magnificent—he had much enjoyed his visit; he had done next to no work and had no troubles. Smith had wired 'Things may blow up—you had better come', so he had gone in case big political things came up, but they didn't. He added that something would happen soon.

He said there was not much progress towards any reconciliation between Russia and Poland. There were deep divisions. Then he spoke of the Katyn 'massacre' and gave me his impartial views about the charges against Russia. The Poles had asked and asked about those 8,000 officers and never got any explanation. Some obscure suggestion that they had disappeared to Mongolia or something of that kind. Sikorski had pressed Stalin personally on the subject and Stalin had been evasive, and it was the fact that when Sikorski left the reception room he had turned to one of his staff officers and said 'Those men are dead!'[1]

Connected with this subject was the question of the Czechs and Russia. Beneš was going to Moscow and Beneš wanted to make a treaty with Russia like our 20-year treaty. He was against this being done because he believed that in present circumstances it would make relations between Russia and the Poles even worse. To have peace in Eastern Europe there must be Russo-Polish-Czech co-operation. That was absolutely essential, but for the Czechs now to make a close treaty with Russia would widen the breach with Poland. Beneš professed to think that it would pave the way to better relations with Poland, but he was convinced that the Poles would take it very differently.

I asked about the Turks. 'They are not behaving at all well at present. Our Tunis victory came too soon for them. That was not what they wanted. They wanted to see Russia and Germany letting each other's blood. But the time is coming—it is not yet—when we shall have to have something of a showdown with them—after the next stage of the military business has been completed maybe. But it is coming. I would not like to see anyone in this country attacking them but I hope there won't be any compliments.'

I said 'They balance things more even than the Swedes. The Turks are sending a military mission to the Germans while the Swedes seem to be cutting down their concessions to the Germans. When are the Swedes going to stop those "leave-trains" by which Germans cross Sweden?'

He said, 'Well, as a matter of fact I think it likely that they will be stopping them in the near future.'

Did I know that there were 20,000 organised guerrillas in Greece, officered by British officers. In Yugoslavia we were supplying arms to both Mihailovitch and the Chetniks on the understanding that if they used them against each other we should stop the supply.[2]

---

1. On 13 April 1943 the Germans announced the discovery of the bodies of 10,000 Polish officers at Katyn. The correct number was 4,510. They had been murdered in April 1940 when the camp at Katyn was in Soviet hands. The Poles asked for an enquiry by the international Red Cross, at which the Soviet government broke off relations with them on 26 April. General Sikorski, the Polish premier, was killed in an aircraft accident on 4 July, while returning from an inspection of Polish forces in the Middle East.

2. There is a confusion here. The chetniks were led by General Mihailovic. The rival force was the partisans, led by Marshal Tito. The chetniks were not fighting the Germans, and British supplies to them ceased at the end of the year.

At this point Bracken came in and, after reproaching me for seeing the Foreign Secretary and not him, said they wanted to send a press-man to Australia (Evatt's suggestion I think) and he, Bracken, would like an MG man to go. He supposed the staff was too small?

I said it was indeed. He asked if there was anyone in Australia who could do it as an MG man.

I said there was a man there, one Cardus,[1] but I thought that he was politically impossible (being too critical of Australia).

Bracken said that Cardus might be fine. He declaimed 'Mr Neville Cardus of the Manchester Guardian' more than once and he said he liked the sound of it. I repeated that Cardus could not do the job they wanted, which was to publicise and lionise Australia. Then he said: 'Well, I wonder whether Mr John Scott would go out there? He's been Regional officer to the MOI. Would you mention it to him when you get back. Please do.'

He finally asked whether I couldn't go and have a talk, so I went at 6 p.m.

4.30 P.M. LORD VANSITTART

I asked him how he was getting on with the 're-education of England' and he said quite well, but he wished that people in denouncing 'Vansittartism' would not attribute things to him which he had never said and never could have said and which they knew quite well he had not said. He was very strong against R R Stokes, Bevan and the other pacifists and applied some very uncomplimentary epithets to them. He expressed great pleasure at the idea of coming to Manchester in September.

He began then on North Africa and expressed the greatest dissatisfaction with our policy or rather, as he said, lack of policy. It may have been all right, at the start after the landing, to admit a plea of military necessity, but that time was past and what we were doing at present was to allow the pro-Vichy, decadent French sort of people to become top-dog, with incalculable dangers for the future. What he feared was quite simply that unless there was a great 'purge' of the bad people both in the administration and in the army—and he kept on reverting to the army—the day would come when this army would land in France and impose a rotten reactionary old-France system on the

1. Neville Cardus, long-time writer on cricket and music in the MG, resident in Australia during the second world war.

French people. The major part of the army would be blacks, who had no views about politics but obeyed orders and didn't mind whom they killed or what they destroyed. That was what was coming unless we changed our methods.

I referred to the AP telegram, about which he didn't seem to know much but he said, when I reminded him of its contents, that it wasn't minor people in the State Dept, in his opinion, who inspired that but people 'much higher up' and that we ought to have put our foot down long ago and told the Americans plainly our view of policy. 'They would have to listen,' he said, 'of course one wouldn't do it crudely or offensively, but we have a right to a policy as well as they and we must press it on them. It is of extreme importance for the future. They can't pull out of the war, you know, now; they must stop in and we can't afford to let them do this sort of thing indefinitely.' I said that in some respects things had improved, had they not? Some of the villains 'purged' and so on? He said, rather grudgingly, 'yes but not enough and not quick enough.' How had it come about, he would like to know, that a man like Peyrouton had ever been accepted even or allowed to have any office at all? And there were crowds of them in the French army, which absolutely needed to be cleared up and reorganised—it was most urgent and necessary.

He had been considering whether he ought not to make a public protest or whether he could remain silent much longer. He might have to expose things in the Lords. He had already hinted at this privately and he had been not obscurely threatened with a Secret Session. 'That's no use to me. I don't want the privilege of telling a few of their Lordships secretly what I think of them and of listening, also secretly, to evasions by Lord Cranborne. What I have to say, if I say anything, will be for the people of this country and for anyone outside too. I haven't made up my mind yet, but if I decide to speak I'll let you know.'

Then Russia and Poland. There again he said that we had no policy. [So Voigt says, from which we may draw a certain inference] He criticised the action of the Russians in breaking off relations with Poland, but he referred also to the Katyn accusations in a very marked way. He did not approve of the Poles appealing to the Red Cross about a matter in territory occupied by the Germans, but one had to remember that the Poles took this business very hard and that many of the Polish officers who had disappeared had relatives and friends serving here in England. He felt very strongly that we ought to have a policy by which we would speak in a quite friendly but firm way to Russia as well as to the USA. The Russians, like the Americans, would have to listen to us, we were entitled to use our influence in trying to solve these quarrels and one side had to make concessions as well as another in an alliance of this kind.

6 P.M. BRENDAN BRACKEN

I called at MoI on my way back to the hotel and found that B, was free. He began at once about the awful War Office which having roped journalists into the army at any cost, was now declaring that it must have 'propagandists' for use as it advanced and they must be good, experienced, skilful journalists. Well, how are they to get them, how was the MoI to provide them, seeing that the War Office has scooped them into the army, had insisted on having them, so that now they were scattered all over the world? The newspapers could not supply such men; they are too hard-up themselves.

.   .   .   .   .

I said the MoI could find out from the papers what good men they had lost and (roughly) where they are, and he said yes that was what they were now trying to do and it was a great labour and should never have been necessary.

Then to the African business. He became very energetic and said it was a most grave business. 'There is a chance, you know, of our actually having a grave split with Roosevelt over this. Roosevelt [B never mentioned Hull] hates De Gaulle; he can't tolerate him or the mention of him and we shall have to be very careful how we handle this. Of course De Gaulle is horribly difficult, and I ought to know. The PM doesn't love him either. At Casablanca the PM thought that with himself and Roosevelt there it was a fine chance for conciliation, and he sent to De Gaulle an invitation to go there. For forty-eight hours De Gaulle refused to go there at all, and the PM doesn't like that sort of thing. For myself (B) I've stopped De Gaulle *twice* from broadcasting according to programme. I had to. There was to be an occasion on which he, Queen Wilhelmina and Beneš were jointly to do a broadcast to the USA. A day or two before the date it became known that De Gaulle was saying the most offensive things about the British and we were sincerely afraid that if he broadcast he would say injurious and dangerous things over the mike. So I told him, with much regret, I couldn't let him use the wireless, and I told him why. He came to see me and he was furious; threatened all sorts of terrible things. But he didn't broadcast, and two days later he wrote me a nice letter, "making it up". As to the USA, "we've got to put up with a lot. We're an old country"—he repeated this—"and they are young and we've got to be patient and try to bring them along with us—that's our job." '

2 July 1943

11.30 A.M. BJÖRN PRYTZ

Things, he said, were undoubtedly going well. But the position was this. Germany would make no offensive against the Russians. She could not. She must wait. The Russians would not attack either this summer—perhaps in the winter.[1] Should we land on the Continent anywhere *this* year? He did not think so. The islands, the fringe, yes! Commando raids on a big scale, yes! But a Continental landing anywhere, even in Italy, No![2]

I said I myself thought he was wrong, but I didn't know. The reason he asked was interesting —

I asked him whether and when the Swedes were going to stop the German leave trains. He said they would like to and they would if they could, but 'the position is precisely this. There is no fighting on the Continent of Europe. The German armies are not fighting *anywhere*—not against the Russians and not against the Western Allies. If then we did anything *abruptly* like stopping the leave trains, who knows whether the Germans might not go for us (we have no Air Force). We think Hitler is capable of it. He *might* calculate that he could bring off a big quick coup and stimulate the Germans again.'

I said, would not that be a pure gamble and would he not fail? He said he might fail, but for the Swedes the question was whether he might try the expedient. He gave the clear impression that *if* the Russians attacked the Germans and if the Allies landed in Europe then the Swedes would take action and that they were looking for the chance.

Of the Turks he said that he thought they would 'come in about five minutes from the end'—'or perhaps two minutes. They are

---

1. Quite wrong. The Germans attacked on 5 July and the Russians on 12 July.
2. Allied forces landed in Italy on 3 September 1943.

afraid of both Germany and Russia, but especially of Russia. They wanted an assurance from Stalin—maybe they were getting it. He thought that Roosevelt's letter to Stalin carried by Joseph Davies related to the question of Turkey. The Turks were in a bad position, one had to admit that—with the Russians all around them and *pushing down into Iran.* I said that I didn't think that the Russians would push into Iran again as they did after 1907.

He said that they would push *somewhere*—if not south into Iran, then north or west in Europe or eastwards, but somewhere yes!

I suggested that Russia would have to pay some attention to British (and perhaps American) influence and policy after the war if they want to work with us at all, and he said maybe, but he thought that they would be able to do pretty well what they liked with that part of the world, and he was obviously unconvinced that we or America would or could stop them. He desperately feared an aggressive-minded Russia after the war.

3 P.M. HERBERT MORRISON

He began by talking about his defeat for the Treasurership of the Labour Party Conference.[1] He said that the result had been a little of a surprise for him. He had thought on the whole he would pull through, but had been rather unlucky in respect of the three big unions which had voted against him. As for one of them it would never have gone against him had George Jagger not died. As for the second, it was Bevin's union. He had heard a report, though he didn't know whether it was true, that Bevin had said 'Well, of course, we always vote for our own members, don't we', the point being that Greenwood was a 'cardboard member' of the union. However, he was not depressed, there had been no personal feeling against him, as the reception which he got on the following day clearly showed. As to the future, he was going to make occasional policy speeches. He would not make many, but it was very advisable that the lines of a policy should be clearly laid down and no one else was doing it. He referred to the PM in this connection and said that he was not illiberal in many things. With regard to monopolies he was liberal minded. He (Morrison) had been shown the passages on this subject in the PM's broadcast about the Four-Year Plan, and what he himself had had to say in his public speeches had been seen by the PM. As a matter of fact the PM was more Liberal in these things than the Tory Party. He had by no means freed himself from the influences of his Liberal days.

---

1. Morrison was defeated by Arthur Greenwood.

He (M) was strongly of opinion that more must be done in the way of actual constructive work before the war came to an end. There was a great deal of planning and preparation going on here and there—that was quite true, but it all remained at present in the preparatory stage and more had to be done to put things into action. One great trouble was the slowing down influence of Kingsley Wood and such like people. Kingsley Wood would say about some particular subject 'Yes, this is very good, very admirable, but we must wait until we see what we ought to do about "A", and then what we ought to do about "B", and so on.' 'And, of course,' said M, 'if one big thing has to wait until half a dozen other big things are settled the result is that nothing will be done at all.'

He referred again, as he had done last time, to the prospects of a General Election at the end of the war and he said 'You know the bulk of our fellows don't in the least understand the political position. They have the idea that the country is waiting to hand them the reins of Government on a platter and that eventually they will decide to do the country the kindness of taking office. Some day they will wake up to realise that the position is quite different and that the Tories have got the whole political position nicely in their hands.' Talking of a statement which he had just made about measures for getting a reasonably adequate vote at by-elections, he said that the machinery would in fact serve if needed for a General Election during the war. He devoutly hoped that such an election would not take place and he didn't think that it would, but you never could tell. There might be circumstances under which it might be necessary. I asked him if he remembered what Churchill had said in the autumn of 1916, when Bonar Law was threatening a General Election in order to get rid of the recalcitrant Tories. He said no, so I recalled the passage in Beaverbrook's Memoirs in which Churchill said that a General Election in wartime was 'the most immoral suggestion he had ever heard'. From this we went on to Churchill's position in politics and in the House, and he entirely agreed that Churchill had had a very easy journey while Prime Minister, being exposed to none of the formidable opposition that Lloyd George had had to meet after he became PM at the end of 1916.

4.45 P.M. PRESIDENT BENEŠ

I asked him how, in his opinion, things were going, and he said well; he thought that the optimism he had displayed in Manchester

—and he showed some amusement, remembering what he had said and the comments—had on the whole been justified. He thought that the bombing was having, and would have, a grave effect on the Germans; it would become worse in the autumn and early winter, and he believed that the strain of this coming winter would be too great for the Germans though he would not say that there would not be a lot of resistance still left in them next year. But he believed that this winter would really be decisive. Moreover, he was of opinion that they would not now *be able* to resist either in the occupied territories or on their own frontiers as had been expected hitherto. The bombing was beyond all expectation and, wherever they stood, there would be wholesale demolition of their equipment, their defences, their troops. The demolition that was external would correspond to an internal demolition of their moral.

.   .   .   .   .

He was sure that the defeat of Italy would have a great moral effect but he did *not* agree that it could have little *military* effect on the German fortress. Far from it. By air we should get within bombing range of Vienna (and of Budapest) and of many other important places. From the neighbourhood of Venice we should both have good bombing targets and we should have a way into Austria south of the Alps between the mountains. (He is as optimistic of the *military* results of defeating Italy as Prytz is sceptical about them.)

The German Generals, he says, know perfectly well now that the war is lost. They will fight on at present in the hope that we shall grow sick of the war or that the Allies will quarrel among themselves. Certainly they will hope to get out of the war on such terms that they can prepare for another. He asserted positively that not only the Generals but the German people 'cherish great illusions'. These were that the British people would be ready at the end of this war to let them off on light terms. He said that the Germans do not believe for one moment that we mean what we say when we say that we are going to destroy the Hitlerite and military system and prevent them from making war again for a long, long time. They think it is all bluff. He insists that this is true of them in general. *He* knows, he says, that we mean business and there is, he says, the greatest shock in the world coming for the whole German people. He doubts whether they will resist up to the point of

allowing Germany to be invaded. (This is also Vansittart's fear.)
He thinks that they will surrender first, believing what they do
about the British. As for Hitler, he says that H suffered a complete
collapse after Stalingrad, that it lasted four months, that he has
recovered or is recovering, and that the General Staff has been
running things 'on its own'.[1] He does not profess to know whether
the Generals will eventually 'by-side' (put aside) Hitler, but he
expects him to be got rid of in some way when peace-offers are
made and he expects that the Nazi leaders, etc., will disappear, or
turn Communist, or discover that they always were pro-British or
something of the kind. When the war has gone further against
them he expects that the Germans will let it be known privately
that they would like peace on certain terms which, he says, will
be 'ridiculous'—evacuation of Norway, Denmark and the Western
Countries, but not so much said about the East. 'The Allies will
make short work of that,' he said. There was another sign of the
way things were going. Had I noticed the change of tone that was
taking place in the Axis press, etc. with reference to the Allies
(e.g. Press of Italy and the British and Americans)? He had had an
instance which amused him. He had just received a copy of the
Kölnische Zeitung which devoted a long leading article to him,
Beneš, and the attitude was greatly changed.

I said—'They're not paying you compliments?'

That amused him again and he said 'Well, not exactly that. But
whereas until now they had treated me as completely negligible,
played out, done for, in this article they attack most violently this
terrible man Beneš, who has always done them damage and been a
most formidable enemy and is now working and scheming against
them all the time, so that they must watch him and his machina-
tions and work against all that he is doing'. 'They wouldn't have
said that about me twelve months ago', he said.

I said that the Russo-Polish breach must be a sad matter for
him. He said, yes, because peace in the East of Europe *must* be
built on Russo-Polish-Czech collaboration, and there was no sign
of it now—no sign of Russians and Poles coming together. He was
going to Moscow [tomorrow] to see Stalin and to try and settle all
Russo-Czech questions. He had been in communication with
Stalin and Stalin had sent word to him 'Come to Moscow and we
will settle everything'. And he could settle everything, but of
course he knew quite well that if he did the Poles would attack

---

1. Not true.

him and declare that he was siding against them with the Russians in the time of their distress. He was not, but he profoundly believed that questions must be settled with Russia *now* before the end of the war, because it would be most dangerous and indeed fatal to leave them unsettled. If the war came to an end with the present dispute between Russia and Poland unsettled then there would be another war—between those two countries. The trouble all arose from the question of territory in Eastern Poland and that *must* be settled before any good could be done. He had gone recently to USA to try to get help in this matter and there they had told him that they were in favour of the Curzon Line in 1918–19, and so was Britain. They were still in favour of it and therefore he should see Mr Eden about it. He had seen Mr Eden and spoken frankly to him, and it seemed to him that now the great Powers Britain and USA should act in order to get Russia and Poland (and anyone else who could help) to settle this question before it became dangerously explosive as it would certainly be.

I asked about Teschen,[1] and he said that the Poles showed no signs of yielding there either. He had laid suggestions before them long ago and he had got, and still got, no answer. He criticised Polish tactics severely. There was the Katyn 'massacre' affair. Well, even if it *were* true that the Russians had done this, small nations had to be *prudent* in the face of the great ones. It was *not* prudent for the Poles to invite the Red Cross to investigate this thing on soil in German occupation. The Russians were bound to resent it and therefore it should not have been done—it was not *prudent*. An analogy—in 1938 the Poles had seized Teschen, which was a horrible stab in the back for Czechoslovakia, but he, the President, had not reproached them with it or accused them or said a single word publicly against them. They had acted very differently regarding Russia. So too in the case of the two Polish Bund leaders who had been executed by the Russians. Even if it were true that they were innocent, well life was cheap in Russia, hundreds were executed every day, and the Poles ought not to have made this the subject of inflamed propaganda campaign. There must be prudence in diplomacy between States.

He was noticeably more 'drastic' about the Germans than he was last time I saw him. Even then he said that the Allies 'must have the courage' to do things at the peace which might seem from one point of view to be 'unjust'. (He meant incorporating the Sudetenland again in the new Czechoslovakia.) 'Now,' he said,

---

1. Seized by Poland in September 1938.

'I hope we have heard the last now about a *just* peace. That's what I told the people I met in the USA—no more talk of a *just* peace; what we have to say now is that we shall make a *justified* peace, which is a different matter.' I thought about the claims of the Poles in the North and said 'What about Danzig and the Corridor —I suppose the Corridor will "go", won't it?'

He said, 'Oh yes, there's no doubt the Poles will have to have satisfaction in the north—they will have to have East Prussia and that should satisfy their aspirations, make them safer in the north and give them proper access to the Baltic'. [It seems to me clear that this was regarded by him as compensation for the Poles losing Eastern Poland and Ukraine, but the Poles, of course, say that they must have East Prussia anyhow.] The Germans would have to be transferred from East Prussia into other parts of Germany.

.   .   .   .   .

21 October 1943

4.45 P.M. SIR ARCHIBALD SINCLAIR

Vainglorious talk about the alleged success of the strategic bomber offensive.

22 October 1943

9 A.M. LESLIE HORE-BELISHA

At the beginning we chatted for some time about the life of the practical politician and especially the question how far the politician should divide his leisure time between reading and thinking on the one hand and social engagements on the other. The issue was, which method would assist the politician most to perform his function in political life. He said that some men seem to devote a large part of their leisure time to lunching and dining and going to parties, and they seemed, in a worldly sense, to get on pretty well with that alone. He disapproved and disliked that method but he thought it was difficult for politicians to get along without devoting a certain amount of time to social intercourse. It was desirable, and even necessary, to get to know a good many people and to know them well. Of course, in time of war things were abnormal, and a War Minister, for instance, could not do much at all in the way of social life. I reminded him of the passage in L G's war book in which L G said that while he was PM he refused all social engagements, whereas Asquith went out constantly to things like fashionable weddings, etc. On this he commented that, after all, these things 'related to Asquith in decay' and were partly due to Mrs A's influence. Talking of her, he went on to say that the political hostesses in London were now again active and probably exerted a good deal of influence. They had largely given up their activity while the country was in great danger, but now that the situation was better and we were beginning to look forward to post-war politics they were busy again, and although they did not make or unmake appointments they were by no means unimportant. Here again was a question for the politician—whether he should ignore them or not. One point was that the members of our genuine aristocracy were in a much easier position in this matter than the man who, so to speak, was 'dragged up from the depths'. The genuine aristocrats could do as they liked, they could accept or reject invitations, cry off, be rude, give offence, but they could not be dropped. They were always 'members of the Club', and could take up, pursue or reject social relationships as they liked. The bourgeois could not. He must either persevere with these relationships all the time or abandon them altogether; if he tried to drop them temporarily he lost them.

He spoke of the 'governing classes' and of the tenacity with which they held their position. As against the suggestions sometimes made that their power was waning, he thought that they were extraordinarily skilful in the taking into themselves and absorbing promising people from the 'non-governing' classes—the middle class and the working class. The more their position was threatened the more persistent and adroit they would be at persuading the new holders of political power to join their ranks.

Speaking of the Government he said that they were tired and jaded men. It was visible even in their faces, e.g., Sinclair, who now lived completely at his office, was burnt out and had 'a face like parchment'. Most of these people had been in office for four years or more and the strain on them was tremendous. It had killed Dudley Pound[1] and Kingsley Wood.[2] Churchill was an exception, but he ordered his day in a way which was extremely trying to his colleagues. He went to bed in the afternoon, got up about six or half-past, and was as fresh as a daisy for a long night's

---

1. Sir Dudley Pound, first sea lord, 1939–43; died 21 October 1943.
2. Sir Kingsley Wood, chancellor of the exchequer, 1940–43; died 21 September 1943.

work. But other wretched people had to stop up with him after they had been working at their desks all day without any rest in the afternoon, and it was very trying for them. He also said that the PM, owing to his long rest in the afternoon, was able to begin work again quite early in the morning.

Talking about the Moscow Conference, he took a rather stiff view about the Russians.[1] He felt extremely sorry for the Poles. He understood we had gone into the war on behalf of the sanctity of international undertakings and he would consider it a grave repudiation if we simply accepted what the Russians had done in Poland when they grabbed the eastern half in 1939. Whatever the rights or wrongs of the Polish Frontier, that was a question which ought to be discussed on its merits at the end of the war, and it should not be decided under the shadow of Russian military occupation or Russian military force. He was convinced that on points of principle of that magnitude, we could not, and ought not, to give way, although we could, of course, support and assist any private discussions between the principal parties at any time. As for Czechoslovakia, he had been told on the best authority that the Czechs had made up their minds that they must live in cordial co-operation with Russia, they must lean on someone, and they were going to lean on Russia and hoped to be able to do it without any loss of independence.

He referred to Russia's joining the Mediterranean Commission.[2] He said that it was a tremendous thing that she should have come into the Mediterranean in this way and that we should have admitted her without any hesitation or questioning. He took the view that when Russia made this proposal and we decided to accept it, we ought then and there to have explained to Russia that as she was bringing her influence into the West with our approval, we assumed that she would accept our presence and influence in the settlement of Eastern European questions. He said that had we made this proposal at that time, he did not see how Russia could have refused it, and we should have made an immense gain.

·   ·   ·   ·   ·

1. The foreign ministers of the three great Allies met in Moscow 19–30 October 1943.
2. This was not much of a concession. Executive authority in Italy was in the hands of the Allied control commission, which was solely Anglo-American. The Allied advisory commission, which was now created in order to please the Russians and on which they were represented, met in Algiers and had no serious role. The Russians followed this model in eastern Europe later, to the accompaniment of much British and American complaining.

12 NOON. BJÖRN PRYTZ

We began by talking of the steps which Sweden had recently taken to demonstrate her neutrality and to show sympathy for the Jews in Denmark. He expressed great satisfaction on the latter point and said: 'We have got almost all of them out'. Apparently there were between 5,000 and 6,000 Jews in Denmark, and 4,500 or more had got safely into Sweden.[1]

He said that the Swedes were still developing their defences as rapidly as possible, and they were going to leave nothing to chance. I reminded him that he had told me a few months ago that Sweden feared lest Hitler in a mad-dog fit should go for Sweden, and I asked whether Sweden still felt any anxieties. He replied: 'Yes, we are not completely confident about the future. It is still possible that Hitler, in spite of the drain on Germany, might strike out at us in a last mad impulse, and, besides, we don't feel too sure about Russia or what would happen if Finland or Norway went out of the war. Suppose, for instance, that Germany wanted to withdraw all her troops from Norway and wanted to take them through Sweden, or suppose that Germany withdrew from Finland and Russia marched in. No one can tell what would happen then, and we have to be prepared.'

He talked about the 'second front' and exhibited the greatest scepticism. He said, 'My people don't believe, and I don't believe, for one minute, that the British and Americans intend to open a second front anywhere in the West until they are sure that it would be something like a walk-over. The 8th Army is the only army they have got that is properly trained, and it would be suicidal for them to attempt to conduct a campaign in Western Europe against the most veteran and experienced soldiers of the war.'

It was clear from what he said that he and his countrymen remain as suspicious about Russia as ever. He referred to the Turks and said bluntly that what they fear is that Russia will seize Constantinople and the Dardanelles. I suggested that this was to credit the Russians with a great lack of wisdom because it would queer their own pitch, completely destroy belief in their good faith and make themselves appear as the new aggressive, treacherous Power. He said: 'Well, look where they are going to get; they will, of course, occupy Bessarabia; they will come right down the Black Sea Coast until they control the mouth of the

---

1. When the Germans prepared to exterminate the Danish Jews, nearly all of them escaped to Sweden. The Danes, rather than the Swedes, deserved the credit for this.

Danube, and then Constantinople and the Dardanelles will be in their power.' I said to have Constantinople in their power did not mean that they would seize it, which was quite a different matter, but he was not convinced.

He said that he was immensely impressed by the action of the Russians in joining the Mediterranean Commission and by our action in assenting to it without hesitation. He said that for many years Russia had been desiring to press forward into the Mediterranean, and British policy had most resolutely tried to keep her out. Now, in one moment, at her mere request, we had abandoned our traditional policy, admitted her to the Mediterranean, and we might see interesting results. It was in his opinion a great triumph for Russia.

.   .   .   .   .

3 P.M. WINSTON CHURCHILL

He referred to the message that he had sent to me on holiday when he was in the USA complaining that Bliven had misrepresented the reception of his broadcast. He said 'He picked the one or two unfriendly references out of a host of good ones, and it annoyed me because I thought that it was unfair, and I know'—he gave a broad grin—'how devoted the MG is to the principle of fair play.' Then he went on to say with great good humour that he neither had nor has any grievance but 'I thought I would give the MG a little dig.' Then he said 'I always read the MG though I don't always agree with it. There are about ten things I disagree about'. I invited him to specify, but he just laughed and went ahead.

Something led him to speak about his keeping fit. 'Not bad for sixty-nine!' he said, and proceeded to say that he attributed it largely to his sleeping, that is, actually going to bed—from 3.30 to 6 or 6.30. 'I wake up fresh', he said 'a new man, ready for anything. I call my sleep my "draught of life".' Then he gave another of his engaging grins, saying 'I don't know whether I'm going to get my sleep today!' it being then about 3.30, with me there and Attlee coming next.

He started first on domestic politics and the prospects. He took a different line from that which he had hitherto taken. He said that though the war might last a long time we must be prepared for something happening suddenly. 'You can't tell; something may happen one fine day to Corporal Hitler and we may be faced with

Peace. We've got to be prepared. And also the country has got to be allowed to have its say. I'm a good democrat and I think that the country must be allowed to choose its representatives for the period of transition. That's what the next stage is to be—the period of transition. Why, this Parliament will be ten years old when the war is over—that's not a Parliament to carry out the new programme! And I'm going to see, I'm going to make sure, that the people gets what it ought to have at the end of the war—and that is "work and food" for all. I regard it as a duty laid upon me.' (He repeated this as the crystallisation of a programme which he had in hand.) I said that I supposed that this would be more than a slogan—that there would be a great deal of preparation and that he could produce the evidence of the means and methods, the arrangements, by which the employment would be obtainable. He said there would indeed be preparation—there would be 'a whole book' of the proposals, showing what was proposed in relation to various industries, age-groups and all sorts of things. One point was that workers over a certain age should be retired altogether, but it would be a detailed worked-out scheme to be put in force quickly.

I asked him if Beveridge's present enquiry into unemployment and his coming report would be concerned in this scheme and he said 'Beveridge! He puts his nose into too many things!'

He referred to Moscow and said that from the first reports it appeared that the conference was going better than had been expected. He hoped very much that the conference would show Russia's desire to be co-operative. The Russians were difficult. You had to put up with a good deal of 'rudeness' from them. 'There's another people also that we have to be very patient with—and that's the Americans. But I am confident that we shall succeed in bringing them along with us and the Russians too.' I asked if the presence of Russia on the Mediterranean Commission meant that Russia would recognise our interest in the eastern problems. He said 'Note that Russia has never yet called it a "Mediterranean Commission". She calls it an Allied Commission—therefore it may have scope beyond the Mediterranean.' But he thought it promising. 'Note also that this Commission is not executive or administrative. That is very important. All rights of sovereignty are reserved to the Governments.'

He expressed himself pleased with the Italian business. 'Well, you see that what I said about the under-belly has come true! The 5th Army is getting on very well indeed. That's because we've got Naples working already—a wonderful piece of work—we're pouring in men and supplies through Naples and the Western ports. The 8th Army isn't going quite so well because of lack of port facilities and its long communications, but it's going all right.'

WPC The Germans may bring down troops on a large scale into Italy—many divisions?

PM   They may and we shall put as many troops in on our side. We're going to get great help from the 'Partisans' in the Balkans. What we can do there is to send in to them supplies, officers, etc. They'll give the Germans a lot of trouble this winter.

On the Second Front he said, referring to Smuts' speech 'Personally I wouldn't have said anything that told the Germans we weren't going to attack till next year, though the German Command must know. To land an army in the West is a most tremendous enterprise—to give it proper supplies and to *keep on* giving it the supplies. You must have reasonably reliable weather conditions. I asked did he mean wintry, frosty land conditions? he said not so much that as steady 'wind and wave' conditions, that was the position to forward the steady delivery of supplies.

Something led him to speak of the Hereford case and he expressed the strongest contempt for the newspaper and the public outcry about the way in which the case of this 'little brat' had been handled.[1] He said with immense energy 'Look at what has happened to the liberties of this country in the war. Men of position are seized and kept in prison under 18B for years without trial and no "have your carcase" rights, and the public and newspapers don't care a hang. There's Mosley,[2] for instance—I think no good of him, but he's been in prison all this time and he's likely to die in prison this winter, and he has never been accused and never tried—a frightful thing to anyone concerned about English liberties. I did it, I sanctioned it, because the country was in danger of destruction and we could run no risk, we had to do it and we were right to do it, but now the great emergency has passed and the necessity is no longer there to the same extent.

---

1. This was the case of a boy convicted before the Hereford juvenile court of stealing. Before the magistrates reached a decision, a police officer stated that the boy wanted other offences taken into consideration. A Divisional Court quashed the conviction on legal grounds. This was not much consolation to the boy who had already been birched. Rayner Goddard conducted a cover-up enquiry for the home office.

2. Sir Oswald and Lady Mosley, who had been interned under defence regulation 18B since the summer of 1940, were released in December 1943.

WPC In that case why not let some of them out? But you are
       doing, aren't you?

PM   Yes, Morrison is letting a lot of them out now, though
       not the bigger ones. And then see how the public,
       which cares nothing about all this, goes into a great
       stir about the wretched brat at Hereford who had
       actually committed all these offences.

WPC Well, Caldecote and the High Court started the uproar,
       didn't they, with their stern words?

PM   Caldecote—that old goose! And on imperfect evidence.
       I can tell you that when Morrison's enquiry has
       finished some of those who have been making all the
       hullaballoo will look pretty foolish.

I said that, brat or not, some very important principles were
involved in the case, but he swept everything aside with repeated
allusions to 18B.

Talking of the future of the Coalition he said 'Don't you be in a
hurry to pull Archie [Sinclair] out of the Cabinet—he's extremely
useful where he is and he ought to be left there.'

When I got up to go I begged him to take an interest in the
Palestine question, pointed out that the White Paper five-year
period would end in March 1944, and that it would be an outrage
if Jewish immigration were to stop then and the Jews to be made
a permanent minority in an Arab State. He said that personally
he certainly did not want that and that he had always been against
the White Paper. Also, that I could take it that the unexpended
quota of immigrants would be made up anyhow.

I replied that this was only a matter of 30,000 and that the
vital thing was the stoppage of immigration altogether—the
fixing of the Jews as a minority. I asked whether it was not possible
at the end of a victorious war to do big things, and enforce big
decisions, which were almost impossible in peace time—that is, to
tell the Arabs that they had got so much that they *must* now accept
a Jewish Commonwealth.

He said it certainly might be easier and that the Arabs had done
little indeed for us in the war.

I interjected 'What except revolt against us in Iraq (Rashid Ali)
and give us trouble elsewhere? and was not the Jewish achievement in Palestine one of the few great successes following the last
war?'

He replied that it was and now, as then, he wanted to see a
great Jewish National Home in Palestine, and that he was glad

to say he had T E Lawrence's personal assurance that he approved of what we had done in Palestine. I said again as I was going that to put the White Paper in force next year and 'fix' the Jewish minority permanently would be a tragedy and a catastrophe.

.   .   .   .   .

Speaking of Italy he said 'Don't worry too much about the King and Badoglio'—pronouncing it 'dog'—'I think it will be all right. They'll get a broader Government presently, probably after we get Rome.' He thought very little of Sforza.

5 P.M. HERBERT MORRISON

He was looking really tired and when I asked him how he felt, he said 'Fridayish' and he would be very glad to get a little rest at the week-end. I asked him whether he really got much respite at the week-ends unless he was away in the country speaking, and he said that, of course, he never had a complete rest but that they sometimes left him a little bit of leisure. He then said that he was coming to the Manchester region in the middle of November (Sunday, 14 November). He was going to confer with the Labour people in Manchester and make one or two speeches in towns round about. I asked him what the subjects were going to be and he said probably in the main domestic and they would include controls. He thought it very necessary to work at that subject precisely and to explain what sort of controls would have to be kept on, and why.

He then referred to his recent Dundee speech. He said he had intended by that to stir things up a bit, and he had indeed succeeded rather more than he had intended. The newspapers had reacted strongly and he mentioned in particular the Telegraph and also the speech in which Capt. Balfour had specifically referred to Ministers. He said he did not himself mind Conservative Ministers expressing themselves strongly. He thought that he himself was entitled to express himself on these things strongly and he saw no reason why they should not do the same. He did, however, think that it was going a bit too far when a junior member of the Ministry directly attacked Ministers for what they had been saying. However, he had not protested and he did not intend to do anything about it.

His Dundee speech, however, had produced some difficulties with the PM, and he told me the story with considerable amusement. A question to the PM on the subject of his speech was put down on the paper and he with his advisers had drafted an answer for the PM to make. He thought it was a pretty harmless answer and that it would have filled the bill. On the morning of the day when the answer was going to be made and only about an hour and a half before it was due, he was at a Labour Party meeting and a letter was brought to him from the PM. This contained a copy of the answer which the PM proposed to make and it was in no way the answer which he had provided for the PM. It was the PM's own and very different. He sent a reply back immediately taking exception to one sentence in particular and asking that it should not be used. Then he returned to his office and presently the PM came on the 'phone to discuss the matter. 'We had a hell of an up-and-down about it. He said "Why are you so provocative", and "Why do you put me in a jam like this?" But it was all in quite good humour. I told him that I must object to the last sentence which he had written, as it amounted to a rebuke of me, and eventually when the answer was given that sentence was taken out in favour of another which was in no way objectionable from my point of view.' He said that the PM was very human and very likable in matters of this kind. When a day or two later a question of some difficult trade or group of people came up, he himself had said 'I think we ought to control them' and the PM had given a violent 'g'r'r'r' like an angry dog. He himself foresaw that there was going to be a very difficult struggle over the maintenance of the necessary controls, because he was sure that Beaverbrook and Rothermere were going to exploit the natural feeling against control of all kinds as soon as the war came to an end and a great deal, for instance, would be made of the 'little man' and the restrictions on his liberty of action.

Returning to the PM, he said that he was undoubtedly moving forward with regard to a programme of reconstruction. He was willing now to admit that there must be certain practical measures to be taken in good time; indeed, after he himself and the other Labour members had been hammering away for a long time they found that the PM was disposed to adopt enthusiastically some of the things which they had pressed upon him, and to push them forward as his own. The PM by the way, was getting quite excited about the internees under 18B. He was much concerned that they had been kept in prison all this time without trial and without accusation. As a matter of fact the few who could be brought to trial had been; the trouble always was that some of the most dangerous had to be confined, but there was not sufficient evidence to bring them before a court of law with confidence that they would be found guilty. There was a good deal of agitation behind the scenes about Sir Oswald Mosley, whose health was said to be such that he might die in prison this winter. Mosley's doctors said that he was in danger. As to that there was no doubt that his health was not good, because he had for a long time suffered from phlebitis. It was said that the clot had now moved from one part of the body to another and there was danger that it might get going with grave results. On the other hand, there were doctors who didn't take so serious a view, and he himself was afraid lest there might be some sort of a 'frame up' to get M out of prison. What he wanted was to be really sure what the man's condition really was. There was also, he said, a fashionable lady, some sort of relation of Mosley's wife, 'fluttering about' and trying to use her influence in important quarters. He didn't know yet what would be done.

We had a considerable talk about Palestine and he expressed himself strongly against the White Paper and on the side of Zionism. He said it was a mistake to suppose that the Jews in Palestine nowadays were all friends of the British. They were not in the least pro-Nazi, or pro-Fascist. Far from it. He thought the nearest analogy was Sinn Fein in Ireland. He mentioned the recent trials for illegal possession of arms and said that it was at any rate no wonder that the Jewish community had tried to arm itself at the time of the Arab outrages before the war, when the Administration quite failed to protect them against murderous attack. He thought they were justified in arming themselves at that time.

23 October 1943

4.45 P.M. A V ALEXANDER

I said he had much to be pleased about on the sea since I saw him last. He slapped the desk, saying 'Touch wood' and added 'I had a bad night last night—a bad night—but there must be ups and downs and the Germans were not done with yet. They were coming out with some new devices which we should have to counter. We should do it, but these things took time. Our scientists, etc. were good and, of course, we had the benefit of ALL the scientists, not just the technical advisers of the Admiralty. They had soon got the answer to the magnetic mine, but this last thing was an Acoustic Torpedo, which was attracted by the sound waves of our ships and, of course, more by the sound waves of the bigger craft (e.g. destroyers) than by smaller ones. Also, we had not yet captured one of the AT's—as we had the magnetic mine and acoustic mine. He did not think, either, that we could hope to capture a dud because they would all be equipped with self-destroying devices if they did not hit the target.

'The Azores gain was very good.[1] The principal gain was that it gave us more variety of routes and we could reach out in various directions where now we were not covered. The agreement did *not* cover any bases in the Cape Verde islands. We did not need these as we were so well supplied on the African coast.

I asked about the Italian fleet.[2] 'We could make some use of some of them already. When we got to Naples we found all the power installations destroyed—a big blow. So we ran six Italian submarines up to the quay side and made them generate the power for the time being.' As for the big ships, it remained to be seen. We had to find out how far they were capable of fighting in a real battle. Hitherto they had shown only the quality of speed. I asked about our supply bases on the Adriatic coast, and he said they were pretty good for our purpose—Taranto, Bari and Brindisi. We could go up the Adriatic a long way if we chose. We were already destroying Axis merchantmen there. He added that the Navy had been indispensable to the Army in the Salerno business—especially Fleet Air Arm and bombarding cruisers. It was always the same—if anyone was in a jam they always came along to the Navy and said 'Do this, that or the other to help us out', and the Navy always did.

THE NORTH The Germans had planted their big ships in the Norway fiords to prevent us from sending supplies to Russia, but we should have to start that again. The Russians made things very difficult for us. They were intensely suspicious and they even seemed sometimes to do things which obstructed our helping them as much as we wanted to do. It would be easier for a bit now that we had damaged the Tirpitz, and something had gone wrong with the Lutzow. I asked about the Scharnhorst and the Gneisenau, and he said that the G had never come out against after its injuries but the S had been in Norway. We had to 'cover' these big ships, but the situation had been so much better that we could 'chance' sending big ships to the Mediterranean. I asked about the Dodecanese and he confirmed that the Italians had failed us at Rhodes. We were in a bad position in the Dodek and other small

---

1. The Portuguese had allowed the use of the Azores as an Allied base.
2. Surrendered by the Italians in September 1943.

islands—we were at the centre of a circle from which the Germans bombed us from Rhodes, Crete and the mainland of Greece.

. . . . .

He was impatient about the demand from the Left for immediate reconstruction measures. Ministers were working themselves to death over the war—sixteen or seventeen hours a day like himself —and that was over their immediate jobs and at the same time they were expected to produce a new world. The Daily Herald was very bad, but anyway he had no influence in that quarter. Even with Reynolds, however, where he might be supposed to have influence, he could do nothing.

. . . . .

He was critical of a Second Front in France. The Germans had twenty or more divisions in Northern France with a strong central position, and ready to move in any direction. They could send more forces direct from Germany to this same centre by the shortest way. He doubted whether it would be much easier to invade France from the south than from the west, though Sardinia and Corsica would help. He inclined towards the other strategy— across the Adriatic and up into Austria towards the north-east. That was the weaker German point. One did not search for the enemy's strongest point and go for him there. People were too optimistic about the war altogether. When you had allowed for our successes in Russia, Italy, U-Boats and bombing, you still had the great German army, a most tough enemy and, as for going into France, if Russia should stand still, did we like the idea of fighting about 200 German divisions? The Germans fought most stubbornly everywhere and they were led with great energy and determination.

As I was leaving he spoke of the future of domestic politics and said it was a tragedy that it required a war for the people of this country to get together and do great things. If they would get together completely in a smaller way for domestic purposes there were some very great things which could be quickly achieved. He referred also critically to some of those who were pushing the Beveridge Plan, saying that it seemed nothing to them where the money was coming from; but to other people, like Ministers, it was a very serious matter.

Index